TRUMAN AND ISRAEL

TRUMAN
AND ISRAEL

MICHAEL J. COHEN

UNIVERSITY OF CALIFORNIA PRESS
BERKELEY   LOS ANGELES   OXFORD

University of California Press
Berkeley and Los Angeles, California

University of California Press, Ltd.
Oxford, England

© 1990 by
The Regents of the University of California

Library of Congress Cataloging-in-Publication Data

Cohen, Michael Joseph, 1940–
    Truman and Israel / Michael J. Cohen.
        p.   cm.
    Includes bibliographical references.
    ISBN 0-520-06804-1 (alk. paper)
    1. Truman, Harry S., 1884–1949—Views on Israel.
2. United States—Foreign relations—Israel. 3. Israel—
Foreign relations—United States. 4. Palestine—Politics
and government—1929–1948. 5. Israel—History—
1948–1949. I. Title.
E814.C627 1990
973.918'092—dc20   89-20237
                                                       CIP

Printed in the United States of America
1 2 3 4 5 6 7 8 9

Politicians treat foreign policy as an elaborate charade, raising issues that promise votes rather than ones that reveal their future intentions in world affairs.
—Robert A. Divine, *Foreign Policy and U.S. Presidential Elections, 1940–1948*

Palestine is the classic case in recent years of the determination of American foreign policy by domestic political considerations.
—H. Bradford Westerfield, *Foreign Policy and Party Politics: From Pearl Harbor to Korea*

To Stan, Francis, Sharon, and Howard

Contents

Photographs following page 146

Acknowledgments

I am grateful to the American Jewish Archives, Cincinnati, for awarding me a Bernard and Audre Rapoport fellowship, which allowed me to research and write in the archives during the summer of 1988.

I wish to acknowledge with gratitude the staffs of the following archives and libraries: The Public Record Office, London; the Harry S. Truman Library, Independence, Missouri (Dr. Benedict K. Zobrist, Denis Bulger); the Library of Congress, Manuscripts Division, and the National Archives, Washington, D.C.; the Washington National Records Center, Suitland–Silver Hill, Maryland; the Weizmann Archives, Rehovot (Nehama Chalom); the Israel State Archives (Dr. Yehoshua Freundlich) and the Zionist Archives, Jerusalem; and the interuniversity library loan service of the University of British Columbia, Vancouver.

I am also grateful to the American Jewish Archives, Cincinnati (Fannie Zelcer); the Seeley G. Mudd Manuscript Library, Princeton University (Nancy Bressler, Curator of Public Affairs Papers), for the papers of Bernard M. Baruch, John Foster Dulles, Louis Fischer, and George Kennan; the University of Vermont (Connell Gallagher), for the papers of Senator Warren R. Austin; the University of Minnesota (Karen Klinkenberg) and Dr. Carol Jenson of the University of Wisconsin, for their help in procuring for me the papers of Max Lowenthal, now in the University Archives, the University of Minnesota; the University of North Carolina, Chapel Hill (Richard A. Shrader, reference archivist, and Carolyn Wallace, Director, the Southern Historical Collection), for papers from the Jonathan Daniels collection; the YIVO Institute, New York (Marek Web); and the American Jewish Committee Archives, New York (Helen Ritter, Ruth Rauch, and Cyma Horowitz).

For the photographs and assistance with their interpretation, I owe thanks to the Harry S. Truman Library and to Max Bengir, Loeb H. Granoff, the U.S. Navy, Addie Rowe, the National Park Service, UPI/Bettmann Newsphotos, David Firestone of the B'nai B'rith philatelic service, and the American Jewish Archives, Cincinnati campus, Hebrew Union College, Jewish Institute of Religion.

I should also like to thank the following for their generous advice and help: Professor Monte M. Poen, Northern Arizona University; Professor Jonathan Sarna and Dr. Abraham J. Peck of the Hebrew Union College, Cincinnati; Professor Charles Liebman of Bar-Ilan University; Dr. Menahem Kaufmann of the Hebrew University, Jerusalem; Fred Lepkin, Vancouver, British Columbia; Frank J. Adler (the Temple, Congregation B'nai Jehudah), Lipman Feld, and Loeb Granoff (son of the late Abraham J. Granoff), all of Kansas City. The story and the opinions set out below, however, are the responsibility of the author alone.

Finally, I should like to thank Alain Hénon of the University of California Press for his constant help and encouragement.

Introduction

This is the story of one man's impact on the fate of the Jewish people in the twentieth century. From 1947 to 1948 President Harry S. Truman arguably played the decisive diplomatic role in the birth of the new State of Israel. On this most historians would agree; but they would disagree in their analyses of his motivation.

Was it a biblical affinity to the "Chosen People" and a sense of historical destiny in helping revive their ancient nationality in the Holy Land? Was it the support of a liberal for a Western-style democracy in a sea of Middle Eastern reaction? Or did Truman, facing domestic political pressures, place his political future above that of his country, as argued at the time by his State Department and since by some historians?

It is these questions that I address in this book. But to assess the motives of any statesman, it is necessary first to study and understand the values and character traits that he brought with him to the job. Thus, I begin by sketching a portrait of Truman's childhood and early career. What were the key values and principles Truman imbibed from his family and early surroundings? What were the pivotal experiences that crystallized his outlook on life, his likes and dislikes, his preferences and prejudices?

Truman came from, and spent his formative years in, the American Midwest. He grew up in a class- and prejudice-ridden, inequitable society with its own snobby aristocracy. He did not follow the cushioned path to power (Groton–Harvard) enjoyed

by his predecessor at the White House and by so many of the
eastern establishment. He spent his youth and early manhood
struggling to make a decent living. He was unable to marry
until he was thirty-five years old and could not afford to have
children until six years later. He did not move to Washington
until his mid-forties, after he was elected to the Senate. And at
the Senate he raised some eyebrows when, to make ends meet,
he employed his wife as his secretary.

I devote the first two chapters of this book to Truman's early
youth and career. The trials and tribulations he experienced
then left permanent scars and lasting trauma, and the mature
Truman cannot be comprehended without some acquaintance
with this period.

During his years in Kansas City, Truman made the friends
that would remain his closest for the rest of his life. He cher-
ished these men, especially his former army buddies, above all
others outside his immediate family. These relationships included his idiosyncratic friendship and business association with
Eddie Jacobson of Kansas City and with the latter's lesser-known
friend, Abe Granoff; his long association with the hitherto
unheralded Max Lowenthal, the éminence grise who drafted
Truman's Palestine policy at the White House from 1947 on.
Lowenthal's private diaries, used here for the first time, disclose
one of the most intimate back-room views of the White House
ever revealed to outsiders.

Jacobson, Granoff, and Lowenthal, along with the better-
known David Niles, Roosevelt's and then Truman's aide on minority affairs (including the Jews), would together have a decisive influence on President Truman's support for the State of
Israel.

Wherever possible I have allowed the characters to tell their
own stories, through their private letters, diaries, and interviews. Truman's life was full of colorful characters—not only
Jacobson and Granoff but also Loy Henderson, head of the
State Department's division for Near Eastern affairs and the
mastermind behind the administration's pro-Arab inclinations;
Secretary of Defense James Forrestal, the bête noire of the Zionists for what they perceived as his anti-Semitism; and a host of
others. If I have managed to flesh out some of the human di-

mensions of these men and the other people in this story and to re-create a sense of what it was really like in the official Washington of the late 1940s, then my purpose has been fulfilled.

This is primarily an American story, which tells of a unique conjunction of circumstances that, seemingly against all odds, persuaded the president of the United States, against the advice of all the official "experts," to lend his diplomatic support to the Zionist cause when it was needed most.

I conclude therefore with the end of the first Arab-Israeli war in January 1949. With Israel's military triumph the State Department (and the British Foreign Office) was finally persuaded that Israel should be supported as an important strategic asset to the West. This was an argument (along with many others) long advocated by the White House. With their agreement on this central proposition the Truman administration had at last arrived at a consensus.

Abbreviations

AJC	American Jewish Committee
AJCA	American Jewish Committee Archives
AZEC	American Zionist Emergency Council
BGA	Ben-Gurion Archives
CZA	Central Zionist Archives
FRUS	*Foreign Relations of the United States*
HSTL	Harry S. Truman Library
ID	*Israel Documents*
ISA	Israel State Archives
MLP	Max Lowenthal Papers, University of Minnesota
NA	National Archives
NEA	Office of Near Eastern and African Affairs, U.S. Department of State
OF	Official Files, Harry S. Truman Library
PPF	Post-Presidential Files, Harry S. Truman Library
PRO	Public Record Office
PSF	President's Secretary's Files, Harry S. Truman Library
SVP	Senatorial and Vice-Presidential Files, Harry S. Truman Library
UNSCOP	United Nations Special Committee on Palestine
WA	Weizmann Archives

PART ONE

Prelude to the Presidency

ONE

The Early Years

INDEPENDENCE, MISSOURI

Harry S. Truman was born in 1884 to a farming family in Lamar, Missouri. The family lived on a succession of farms. In 1887 they moved to a farm owned by Harry's grandmother in Grandview near Independence, a small town some ten miles east of Kansas City. In 1896 the family bought a house in Independence, where the young Harry would spend his formative years. Settled in 1827, Independence was once known as the last staging area for wagon trains preparing for the long trek across the plains.

Independence was a snobbish little town with its own hierarchy and "aristocracy." It was divided socially along the lines of its churches. At the top of the social pole came the Presbyterians, then the Campbellites (the "Christian Church"); next came the North and South Methodists, and after them the Baptists. The German immigrants had their own Lutheran church, and the large Catholic church was attended mostly by out-of-town country folk.[1]

The Presbyterians kept to their own social circle, and their children invited only their own denomination—with sometimes a Campbellite or two or a couple of Catholics—to their parties. It was a social rather than a religious discrimination.[2] As a boy of six Harry Truman was invited by the Presbyterian minister to attend his Sunday school. His parents agreed, and it was there that he later met and fell in love with Bess Wallace, his future wife.[3]

But at the age of eighteen Harry joined the Baptist church at Grandview, a membership he retained throughout his life. He was not apparently a regular churchgoer, unattracted by the more ceremonial forms of worship. After he became president he attended church only rarely, explaining that he attracted too much attention and distracted the other worshippers.[4]

In 1910 Harry began courting Bess Wallace, the daughter of one of the richest families in town, members of the local "aristocracy." In 1903 Bess's father had committed suicide, and Mrs. Wallace had felt so humiliated that she had moved to Colorado for a year. When she returned, she matriarchically clung to Bess and frowned on the advances of the young Truman. Bess was the "family princess," and Mrs. Wallace would not allow her to marry Harry.[5] The haughtiness of the Wallaces induced in the young Truman an inferiority complex, and he was forever hoping to prove his worthiness to them.[6] In 1918, after a courtship of eight years, Harry and Bess were finally married. Harry had just returned from the war in Europe; he was now thirty-five years old.

The social divisions and tensions of Independence at the turn of the century undoubtedly left their mark on the young Harry. They instilled in him a burning ambition to make good, to make his fortune, if only to be worthy of the Wallace family. In growing up, Harry faced other, not inconsiderable, material hardships and physical handicaps.

The young Truman suffered from bad eyesight and by the age of nine needed to wear spectacles, unusual indeed for those times. He had a "flat eyeball," which restricted his vision even more than ordinary shortsightedness.[7] Any child who wore glasses was ridiculed for it, and Harry was often called "four-eyes." His glasses removed him from the normal rough and tumble of games and sports. He came in for further derision when he took up the piano and began music lessons.[8]

As a boy Harry swept out at the local drugstore and did other chores to help out the family. His parents were very strict with him, which is perhaps why, a childhood friend suggested, he later broke out and swore like a trooper.[9]

In 1901, when Harry was sixteen years old, his father, John

Anderson Truman, lost his savings in the grain futures market. In his young manhood Harry would dream up several business ventures and investment coups to get rich quick. But these were never to be successful (in 1915 he invested and lost money in a zinc-mining venture; in 1916 he helped organize an oil-drilling company but sold his share just before the company struck it rich).[10]

In 1903 Harry's parents moved to Kansas City. After a series of relatively menial jobs—in the mail room of the *Kansas City Star*, as timekeeper for the Santa Fe Railroad construction project, as bank clerk and bookkeeper—Harry was recalled in 1906 to help run the family farm in Grandview. Here he stayed, working the long, strenuous hours of a crop and cattle farmer, until 1917, when the United States entered the war.

His childhood friends believed that Harry had had a relatively happy childhood. But evidently it was not without its share of economic struggle and frustration. As a result Truman became something of a social climber. In 1909 he joined the Masonic Order, Lodge 450, in Belton, Missouri, and in 1911, at the age of twenty-seven, he organized the first Masonic lodge in his own suburb of Grandview. In the summer of 1919, just a year after his return from the war in Europe, Harry paid out $225 to join the Kansas City Club, "so he could circulate in the upper-level business community."[11] In addition, he became president of the Kansas City Reserve Officers Association, "a meeting place for high-class persons," which "united community leaders in a selective brotherhood."[12]

TRUMAN'S RELIGIOUS CODE

For Harry Truman religion was a matter of private conscience. He liked to boast that he had read the Bible right through twice by the time he was twelve years old. But one of his earlier biographers, a man who knew Truman intimately and married his only daughter, suggested that his intimate knowledge of the Bible probably showed "less predilection for religion rather than an affection for the big type in which such Bibles were printed."[13] A student of Truman's religious views has concluded that although he "maintained an almost Fundamentalist reverence for the Bible and liked to read and quote it, there is little evidence that he had any academic interest in complex theological issues."[14]

His affinity to the Bible was strengthened when he joined the Masons in 1909, as Masonic studies used what Truman would later call "a system of morals based entirely on the Scriptures." The themes of "honor and integrity" were implicit in a prayer he said daily throughout his adult life: "Help me to be, to think, to act what is right; make me truthful, honest and honorable in all things; make me intellectually honest for the sake of right and honor."[15]

For Truman the Bible was neither legend nor myth but literally the story of everyday, God-fearing people. He told one biographer: "The stories in the Bible, though, were to me stories about real people, and I felt I knew some of them better than *actual* people I knew."[16]

He preferred the New Testament, especially the Gospels, to the Old. Overall, he regarded the Bible more as a manual that provided a moral code for everyday behavior, one by which all good men should abide. In some contrast to Machiavelli, Truman seemed to believe that public servants and politicians should manage public affairs according to the precepts of private (religious) morality. "He liked to read and quote the Scriptures, often reciting verses from memory to fit political situations." His favorite quotation for many occasions was the Sermon on the Mount, and he believed that "every problem in the world would be solved if only men would follow the Beatitudes." His speeches, dotted with quotations from the Scriptures, at times carried a spirit of "Calvinistic determinism and even moralism."[17]

Of course it was a naive view, and as Truman himself must have been only too aware, his own behavior frequently fell short of religious prescription. But Truman was no cynic. The Bible provided him with an indispensable set of values without which he would have been lost. It was a moral guide, one that he tried to keep to, in his own way, throughout his life.

It has been claimed frequently that Truman's intimate knowledge of the Bible imbued him with a special affinity, even affection, for the Jews, God's "Chosen People." Truman himself did nothing to discourage this view. In an interview given in 1959, he stated: "As a student of the Bible I have been impressed by the remarkable achievements of the Jews in Palestine in making the land of the Holy Book blossom again."[18] But as will be noted at length below, Truman's attitude toward the Jews was complex and ambivalent. The interview he gave in 1959 cannot be taken as a true expression of his private views either as a young man growing up in the Midwest or even as president during the turbulent years that preceded the establishment of Israel. Truman's real feelings are reflected perhaps more accurately by a private memorandum penned by him as president in June 1945:

The Jews claim God Almighty picked 'em out for special privilege. Well I'm sure he had better judgement. Fact is I never thought God picked any favorites. It is my studied opinion that any race, creed or color can be God's favorites if they act the part—and very few of 'em do that.[19]

RACISM AND ANTI-SEMITISM

Just as Truman's personal ambitions were fed by childhood frustrations, so his world outlook was shaped by the environment in which he grew up. Some letters (discovered rather belatedly in 1983) that Truman wrote to his then fiancée, Bess Wallace, have revealed a side of Truman that few people apart from his immediate family and some intimates had previously dreamed existed.[20]

Independence was a Southern border town, one of whose more prominent organizations was the United Daughters of the Confederacy. Harry Truman's racial attitudes stemmed from "his family's Southern roots and prevailing views in turn-of-the-century Independence, still divided over the Civil War." "As a struggling young Missouri farmer, he used the language of the times to speak derogatorily of blacks, Italians, Jews and orientals." Everyone had servants, blacks of course. Like his neighbors, Truman always used the word "nigger" in private.[21]

In June 1911, in proposing marriage to Bess, the twenty-seven-year-old Harry wrote:

Uncle Will says that the Lord made a white man from dust, a nigger from mud, then he threw up what was left and it came down a Chinaman. He does hate Chinese and Japs. So do I. It is race prejudice, I guess. But I am strongly of the opinion that negros [*sic*] ought to be in Africa, yellow men in Asia and white men in Europe and America.[22]

But Harry Truman's racist comments were not simply an acquired habit, caught from his contemporaries. They were fueled by his own frustrations and an evident feeling that foreigners were making their fortune in the "promised land" at the expense of its natives, such as himself. Thus, when planning a trip to South Dakota in 1911 to look for farming land to buy, he wrote to Bess:

I'll bet there'll be more bohunks [a derogatory term for Eastern or Southeastern Europeans] and "Rooshans" up there than white men. I think it is a disgrace to the country for those fellows to be in it. If they had only stopped immigration about twenty or thirty years ago, the good Americans could all have had plenty of land and we'd have been an agricultural country forever.[23]

Truman's early business relations with Eddie Jacobson, a Kansas City Jew, first in running an army canteen and, after the war, in their joint haberdashery venture, are of great significance and will be dealt with in some detail. Truman and Jacobson developed an intimate relationship, based on mutual trust, which usually remained above any racial prejudice. Eddie could hardly have imagined, and would have no doubt been shocked to read, some of the comments his business partner and friend was writing in private about the Jewish race.

Truman held a stereotyped image of the Jews, immigrants par excellence, to whom he attributed the negative character traits traditionally believed by anti-Semites. In February 1918 he boasted to Bess from Camp Doniphan, Oklahoma (whence he was waiting to be shipped to France), about the success of his army canteen: "I go count nickels and dimes up to four hundred dollars a day more or less. I guess I should be very proud of my *Jewish ability*. My thirst emporium is the only one in camp that's open. The rest are insolvent or can't make a clear statement of their financial standing."[24]

Truman's success with the canteen earned him a string of nicknames—"Lieutenant Graball," "Graballsky," and "Lieutenant Trumanheimer"—the latter evidently alluding to his "Jewish" business acumen.[25] This nicknaming was apparently all part of the regular camaraderie of army life, and Truman took it in good humor. One incident provided him with material for a letter to Bess: "Did I tell you I met a very pretty girl in Guthrie who was nice to me until someone told her my name was Trumanheimer, and then she wouldn't look at me anymore. She thought I surely must be of Hebraic descent with that name."[26]

In March 1918, when his unit shipped out of New York for Europe, he again expressed his resentment of foreigners, focusing on Jews. In a letter to Bess he called New York a "kike" town.[27] To his first cousin Mary Ethel Noland, he was more explicit: "This town has 8,000,000 people, 7,500,000 of 'em are of Israelitish extraction. (400,000 wops and the rest are white people)."[28]

The Kansas City journalists who in 1983 first published extracts from Truman's letters to Bess suggested that "politics, wide reading and two world wars" had moderated Truman's earlier racial views.[29] It should be remembered, however, that Truman was a mature young man already in his late twenties when he was writing these letters. Moreover, his later private letters, written from Washington when he was a U.S. senator in the late 1930s and 1940s, do not indicate any significant change in his stereotyped images of Jewish character traits. Of course, Truman had always kept his racist comments private, and once he entered politics his public reserve would be but a matter of good common sense.

But the very word "Jewish" evidently retained negative connotations for Truman. Time and again he would make a point, quite gratuitously, of noting the Jewish origin of someone he was writing about. In 1935 he described to Bess a poker game in Washington, at which a Costa Rican minister had "screamed like a Jewish merchant."[30] In 1940, wanting to fire one of his campaign workers, Al Holland, he wrote that he would "cut the smart Hebrew loose" as soon as he could.[31]

EDDIE JACOBSON
AND THE HABERDASHERY VENTURE

Harry Truman's first contact with Jews was most likely with the Viner family, neighbors of his family in Independence. According to the daughter, Sarah Peltzman, young Harry was always over at their house and had a soft spot for the Passover matzo (unleavened bread). Mrs. Peltzman told one interviewer that Harry had been the Viners' *shabbos goy* (literally, a "sabbath gentile," one who performed chores, such as switching on the electricity, forbidden to an orthodox Jew on the sabbath).[32] She also recalled that as a county judge in the 1920s Truman had done the Jews many favors, such as surfacing the road to the local Jewish cemetery.[33]

Eddie Jacobson and Harry Truman first came into contact with each other in 1905 in Kansas City. Twenty-one-year-old Harry, then a bookkeeper at the Union National Bank, occasionally went by the dry goods firm where fourteen-year-old Eddie worked as a stock boy. During the next decade or so, Eddie was to develop the proficiency in merchandising that would later underpin his and Truman's joint business ventures, first in the army and then after World War I in Kansas City. In those prewar Kansas City days, however, neither man had either the inclination or the capital to start up a business.[34] Eddie and Harry lost track of each other after 1906 but were to meet again more than ten years later under entirely different circumstances.

In 1905 Truman "indulged old military aspirations" and became a charter member of the newly formed Battery B of the Missouri National Guard. He entered as a private but by September 1906 was promoted to corporal.[35] Eddie Jacobson enlisted in 1917 as a private in the 2nd Field Artillery of the Missouri National Guard. He and Truman were reunited when Eddie was assigned to Battery F, in which Truman had become junior first lieutenant. In August 1917 their regiment was mustered into the U.S. Army as the 129th Field Artillery of the

Thirty-fifth Division.[36] In 1918 Truman became captain of Battery D of the 129th.

It is worth digressing at this point to note the significant impact that Truman's army experience had on his life. It would not be an exaggeration to say that Truman formed his deepest and most enduring relations (apart from those with his immediate family) in the U.S. Army, especially during his short period of service in World War I. During the war, he proved his leadership qualities and earned the lasting admiration of the men under his command. (In May 1918, soon after arriving with his battery in France, Truman was promoted to captain, thanks largely, so Truman believed, to his and Jacobson's work in the canteen.)[37]

By the war's end he had gone "from shy boyhood to gregarious adult."[38] His business and social success in the army undoubtedly had a cathartic effect upon a man who had experienced no small amount of social segregation and prejudice in his youth. For the rest of his life Truman's old army buddies enjoyed a place of special prominence and privilege.

After the war Truman had his teeth ground by former lieutenant George Arrowsmith and his hair trimmed by former private Frank Spina. Veterans of his artillery battery held annual stag reunions in a Kansas City hotel on St. Patrick's Day.[39] On more than one occasion the proceedings got so out of hand that the intervention of the local police was required. When he and Eddie Jacobson opened their haberdashery, the store served as much more than a place where he earned a living. It became a meeting place for his old army "buddies" and "a base from which he moved about the city visiting with other men and encouraging them to come to the store."[40]

Vic Messall, Truman's secretary in the Senate from 1935 to 1941, recalled later that "one of Truman's first acts was to give him a list of Battery D veterans, all of whom were to get special consideration if they asked for anything."[41]

When president, Truman welcomed Battery D veterans into the White House, no doubt finding welcome relief in breaking out a bottle of whiskey and indulging in a raucous session with "the boys." After being reelected in his own right in 1948, Truman started off his inauguration day at 7:00 A.M. with a break-fast at the Mayflower Hotel with ninety-eight former members of Battery D. The men presented Harry with a gold-headed cane. After the inauguration ceremony the Trumans took part in a long parade on foot down Pennsylvania Avenue, with the Battery D veterans serving as an honor guard.[42]

In August 1917, when Battery F wanted to raise money for its mess fund, Eddie Jacobson proposed a dance and a movie. The battery ended up netting a profit of $2600, no small amount for those days. When the 129th Field Artillery was formed and transferred for training to Camp Doniphan on the Fort Sill reservation in Oklahoma, it seemed only natural for the regimental commander to place the regimental canteen under the "responsible supervision" of Lieutenant Truman. In turn, Truman asked Private Jacobson, "a man with merchandising experience," to help him.[43]

Truman kept the books, and Jacobson purchased the merchandise. Eddie knew about purchasing in large lots, and Truman had had his experience as a bookkeeper in the Kansas City bank. They bought the kinds of goods that the army did not provide, including "large quantities of a soft drink called Puritan."[44] To build up their stock, they collected $2 from each of the eleven hundred men in the regiment and within six months were able to repay the men their initial "investment" and to show a $15,000 dividend. Each battery and company supplied clerks to work in the store. Harry and Eddie protected themselves against pilfering (apparently a common pastime) by sewing up the clerks' pockets.[45]

The canteen was a resounding success and ensured Truman's promotion to captain. He was well pleased with himself. With good cause he boasted to Bess: "They say I have the best canteen on the reservation, and every regiment has one. I declared a dividend to the Batteries of three thousand dollars last week. The regiment appointed a committee to audit me. I came out with flying colors."[46]

Eddie was glad to help Truman out in other ways, as he recalled much later: "Each day Harry would write a letter to his girl, Bess Wallace, and I would write one to my sweetheart, Bluma Rosenbaum, who is now my wife, and when I went into town, I would mail them."[47] Little known to Eddie, the letters he was faithfully mailing for his lieutenant contained recurring references to his partner's Jewish origins. Truman still found the fact of someone's Jewishness sufficiently noteworthy to put in a letter: "I have a Jew in charge of the canteen by the name of Jacobson and he is a crackerjack. Also the barbershop is run by a Jew, Morris Stearns by name."[48]

On Truman's part there was an element of condescension in the relationship, perhaps because of his seniority in rank. He referred to Eddie as his "Jew clerk."[49]

They were both shipped out to France in April 1918. The canteen was wound up, and Harry's and Eddie's business association was interrupted. Harry was transferred to the command of Battery D, and he and Eddie saw each other but occasionally. But after the war they sailed home together with the regiment and were both discharged from the army at Camp Funston, Kansas, on May 6, 1919, two days after Harry's thirty-fifth birthday.

Harry remembered Sergeant Jacobson and their success with the canteen at Camp Doniphan. After he and Bess were married (on June 28, 1919), Truman met with Jacobson, and they began planning and talking seriously about a joint business venture. The idea of a men's clothing store was Eddie's.[50] Their preparations took all summer and autumn, and in November 1919 they were finally ready to open. Their shop was at a choice location, across the road from Kansas City's major hotel, the Muehlbach. They divided their functions as in the canteen— Eddie did the buying, Harry was the salesman and kept the books.[51]

The store was open every night and became a natural meeting place for the town's veterans. The loving cup that Truman had received from Battery D was prominently displayed, and the men from the unit visited the store regularly; an average night would find some twenty to thirty men congregated there.[52] The store became much more than a place of business; it was a social club where the men could pick up the latest news, and it also served as an "unemployment agency, schoolroom, small loan center, confession booth and club. As time went on it seemed to become more of the others than the store."[53] But of course, when they needed to, Harry's friends also bought their shirts, ties, and underwear there.

Unfortunately, the haberdashery failed during the postwar depression of 1920–1921. It was rumored that Truman's excessive extension of credit to his friends was the cause of his business failure. (Such rumors were used later to ridicule him as president, when it was claimed that he could not even run a haberdashery.) Truman was undoubtedly generous and good for a loan here and there, but the failure of the store was caused by postwar price deflation, not by overextended credit.[54] Businesses with larger credit reserves and more experienced managers survived, but the Truman-Jacobson store had little chance. They had overstocked on luxury items, for which demand dropped as soon as business declined and unemployment rose. The depression also created an energy crisis, which prevented them from staying open for the all-important after-work evening hours. Although Eddie insisted on a strict cash sales policy, Truman's loans and credit to old comrades did not improve matters. The partners did not have sufficient reserves to tide them over, as their stock declined in value to way below what they had paid for it.[55]

They tried in vain to raise capital until they could write off their inventory losses and restart at new price levels. But by February 1921 the store needed more money than the banks were willing to loan without additional collateral. They tried changing the business from a partnership to a corporation to enable them to sell stock. Truman claimed later that they raised twelve thousand dollars in this way. They took in a third director, who was also, inevitably, from the 129th Field Artillery—a captain of the regiment's supply company, Harry Jobes.[56] But it was all in vain; in 1922 they were forced to close.

The haberdashery episode undoubtedly greatly influenced Truman's life and subsequent career. First, it left him with a rankling bitterness against Republican politics, whose economic and social policies he blamed for the store's failure.[57] Second, and more germane to our subject here, the entire experience, including the bankruptcy, served to cement Truman's bonds with Eddie Jacobson and to elevate their military sergeant-captain relationship to one of true partnership and friendship.

After closing the store in 1922, the partners owed thirty-five thousand dollars—the incorporation of the business in 1921 had not affected the liabilities they had incurred prior to that. The merchants to whom they owed the money agreed to a settlement on a percentage basis of their remaining stock. But they also owed money to the banks for loans negotiated, as well as for the balance of the store rental.[58]

The final settlement of all the bills took some fifteen years. This was facilitated during the Great Depression in the 1930s by the failure of the banks that held the credit notes. When the bank holding their major credit note failed, Truman's brother Vivian bought it at a sheriff's auction for one thousand dollars, about one-tenth of its value as determined by the courts. Vivian resold it to Harry, thereby canceling it out.[59]

The salient point to be noted here is Jacobson's role in the bankruptcy. By law the haberdashery had been an unlimited partnership, meaning that both partners, together or individually, were personally liable for any bills that the store's revenue could not cover. This meant either partner would have to pay all of their joint debts should one of them run out of money.[60]

Both men encountered hard times. Eddie took to the road as a traveling salesman and was to struggle to make a living for the next two decades.[61] Eddie was hit much harder than Truman, who was soon to find his place in local politics. Soon after their store's failure, when the two former partners were having lunch, Truman commented on Eddie's frayed clothes and said: "Here's some money and don't spend it on anything but clothes."[62]

Both men made payments on their debt from time to time as they could, sometimes as little as twenty-five dollars. In 1925 Eddie was finally forced into bankruptcy by his creditors, with debts listed at more than ten thousand dollars. He and his family had to move in with his wife's parents. Truman held out. As he told an early biographer: "Our creditors drove Eddie into bankruptcy, but I became a public official, and they couldn't do that to me."[63]

One could draw the conclusion from Truman's memoirs that he alone was left to repay the remainder of the haberdashery's debts. He wrote that as a result of Eddie's bankruptcy "there were those who tried to force me into bankruptcy at the same time. I resisted, however, and continued to make such payments as I could."[64] Indeed, Truman was the only one now legally liable for the outstanding debts. But the little-published fact is that Eddie Jacobson secretly continued to make payments to Harry for his share of their joint debt. Eddie did not remember exactly how much he repaid Truman but did recall twice giving him sums of five hundred dollars.[65] Jacobson's loyalty was the more admirable, considering his own impecuniosity and the fact that after the declaration of his own bankruptcy in 1925 he was under no obligation, except moral, to his former partner. The point was not lost on Truman, who in the future would have plenty of opportunity to repay the loyalty of his old friend and partner.

Eddie Jacobson looked back on their business partnership as an idyllic period: "Those were happy years. We were not only business partners, but close friends, frequently in each other's homes." Harry visited the Jacobson home regularly for dinner and a card game afterward. Once he joined the Jacobson's daughter Gloria in a piano duet.[66] But, according to Jacobson's wife, Bluma, their hospitality was never reciprocated: "Eddie and I were never at the Truman house. We went maybe two or three times on picnics and on the Fourth of July, but the Trumans never had us at their home. The Wallaces were aristocracy in these parts, and under the circumstances the Trumans couldn't afford to have Jews at their house."[67]

The restrictions imposed by his mother-in-law, however, did not impair Truman's friendship with Jacobson. Their mutual trust was apparently absolute: "There was never anything signed. In all their relationship there was never anything signed. They just felt that close to one another that they could trust each other, which they did all through their lives."[68] According to Bluma, their relationship also weathered their business failure: "[Eddie] and Harry never quarreled. Even when the haberdashery, even when the business was bad, when it was going to go broke, they never quarreled. The newspapers always said that Harry had a very quick temper, but we never saw it around here."[69]

Eddie was later to benefit from the course of events that ultimately brought Truman to the presidency. He had reopened a men's store in Kansas City, and his well-known association with Truman, judiciously publicized by a well-photographed visit or two by his friend who had become president, ensured that business was brisk and profitable.

One final comment about the Truman-Jacobson relationship and Zionism. Jacobson belonged to the Jewish denomination predominant in Kansas City, the Reform Temple of B'nai Jehuda, whose rabbi was pronouncedly non-Zionist. Until World War II, the temple was the only Jewish communal organization to which Jacobson payed dues. After the war, inspired by the horrific news about the Holocaust, Eddie also joined B'nai B'rith, a major national Jewish organization founded by German Jews in 1843 "for charity, mutual aid and welfare."[70]

Eddie Jacobson had no interest in or acquaintance with Zionism. Notwithstanding his great services for the State of Israel after World War II, he was never to consider himself a political Zionist, nor did he ever join any Zionist organization.[71] Eddie's closest Jewish friend was Abraham Granoff, a lawyer, who regularly accompanied Jacobson on his visits to the Truman White House. Granoff recalled later that Eddie had hardly ever read a newspaper or magazine. Granoff had regularly briefed him on the issues they were to raise with the president. In all of their long friendship Granoff could not recall ever discussing with Eddie "Israel, Palestine, Jewish history, the butchery of six million Jews, its historic impact on the world. . . . We used to play gin rummy a couple of hours on a Saturday afternoon. . . . We never talked about Jewish affairs, or anything, communal affairs. He was a paying member of B'nai B'rith, but that's all; he never did attend a lodge meeting."[72]

On all their visits to the Truman White House on behalf of the Zionist cause, both Jacobson and Granoff were guided by one key principle: there should never be any conflict between what they asked of the president for the Jews and their duties as American citizens. Only on this basis could they justify their own lobbying and the president's actions for their people. Jacobson claimed later: "The President always listened to me because he knew I would tell him the truth. But I want to make it clear that whatever President Truman did for Israel he did because he thought it was the best thing for this country."[73]

The Truman-Jacobson relationship was a purely business and social association. In the parochial ambience of post–World War I Kansas City, Jacobson and a few other of his Jewish friends "were the sort of Americanized Jews who enjoyed a good poker game with their old Army buddies."[74] Truman then had little or no knowledge of Jewish or Zionist problems, and Eddie Jacobson would not have been the person to have enlightened him.

TWO

Truman's Entry into Politics

Truman owed his early political appointments, both locally and nationally, to "Boss" Tom Pendergast of Kansas City. His complex and frequently uneasy relations with the Pendergast machine, which controlled all political patronage in Jackson County, deeply influenced Truman's character and are directly relevant to his later modus operandi as president. The humiliations heaped on him by fellow politicians and the media merely reinforced his already strong determination to be his own man.

THE PENDERGAST CONNECTION

Truman had begun to consider a political career during the war. Apparently his speculations were once overheard by a fellow officer, Lieutenant James Pendergast. James was the son of Mike Pendergast, political boss of eastern Jackson County; Mike was a nephew of Tom Pendergast, who controlled the whole county. After the war, James and Mike visited the haberdashery and asked Harry to run for eastern judge. But at that time (in 1921) the business was still going well, and Truman did not take up the offer. But the Pendergasts returned the following spring with the same proposition, and this time Truman accepted with alacrity. With the collapse of the haberdashery, he was in sore need of employment; he soon announced his candidacy.[1]

Truman later recalled his family's long involvement in local politics and that he had been Grandview postmaster before

World War I. At every local election since 1906 Harry had been a Democratic clerk.[2]

Truman had the assets the Pendergasts were looking for. He was well known throughout the county because he had lived there since he was a small boy and had relatives scattered throughout the rural precincts.[3] He was a member of one of the oldest families in eastern Jackson County, which contained both Independence and Grandview.[4] As put eloquently by an early biographer:

There was, in 1922, no veteran in Jackson county who, in his hard luck at so central a location as well as in his continuing comradeship served better as a rallying point for those veterans whose solidarity in America sometimes increased as the bright promises of the peace seemed personally more and more dull. Some of those veterans had been talking in the store about politics. Harry was a Baptist. He brought his increasing prominence as a Mason to the ticket of the Irish Catholic bosses.[5]

As a county candidate for the city politicians Truman was also well known as a farmer. He was not tainted by the image of being a city politician with pretensions of telling "the country boys" what was best for their district.[6]

Another one of Harry's attractions for the Pendergasts was his obvious popularity among the war veterans; he had been an officer "whose men didn't want to shoot him"![7] Truman seemed to be popular enough to win in rural Jackson County, despite the antagonism that had set in against "the city boss and the inefficient, corrupt court which he had dominated."[8]

Jonathan Daniels has claimed that the significance of the veteran vote of the 129th Field Artillery in Truman's first election can be calculated mathematically: "Truman's war associates went from Jackson County to fight and came back to Jackson County to vote." A total of 2269 officers and men had served in the regiment from August 1917 to May 1919. Truman won the 1922 election by a margin of 282 votes. Even allowing for those killed and those who moved from Jackson County after the war, it seems fairly safe to assume that without the veteran vote, Truman could not have won. Local historians add that he might

not have won even then "if the 129th in the person of a highly
nervous ex-private with a very large .45 calibre automatic had
not been on guard at the ballot box in a precinct at Mount
Washington in the Intercity district."[9]

With the Pendergasts behind him Truman was elected in
1922 as eastern judge of the Jackson County court. The judges
of the Missouri county courts had no judicial powers but were
actually county commissioners, who controlled the expendi-
tures in the construction of the county's roads and highways
and oversaw the maintenance of all buildings constructed by
the county. (The Pendergasts controlled huge cement contractors, whose fortunes depended on county contracts.) The county
courts were an important part of the local political system as
they had so much patronage and funds at their disposal. Truman's court alone disposed of nine hundred jobs. The courts
also levied local taxes and managed and controlled all chari-
table institutions operated by the county.[10]

In 1924 Truman was defeated in his bid for reelection. It was
the only election he ever lost. But in 1926, again with the Pendergast machine behind him, he was elected as presiding judge
of the Jackson County court, in which capacity he served for
two four-year terms, from 1927 to 1934.

In 1934 and again in 1940, with Pendergast backing, he was
elected U.S. senator for Missouri. Truman and Pendergast were
locked into a mutually beneficial partnership to which Truman
applied the same rules of loyalty as he had in his business partnership with Eddie Jacobson: "Harry Truman would never
have reached national prominence without the boss's support,
and likewise, Tom Pendergast could not have strengthened his
hold on Jackson County and the State of Missouri without Truman's loyal assistance."[11]

The Pendergast machine engaged in the rankest forms of
graft and corruption and when it felt the need did not shrink
from engaging gangsters to impose its will. The machine not
only cast votes for absentees but even rallied the deceased. One
popular quip in circulation was: "Now is the time for all good
cemeteries to come to the aid of the party."[12] Local elections
were rigged. Ballots were interfered with and changed. The

machine's efforts to enhance its power, through police intimidation and fraudulent manipulation of the electoral process, reached their peak in the Kansas City elections of 1934; hired gangsters roamed the streets intimidating voters with no interference from the police. The machine hired attorneys to hamper or block legal process and threatened federal judges, juries, and their families. In thirteen successive trials in the 1930s not a single defendant was acquitted.[13]

Truman's association with the Pendergast machine attached to him a stigma that remained into his presidency. Critics maintained that his political success was based on fraud. When he was elected to the U.S. Senate, he was dubbed "the Senator from Pendergast." Truman may have been dismayed by and concerned about the machine's image, but he held his silence. It has been suggested that as a judge, Truman compensated by redoubling his efforts to do a good job in the county court.[14]

It has been claimed that the Pendergast machine was "an insuperable fact of life in Kansas City," one that candidates for any local office ignored at their peril.[15] One might speculate that Truman would have preferred to remain in the haberdashery business had it only been more successful. But in 1922, with huge business debts looming, Truman had perhaps felt he had little choice. He was thirty-eight years old, married for barely three years, living with his mother-in-law, and unable yet to contemplate having children (his only child, Margaret, would be born in 1924).

It was the most complex of relationships, one that would have ruined the reputation of a person who lived by anything less than the straitlaced, self-imposed moral code of Harry Truman. He believed that he would be able to ignore the sordid facts of local political life and remain personally untainted. In his own eyes he not only succeeded in doing so but also believed that he had brought great benefit to the citizens of Jackson County. It was perhaps the supreme test for a self-professed righteous man, who endeavored to live by the prescriptions of the Holy Scriptures.

In private Truman once wrote: "I think maybe machines are not so good for the country."[16] But in practice he believed that patronage was "one of the honored prerogatives of the system," and in its disposal he was consistently loyal to the machine.[17] Truman liked to think that his own ways of employing the machine's control were benign.[18]

Truman drew a fine but strict distinction between the graft and corruption that had marked the Jackson County court, which he was determined to stamp out, and the court's patronage, which he believed belonged by rights to the victorious political machine that had won the election. Truman refused to give automatic preference to contractors recommended by Boss Tom but saw nothing wrong in giving jobs to the boss's men, provided they were up to the job. Of course, some appointees might turn out badly, but this was a calculated risk, part of the game.

Truman managed the court so efficiently and achieved so much while in office that he won an enormous popular following and built up an excellent reputation. Ironically, it was the very nature of Truman's regime that strengthened the machine's grip.

The general verdict seems to be that although Truman was part of a machine that at times dealt in the lowest forms of graft and corruption "the future president of the United States was actually an honest reformer, reminiscent of some of the prewar progressive traditions. He successfully worked towards cleaning up the graft in the county government and increasing the court's efficiency. At the same time he was able to survive as a key member in the machine."[19]

But Truman was evidently forced to give way to the machine more than he liked to admit in public. The recently discovered "Pickwick papers" (notes Truman wrote in the Pickwick Hotel in the early 1930s) reveal that Pendergast was not so magnanimous, nor Truman as independent, as later accounts would have it. Making an "internal audit" of his county administration, Truman claimed that in addition to spending some $7 million for the taxpayers' benefit he "gave away about a million in general revenue to satisfy the politicians." He justified this by adding that had he not done so "the crooks" would have taken half the $7 million as well.[20]

IN WASHINGTON

Truman's experience in the Senate was in some respects a repeat of his county court experience. Although he acknowledged his continuing debt to Pendergast, he yearned to become, and to be regarded by others, as his own man.[21] The logic whereby Truman may have justified his position has been described aptly by Robert H. Ferrell: "Truman was never daunted by what he could not control, and the chicanery surrounding his election to the United States Senate was no exception. He knew that once elected he could pursue his own honest ends. The Pendergast machine was corrupt—but then so was the St. Louis machine, and he preferred the approval of Tom Pendergast to that of the party leaders in St. Louis."[22] He was able to live with his conscience by following the same principles he had in the county court: "Pendergast would receive the patronage Truman saw as the Boss's due, but the Senator would seek an independent role in national affairs."[23]

When Truman wanted to appoint a Kansas City man, Bud Faris, to be his first Senate secretary, he asked him to obtain a written endorsement from Pendergast. When Faris brought the note to Truman, the latter said: "Well, that's fine. You know, that solves a lot of things."[24]

Pendergast allowed Truman certain license, but in the exchange, the boss gained more than he lost. The federal patronage that Truman brought in, particularly Works Progress Administration jobs, enabled Pendergast to extend his influence throughout Missouri.[25]

It was generally believed that Truman would not run again for the Senate in 1940 because of the demise of the Pendergast machine and Boss Tom's imprisonment the previous year. (At Tom Pendergast's trial in 1939 it had been established that between 1927 and 1937 he had failed to report income in excess of $1 million and had evaded paying over $550,000 in income taxes. He was sentenced to fifteen months in prison, a fine of $10,000, and a payment of $434,000 in taxes, interest, and penalties).[26] Roosevelt intimated that he would give Truman a lucrative job with the Interstate Commerce Commission.

But Truman evidently balked at the idea of being "bought

off" by the president. He felt that he had done a good job and deserved to be returned to the Senate in his own right. Moreover, the opposition in Missouri that had raised its head after the fall of the Pendergast machine aroused Truman's fighting spirit. Truman sent word back to the president that even if he received just one vote he intended fighting "for vindication and re-election to the Senate."[27]

In a display of independence Truman voted for the reelection of the Missouri district attorney, who had campaigned in the courts against the Pendergast machine, bringing down on his head a storm of criticism and rebuke from Missouri Democrats. The following extract from a letter to Bess illustrates well Truman's impatience and frustration and provides a clear indication of his future attitude toward politics: "I don't care much of a damn what they do or don't, from here out I'm going to do as I please—and they can like it or not as they choose. I've spent my life pleasing people, doing things for 'em, and putting myself in embarrassing positions to save the party and the other fellow, now I've quit. To hell with 'em all. Now I feel better anyway."[28]

Nonetheless, the media continued to regard Truman as an anachronistic creation of the Kansas City machine. The *St. Louis Dispatch* called him "Ambassador of the defunct principality of Pendergastia."[29]

Truman remained loyal to Pendergast long after his downfall in 1939. For all the complexes that came with his being regarded as a Pendergast man, his sense of loyalty (not to mention indebtedness) was as rock solid as that to any of his old army buddies. As he grew older, Truman's "modesty combined with his loyalty to make him blind sometimes to the insensate selfishness which . . . grew in Pendergast like a disease."[30] He was criticized sharply by some when in January 1945 as vice-president he employed a U.S. Air Force plane to fly to Tom Pendergast's funeral. But others admired Truman's loyalty and his courage in standing by an old associate, down on his fortune, literally to the end.

But Truman's loyalties were parochial and at times, as in the Pendergast case, went far beyond the bounds of good taste or political common sense. Even his elevation to the presidency did not persuade Truman to cut himself loose from the Pendergasts. Jim Pendergast was a frequent guest at the White House and on occasion flew with Truman on the presidential plane, the "Sacred Cow." The battered Pendergast machine quite obviously drew encouragement and sustenance from such privileges.

In the 1946 congressional elections Truman mobilized the Pendergast machine to oppose the election of a local congressman to the Fifth District of Kansas City, even informing the press that he had done so. The congressman, Roger Slaughter, was duly defeated, but in May 1947 a grand jury found that there had been a fraudulent miscount of votes. An editorial in the *Washington Evening Star* summed up the whole sorry episode admirably:

Now no one suggests that Mr. Truman, personally, had anything to do with the fraud, or that he personally approved of what was done. Still, the fact remains that the election was obviously stolen. . . . Furthermore, if Mr. Slaughter is right—and the President does not deny it—Mr. Truman continues to be a dues paying member of the Pendergast organization and permits the machine to list him on its letterhead as its vice-president. . . . The whole affair is a sordid business, the worst thing that can happen in a democracy, and the President, having enlisted the support of Pendergast in the first instance, cannot escape some measure of connection with it.[31]

In conclusion, two points relevant to our theme may be underlined here. First, Truman's steadfast loyalty to Pendergast, even if politically unwise, was entirely in character, a reflection of the values that Truman held supreme. It was a blind, almost canine loyalty, one that for all its differences was akin to that he retained for Jacobson or for his former army buddies. He remained stubbornly confident that so long as his own two hands were clean he could not be held personally responsible for the machine's misdoings.

Second, it is equally clear that for all his devotion Truman was deeply troubled, at times to the point of humiliation, by the restrictions on his liberty imposed by the Pendergast machine. Thus, his early political career reinforced the strong urge in Truman to prove himself independent, to make it on his own, and, just as important, to be accepted in his own right, for his own virtues.

This is of special relevance to the issues discussed in this book. For when faced by various pressure groups during his presidency— for example, as in the case of Palestine, the State Department on the one hand and the Zionist lobby on the other—Truman would balk at being told what to do. He was ultrasensitive to any infringement on what he considered his prerogatives. He had already had more than enough of that for one lifetime. The "striped-pants boys" (as Truman called them) of the State Department would earn a special rebuke in Truman's memoirs.[32] But Truman also vented vitriolic diatribes against the Zionists (like his earlier comments about Jews, these were reserved for private forums or personal letters), and there would come a time when Truman refused to receive any Zionist in the White House.

Ironically, the president who has gone down in history as being one of the greatest friends of the Zionists was at times, in private, reduced to a bitter frustration that brought to the surface unsavory prejudices.

THREE

The Jewish Problem
First Acquaintance

JEWISH REFUGEES

With the Nazi takeover in Germany in 1933 and the gradual incursions, both legal and physical, on Jewish rights, a great many Jews began to flee the country. The movement increased drastically after the Kristallnacht pogrom of November 1938, but once war broke out in 1939 the efforts of panic-stricken Jews to escape were increasingly futile. As the Germans conquered large areas of Europe, they all but closed off the continent to all further Jewish emigration.

The persecution of the Jews by the Nazis and the horrors of the Holocaust cannot be said to have been issues of major concern to Harry S. Truman. During his two terms as U.S. senator, from 1935 to 1945, Nazi policies toward the Jews reached their tragic climax.

But like many of his illustrious contemporaries, Truman did not monitor the development of the Jewish tragedy. He never criticized the Roosevelt administration for its procrastination on Jewish problems, nor did he press for or join any initiatives to take any special measures to help the Jews in their plight. True, in his few dealings with the State Department, Truman was wont to deride the excessive red tape. This was a routine complaint of his against bureaucracies, however, and it did not seem to occur to him that a more purposeful and vigorous direction was needed from the political echelons. As will be seen below, appeals to him to make some special effort on the Jews' behalf were met with the administration's stock reply that nothing should be done that might impede the Allied war effort.[1]

Senator Truman did not initiate or take part in any general campaign to help Jewish refugees from Europe. His association with the Jewish refugee problem, both in the 1930s and during the war itself, was almost entirely the result of his senatorial duties to his constituency in Missouri. His efforts resulted from specific appeals, especially from old friends and associates, for example, former soldiers of Battery D or political supporters.

Any Jew with direct or indirect access to a senator stood an immeasurably better chance of getting an endangered relative out of Europe to the United States. On reading Truman's senatorial refugee files, one is reminded of the dictum about the importance of "whom you know." For example, one family helped by Truman was that of Alex Sachs. Sachs was a civil engineer who in 1932 had been recommended to Truman for the Democratic nomination for Jackson County highway engineer. Sachs and Truman worked closely for the next two years and developed a mutual admiration. Truman's county roads program was the first great success of his political career. During the 1930s, Senator Truman and his staff helped several of Sachs's distant cousins to obtain immigration visas into the United States. As a former close associate of Truman's, Alex Sachs was then approached by several local Jews, who asked if he would write to the senator from Missouri for aid in getting members of their families out of Europe. In 1977 Howard Sachs, the son of Alex, checked Truman's senatorial files and found more than a dozen immigration case files in which his father's name had been used to obtain Senator Truman's help.[2]

Another obvious source for appeals was Eddie Jacobson. Dave Finkelstein, a friend of the Jacobsons "for over 30 years," wished to bring to the United States his fifteen-year-old nephew, Heinz. Jacobson spoke about Finkelstein during a visit by Truman to Kansas City and followed it up with a letter that was not entirely devoid of flattery: "They have been trying for over a year to get some action on this matter but I really think it takes a 'Big Shot' like yourself to kick things along."[3] Truman wrote soon after to the U.S. consul general in Berlin, expressing his personal interest in the boy's application for an immigration visa; within the month he received a reply that it had been granted.[4]

Another interesting file is that on the Blumenfeld family, who were also trying to flee from Germany to the United States. The Blumenfelds were cousins both of the Jacobsons and another Kansas City resident, Lee Erb. Erb wrote to Truman to appeal on their behalf "with Ed's knowledge and approval." Erb complained about the procrastination of the U.S. consulate officials in Germany. They had asked for documents from the Kansas City sponsors (tax bills, affidavits) giving evidence of their ability to support the refugees in the United States. Although Erb had sent them affidavits proving that his own wealth was assessed at more than thirty thousand dollars, the officials were not satisfied. In his letter to Truman, Erb suggested: "It may be that our Consul General in Berlin is not any more favorable to having our people come here than Hitler is to have them remain. I can't help but feel that the objections raised are without substantial merit, but I am attempting to comply nevertheless."[5]

Anything to which Eddie Jacobson's name was attached produced instant action on Truman's part. Within a week he had written again to Douglas Jenkins, the U.S. consul in Berlin, giving his opinion that Erb was a man of "excellent reputation" and informing Jenkins that he would like to see Erb's family accommodated. For good measure Truman added the observation that apart from being related to Erb the Blumenfelds were "cousins of Mr. Eddie Jacobson, an outstanding businessman of Kansas City, and a close personal friend."[6] Truman's definition of Jacobson's standing in the Kansas City business community at that time was hardly accurate to say the least.

Ironically, Truman had an account to settle with the Erb family in Kansas City. He wrote to Eddie Jacobson about the appeal he had received from Lee Erb and reported that he had already written to the consul general in Berlin. Then he added:

But Ed, Lee has been doing everything he possibly could to put my sister's filling station out of business out there on [Highway] 71, and I don't like his attitude.

I wish you would tell him that I want to see him succeed in business and do as well as he can, but I don't think he should do some of the things he has been doing to make it unpleasant for the young men who are working for Mary.[7]

Jacobson duly passed on Truman's letter to Erb, who quickly wrote to reassure Truman that he had checked out his assertions and could state unequivocally that the senator had been misinformed.[8]

Four days later Erb wrote to Truman again, informing him that the Blumenfelds' papers had again been returned by the consulate, as they had omitted to insert specifically the surnames of his cousin's wife and daughter. This example of crass bureaucratic procrastination brought Erb to the conclusion that without the senator's further aid, "unmerited technical objections will be urged for the purpose of delay." The matter was already one of some urgency, Erb concluded, since none of the family was permitted to work, and they were dependent on charity.[9] Truman wasted no time at all and wrote once again to the consul general, enclosing an additional affidavit stressing his personal interest in the case: "Mr. Erb is a close neighbor of mine at home in Jackson County, Missouri. I know him and I know that he can assume the responsibility and meet it regarding this family."[10]

Curiously, Truman seems to have overlooked or misinterpreted Erb's complaints against the State Department officials. When he reported to Erb on his renewed approach to the Berlin consulate, he referred to the obstacles raised by the *German* officials. Whatever the case, his next letter to Erb provides one of Truman's first recorded critiques of the Nazi regime: "You are perfectly correct about all the technicalities that the German Government is using to harass the Jewish people. I don't approve of it and I am morally certain that they will be properly taken care of for their attitude at some time in the future."[11]

Once war broke out, the situation of the Jews changed radically for the worse. Jews in Germany, and then in other countries conquered by the Germans, came under immediate physical threat. Furthermore, after the United States joined the war against Germany in December 1941, American consulates across Europe were closed down, making it impossible for refugees to obtain immigration visas. On top of all this, as great an obstacle was presented by the protracted procedures and excessive red tape of the immigration division of the State Department, which during the war managed to keep immigration well below the meager visa quotas officially allocated.[12]

The wartime correspondence in Truman's refugee files offers a poignant glimpse into the variegated problems arising for the Jews out of the German occupation of Europe. It gave Truman a firsthand acquaintance with the trials and tribulations of the Jews in their persecution, no doubt providing something of an education for the senator from Missouri. To distress was added frustration, as all too frequently Truman's efforts were in vain.

In February 1940 Truman received an appeal from Dave Berenstein, a Jewish attorney and political supporter from St. Louis, who later that year would manage Senator Truman's election campaign in that city. Berenstein wanted Truman to help secure a "derivative citizenship certificate" for a mutual friend, Sam Ferer. Ferer's citizenship rights derived from his father, but the only evidence that the American authorities would accept was available from a now-inaccessible village in Poland. Since that country was now under Nazi rule, it was patently impossible to secure the said document. The request illustrated the willfully obtuse attitude of the Immigration and Naturalization Service.

Truman duly wrote to the commissioner of immigration and naturalization at the Department of Labor, declaring that "Mr. Ferer has more than enough evidence to show that he is the son of Aaron Ferer and that through his father he is entitled to American citizenship." After some nine months the naturalization service issued a naturalization certificate to Ferer.[13]

In mid-1941 another appeal arrived, invoking the name of "your friend Jacobson." Paul Levy, a men's and women's outfitter from Butler, Missouri, had approached Jacobson about getting his brother, Siegfried Loewy, out of Germany. He then asked Senator Truman to send a cable to the U.S. consul in Stuttgart so that his brother could "obtain his visa immediately, and get out of that God-for-saken country." But Truman was powerless to help, since all American consulates in Axis or occupied countries were being closed. Truman's secretary, Harry H. Vaughan, wrote to Levy in Truman's absence that should his brother manage to get to a country from where he could apply for an American visa, Truman's office would be pleased to take up the case again with the State Department's visa division.[14]

Two particularly distressing cases illustrate the fate of Jews in France during the war. One involved C. W. Evans, an old friend of Truman's and a political fund-raiser. He wrote to Truman in June 1941 about a client of his, Izzie Jacobs, for whom he was trying to secure immigration visas for some family members in unoccupied France. Jacobs had received a cable from the family in Marseilles indicating that visas were available for July 13 and that tickets were booked on a boat sailing on August 15, 1941. But the consulate could issue the visas only with Washington's consent. The cable from France to the Jacobs family asking them to have Washington cable the visas to the U.S. consulate at Marseilles concluded on an urgent note: "Personal intervention by influence of personality at Washington even better. Most urgent. . . . Do all you possible. Last chance to save us. Absolutely desperate. Do everything by cable. I shall repay. Horenslup."[15] Evans's letter urged Truman to intervene, stating the deepest appreciation on the part of himself, the Jacobs family, and another family involved in the case.

But it took more than a year for the State Department to report back to Truman on the Horenslup family, and by that time it was too late to help them.[16] The correspondence does not clarify the reason for the protracted delay, but one may assume that it was either because in the meantime the consulate had closed or that the family had been deported (the first deportations of French Jews to Auschwitz, Poland, began in March 1942. In July the French leaders Laval and Pétain agreed to Gestapo deportation plans, and the really large-scale deportations of French Jews began in October 1942).[17]

In September 1942 Truman received a letter from William Friedman, a wealthy St. Louis businessman. Friedman appealed for help in the case of a Jewish refugee girl who had been living with his family for the previous five years. In 1940 the girl's mother, Lili Westerfeld, had been deported from Germany to a concentration camp in unoccupied France.

In August 1942 Mrs. Westerfeld had advised her daughter in the United States that the U.S. consul at Marseilles had invited her to his office to collect an immigration visa. But she doubted that she would be allowed to travel there and feared she would soon be transported to Poland. The Friedman family was willing to pay for Mrs. Westerfeld's ticket and to support her in the United States. They asked Truman to cable the U.S. consul at Marseilles, urging him "to use his influence with the French authorities to permit Mrs. Westerfeld to make the trip to Marseilles."[18]

Shortly after mailing his letter, Friedman cabled Truman that he had received news that Mrs. Westerfeld had indeed been deported to Poland. He now asked Truman if there was anything either he or the State Department could do. In response to Truman's inquiry the State Department informed him that since Mrs. Westerfeld was not an American citizen neither the department nor any of its consular staff abroad could do anything on her behalf, and the question of her leaving Europe would rest with the appropriate foreign authorities. In reply to a further inquiry from Truman that same November, the State Department informed him that no further action in France was possible because of the closure of all American consular establishments in that country.[19]

Truman's senatorial immigration files contain not only cases involving Jewish refugees in Europe but also some concerning U.S. residents who had run into trouble with the American immigration authorities. Again, Truman's interest was largely a question of doing favors for old friends, when he could.

PUBLIC APPEALS

The number of Jews fortunate enough to escape from Europe to the West was infinitesimal. The vast majority were trapped inside Nazi-occupied Europe, and some six million perished in what would become known as the Holocaust.

The mass killing of the Jews of Europe began with the German invasion of Russia in June 1941. Special "killing squads" (*Einsatzgruppen*) accompanied the Wehrmacht on its conquest. The "final solution" to the "Jewish problem" was given bureaucratic sanction at the Wansee Conference in January 1942. The conference planned for the murder of Europe's entire Jewish population of eleven million. The Jews were to be gassed to death in specially constructed extermination camps. News of the conference and its agenda was leaked to the West gradually during the spring and summer of 1942. The Allies' first official cognizance that the Jews were the chosen victims of the Nazi death machine came in December 1942 with Allied broadcasts and warnings of retribution for the Nazis' crimes against the Jews.

Several of Truman's Jewish constituents wrote, appealing to him to speak out against German atrocities and to initiate some special effort to alleviate the fate of their Jewish brethren in Europe. With one single exception Truman's responses were coldly correct, spelling out impassively the administration's official line.

In April 1942 Truman received an official appeal from the national chairmen of the United Jewish Appeal, the major Jewish fund-raising body in the United States. Although the nature of the Holocaust was still a matter of general rumor in the West, Nazi persecution threatened millions of European Jews. The appeal stressed the general need for rescue efforts, although it lacked the sense of life-and-death urgency that would come when the Nazis' final solution became a matter of established fact:

While all of us are deeply concerned with our responsibilities in our country's war effort, we nevertheless are desirous of making any additional contribution possible toward the strengthening of the structure of humanity which is the framework of our democratic way of life. . . . We are also mindful that the rescue of large numbers of victims of Nazi persecution whose devotion to democracy has been tested in the crucible of Nazi persecution may make a distinct contribution to the winning of the peace which all of us wish to secure together with victory on the field of battle. . . .

It is our sincere hope that we may have a message of encouragement from you as we go forward with the tasks which are our solemn responsibility as Americans and as Jews.[20]

Truman's reply was somewhat perfunctory and closed with a mild admonition of which the administration would have been proud:

You are doing great work in endeavoring to keep up the morale of the Jewish refugees and also in your endeavor to unify the efforts of the American Jews for the proper care of their brethren in distress.

I congratulate you on it most highly. In doing this extra war work however, remember that the main effort is now for the United States to win the war as quickly as possible.[21]

Even when a year later Truman received a letter referring to what was by then common knowledge, that is, the "deliberate extermination of Jews," his response was again hardly imaginative or sympathetic and barely more than bureaucratically neutral: "I am sure that what can be done is being done to relieve this shocking situation by providing the means for these people to go to places of refuge. However, as you will readily realize, with most of the world at war it is a very difficult thing to accomplish, and the results, as compared with the need, are pitifully small."[22]

Truman *did* come out, exceptionally, in a strong public statement against the Nazi persecution of the Jews. He was apparently prevailed upon to make this statement by leaders of the American Jewish community, which in March 1943 organized the Joint Emergency Committee on European Jewish Affairs. During the spring of 1943, just before the Bermuda Conference (discussed later), the committee held forty mass rallies in twenty different states to "publicize the Holocaust and to mobilize public opinion behind the rescue proposals" that had already been adopted at a mass rally in New York City on March 1.[23]

The occasion of Truman's speech was the "United Rally to Demand the Rescue of Doomed Jews" held in Chicago on April 14, 1943, just five days before the official opening of the Bermuda Conference. Because of the uniqueness of Truman's public tirade against Hitler's anti-Jewish policies, the text of his speech is quoted here at length:

Through the edict of a mad Hitler and a degenerate Mussolini, the people of that ancient race, the Jews, are being herded like animals into the ghettos [on April 18, 1943, the Jewish resistance in the Warsaw ghetto rose in revolt against the German deportation and extermination policy. The Germans invaded and destroyed the ghetto], the concentration camps, and the wastelands of Europe. The men, the women and the children of this honored people are being starved, yes! actually murdered by the fiendish huns and Fascists. Today these oppressed people, still with spirit unbroken look for succor to us, we people of the United States, whose flag has always stood for liberty, freedom and justice for all. . . . So on down through the pages of the history of America, you find these efforts of the Jews—as of all Americans—striving for all those things that have made America great. . . . No one can any longer doubt the horrible intentions of the Nazi beasts. We know that they plan the systematic slaughter throughout Europe, not only of the Jews but of vast numbers of other innocent peoples. The streets of Europe, running with the blood of the massacred, are stark proof of the insatiable thirst of the Nazi hordes. . . . Today—not tomorrow—we must do all that is humanly possible to provide a haven and place of safety for all those who can be grasped from the hands of the Nazi butchers. Free lands must be opened to them. Their present oppressors must know that they will be held directly accountable for their bloody deeds. . . . This is not a Jewish problem. It is an American problem—and we must and will face it squarely and honorably.[24]

Truman received an immediate accolade from a prominent member of his Jewish constituency, James H. Becker: "Our hopes were buttressed by the glowing, trenchant words spoken by you. All of us appreciated your coming and your participation."[25] Becker was chairman of the program committee for the "United Rally to Demand the Rescue of Doomed Jews" and a member of the American Jewish Committee. (This committee was the oldest American Jewish defense organization, founded by German Jewish immigrants in 1906 in reaction to the Russian pogroms. It included some of the most prominent members of the German Jewish elite in the United States and conducted its affairs in "an oligarchic, *noblesse oblige* fashion until the 1940s, limiting membership to a select few.")[26]

One is struck by the contrast between this unique, public expression of Truman's outrage against Nazi racist policies and the correctness of his private correspondence. It is quite possible that his public speech was written for him by the Joint Emergency Committee. But in any case, the speech can leave no doubt that Truman was by now well aware of the nature of the Holocaust then proceeding in Europe. Public rallies, at which a good impression might be easily made, were one thing, however, and in truth they cost very little.

In his private correspondence Senator Truman equally left no doubt that he was squarely behind the administration's policies or the lack thereof. Whereas he had closed his Chicago speech with the statement that Jewish persecution was an "American problem" that should be dealt with "squarely and honorably" and had urged action "today—not tomorrow," when it came to a direct appeal to raise his voice in the Senate, he now urged patience.

In December 1943, nine months after the public rally, Rabbi Phineas Smoller, leader of the United Hebrew congregation in Joplin, Missouri, sent Truman a petition, addressed to President Roosevelt and the members of the Senate, on behalf of the one hundred Jewish families in his congregation:

We appeal to you to lend your personal support, in the Senate, to the relief of the plight of Europe's remnant of Israel, and to aid in the formulation of such opinion in the Senate as will impress itself, through our State Department, on the British Government, towards the end . . . that the people of the Jewish Faith, everywhere in the world, shall be assured of the benefit of the Four Freedoms.[27]

Truman's reply was perfunctory, almost patronizing, and concluded with the usual admonition:

I do not think it is the business of Senators who are not on the Foreign Relations Committee to dabble in matters which affect our relations with the Allies at this time. There is nobody on earth who dislikes more than I do the actions of Hitler and Mussolini; but it is of vital importance that the Jewish Congregations be patient and support wholeheartedly the foreign policy of our government. I think you will find that every effort is being made by the government to accomplish just what you have in mind.[28]

THE "BERGSON BOYS"

The so-called Bergson boys represented a small circle of young Palestinian Jews, headed by Hillel Kook (alias Peter Bergson), active in the United States. They were followers of the Zionist Revisionist Vladimir Jabotinsky and secretly members of the Palestine underground army, the Irgun. In December 1941 the group had set up a Committee for a Jewish Army, whose goal was to induce the Allies to mobilize an independent army of Palestinian Jews and stateless Jewish refugees to fight Hitler. It was presumed that such an army would establish rights to a Jewish state in Palestine.

The committee achieved great publicity successes through full-page advertisements in the press and dramatic stage presentations. Its chairman, the celebrated Dutch author Pierre van Paassen, wrote the text of many of the ads; the stage spectacles, such as *We Shall Never Die* and *A Flag is Born,* were written by Hollywood screenwriter Ben Hecht.[29]

Bergson was not always scrupulous in his methods and habitually canvassed the support of prominent public figures without explaining to them properly what they were about to sign their name to. Having gained someone's initial support, Bergson did not always trouble to secure the individual agreement of each signatory to a new advertisement.[30] The committee also fell afoul of the American Jewish establishment, which accused it of "recklessness and sensationalism, as well as gross effrontery in presuming to speak for an American Jewish constituency."[31]

In January 1942 Truman was approached indirectly to join Bergson's Committee for a Jewish Army. Congressman Andrew L. Somers wrote to tell him that he had become interested in a movement that he felt would "go far to end the persecutions of the Jewish Race by governments in the future." Somers had delivered a series of speeches across the country in favor of a Jewish army for Palestine and had also presented a resolution to President Roosevelt in which he asked him to direct the secretary of state to prevail upon the British to authorize such an army.[32] (In October 1940 the British government had approved the mobilization of a Jewish division, which was to be composed partly of Palestinian and partly of American Jews. The Foreign Office, fearful of adverse reaction among Arabs, was able initially to get the scheme postponed and ultimately, in October 1941, canceled.)[33]

Somers's was not the first approach to Truman on this subject, and predictably, and typically, Truman begged off. His reply once again adhered faithfully to the official administration line:

I have had a great deal of correspondence about this suggestion but so far as the United States is concerned I think the best thing for the Jews to do is to go right into our Army as they did in the last war and make the same sort of good soldiers as they did before.

It is an honorable undertaking to organize an Army for Palestine but I think American citizens ought to serve in the American Army.[34]

Following further contacts with Bergson, however, in May

1942 Truman was prevailed upon to join his committee, as were several other legislators. Their membership probably involved nothing more than lending their names to the full-page ads published by the committee. On November 2, 1942, the twenty-fifth anniversary of the Balfour Declaration, Truman's was one of the signatures of sixty-eight senators and 194 congressmen appended to a statement commemorating the event.[35]

Truman's membership in the Committee for a Jewish Army lasted barely a year. He resigned abruptly in May 1943 in protest against the committee's forthright condemnation of the Bermuda Conference.

The conference, held in April 1943, had been planned by Britain and the United States ostensibly to find shelter for Europe's refugees (Jews were not specifically mentioned). There was an implicit agreement between the two allies that Britain would not press the United States to relax its rigid visa policy and the United States would not press Britain to allow more Jews into Palestine. The principal "achievements" of the conference would be the evacuation of five thousand Jewish refugees from Spain and the revival of the prewar Intergovernmental Committee on Refugees, which proved to be just as ineffective as it had been before the war.[36] Historians have been almost unanimous in their condemnation of the conference: "The Bermuda Conference was, in fact, no more than a pretense. It was a diplomatic hoax intended to defuse the pressures for rescue that had built up in England and the United States."[37]

When the details of the Holocaust started emerging at the end of 1942, the Bergson group began concentrating on public pressure to mount rescue efforts. It now constituted another public body, called the Emergency Committee to Save the Jewish People of Europe. In the spring of 1943 this committee led a public campaign to discredit the Bermuda Conference. On May 4, 1943, it published a full-page ad in the *New York Times* headed "TO 5,000,000 JEWS IN THE NAZI DEATH TRAP BERMUDA WAS A CRUEL MOCKERY." The ad accused the State Department of procrastination and put forward the committee's own ten-point rescue program.[38]

Truman took great umbrage and wrote to Bergson two days later, criticizing the use made of senators' names, including his own, without receiving prior approval: "While there is nothing to indicate that this group of distinguished citizens endorses the specific advertisement, the inference might be made that they do. . . . The Committee and I must come to an understanding at once that greater caution be exercised in publishing the names of Senators who favor our cause."[39] But the key point was that Truman did not share Bergson's jaundiced view of the Bermuda Conference, especially since a Senate colleague of his, Scott Lucas, had been one of the three official American delegates: "My colleagues and I have great respect for Senator Lucas and we do not deem it fair to him to prejudge or condemn the work of the committee until after it has had sufficient opportunity to make a report. . . . I must therefore withhold my judgement until such time as I know what exactly took place in the conference."[40]

On that same day (May 6, presumably *after* Truman had sent his first letter to Bergson) the Senate debated the castigation of the conference in the *New York Times* ad. Senator Scott Lucas had taken the attack personally and made it an issue on the Senate floor. Lucas alleged that none of the senators whose names appeared in the ad had in fact been notified in advance. He also read out a letter from Senator Edwin Johnson, chairman of the Committee for a Jewish Army, to Bergson, in which he admonished the latter for impugning Lucas, an "esteemed colleague."[41]

A battery of senators, including Truman, then asked Lucas to yield the floor so that they could also dissociate themselves from the ad and express their confidence in the senator. As one historian concluded acidly: "The integrity of the senatorial club had to be preserved."[42]

Truman had *not* decided of his own accord to resign from Bergson's committee after reading the offending ad. The debate on the Senate floor made up his mind for him, and the next day he sent Bergson his written resignation:

Senator Johnson informs me this advertisement was never submitted to him for approval, and I have the same information from a number of other Senators.

I am withdrawing my name from your Committee, and you are not authorized under any circumstances to make use of it for any purpose in the future.

This does not mean my sympathies are not with the down-trodden

Jews of Europe, but when you take it on yourself without consultation to attack members of the Senate and House of Representatives who are working in your interest I cannot approve of that procedure.[43]

Truman was apparently the only senator to resign as a result of the incident surrounding the *New York Times* ad. Bergson, realizing for once that he had gone too far, made a public apology on May 8.[44] But Truman did not retract and probably felt himself better off out of Bergson's company. The fraudulent use of the senators' names undoubtedly offended Truman's code of ethics. Moreover, Truman could derive political comfort from the ostracism of the maverick Bergson group by the mainstream of American Jews.

Truman took care to send a copy of his resignation letter to Rabbi Stephen Wise, chairman of the American Zionist Emergency Council. Their exchange provides a classic example of the damage done to the Zionist cause in the United States by the divisions within the Jewish community. As Rabbi Wise soon discovered, it was not just the Bergson group that Truman was divorcing himself from but the Jewish cause itself.

In his letter to Truman, Rabbi Wise expressed a fear common to the Jewish establishment:

The activities of Mr. Bergson have been a source of considerable embarrassment to the organized Zionist movement in this country. . . . Unhappily the recent reaction to the efforts of Mr. Bergson is liable to obscure the appalling plight of the Jews of Europe. And while it is true that no report has been issued as yet on the proceedings of the Bermuda conference, there seems to be little indication that the situation is likely to be tackled in a large and effective way.[45]

Wise hoped that Truman would not allow Bergson's "irresponsible acts" to affect his "understanding approach" to Jewish problems. But Truman seems to have allowed the incident to grow all out of proportion. Although he evidently knew of the plight of millions of European Jews—as evidenced by his speech at the Chicago rally just six weeks before—Truman now washed his hands effectively of any further involvement on the specious grounds of the harm caused to American military interests. In a letter full of hyperbole Truman replied to Wise:

It is fellows like Mr. Bergson who go off half cocked in matters that affect strategy of the whole world that cause all the trouble.

No one feels more sympathetic towards the Jews than the members of the United States Senate who signed that Committee petition, but when an ad such as Bergson put in the New York Times can be used to stir up trouble where our troops are fighting it is certainly outside my policy to be mixed up in such an organization.

That ad was used by all the Arabs in North Africa in an endeavor to create dissension among them and caused them to stab our fellows in the back.

We want to help the Jews and we are going to help them but we cannot do it at the expense of our military maneuvers.[46]

The pretext of harming American (or British) military interests was used frequently during the war to excuse lack of any meaningful Allied action to save Europe's doomed Jewish communities. Truman was quite simply taking a page out of the administration's book. As has been noted already, Truman showed great sympathy for Jewish suffering, but he also "displayed great caution not to commit himself to any line of action which deviated from the Roosevelt Administration's policies" vis-à-vis the Holocaust.[47]

Thus, for all of his professed sympathy, whether public or private, for the Jewish tragedy, Truman proved unwilling to step out of line with official policy or translate his occasional rhetoric into action. His efforts on behalf of the Jews remained parochial—individual acts to help out old friends or associates—or were moves that were politically beneficial. His "refugee Zionism," which would become prominent in his early presidential policy on Palestine, has been assessed as merely reflecting Truman's dual position as "Congressman and sympathetic average American citizen."[48] Like most of his contemporaries in politics, it would appear that Truman failed to appreciate the wider historical significance of the Holocaust.

FOUR

Truman and Zionism

THE 1939 WHITE PAPER

Truman's first act of support for the Zionist cause is generally dated to May 1939, when he is alleged to have made a short speech on the Senate floor in condemnation of the British white paper on Palestine issued that same month by the Chamberlain government in Britain. Abba Eban has claimed, with perhaps some exaggeration, that "there is no evidence that Truman was even aware of the Zionist problem until he made [this] brief speech."[1] (The 1939 white paper determined that Palestine would become an independent, democratic (i.e., Arab) state within ten years; that Jewish immigration would be restricted to seventy-five thousand over the next five years, after which all further immigration would require Arab consent; and that land sales to Jews would be prohibited in most of Palestine and severely restricted in certain parts.)[2]

In fact, Truman did *not* speak on Palestine in 1939 on the Senate floor as historians have hitherto claimed.[3] Truman asked to have a newspaper article printed as an appendix to the *Congressional Record,* and it was his covering note, also printed as part of the "Extension of Remarks," that has been mistaken for a speech on the Senate floor. (An "Extension of Remarks" consists of material not actually delivered on the floor of the Senate or House but included in the *Congressional Record* at the request of members of Congress.)

The article that Truman had inserted into the official record was written by Barnet Nover and had appeared in the *Washington Post* on May 18, 1939. In his covering note Truman took his cue from the article's invocative title: "British Surrender—A Munich for the Holy Land." Like Winston Churchill across the Atlantic, Truman referred to the Palestine white paper as yet a further expression of the Chamberlain government's disastrous appeasement policies: "Mr. President, the British Government has used its diplomatic umbrella again, this time on Palestine. It has made a scrap of paper out of Lord Balfour's promise to the Jews. It has just added another to the long list of surrenders to the axis powers."[4]

In the early 1940s Truman seems to have had some contact with Chaim Weizmann, president of the World Zionist Organization, but not in connection with furthering the Zionist cause with the administration. Weizmann was trying to interest the U.S. government in his chemical process to produce synthetic rubber out of grain alcohol. Blocked by the American oil companies and other vested interests, Weizmann turned to his friend Paul Uhlman, head of the Uhlman Grain Company of Kansas City and a generous donor to Weizmann's scientific institute in Rehovot, Palestine. Uhlman put Weizmann in touch with Senator Truman, and apparently a government plant was eventually set up in Atchison, Kansas, that used the Weizmann process.[5] (The *Letters and Papers of Chaim Weizmann* contain nothing on any contact between Weizmann and Truman during the war.)

In early 1941 Truman lent his name, along with those of numerous other prominent persons, to the pro-Zionist American Palestine Committee, just reconstituted by the American Zionist Emergency Council. He was thanked by Rabbi Stephen Wise for lending his support to the Zionist cause.[6]

All this did not add up to any active commitment. And when in 1944 a pro-Zionist resolution, recommending that Palestine be converted into a Jewish commonwealth, was brought before the Senate, Truman opposed it (as he did later as president). On this issue, as on those of a Jewish army and Allied rescue efforts, Truman adhered faithfully to the Roosevelt policy of inaction. He engaged in, as Roosevelt himself has been accused of doing on Jewish issues, "the politics of gestures."

THE TAFT-WAGNER RESOLUTION

Truman's commitment to Zionism was put to the test in 1944, an election year, when the American Zionist Movement lobbied congressmen in support of its cause. The lobby had begun early in the year because of the pending deadline (March 1944) set by the 1939 British white paper on the ending of all further Jewish immigration to Palestine unless with Arab consent. The Zionists hoped that congressional endorsement of their goals would deter the British from implementing the immigration restrictions.[7]

In January 1944, largely as a result of the Zionist lobby, the Taft-Wagner Senate resolution was drafted, pressing for the abrogation of the 1939 white paper restrictions and urging the establishment of Palestine as a Jewish commonwealth. (In May 1942 the American Zionist Movement, at an extraordinary conference attended by David Ben-Gurion and Chaim Weizmann, had passed the Biltmore resolution, which urged the establishment of Palestine as a Jewish commonwealth as part of the new world order after the war. In 1943 a general conference representing most of American Jewry had endorsed the Biltmore resolution.)

With the Taft-Wagner resolution pending, Truman was lobbied by a number of his Jewish constituents for his support. Truman followed loyally the line set by the administration that any American intervention in the British sphere of influence in Palestine during the war would harm Allied military interests in the Middle East, particularly in the Arab world. Truman had a form letter drawn up, copies of which he sent out to all those who were lobbying him. After expressing his familiarity with the Palestine resolution, Truman referred to it as "one which affects the foreign relations program between Great Britain, the United States, and the Middle East." His letter continued:

My sympathy of course is with the Jewish people, but I am of the opinion that a resolution such as this should be very circumspectly handled until we know just exactly where we are going and why. . . .

. . . with Great Britain and Russia absolutely necessary to us in financing the war I don't want to throw any bricks to upset the applecart, although *when the right time comes I am willing to help make the fight for a Jewish homeland in Palestine.*[8]

Truman's form letter did little to convince or reassure his constituents. His unwillingness to stand up now against the 1939 white paper (as he had formally in 1939) produced a backlash of local Jewish public opinion. The leaders of the pro-Zionist Jewish community of St. Louis were particularly incensed, especially when they contrasted Truman's lukewarm correctness with the "warm and energetic support given by the other Senator from Missouri, Bennett Champ Clark."[9]

One significant letter that reached Truman was written by M. J. Slonim, president of the St. Louis branch of the American Jewish Committee, claiming to represent sixty thousand Jews in the greater St. Louis area. Slonim's letter, which accused Truman of not living up to his reputation as "one of the dearest friends the Zionist cause has in the House of Congress," was not entirely devoid of the inevitable flattery. Slonim had been approached about Truman's attitude on the Senate resolution by a number of people who could not understand how Truman could "hesitate about supporting a resolution which [would] most vitally affect the position of the Jewish people throughout the world." Slonim's letter continued:

I gather from your letter that in your opinion, the matter of the Jewish Commonwealth should be postponed for diplomatic reasons. . . . I would agree with such an attitude if nothing were done during hostilities to change the status of the Jewish people in Palestine. This as you well know, is not the case. . . . We feel that the British are now making commitments to the Arabs and are crystallizing the Jewish position in Zion. . . . You, Senator, more than most Americans, know that without Palestine the Jews have little to look forward to in most parts of this brutal world. *Over three million Jewish civilians have been exterminated in occupied Europe. . . . We are all one hundred percent for the war effort of course. But, we cannot understand how the appeasement of the Arabs, who have done virtually nothing for the Allied Nations, can achieve anything worthwhile.*

I plead with you—who are a true friend of our people—to abandon all hesitation and to help us now with this historic resolution in the Senate.[10]

All appeals notwithstanding, Truman upheld the administration's opposition to the Taft-Wagner resolution. But the Zionists were encouraged when on March 9 President Roosevelt received their leaders, Rabbis Wise and Abba Hillel Silver, and authorized them to state that the American government had never officially endorsed the 1939 white paper (formally this was correct, though neither had the Roosevelt administration protested it nor intervened with the British government in any way whatever). But Zionist euphoria was short-lived, as one week later the State and War departments with Roosevelt's approval succeeded in having the Senate resolution shelved on the grounds that it constituted a "security-military" threat. Unknown to the Zionists, Roosevelt thanked Speaker Sam Rayburn in private for having the resolution blocked and at the same time sent letters to Arab capitals minimizing his own statement on the white paper and reassuring the Arabs that "no decision altering the basic situation of Palestine should be reached without full consultation with both Arabs and Jews."[11] In a speech on the Senate floor at the end of March Truman followed the administration's lead and, using the text of his form letter, opposed the current raising of the Palestine issue.[12]

This was but the first foray, however, in a long political campaign. During the summer of 1944, both Republicans and Democrats held their party conventions. The Zionists, inspired by Rabbi Silver, applied their new strategy of "initiating Democratic and Republican competition for the Jewish vote . . . thereby shaking Roosevelt's assumption that the Jews were safely in the Democratic bag."[13]

Rabbi Silver, with his excellent Republican connections (Senators Robert A. Taft and Arthur Vandenberg), and Rabbi Wise, calling on his good connections and long-time association with the Democrats, succeeded in procuring from both party conventions a commitment to the Zionist platform. But the Democrats upstaged the Republicans. Whereas the latter called for a "free and democratic Commonwealth" in Palestine, the Democratic plank favored the establishment of a "free and democratic *Jewish* commonwealth."[14]

In October 1944 both presidential candidates, Roosevelt and Dewey, endorsed their parties' Palestine planks. Roosevelt was duly reelected, and Harry Truman found himself suddenly elevated to national prominence as vice-president.

The Zionists' success with both parties augured well, and in November 1944 they determined to renew the campaign for the congressional resolutions. Senators Taft and Wagner reintroduced their resolution (in the House, Representative Sol Bloom [Democrat, New York City] introduced the Wright-Compton resolution with a similar text).

But when the Senate's Foreign Relations Committee began its consideration of the resolution, the State Department again advised that the present time was not suitable. Secretary of State Edward Stettinius himself lobbied vigorously against it and referred to "rising Soviet interests in the Middle East." On December 11, 1944, the committee voted by ten to eight to table the resolution. The president persuaded Senator Wagner to go along with the deferral, speaking of his fears of an Arab "massacre" of the Jews and of how Wagner's resolution might restrict him, the president, at the pending Yalta Conference.[15]

On April 12, 1945, President Roosevelt died, and an overawed Harry Truman succeeded automatically to the presidency of the United States. As noted already, during the war Truman had adhered consistently to Roosevelt's hands-off policy toward Zionism and Palestine. Like the late president, Truman regarded that country as lying within the British sphere of interest and believed that overzealous support of Zionism might alienate the Arab world from the West. Although having every sympathy for Jewish sufferings during the war, Truman did *not* favor the establishment of a Jewish state in Palestine.

The last episode of the Taft-Wagner resolution campaign occurred during the fall of 1945 under Truman's presidency. With the war over the "security-military" argument could hardly hold much water. Across the Atlantic, notwithstanding its election promises to the contrary, the British Labour government still adhered to the 1939 white paper regulations. With Britain so dependent now on her Atlantic ally, the Zionists decided to raise the pro-Zionist resolution in Congress again.

But another factor, all-important in Truman's eyes, was working against the resolution. As Senator Vandenberg confided to a Zionist, the phrase "Jewish Commonwealth" had seemed to him and to other senators "too ambitious, at least for the moment." The terminology confirmed for many senators the jibe of the anti-Zionist American Council for Judaism that the Zionists' goal was "a racial and theocratic state."[16] Any conception such as this was anathema to Truman. (On the American Council for Judaism, see chapter 6.)

The council's views were shared by the leaders of Kansas City's Reform community, the B'nai Jehuda. Among its members the temple counted Eddie Jacobson and Alex Sachs, who had served with Truman in the 1920s when the latter had been a county judge. Truman had frequent contact with these Reform Jews and identified most with their views, at least until 1947.

On September 27, 1945, Truman received a letter from Sachs, who had been inspired to write by a spate of newspaper articles that had appeared in the local press. One of them, a syndicated edition of Drew Pearson's column that ran in the *Kansas City Times,* had reported that Truman was not ready yet to support "an outright Jewish state" but would prefer Palestine to "be governed by all religions."[17] Sachs reassured Truman that his opposition to a Jewish state would enjoy the support of the majority of liberal Jews:

Those to whom I have talked, have only the highest commendation for you on your stand opposing a Jewish State—and for urging every assistance for the refugees to enter Palestine.

As you have already discovered, your opposition to a Jewish state will not be popular with the large group of ardent Zionists who have already voiced their disapproval.[18]

Truman, already exasperated by the Palestine imbroglio, replied: "It has such a strong bearing on the foreign situation, particularly in the Near East that it is almost dynamite to us and Great Britain. What I am trying to do is to make the whole world safe for the Jews. Therefore, I don't feel like going to war for Palestine."[19]

The new joint resolution was introduced by Senators Taft and Wagner on October 26, 1945. The salient part read: "The United States shall use its good offices to the end that the doors of Palestine shall be opened for free entry of Jews into that country and that there shall be a full opportunity for colonization so that they may reconstitute Palestine as a free and democratic Commonwealth in which all men regardless of race or creed shall enjoy equal rights."[20] The Zionists had been forced to defer to the objections raised in 1944 and to the claims of the American Council for Judaism that their goal was to set up a "racial and theocratic" state in Palestine. The prefix "Jewish" had been removed from "Commonwealth," as had the term "Jewish People" from the 1944 version. A new sentence, assuring equal rights for all "regardless of race or creed," had been inserted.

President Truman's own role in this episode was ambiguous and confused—perhaps typical of his Palestine policy (or lack of one) during the first years of his presidency. At the Potsdam Conference (held July 17–August 2) he had pressed the British side to lift the white paper restrictions and to allow large-scale Jewish immigration into Palestine. But he had evidently been lectured by the British (or by his own State Department or both) on the potential military repercussions of such a move, that is, a large-scale Arab revolt.

On his return to the United States on August 16, Truman said at an impromptu press conference that he had pressed Churchill and then the new Labour prime minister, Clement Attlee, to allow as many Jews into Palestine as possible. But he now added that any solution would have to be worked out together with the British and the Arabs and would have to be done on a peaceful basis, for *"he had no desire to send half a million American soldiers to keep the peace in Palestine."*[21]

The British had apparently convinced Truman that the establishment of a Jewish state in Palestine would require military support from the West. One constant in Truman's Palestine policy would remain his absolute refusal to commit American troops to Palestine. This was a theme to which he returned repeatedly in those first postwar years. He reiterated it, for instance, for the benefit of Senator Joseph H. Ball, who on November 19 forwarded to the president a resolution of the Minneapolis Histadruth (Labor Union) Committee favoring the establishment in Palestine of a Jewish state. Truman responded with some acidity:

I told the Jews that if they are willing to furnish me with five hundred thousand men to carry on a war with the Arabs, we could do what they are suggesting in the Resolution—otherwise we will have to negotiate a while.

. . . I don't think that you, or any of the other Senators would be inclined to send a half dozen Divisions to Palestine to maintain the Jewish State.[22]

It is not clear to whom Truman was referring when he wrote that he had "told the Jews" already. Truman's intentions would be made public only at the end of November. In the meantime, the Zionists were apprehensive and confused. Rabbi Silver wrote to Senator Wagner:

What our Government intends to do in the matter is still a mystery to us. The promises and the endorsements of the Zionist program are all there—but no action—no directives to our State Department. President Truman's recent statement on Palestine at the press conference on August 16 was very ambiguous and left the Jews of America baffled and confused. . . . The Zionist leaders have not had an opportunity to discuss the subject with the President since last April and then only for a few brief moments.[23]

It is not altogether surprising that Truman's policy was unclear, since he himself was receiving different messages from different sections of the Jewish community. It was perhaps only natural that the president should choose to listen to the establishment Jews, especially since their ideas coincided with his own. The heads of the American Jewish Committee (AJC), Judge Joseph Proskauer (president) and Jacob Blaustein (chairman, Executive Committee), had tried to obtain an audience with Truman before he had left for Potsdam, but their interview had been put off until the end of September. In the meantime, Judge Proskauer had sent to the White House a background memorandum clarifying the AJC position, one clearly at odds with the Zionists' goals and with the sense of the congressional resolutions:

2. We distinguish sharply between the importance of Palestine as a place of homeland and refuge and the question of statehood for Palestine.

3. We have contended that it was ill-advised to agitate for Jewish statehood in Palestine under existing conditions. . . . in a conference with Mr. Blaustein and me shortly before he left Washington for the last time, President Roosevelt stated to us that he had come to this belief and that he saw in the extreme Zionist agitation grave dan-

ger for the world and for Palestine itself. He added the belief that Great Britain could not presently consider Jewish statehood. . . .

4. Accordingly, we stress at this time as the main objective for Palestine the modification of the British White Paper and the liberalization of Jewish immigration into Palestine, for that may become necessary for the relief of many thousand stricken European Jews.[24]

The AJC formed a useful, at times decisive, counterbalance to the Zionists. The view of the AJC, as formulated in a further memorandum sent to the White House, was that "while the population of Palestine remain[ed] two-thirds Arab, it [was] futile to raise [the] question of statehood, irrespective of its ultimate merits or demerits." The potential of Palestine as a Jewish refuge should not be confused with the separate issue of a Jewish state, the memorandum concluded. Judge Proskauer and Blaustein repeated these views when they were received by President Truman on September 29, 1945.[25]

On October 2 Truman also received at long last the Zionist leaders Rabbis Wise and Silver. The president was quite obviously preoccupied, if not overwhelmed, by the multifarious problems arising from Cold War tensions. He told the Zionist leaders to have patience, that he would not be rushed or bound by past commitments. He referred to excessive "ethnic pressure" on him from Poles, Italians, and Jews. He soon returned to his objections to a religious state, "be it Jewish or Catholic." But when the Zionists refuted them, Truman then stated somewhat disingenuously that he had no objection to the Zionist conception of a Jewish state. But he also made it quite clear, yet again, that he would not contemplate the commitment of American troops to Palestine.[26]

Literally minutes later, Judge Proskauer and Jacob Blaustein were ushered in, and they assured Truman that whereas they favored Jewish immigration into Palestine they were opposed to Jewish statehood. According to Blaustein's notes of the meeting, Truman expressed his irritation with the Zionist leaders, who had been "insisting as they do constantly for a Jewish State. Truman said that positively is not in the cards now (or any time in the foreseeable future) and would cause a third World War."[27]

Nonetheless, when at the end of October 1945 Senators Wag-

ner and Taft showed the draft resolution to Truman and his
secretary of state, James Byrnes, they were told that the administration had no objection to its introduction.[28] The vacillations
of 1944 were about to reoccur.

At the beginning of November 1945, following the visit of
Prime Minister Attlee to Washington, the United States and
Britain announced the formation of a joint Anglo-American
committee to investigate the problem of the Jewish refugees in
Europe and "to make estimates of those who wish, or will be
impelled by their conditions to migrate to Palestine or other
countries outside Europe."[29] Truman, who had always been
concerned primarily with solving the Jewish refugee problem,
changed his mind on the congressional resolutions, which he
now perceived as preempting the joint committee's work (although he had known about the pending appointment of the
committee, a British initiative, long before his end-of-October
meeting with Senators Taft and Wagner).[30]

The Zionists' suspicions were aroused as discussion in the
Senate dragged out through October and most of November.
Their apprehensions that the administration was again behind
the delay were confirmed privately on November 23, again by
Senator Vandenberg, who so informed Silver through Philip
Slomowitz, editor of the *Jewish News* of Detroit:

We shall try to settle the Palestine Resolution Monday morning. History is repeating itself. The President and the Secretary of State are
again telling us in executive session the Resolution should *not* pass;
that it will greatly embarrass the Truman-Attlee Commission . . . [and]
that *if* we pass it, we must be prepared to answer a British request for
American troops to handle the situation (which none of us would do);
that a notice is on the way already from the nations in the Pan-Arab
League stating that diplomatic relations may be severed with us as a
result of what the President has already done. . . . The tragedy is that
we took the precaution to get clearance in advance from "down town"
before the Resolution was ever introduced.[31]

On November 29 Truman conveyed his opposition to the
pro-Zionist resolution through Secretary of State Byrnes, who
spoke to a closed session of the Senate Foreign Relations Committee. The administration's reversal created something of a
political quandary for those senators from states with large Jew-

ish electorates (New York, Connecticut, Pennsylvania, Illinois, and California), who were relying on the passage of the resolution to boost their chances of reelection to the Senate the following year. They made their displeasure so plain that Byrnes emerged from the secret meeting "white-faced and tight-lipped."[32] Truman announced at a press conference that day that he no longer supported the Taft-Wagner Senate resolution. The adoption of that resolution, he claimed, would be tantamount to admitting that there was no need for an Anglo-American commission to ascertain the facts.[33]

A few days later, on December 4, Truman gave separate interviews to J. David Stern, publisher of the *Philadelphia Record* (and a supporter of the Bergson group), Lessing J. Rosenwald, president of the AJC, and Chaim Weizmann, president of the World Zionist Organization. Truman made it abundantly clear to all three that he was preoccupied with the fear that Zionist aspirations would lead to a racial or theocratic state, a possibility totally at odds with Truman's (American) model of a pluralistic, secular society.

Stern was permitted to quote the president as being opposed to the establishment in Palestine of a Jewish state as Truman did not feel that any state should be established on racial or religious lines. Truman opposed "a state based on Judaism for the same reason that he would oppose basing it on the Moslem religion or the Baptist denomination."[34] Truman still favored "making Palestine a haven for Jews as well as opening the country to immigration, but he did not favour making Palestine a Jewish state. . . . the government of Palestine should be a government of the people irrespective of race, creed or color."[35]

Rosenwald had secured an interview after weeks of nagging Dean Acheson at the State Department and his contacts at the White House, Judge Samuel Rosenman and Matt Connelly. Rosenwald told Truman that Palestine should remain "a country in which people of all faiths can play their full and equal part." He also pressed the president to see to it that all members of the United Nations adopted liberal immigration policies.[36]

Weizmann was escorted to the White House by the British ambassador, Lord Halifax, who also sat in on the interview. Weizmann expounded on his vision for the future, claiming that a Jewish state could eventually absorb four million Jews. Truman barely reacted, except to ask Weizmann if it would be a religious state. Weizmann retorted emphatically, "No!"[37] But Truman was evidently not convinced. When Weizmann claimed that one and a half million Jews were now waiting to go to Palestine, Truman interjected that "he did not think that the Jewish problem should be viewed in terms of Palestine alone and he deprecated use of the phrase 'Jewish state' in favor of 'Palestine state.' There were many Jews in America, representations of whom he had been receiving just before he had seen Weizmann, who were not at all keen on the Palestine solution."[38]

But the president's opposition was not sufficient to block the pro-Zionist resolutions this time. In 1945 the Wright-Compton (House) and the Taft-Wagner (Senate) resolutions were submitted as concurrent, not joint, resolutions and therefore did not require the president's approval. On December 17 the Senate adopted the resolution by a comfortable majority.

The Zionists had gained a significant victory, though it proved to be Pyrrhic. They hoped that the expressions of congressional will would serve as a policy directive to the State Department and as a beacon to the Anglo-American committee on Palestine.[39] As will be seen in chapter 8, this was not the case on either count. The resolutions had no practical impact whatever on America's Palestine policy.

Perhaps of greater significance was the campaign behind the resolutions. The Zionists were influential in persuading non-Zionist opinion, both Jewish and non-Jewish, to link the fate of Palestine with that of the Jewish refugees. But the non-Zionist influence is reflected in Truman's inclination at this time to continue with his refugee Zionism, that is, to treat Palestine as a refuge but *not* as the site for a Jewish state. In maintaining this position, Truman had been persuaded that he would be able to please the mainstream of American Jewry, as represented by the American Jewish Committee and the American Council for Judaism.

Part Two

The Presidency

FIVE

The Shaping of Truman's Palestine Policy
The Zionist Lobby

The Zionist lobby came into its own during the Truman presidency, in the diplomatic struggle that preceded the establishment in May 1948 of the State of Israel and in the ensuing months, during the first Arab-Israeli war.

The Zionist Organization of America and its proxies are generally considered the primary forces behind the lobby, especially in the influence they brought to bear on the White House. The strength, or weakness, of the Zionist lobby was to depend on its ability to mobilize the support of the American Jewish community and, further, to persuade the administration of its ability to withhold two assets—the Jewish vote and Jewish finance—considered vital to the electoral success of any, but especially a Democratic, presidential candidate. The importance of the lobby was brought home to Truman through several agencies, direct and indirect, formal and informal, particularly during what was derisively called "the silly season," that is, election time.

But the lobby worked also in another, equally vital, sphere, among advisers and aides, mostly without officially specified positions, who played a key role in shaping President Truman's Palestine policy. This group enabled Truman to believe in what he was doing and not simply to feel that he was bowing to electoral blackmail. Even so, until the pro-Zionist advisers assumed primacy in 1947, Truman felt that he was being imposed upon, as shown in no uncertain manner by his frequent outbursts.

THE JEWISH VOTE

In November 1947, one year before the presidential elections, Clark Clifford, Truman's key adviser on Palestine at the White House, submitted to the president a memorandum on the importance of the Jewish vote. The key passage ran: "The Jewish vote, insofar as it can be thought of as a bloc, is important only in New York. But, (except for Wilson in 1916) no candidate since 1876 has lost New York and won the Presidency, and its 47 votes are naturally the first prize in any election."[1]

Ironically, Truman would go on to be the first president since Wilson to be elected *without* taking New York. But the New York vote was quite obviously the major prize for which any presidential candidate must strive, or neglect at his peril. The difference between winning or losing this single state was 94 electoral votes, and the presidential candidate needed just 266 for election. The Jewish vote was important not only in New York but also in the large states of Pennsylvania (36 votes), Illinois (27 votes), and Ohio (23 votes).[2]

In New York State Jews made up an estimated 14 percent, and in New York City an estimated 20 percent, of the population. But because of their political energy and their close association with the Democratic party, they cast a far higher proportion of the total votes given to the Democrats at election time. Nationally, the Jews represented about 3 percent of the vote, yet they cast an estimated 4 percent of the votes in presidential elections. This seemingly insignificant difference of one percentage point in fact added up to some three-quarters of a million votes, enough to make the difference in a close election. Their significance is magnified when one takes into account that these votes were cast as a bloc and were concentrated in the big electoral-vote states.[3] In sum, the power of the Jewish vote lay not necessarily in its absolute numbers "but rather in its ability to swing votes, and thus to determine the results of the election."[4]

Of course, Jewish leaders were aware of this electoral leverage at their disposal. Bernard Baruch, a prominent Jew, master financier, and éminence grise to more than one president, though not a Zionist, suggested (with some hyperbole) that the New York Jewish vote of itself outweighed the assets of the entire Arab world: "You let me have the Jewish vote of New York and I will bring you the head of Ibn Saud on a platter! The Administration will sell all seven Arab states if it is a question of retaining the support of New York alone; never mind the rest of the country."[5]

Jews in the United States stood out in every political arena save one—that of holding elective office. In relation to their level of general activity in politics, few Jews occupied positions of "primary" power. Therefore they had to depend on primarily non-Jewish legislators and executives to further the causes in which they were interested. Thus, as a minority, they worked hard at "putting responsive people at the controls of [the] system."[6]

In the 1944 election nine out of every ten Jews had voted for Roosevelt. This was a valuable legacy passed on to President Truman (in 1948, Governor Dewey received only 10 percent of the Jewish vote, even if he did win New York). The Jews never forgot that it had been the Republicans who had harbored anti-Semites in the 1920s and 1930s, who had called the New Deal the "Jew Deal," and who made up the majority of the membership of New York's exclusive Colony Club, which barred Jews.[7]

Moreover, it was far easier to buy one's way into the Democratic party than into the Republican. Many "nouveaux" Jews by a well-placed donation or two could obtain an invitation to the governor's mansion or even the White House, where they might rub shoulders with the great. As noted bluntly by Stephen Isaacs: "The Democrats are always poor, they're always scrounging for dough, and this makes them much more vulnerable if a guy is interested in that kind of success."[8] As will be seen below, more than one or two Jews excelled in the financial approach to politics.

This was a new milieu for President Truman, and he never quite reconciled himself to the need to curry favor with the Jews. He had not had to cope with such considerations before. Jews in Missouri had not been important politically and had never lobbied as a bloc. They had accounted for only about 6 percent of Pendergast's Jackson County electorate and had "regarded Zionism and such foreign movements with suspicion."[9] Truman's old buddy and business partner Eddie Jacobson was the quintessential noncommitted, assimilated American Jew. The two men had never discussed Zionism (it is difficult to ascertain which of them knew less about the subject), and their only dealings with Jewish problems had been on an entirely individual basis, trying to help friends or relatives rescue family members trapped in Nazi-occupied Europe.

Zionist and Jewish leaders pondered and discussed the ways in which Jewish electoral weight could be used to bring in concrete dividends. The Jewish community itself was split on this issue, reflecting the intrusion of differences among its various political affiliations.

One early assessment, written in April 1945 by Marcus Cohn, an official of the American Jewish Committee, suggested that Jews would have to try an approach different from the one that they had employed with President Roosevelt. He believed that Truman was liberal-minded and was "not only not anti-Semitic but truly appreciat[ive of] the meaning of religious freedom and the contribution that Jews have made to western civilization."[10] Cohn analyzed astutely the significance of Truman's parochial background. Truman was regarded as a "small-town politician" who did not possess Roosevelt's "complete grasp of national affairs" or "aristocratic background" and was "totally lacking [in] . . . knowledge of Jewish affairs." Therefore, as with congressmen, the approach had to be at "the district or state" level. Thus, in Cohn's opinion all emphasis should be laid on Truman's home state of Missouri:

The greatest contribution to the effectiveness of our work on the national and international scene can now be made by organizing strong St. Louis and Kansas City chapters which will have within them members whose names mean something to Truman and the people who will surround him. I cannot emphasize this point too much: Missouri, Missourians, and Missouri organizations mean a great deal to Truman and his staff. Organizations which do not have large and potent memberships from Missouri will probably mean nothing.[11]

Marcus Cohn was advising the heads of the American Jewish Committee, a body whose goals were somewhat different from those of the Zionists. But they were eventually to implement his advice, with great effect. In 1948 Truman's former business partner, Eddie Jacobson, would be mobilized from Kansas City. Likewise, and with yet more significant results, Missourian Clark Clifford would bring to the Palestine desk at the White House Max Lowenthal, a man with whom Truman had been familiar since the mid-1930s and who long ago had earned the president's friendship and respect.

The militant Zionists Rabbi Abba Hillel Silver and Emmanuel Neumann advocated a complete departure from what has been called the "Court Jew" school of Jewish politics as practiced by Zionist leader Rabbi Stephen Wise and Judge Joseph Proskauer, president of the American Jewish Committee.[12] So long as Rabbi Wise was in control of the Zionist Organization of America, he had opposed using the Jewish vote as an instrument of Zionist diplomacy. In contrast, Silver and Neumann believed that little would be achieved unless the administration became convinced that "it would suffer politically if it continued to disregard its pledges to the Jews."[13]

Silver believed that instead of attempting to ingratiate themselves with the administration the Democrats and Republicans should be made to outbid each other for the Jewish vote. Indeed, at the end of 1944 it was at Silver's instigation, against Wise's opposition, that the Zionists had wrung support from the conventions of both parties for the Taft-Wagner resolution (see chapter 4).

But perhaps because the Roosevelt administration had with so few qualms reneged on its election promise to support the pro-Zionist resolution in Congress, Silver still claimed that the Jews went to the polls tied to the Democrats. In his opinion the danger was that the Democrats would take the Jewish vote for granted.

Silver was a Republican supporter and close to Senator Taft. His advocacy of a policy of neutrality might easily be interpreted as a call for the Jews to abandon the Democrats.[14] Certainly, this was how Truman interpreted the attacks by Silver, who became shortly persona non grata at the White House.

But whereas establishment Jews might wring their hands at the damage they believed Silver had done to their cause, he was convinced that the administration's discomfort was because of his own success in agitating the Jewish masses against the president's Palestine policy, or the lack of one. Silver would have argued that he had made the White House sit up and take notice of the Jews and that the president's anger barely covered up his fear of, or at least respect for, Jewish influence at the polls.

In retrospect, one can see that it was a combination of the Silver brand of militancy and the Wise brand of quiet diplomacy—carried on after the war by Chaim Weizmann and most directly by Eddie Jacobson—that would prove such a formidable, convincing machine. Silver worked the Jewish masses and made party bosses and officials right up to and inside the White House fearful of losing the Jewish vote.

When Weizmann first met President Truman in December 1945, the latter was opposed to the central Zionist goal of a Jewish state, which he feared would become a racialist, theocratic entity. But by the time Weizmann met the president at critical junctures in the Zionists' diplomatic struggle—in November 1947 and in March 1948—Truman was well briefed by a pro-Zionist White House staff, whose principal creative figure was Max Lowenthal.

So well did the Zionist lobby function that some Zionist officials feared it would produce an overkill or reach its peak prematurely. Once the Zionist cause was taken to the hustings, it was feared that the administration might outplay the Zionists at their own game—that it would appease the Jewish voters with empty rhetoric, behind which remained the same noncommitment. If one believed, as Silver did, that the administration's support for the Zionist cause was in purely cynical self-interest, there was an inherent danger in allowing Zionism to become a plaything in the hands of the politicians:

Granted that the President's main interest in Palestine springs from internal American reasons, it is feasible that at a certain point of time he will attempt to pander to the Jewish vote by empty declarations which cost him nothing, without making any real attempt to ram an acceptable solution down the British throat. This may be particularly the case in view of the known fact that the President's views on the Palestine question have never found complete favour with the State Department and that the latter's views on Middle Eastern policy . . . tend to coincide with the British views.[15]

A case in point was the so-called Yom Kippur statement issued by Truman in October 1946 (see chapter 8). As Silver himself noted:

The need of the Administration forces to counteract the widespread resentment and indignation of the Jews of the United States in the face of the Administration's political inaction prompted them to issue this statement. Mr. Crum and Mr. Niles seemingly persuaded the President to issue the statement as a *smart pre-election move.*

The danger now is, of course, that having cashed in on whatever good will this statement may have produced among the Jews of America, the White House will be content to let the matter drop—as it has done time and again in the past after similar maneuvers on the eve of elections.[16]

The anti-Zionists in the Jewish community bitterly resented the Zionist lobby, fearing as always an anti-Semitic backlash. Lessing J. Rosenwald, president of the recently formed American Council for Judaism (see chapter 6), told the third annual conference of his organization in February 1947:

Zionists *created a Jewish issue in the elections.* A vast, powerfully organized, unholy effort was made to introduce consideration for a so-called Jewish bloc vote, and a threat to use that bloc for punitive means.

In more than one statement, I denounced that claim in behalf of the American Council for Judaism. I denounce it now. It is a fraud upon the public. And it is one of the most evil and gravest injustices done to the Jews of the United States. Those responsible for the effort and for those claims have much for which to answer.[17]

Some inside the Zionist camp itself also thought that Silver's aggressive tactics could easily become self-defeating. The correct strategy, as seen by Lionel Gelber, one of the more astute Zionist diplomats, was to elevate their cause above pure electoral self-interest and persuade the president that support for Zionism was consistent with the American national interest and, indeed, was a historic ideal worthy of American support. It is no coincidence that Gelber's memorandum is to be found in the David Niles Papers, now located after a long hiatus in the Harry S. Truman Library.[18]

As Gelber saw it, it was more than a little ironic that militant

Zionists such as Silver shared British cynicism about Truman's motives. Referring to Zionist criticism that the Yom Kippur statement was "nothing more than a base, insincere, short-lived electoral move," Gelber commented:

Mr. Truman has made a welcome step in our direction. He is rewarded with skepticism in almost identical language from the rival quarters of both the Zionists and the British. The effect of this may be adverse. A simple, harassed man, Mr. Truman is likely to drift back into the sulking corner of the early summer when he pleaded for someone to come to him with an "American" question for a change. Finding favor on neither side, he may, after the elections, call a plague on both our houses—the British and the Zionists alike.[19]

Even if he did support them primarily "out of domestic political exigencies," wrote Gelber, "surely it [was] good psychology to encourage President Truman to think well of himself, to be applauded so far as possible for what he has done, in order to embolden him to do more." After all, wasn't the recognition of Jewish voting strength by both parties a legitimate exercise of the Western democratic process? If the Zionists now proclaimed that on the evidence of his past behavior they expected Truman to "lie low as soon as the election [was] over," the president just might do precisely that. Obviously, they wanted the president to make good on his word, but perhaps they should emphasize "the high statesmanlike character of [the government's] new long-term commitment to political Zionism." If the Zionists were to "lay stress at once and in full volume on the historic significance of American support for [their] political program," they would "drive that home to Washington, the nation and the world, while President Truman himself [would] be less able, and conceivably less inclined to recede."[20]

That Truman was embittered and exasperated by Jewish pressures is a matter of record. But it should be noted that his anger was aroused by the public attacks by the Zionist lobby, primarily those of Rabbi Silver. This did *not* lead to any break with his Jewish pro-Zionist advisers inside the White House (David Niles and Max Lowenthal) or with those Jews whose generous donations would provide the financial underpinning for his 1948 reelection campaign. A clear dichotomy was established between the militants or "extremists," such as Silver—whose actions were ascribed to his Republican politics—and the "moderates" (Weizmann, Rabbi Wise, and Nahum Goldmann), who restricted their activity to quiet diplomacy, even when it appeared that Truman's administration had reneged on their cause.

Presidential adviser Judge Sam Rosenman believed that the official Zionist leadership had bothered the president too much and should have limited its appeals to only the most critical of issues. Not only that, but, in evident reference to Silver, the Zionists had offended a man who was sensitive to pressure with criticism he believed to be unwarranted. Truman's response—to close the White House for long periods to Zionist visitors—was frequently exploited by their opponents in the State Department. Fortunately, David Niles and Clark Clifford watched closely over Zionist affairs.[21]

Truman was incensed particularly by a press conference that Rabbi Silver gave at a special session of the United Nations in May 1947 at which he accused the United States of being willing to sacrifice Jewish interests to win Arab support. David Niles told Eliahu Epstein, the Zionist representative in Washington, that few speeches had so angered the president, especially since Silver had chosen the international forum in which to castigate his own government, thereby giving satisfaction to its enemies.[22]

As noted already, Truman had developed something of an allergy to anything that smacked of outside pressure or dictates. He took care repeatedly to insist that his Palestine policy would *not* be influenced by the Zionist lobby. For example, John M. Redding, publicity director of the Democratic National Committee in 1948, told Truman that he had "Zionist Jews" in his office every day and that the pressure was building. According to Redding, Truman's reply was that putting pressure on the committee would not help the Jews, and the issue would be handled at the White House without politics.[23]

Truman could be blunt with the Jewish lobbyists. In May 1948, just before his recognition of the State of Israel, Truman wrote the following to General Julius Klein, the venerable president of the Jewish War Veterans Association: "As far as I'm concerned, I don't think there has ever been any more lobbying and pulling and hauling than has been carried by the Jews in this Palestine difficulty. . . . I have no objection to their lobbying—neither have I any objection to the Arabs doing so if they feel like it but, in neither case does it affect my decisions or judgement."[24]

These are sentiments that Truman evidently liked to have people believe he would work by. But the reality was different, and no one at the time really thought otherwise. On one rare occasion Truman confessed his remorse for having succumbed to such pressures to none other than the British foreign secretary, Ernest Bevin. It was the more ironic since Bevin had aroused Truman's ire more than once with accusations exactly to that effect. According to Bevin's record of their conversation, on December 8, 1946, President Truman had said he thought it would be easier for him to help Bevin on Palestine now that the American (1946 congressional) elections were over. Truman went out of his way to explain how difficult it had been with so many Jews in New York and spoke contritely of the awkward position in which this had placed him.[25]

During the summer of 1946, Truman had indeed almost reached the breaking point. He became irritable with anyone who tried to broach the Palestine problem with him. His frustration was heightened as he began to realize that the problem was not given to any quick and easy solution, such as the mass migration of Jewish refugees into Palestine. He complained frequently that the Jews were ungrateful for what he was doing on their behalf and threatened to wash his hands of the problem completely, "leaving the British and the Zionists to sort out the mess by themselves."[26] According to Henry Wallace, secretary of commerce, at a cabinet meeting in July 1946 Truman had snapped: "Jesus Christ couldn't please them when he was here on earth, so how could anyone expect that I would have any luck?" and had added that "he had no use for them and didn't care what happened to them."[27]

The following exchange between Wallace and Bronx Democratic boss Ed Flynn is perhaps instructive on the attitudes of politicians toward Jewish pressures. (Flynn was credited with a key role in securing Truman's nomination as vice-president in 1944 and was considered an important conduit to the Truman

White House on the Jewish vote.) In 1943 Flynn had confided to Wallace his belief that Jews had a pervasive influence in the United States, especially in the entertainment business. He had advised Wallace to read a book on the Jews by Hilaire Belloc (a noted anti-Semite) and stated that the Bronx was 60 percent Jewish, but "every time a Jew [stuck] up his head in the Bronx he knock[ed] it down."[28]

By 1947 President Truman, like many of his contemporaries, was becoming "emancipated" from the sentiments of compassion and sympathy for Jewish sufferings during the war. In November 1946 one of Truman's inner circle, David Niles, told David Ben-Gurion: "The feeling of guilt for the Holocaust is no longer so great as when the Nazis' acts were first revealed, and the longer the solution to the DP [displaced persons] problem [is] put off, the more public interest [will] lag."[29]

Truman's exasperation was expressed in a private letter to Eleanor Roosevelt, written in August 1947, as pressure was building prior to the UN Special Assembly on Palestine. In a passage that all but compared the Jews to their erstwhile persecutors, Truman wrote: "I fear very much that the Jews are like all underdogs. When they get on top they are just as intolerant and as cruel as the people were to them when they were underneath."[30]

Mrs. Roosevelt was apparently not sufficiently moved to respond to this comment. Indeed, she herself resigned soon after as cochairperson of a dinner to be given by associates of the *Nation*, when that group circulated a letter asserting that a "gigantic doublecross" was in the making and that President Truman had decided to yield to the Arabs.[31]

But however much Truman may have been agitated by the public pressure and criticism aimed at him by the Zionist lobby, he was still in need of Jewish finance, especially in election years.

JEWISH FINANCE

Unlike many of the presidents both before and after himself, Harry Truman did not bring to the White House any family or self-made wealth. Nor did the Democrats enjoy the largesse of the big industrialists to the extent that the Republican party did. Therefore, simply put, Truman depended on private donations to fuel his election campaigns, and many of the most significant of these came from Jews. And Truman was never a man to forget a debt, no matter what he might feel about Zionists of the Silver ilk.

Unknown to the general public, several Jews made large contributions to politicians in outlying states, such as Arizona, Iowa, Oklahoma, and Oregon. Bernard Baruch helped line the Democrats' coffers in the east as did Pat McCarran in Nevada in the west. Although these funds did not buy votes or sway officials against their constituents' wishes, they did ensure easier access to congressmen and senators.[32]

Large donors were entitled to certain privileges, such as invitations to the White House and meetings with the president. Thus, during Truman's first term, there grew up a small, almost clandestine circle of wealthy Jews, *not* of the older Jewish establishment, who had entrée into Truman's inner sanctum. Furthermore, as will be seen, a few of these new arrivals fancied themselves as informal, substitute ambassadors for the official Zionist representatives, subtly pulling strings behind the scenes and by virtue of their influence at the White House enjoying positions of prestige in the fledgling State of Israel.

One of the earliest donors of this kind was an American Zionist, Dewey David Stone. In 1944, when it became known that Vice-President Wallace would be dropped from the Roosevelt ticket, Dewey was informed that Senator Truman might run as a vice-presidential candidate. Just prior to the party convention, Stone received a phone call from his attorney, William Boyle (later executive vice-chairman of the Democratic National Committee), asking him for twenty-five thousand dollars to finance Truman's publicity. Stone did not even know who Truman was, but he told Boyle that if he wanted him to "take a gamble" he would make the money available. Thus, when Truman became president, Stone was one of the few to whom Truman owed a political debt.[33]

Stone apparently did not meet Truman until 1948, when Truman's campaign for reelection was in desperate straits. Stone mobilized Abraham Feinberg, perhaps the central figure in the small group of Jews who were to help finance Truman's reelection.[34] Abe Feinberg was a self-made man, who had made a fortune during World War II in the hosiery business. He founded the Julius Kayser Company in the 1950s and branched out later into banking and real estate. In 1967 he obtained the Coca-Cola franchise for Israel.[35]

Through mutual business connections Feinberg became friendly with Robert Hannegan, former Democratic governor of Missouri and a close political associate of Truman's. Hannegan had been a powerful party boss in St. Louis politics and had helped Truman secure a Senate seat in 1940. In 1944 Hannegan became chairman of the Democratic National Committee, from which position he helped Truman get the vice-presidential nomination from Roosevelt. Feinberg believed that "the use of threatened pressure" by the Zionist organizations was unproductive. His strategy was to use his money to gain access to the White House, where he might engage in "quiet diplomacy." In 1944, when Feinberg asked for an introduction to President Roosevelt, Hannegan suggested he meet the vice-president first. Feinberg first met Truman at the end of that year, when the latter spoke at a fund-raising dinner in New York for a Jewish hospital in Denver. The two immediately struck up a warm friendship, although Feinberg was not apparently called on (by Dewey Stone) until 1948 to help refloat Truman's election campaign.[36]

In September 1948 Truman's reelection campaign was on the verge of collapse. His election coffers were empty, and opinion polls could not have been less encouraging. According to Feinberg, some potential donors, including himself, were called to the White House. Truman and his advisers were then planning his famous whistle-stop train tour, a move destined to turn the election campaign and confound the universal predictions of a Dewey victory. Truman stood up on the "famous Truman portico" and delivered himself of the following: "Boys, if I can have the money to see the people, I'm going to win this election. If I had money, I would put my own money in first. Now, you all go back to the Democratic Committee and see what you can do about it."[37]

Two Jews were in the group at the White House—Feinberg

and Edmund I. Kaufmann, a close friend of David Niles, owner of a nationwide chain of jewelry stores, and one of the richest men in Washington. Kaufmann could not go to the meeting at Democratic headquarters mentioned in Truman's speech but Feinberg was able to.

A few, slightly conflicting, versions of the meeting exist, and the following is a composite synthesis. Senator Howard McGrath, chairman of the Democratic National Committee in 1948, presided. Few people in fact turned up, and no one offered to become financial chairman. McGrath sat stunned.[38] According to Alfred Steinberg, Senator Louis A. Johnson asked for a short break, during which he went over to the White House to talk to Truman. Johnson had wanted a cabinet position for years, and now, in return for taking on the position of financial chairman, Truman promised him the coveted position. According to Steinberg, Johnson paid the party's initial expenses out of his own pocket.[39]

Feinberg's recollection is somewhat different, and the more colorful. Recollecting the scene twenty-five years later, Feinberg described the meeting as a "wake." He recalled that he had been the youngest in the group and the brashest. He remembered saying: "The President has done a great deal for my people. I feel that we owe him a great deal. We certainly owe him a chance, and I will pledge on behalf of Ed Kaufmann and myself that within two weeks we'll have $100,000 towards this trip."[40] In 1948 that was an incredible sum of money for one man to promise. Senator Johnson rushed after Feinberg to the elevator, asking him if he was serious. Feinberg replied, "I never make a promise I can't keep." Johnson responded that in that case he would take on the finance chairmanship.[41]

Feinberg apparently raised the money not in two weeks but in two days. He mobilized his friend Ed Kaufmann, owner of stores in eighty cities nationwide, who wrote not only to his friends but to his store managers throughout the country, asking them to call meetings to raise funds for the Truman campaign. Kaufmann himself visited several places and remembered raising fourteen thousand dollars one evening at the home of a friend in Providence. Kaufmann personally committed twenty-five thousand of the one hundred thousand dollars promised by Feinberg. After the election he wrote to David Niles listing his preelection efforts and surmising that if he was called on again and given sufficient time he would be able to raise five hundred thousand dollars unassisted just through his friends and his stores.[42]

Whatever moved Johnson to take on the financial chair (it may have required both Feinberg's and Truman's promises to persuade him to assume the job), Feinberg's role was obviously a key element, one that President Truman did not forget. Truman apparently credited Feinberg with having made the whistle-stop tour possible: "If not for my friend Abe, I couldn't have made the trip and I wouldn't have been elected."[43]

To an extent, Truman's triumph became Feinberg's too. It had become common knowledge at the time that Feinberg had raised a large amount for Truman when he had needed it most. Thus, Feinberg's activities began a process that made the Jews into "the most conspicuous fund raisers and contributors to the Democratic Party." As one non-Jewish political strategist stated: "You can't hope to go anywhere in national politics, if you're a Democrat, without Jewish money."[44] In addition—as Abba Eban, Israel's first ambassador to the United Nations, recalled—after the 1948 elections Abe Feinberg and Dewey Stone enjoyed fairly free access to the president in times of crisis.[45]

Feinberg liked to think that he had fulfilled a special role for the Jews and for Israel. Even though Eliahu Epstein, the Zionist representative in Washington and later Israel's first ambassador to the United States, was liked by all, whatever he did had to be passed through all the formal channels. In contrast, Feinberg had entirely informal contact with the White House. Through him Truman was able to obtain an intimate picture of what was going on, so that he could more readily understand problems when they came to him through ordinary departmental channels. Israeli leaders, learning of Feinberg's connections inside the Truman White House, were only too eager to bypass regular channels and work through him.[46]

But even with the sums raised by the big donors, Truman's whistle-stop tour was plagued with pecuniary difficulties. His 1944 vice-presidential campaign had provided a dress rehearsal of sorts for the 1948 tour. At that time a small committee of

Truman's friends in Kansas City had organized themselves to raise funds—for such emergencies as "paying the railroads to move the bobtail special to the next stop." The committee had been headed by Truman's Kansas City friend Tom Evans, owner of a chain of drugstores and a radio station. Some 60 percent of the money raised was in modest contributions, and one of the more active fund-raisers had been Truman's old partner, Eddie Jacobson.[47] Eddie Jacobson's wife, Bluma, later recalled her husband's fund-raising activities: "Eddie was really a whiz at raising money. I don't know how he did it, but he'd pick up the phone and call somebody, and while we never got great amounts, we always got enough money to get the train moving again. . . . I don't think there was anything in the world that Eddie wouldn't have done for Harry, and raising money in that campaign—he was, I think he was only sorry he couldn't do more."[48]

Tom Evans was given the position of chairman of fund-raising for the western half of Missouri during the 1948 campaign. He has left a graphic personal recollection of some of the mishaps that occurred when funds dried up. Truman would literally run out of money to pay the railroad company to carry him further on his whistle-stop tour. On occasion local notables would take up a collection on board the train, as happened in Oklahoma City.[49]

Truman was made acutely aware of the precariousness of his position. And at times there were no local affluents to call on. Then Tom Evans in Kansas City would receive a phone call: "Look, we need $5000 by four o'clock tomorrow afternoon and we've got to move the train out of the station and we can't move until we pay the railroad." Evans would phone Eddie Jacobson, and they would begin calling up friends. Evans recalled that this happened at least eight times, and they had raised amounts from fifteen hundred to five thousand dollars and then wired the money. Once, on a weekend, they had to scrape up a sum in cash, and Eddie Jacobson flew to meet Truman with the money in his pocket.[50]

Truman's campaign coffers were so short on cash that his radio speeches were sometimes cut off in mid-course. This was in contrast to the long addresses made by Truman's opponent, Dewey. Listeners wondered why the president was treated so disparagingly. At times it was because of the sheer lack of money to pay for a few extra minutes. But it was also done on purpose by Louis Johnson "to dramatize the meager funds of the Democrats." On one occasion a radio executive told Johnson they would have to interrupt Truman soon unless he came forth with more money. "Go ahead," smiled Johnson, "that will mean another million votes."[51]

THE PRESIDENTIAL ADVISERS

The two key advisers working on the Zionists' behalf inside the White House itself were David Niles and, from 1947, Max Lowenthal. Both men were quintessential back-room boys.

David Niles

David Niles was a bachelor, the son of Jewish immigrants who had settled in Boston. He and Judge Sam Rosenman were the only Roosevelt aides to be retained by President Truman. According to acquaintances, Niles was a lonely man, whose "whole life was the President," whether Roosevelt or Truman. Niles would become truly devoted to Truman, perhaps because of the momentous events for the Jewish people that they saw through together.[52] Niles would spend the week in Washington and commute back home to Boston on weekends.

Niles's attitude to Zionism was influenced by Rabbi Stephen Wise, with whom he shared a strong dedication to the Democratic party. He shared Wise's dislike of Rabbi Silver and his resentment of Silver's attacks on the Truman administration. Niles tried to undermine Silver's position and to promote that of Wise.

Niles's interest and activity in Boston had been in progressive politics and the Ford Hall Forum (a rostrum for progressive politics), which he had directed for several years. At the forum he had made the acquaintance of President Roosevelt, a frequent speaker there.[53] Niles was presidential aide to Roosevelt and Truman, maintaining "close liaison with liberal and labor organizations of all kinds, but particularly those that were influential along the Washington–New York–Boston axis."[54]

Niles served Roosevelt as a buffer between the White House

and minority pressure groups, especially the Jews, who were agitated over the fate of their peoples in Europe and by British policy in Palestine. Niles also advised the president which Jewish leaders to receive and which might be rejected politely without causing too much political damage. Niles came to see himself "not as a representative of the Jews to the White House but rather as a protector of the president from the divergent pressure groups."[55]

According to Niles's assistant at the White House, Philleo Nash, when Truman became president Niles supplied him with the key to Jewish and labor politics along the northeastern seaboard. Truman was "baffled by New York City's intricacies and machines. The ideologues troubled him and he relied on Dave [Niles] to handle them."[56] Abe Feinberg would report regularly to Niles and Max Lowenthal on the various Jewish groups around New York and on people who were financing the election campaigns in the area.[57]

Under the 1939 reorganization of the White House the administrative assistants were intended to have "a passion for anonymity." But in Niles's case it developed into a mania. Perhaps because he was acutely aware that he was working in a highly controversial area, he took in no assistants or colleagues when he met with the president and seldom, if ever, attended staff meetings. He operated primarily on the telephone, committing as little as possible to paper. Each year he "stripped" his files "in celebration of the New Year." Truman's handwritten scrawls on the various communications he sent to Niles reflected the president's complete trust in him.[58]

This modus operandi had its advantages and disadvantages. It avoided the perennial difficulty of the White House staffer: "getting caught between a presidential decision and a cabinet officer."[59] It enabled Niles to get things done quickly, to cut through bureaucratic red tape and, at times, to bypass other government departments. It could be a serious disadvantage, however, if Niles was absent for a period from the White House; for example, he fell ill in March 1948 during the crisis that preceded the American switch from the UN partition plan to trusteeship for Palestine.

Niles's discretion also aroused animosity and neurotic suspicions not only at the State Department but among other White House staff, who did not share Niles's commitment to Zionism. George Elsey, another of Clark Clifford's assistants, was one White House aide who evidently resented, and later derided, Niles's role. Elsey referred to him as a "most secretive individual who slunk rather furtively round the corridors of the White House and the Executive Office building," never telling his White House colleagues what had transpired in his private meetings with the president. Elsey deduced that the reason for Niles's secretiveness was that he did not in fact enjoy nearly so much influence with the president as he claimed. He also believed that Niles's methods were self-defeating, since none of his White House colleagues respected his opinions, which were inevitably and predictably pro-Zionist.[60]

Loy Henderson, who as chief advocate of the Arab cause at the State Department was Clifford's antagonist, also saw in Niles the archetype of the furtive conspirator. Henderson regarded Niles as "the most powerful and diligent advocate of the Zionist cause," without whom the State of Israel would not have gained recognition at the United Nations as and when it did. Henderson believed that the wily Niles was hiding in the corridors of the White House to ambush each move the State Department made. When Henderson's memoranda on Palestine were sent over to the White House by Under Secretary of State Lovett, Niles would intervene to "deride the memoranda and cast personal aspersions" on Henderson. Henderson claimed to have known in advance that every memorandum he sent to the White House would find its way immediately through Niles to the Zionists. Henderson went so far as to suggest, nearly thirty years later, that Niles would have loved dearly to replace him because "he wanted men he could control."[61]

Max Lowenthal

Truman met and acquired considerable respect for Max Lowenthal during his first term in the Senate. Lowenthal would have a major influence on Truman's Palestine policy after World War II: Truman in fact would credit Lowenthal as being the primary force behind the American recognition of Israel. Yet

Lowenthal took good care to keep out of the limelight, and therefore until recently his role at the White House in formulating Truman's Palestine policy has almost escaped the attention of historians.[62]

In interviews given to a member of the Truman Library staff in September and November 1967, Lowenthal was discreet to the extreme. He claimed to have heard about Truman's recognition of Israel in May 1948 "secondhand from someone in the White House," whose name he could not recall. Lowenthal added that he had never discussed Israel with Truman during that period "*at all.*"[63]

Truman's private papers enable us now to penetrate the smoke screen of discretion. Lowenthal's private papers, which include meticulous, typed diary notes on the Palestine issue, were recently made available by the University of Minnesota and are used here for the first time; they permit a close look at the everyday workings of the "Zionist lobby" inside the White House. We also refer to the evidence of Eliahu Epstein, at that time head of the Zionists' Washington office.

From 1947 to 1948 Lowenthal was employed by Clark Clifford to provide legal advice on the Palestine question. In fact, he did much more than that. He visited and obtained material from the Zionist office in Washington regularly. On the basis of the briefings he received there, Lowenthal drafted the memoranda on Palestine that Clark Clifford would present to the president and to the State Department.[64]

Lowenthal pressed his views at numerous informal oral briefings of the president. Yet he never appeared on the White House staff list, nor was he given an office of his own—although he had the occasional use of a desk.[65]

Lowenthal (1883–1971) was a protégé of Louis D. Brandeis, a Zionist and the first Jew to be appointed a Supreme Court justice. Brandeis was regarded universally as one of the great judges in the American liberal tradition.[66] Lowenthal graduated from the Harvard University Law School in 1912, and after a short period as clerk to Judge Julian Mack on the U.S. Court of Commerce he practiced law in New York from 1913 to 1929, becoming a law partner of Robert Szold. (Szold engaged in various economic activities on behalf of Palestine.) From

1933 to 1934 he served as counsel, and from 1935 to 1942 as chief counsel, to the Senate Interstate Commerce Committee. There he and Truman first met, in 1936, on the committee's subcommittee on railroads.

Their point of common contact was Burton K. Wheeler, a senator fascinated with the banks' financing of the railroads and concerned about the large number of railroad bankruptcies during the Depression. In February 1935 Wheeler had introduced a resolution into the Senate calling for "an inquiry into the financial difficulties which were crippling the major railroad systems of the country." The Senate authorized the Interstate Commerce Committee to proceed with the inquiry, and Wheeler named a subcommittee to investigate with himself as chairman. Max Lowenthal and Sidney J. Kaplan were named as counsel and assistant counsel, respectively, to the subcommittee.[67]

Lowenthal was then a young labor attorney, described accurately by Jonathan Daniels as "self-effacing but ubiquitous." He had come to Wheeler's notice through a book he had written on corporate reorganization. For his main illustration Lowenthal had taken the reorganization of the Chicago, Milwaukee, and St. Paul railway of 1925–1928.[68] Truman was not a member of the subcommittee but asked Wheeler if he could attend its meetings. Wheeler obliged gladly, and when some other Senate members lost interest, Truman was officially appointed a member.

When Wheeler went home to Montana for a rest, Truman assumed the chair of the subcommittee—just as his home railroad, the Missouri Pacific, came up for discussion. Lowenthal and his staff suggested to Truman that some matters concerning the railroad might prove embarrassing. Telegrams and telephone messages from Missouri asked Truman to stop the hearings on the Missouri Pacific, or to go easy. Truman told the attorneys to treat their findings in this case just like those in any other and to hide nothing. Lowenthal, who had shared the general image of Truman as a Pendergast errand boy, was suitably impressed.[69] The foundations were thus laid for a long friendship and political association, based on solid mutual respect.

Vic Messall, Truman's secretary in the Senate during his second term and therefore a close observer, has commented that

"Lowenthal was a mystery man. . . . He exercised power behind the scenes and had a great deal of influence on Wheeler, and subsequently on Truman. Truman was a good listener to what Mr. Lowenthal had to say."[70]

The result of the subcommittee's five years of research and hearings was the Truman-Wheeler Transportation Act of 1940, which "bound errant bankers and lawyers to stricter business ethics" and "protected unsuspecting people who bought railway bonds and stock in the belief that they were getting certificates of value." Truman gained a reputation of being a populist and anti–Wall Street.[71]

The Truman-Lowenthal association was important in several respects. First, in the sphere of American politics Lowenthal (who would later set up the political action committee of the Congress of Industrial Organizations) would play a vital role in 1944 in persuading labor leader Sidney Hillman that Senator Harry S. Truman would be a vice-presidential candidate acceptable to organized labor.[72]

Second, Lowenthal introduced Truman to Judge Brandeis. Brandeis, then in his eighties, held weekly teas, which had become something of a Washington institution. Lowenthal was a regular guest and on one occasion suggested to Truman that he come along. The elderly justice took an immediate liking to Truman, "the Senator with the flat Missouri twang," who was from then on a regular visitor.[73]

At Truman's first tea the main subject of discussion, at least with Truman, was transportation and the grip on it by the banks and the lawyers in their service. Brandeis claimed that the great law firms resorted "to tricks that would make an ambulance chaser in a coroner's court blush with shame."[74] There was also a sprinkling of Harvard lawyers expounding on constitutional law and the philosophy of the New Deal. Truman was obviously flattered by the special attention Brandeis paid him. He reported back on one such tea party to Bess: "The Justice spent more time with me than with his other guests and seemed very much interested in what we are doing to the railroad and insurance companies. Both he and Mrs. Brandeis are as nice as they can be. . . . It was a rather exclusive and brainy party. I didn't exactly belong but they made me think I did."[75]

It is reasonable to assume that the subject of Zionism occasionally came up at Brandeis's California Street apartment. Although Truman makes no mention of any conversations on Zionism with Brandeis, one may speculate that at the weekly gatherings Truman first heard about the basic tenets of Zionism and, in view of the Jews' demise during the 1930s, about its potential as a solution to the Jewish problem. Such an assumption has been made by a recent Brandeis biographer: "It seems evident that Truman was yet another president influenced by Brandeis."[76]

Alben Barkley, who would go on to become Truman's vice-president, was another regular at Brandeis's at-homes. He did credit Brandeis specifically for his own interest in Zionism and Palestine.[77] Brandeis had been the leader and was now elder statesman of the American Zionist movement. He remained actively interested in the cause, especially during the 1930s, when news of Hitler's anti-Jewish policies filtered out. Lowenthal, too, under Brandeis's influence was solidly pro-Zionist.

In 1947 Lowenthal was able to step straight into a key position in the White House as Clifford's chief adviser on Palestine affairs, a position from which he greatly influenced the president's policies. In 1952, nearly four years after the creation of Israel, Truman tried in a private letter to persuade Lowenthal to take some of the credit he thought was due to him:

I know exactly how you feel about the idea of your not wanting to be considered as benefactor to the State of Israel but I don't know why you should because *I don't know who has done more for Israel than you have.* In fact, you are the one I talked with when we were trying to work out the recognition for the State of Israel, and you know how those Israelites have placed me on a pedestal alongside of Moses, and that is the reason I wrote you as I did because I wanted you to have the credit.[78]

Inevitably, the presence in the White House of two fervent advocates of the Zionist cause, both of whom appeared to enjoy a special relationship with the president, aroused suspicions and resentment among other White House aides. Interesting speculations may be made on the significance of the following unsigned memorandum that assesses the "objectivity" of Lowenthal's advice. Equally thought provoking is the fact of this memorandum's presence in the private papers of Clark Clifford:

It is well to be aware, in reading Mr *Lowenthal's* voluminous memoranda, of the adroitness with which carefully-screened facts are assembled to "prove" whatever point he is trying to make at the moment. . . . One should not be misled into accepting the course of action Mr Lowenthal advocates without question merely because the "facts" are presented in what appear to be convincing argument. One must be aware that one premise is implicit in all his memoranda. That premise is:
"The United States should support the Zionist cause, come what may."[79]

The Niles-Lowenthal duo inside the White House was undoubtedly influential. In particular, Lowenthal's skillful drafts provided the reasoned, solid argumentation for the Zionist cause, right up to the highest level. They would prove constantly to dismay the State Department, whose permanent staff believed that the president's aides were unfairly, even unpatriotically, introducing extraneous factors into the administration's Middle East policies.

Truman was torn between State Department arguments about the "national interest" and the political and emotional pressures emanating from his aides inside the White House. He never quite resolved his dilemma. Another presidential aide, Oscar Ewing, recalled later that Truman had once told him:

I am in a tough spot. The Jews are bringing all kinds of pressure on me to support the partition of Palestine and the establishment of a Jewish state. On the other hand, the State Department is adamantly opposed to this. I have two Jewish assistants on my staff, David Niles and Max Lowenthal. Whenever I try to talk to them about Palestine, they soon burst into tears because they are so emotionally involved in the subject. So far I have not known what to do.[80]

THE BRAIN TRUSTS

Apart from the advice the president received from his official White House aides (albeit with vaguely defined authorities), the White House was also under constant bombardment from a bevy of self-appointed bodies that, for want of a better term, may be referred to as "brain trusts." The White House aides frequently sat on these bodies or at the very least were briefed regularly by them.

One of the earliest groups to ply the White House with pro-Zionist advice was one organized in Washington in 1942 by the Anglo-Jewish magnate Israel Sieff, a director of the Marks and Spencer chain. His was an informal group of well-placed Jewish friends, including Ben Cohen, a presidential adviser. Also joining were Robert Nathan, a young economist on assignment to U.S. intelligence; David Ginsburg, a lawyer and New Deal bureaucrat; and on occasion David Lilienthal of the Tennessee Valley Authority. David Niles too joined in occasionally. This little group was strategically placed to carry the Jewish and Zionist lines to the highest quarters in the administration, either directly or through well-calculated remarks "among well-placed colleagues in the corridors of power and the salons of social Washington."[81]

Early in 1947 a regular brain trust was set up by Oscar Ewing, vice-chairman of the Democratic National Committee from 1942 to 1947 and administrator of the Federal Security Agency from 1947. Ewing was a resident of New York City and a lawyer who had personal contact with many Jewish and Zionist organizations. As such, he had no need to be educated about the importance of the Jewish vote. During Truman's whistle-stop tour in 1948, Ewing would hold the key post of "anchorman" in Washington.

The brain trust that Oscar "Jack" Ewing chaired was modeled on the one set up by Sam Rosenman in 1933 to advise President Roosevelt on the "New Deal," a program to solve America's economic and social problems. The liaison with the White House was Clark Clifford, who worked in harmony with Ewing. Among the members of the trust were Louis Schwalenbach, also associated with the New Deal, a former senator of Washington State, and labor secretary under Truman; Charles F. Brannan, agriculture secretary, a Mormon dedicated to the Zionist cause; Oscar Chapman, deputy secretary and then secretary of home affairs, a close friend of Truman's and also dedicated to the Zionist cause; and Leon Kayserling, vice-chairman of Truman's

Economic Advisory Council, who was the only Jew in the trust.

The trust met regularly on Monday evenings under a veil of secrecy at the Wardman Park Hotel in Washington. Shortly after its establishment it discussed the Palestine issue and its possible repercussions on the elections to Congress and for the presidency. The trust impressed on Truman the danger to the Democrats' election chances if they did not make good on their 1944 election promises to support a Jewish commonwealth. Truman confessed his dilemma in the face of conflicting recommendations from the State Department. Ewing was supplied with copies of State Department memoranda, and the trust responded with critical analysis.[82]

Finally, yet another small informal group used to meet to discuss Palestine during the crucial months of May to June 1948, prior to the Democratic Convention. It met on the back balcony of the White House. This was emphatically a "political group," gathered to consider the domestic political ramifications of the Palestine issue. Sam Rosenman was invited along, as were Frank Walker, Clark Clifford, Matt Connelly, Abe Feinberg, and Bob Hannegan.[83]

Undoubtedly, such informal gatherings multiplied at election time. Yet the process was continuous, and the White House through its busy and assorted "aides" never wanted for advice on the Palestine question. All together the quantity of well-argued advice coming in through various unofficial channels was enormous and would provide an efficient counter to that coming from the president's official foreign policy-making body, the State Department.

CHRISTIAN PRO-ZIONISTS

Had the Zionist lobby been forced to work in a vacuum, totally isolated from any moral or material support from other ethnic sections of America, its achievements would no doubt have been considerably more modest. Fortunately, extensive support from Christian Zionists, much of it "genuine and indigenous to the American culture," provided a solid, positive context within which the Zionists could function: "Christian Zionist activities made crucial, albeit unquantifiable, contributions to the growth of Zionist influence in the years immediately preceding the establishment of Israel."[84]

Although the Zionists naturally worked hard to stimulate sympathetic Christian opinion, much Christian support was entirely spontaneous, found frequently among communities remote from Jewish centers or congressmen with no Jewish constituencies. Christian Zionist sentiment reflected not only "Zionist proddings" but a number of other factors both humanitarian and moral. There was a widespread belief in the moral claim of the Jewish people to the Holy Land and "a wish to help realize Scriptural prophecies," made the more urgent by the universal revulsion against the horrors of the Holocaust.[85]

Quite apart from the financial or moral contribution they made to the Zionist cause, Christian pro-Zionists were also highly influential in those Jewish circles that were apprehensive of any move that might prove "distasteful or ill-advised to the non-Jewish majority." To the degree that many Jews sought to identify themselves with the values of the Christian majority, Christian Zionist support for Zionism provided the prerequisite certificate of legitimacy for large sections of the Jewish community, especially the more established.[86] The Zionists were well aware of these factors and took pains to nurture Christian Zionism. The "shaping and mobilization of favorable non-Jewish opinion" became a conscious goal of the Zionist leadership and an integral part of Zionist policy during the war.

In April 1941 Emmanuel Neumann of the American Zionist Emergency Council (AZEC) revived the American Palestine Committee, a society of Protestant notables that had been languishing without direction for years. Senator Wagner of New York agreed to head the committee and enlisted twenty-six members of the Senate, including the majority and minority leaders, Secretary of the Interior Harold Ickes and General Robert Jackson, respectively. The AZEC allotted $50,000 of its budget to the organization, a figure that grew to $150,000 during the two critical years preceding the establishment of the State of Israel. By 1946 the committee could boast a membership that listed fifteen thousand influential Americans, including sixty-eight senators, two hundred congressmen, and several state governors. Across the country seventy-five local chapters were organized.[87]

Wagner's committee became "the preeminent symbol of pro-Zionist sentiment among the non-Jewish American public."[88] Zionist control was discreet but tight. The committee's correspondence was drafted in the AZEC headquarters and sent to Wagner for his signature. Mail addressed to Wagner as head of the American Palestine Committee, even if it came from the White House or the State Department, was opened and kept in Zionist headquarters; Wagner received a copy.[89] The AZEC placed ads in the press under the committee's name without bothering to consult or advise it in advance, until one of its members meekly requested advance notice.[90]

Among certain sections of the Christian clergy the Old Testament's prediction of the Jewish return to the Holy Land was frequently an article of fundamental belief. Such clergy were favorably predisposed to the Zionist cause. In late 1941 Neumann therefore organized the Christian Council on Palestine. By 1946 the council numbered almost three thousand Protestant clergymen. Their prestige and authority were used by the Zionists in many appeals to the American public and to the administration.[91]

In 1948 the American Palestine Committee and the Christian Council on Palestine were merged into the American Christian Palestine Committee. Once more, Robert Wagner was chosen to head the new committee.

Christian Zionist support for the Zionist cause, both spontaneous and organized, would prove a valuable, even if unquantifiable, asset in the Zionist diplomatic struggle. At the very least, it provided a crucial counter to the aspersions cast both by anti-Zionist Jewish elements and by the State Department that the Zionists were a narrow, parochial lobby, not representative of even the Jewish community let alone the larger, non-Jewish one.

SIX

The Anti-Zionist Forces

THE STATE DEPARTMENT

The senior officials of the State Department have been described as a "largely elitist, continuous, and homogeneous group." They sought to promote abroad what they regarded as the "American national interest," which meant not only national power and prestige but equally "profitable business opportunities for American private interests." At home the department regarded its position as foremost within the administration and strove jealously to preserve its status.[1]

The State Department viewed Palestine as an integral part of the Arab world. Thus, anything non-Arab was by definition "inherently foreign." The Department's Division of Near Eastern and African Affairs (NEA) did recognize the existence of the Jewish community in Palestine (Yishuv) and Palestine's status as terra sancta to three religions, but these non-Arab factors were regarded as "incidentals, hardly enough to change the Department's view that Palestine was, and must remain, an Arab area." The department downplayed the reality of entrenched minorities and communal differences in the Middle East and naively expected that those minorities would simply be absorbed by the "native majority," much the same as waves of new immigrants were, or at least were supposed to be, assimilated in the United States.[2]

After World War II the department viewed the Middle East with optimism as an area "for an easy, almost automatic, American harvest of influence." This would be reaped because of the weakness or preoccupations of other powers elsewhere; accumulated Arab goodwill, arising from nonimperialist influence and aid; and from Ibn Saud's preference for the American connection. Such hopes led the department to conclude that "the native majoritarian nationalisms of the Sunni Arabs were necessarily benevolent and progressive, not to say overdue, from World War I; while the political Zionism represented chiefly by the Jewish minority in Palestine and in the United States was retrograde, a chimera in the 'Arab world' and, in the context of pro-Zionist American politics, an albatross around the Department's neck."[3]

The department dismissed out of hand any commercial benefits that the Yishuv might yield. It made only superficial attempts to study the extent of Jewish investment in Palestine, although during the interwar decades Palestine was by far the largest American economic interest in the Middle East. In 1939 the American consulate at Jerusalem reported that 78 percent of all American citizens in the Middle East resided in Palestine and that 84 percent of these were Jewish. Of a total American investment in Palestine of $49 million, $41 million came from American Jews.[4] But such statistics made little if any impression at the State Department, possibly because the nationals and their capital were Jewish and the Yishuv's economy was deemed artificial, propped up by Jews (mainly American), "who were only promoting their own narrow and parochial nationalistic aspirations."[5]

But during World War II, the commercial exploitation of Saudi oil and the influence of Aramco on the Washington establishment soon dwarfed any other American economic interest in the Middle East, even if during that period American dependence on foreign oil continued to be minimal.

In the department's view Palestine's importance lay in its negative, destabilizing role in what it claimed would otherwise have been a serene, tranquil Middle East. Zionism jeopardized the consummation of an Arab-American entente. The greatest departmental fear, played upon incessantly and to great effect by the Washington oil lobby, was that the administration's support for the Zionist cause would turn Ibn Saud against Aramco and drive the Arabs into the arms of the Russians.

State Department officials were unable to reconcile what they regarded as their foreign policy–making duty with White House pressures and actions arising from what they saw as the president's personal political ambitions. Upon his arrival at the White House, Truman was submitted to a deluge of State Department warnings about the harm that would come to American interests in the Arab Middle East should he succumb to Zionist pressures.[6]

Even on Truman's appeal to admit the one hundred thousand Jewish displaced persons into Palestine (what has been referred to above as "refugee Zionism"), the State Department differed fundamentally. Dean Acheson, under secretary of state from September 1945 to January 1947 and given direct responsibility for Palestine by Secretary of State Byrnes, wrote later: "The number that could be absorbed by Arab Palestine without creating a grave political problem would be inadequate, and to transform the country into a Jewish State capable of receiving a million or more immigrants would vastly exacerbate the political problem and imperil not only American but all Western interests in the Near East."[7]

The department resented the intrusion of domestic politics in foreign policy, which it regarded as its special preserve. It lamented the continued existence of so many "hyphenated" Americans and denied the legitimacy of any "ethnic vote" for several reasons, including "the legitimate fear of national disunity in wartime."[8]

The significance of the Jewish vote was apparently brought up by Truman quite unabashedly at a conference of U.S. chiefs of mission to the Middle East held in Washington in October 1945. When the ministers all dwelt on the threat to American national interests caused by continued American support for Zionism, Truman is reported to have replied: "I'm sorry gentlemen, but I have to answer to hundreds of thousands who are anxious for the success of Zionism; I do not have hundreds of thousands of Arabs among my constituents."[9] The White House resented what it regarded as the State Department's myopia on this point. The president was elected by the *whole* nation, including a sizable Jewish minority. Therefore, he was bound to serve the interests of his Jewish constituency too, not only because of political self-interest but also on good moral and constitutional grounds.

On occasion, as with the State Department's trusteeship proposal of March 1948 (see chapter 10), the White House went so far as to accuse the department of deliberately sabotaging the president's electoral chances. For example, when State Department adviser Charles Bohlen was chided for "working in a vacuum" and failing to consider the domestic political effects of the department's actions, he retorted that this was *exactly* his intention—officials were supposed to be outside the influence of politics. Matt Connelly, presidential press secretary, replied that even though the State Department denied the legitimacy of American politics intruding on policy making, it had accepted it when applied to the British. When the Labour government argued that it was unable to get the support of the British people for its policy in Palestine and was therefore pulling out, the State Department had backed it.[10]

With the wisdom of hindsight Loy Henderson admitted, albeit in private, that Truman had been right to give due consideration to domestic politics. Even had the president wished to keep politics out, he had in effect been a prisoner of the American political system. In a letter written to Dean Rusk in 1977, Henderson stated:

In so far as internal political considerations played a role, we should bear in mind that many of the leaders of the Republican Party, including Dewey . . . were almost constantly criticising Truman for failure to give full support to the Zionists. If Truman had taken positions that would have resulted in a failure to establish the Jewish State, he would almost certainly have been defeated in the November [1948] elections since the Zionists had almost the full support of the Congress, the United States media, and most of the American people. The new Republican Administration would then have gone along with the Zionists.[11]

Truman's first appointee as secretary of state, James Byrnes, washed his hands of Palestine, thereby conceding to the White

House a monopoly. In July 1946, when Ben-Gurion tried to get State Department assistant Ben Cohen to secure him an interview with Byrnes, Byrnes sent a message back that he wanted Ben-Gurion to know that the Palestine issue was out of the hands of the State Department and in those of the president. Byrnes resented Zionist criticisms of the State Department's Palestine policy and decided that he would no longer take responsibility for it. When David Niles reported this to the president, Truman wrote by hand the following jocular note: "Dave:—I don't blame him much. Imagine Goldmann, Wise & Co. each running in after a round with a bandit like Molotov on Trieste & the Tyrol!—reparations, displaced persons, and hell all around. Think probably I'd tell him to jump in the Jordan." [12]

At the upper levels relations between White House and State Department staff degenerated to a state of open feuding and mutual acrimony. In January 1947 Niles warned the Zionist representative in Washington, Eliahu Epstein, that the Zionists had to maintain correct relations with the State Department and must not underestimate Loy Henderson and NEA. Niles and his colleagues at the White House sought regular reports on the Zionists' interactions with the State Department. [13]

In 1948 the White House aides would successfully seek the head of Loy Henderson, director of NEA, and have him removed from Washington as ambassador to distant and neutral India. For his part Clark Clifford believed that he and Niles were on the State Department's blacklist. As Clifford told Niles in May 1948, they had better be careful as "the State Department was gunning for both of them." This made Niles only the more determined to neutralize Henderson first. He replied: "That's really something, that people in the Government, in the Government under the President, are gunning for men on the President's own staff." [14]

During the first two weeks of May 1948, tensions between the White House and the State Department reached the breaking point. Niles reported to Max Lowenthal about "the way people in State are bitching things up . . . instead of abiding by decisions." Lowenthal replied: "No matter who is President there either has to be a house-cleaning in State (a herculean task) or someone in State on Palestine matters who is trustworthy." [15]

THE HILLDRING EPISODE

Lowenthal's last comment reflects some disillusion with his and
Niles's failure to place their own appointee in the State Department to look after Zionist affairs. Their efforts had focused on
General John Hilldring, who at war's end had served as assistant secretary of state for the occupied areas in Europe.
In that capacity he "had demonstrated a humane and compas-
sionate attitude toward the displaced persons in the camps
in Germany and Austria and understood the Jewish yearning
for Palestine." By chance General Hilldring had retired from
that position on September 1, 1947, and his special assistant,
Herbert A. Fierst, who kept close contact with David Niles,
had suggested to the latter an appointment for Hilldring on
the U.S. delegation to the UN General Assembly session on
Palestine.[16]

The timing was providential, since Niles had just heard that
the key advisers to the delegation on the Palestine issue were to
be Loy Henderson and George Wadsworth, former ambassador to Iraq, both reputedly philo-Arabs. Niles recommended
Hilldring to Truman:

I understand that the key advisers on Palestine to the United States
Delegation at the Fall Session will be Loy Henderson and George
Wadsworth. Because both are widely regarded as unsympathetic to
the Jewish viewpoint, much resentment will be engendered when
their appointment is announced and later. Moreover, on the basis of
their past behavior and attitudes, I frankly doubt that they will vigorously carry out your policy. But your administration, not they, will
be held responsible.

It may not be feasible to oppose Henderson and Wadsworth as advisers to the Delegation. In any event, I believe it is most important
that at least one of your advisers be a vigorous and well-informed individual in whom you, the members of the United States Delegation,
and American Jewry have complete confidence. There is only one
person I know who will fit the bill completely—General Hilldring.[17]

Truman accepted Niles's recommendation, and Hilldring
was appointed an alternate representative to the U.S. delegation on September 10, 1947. In his function as liaison between
the UN delegation and the White House, Hilldring rendered

yeoman service to the Zionist cause. But it should be emphasized that he did *not* counter the influence of Loy Henderson or really challenge NEA's domination of the delegation. The end of the UN General Assembly also meant the end of Hilldring's temporary posting, and the White House was again left without a sympathetic channel to the State Department.

The second, less known and most fascinating, phase of the Hilldring episode would take place in the spring of 1948, when Niles and the Zionists tried to "infiltrate" Hilldring into the State Department (see chapter 11).

Obviously, the considerations guiding State Department policy on Palestine were frequently in direct conflict with those guiding the White House. The resulting lack of harmony and productive cooperation led to attempts by each side to present the other with swift faits accomplis, which were at times crude and even bordering on the unconstitutional. Undoubtedly, they interfered with the smooth process of good government.

THE OIL LOBBY

During the war, the Americans alleged that they were providing a disproportionate share of the oil for the war effort and that American reserves were being dissipated for the benefit of Great Britain. In March 1943 the Presidential Committee on International Petroleum Policy had reported that future American demand for oil—both for defense and for vital economic needs—would exceed domestic production.[18]

At the end of 1943 the United States instigated talks with Britain on a reallocation between the two of Middle Eastern oil reserves. A new agreement, arrived at under U.S. pressure in 1944, weighed heavily in America's favor. The United States gained control of 42 percent of the Middle East's proved oil resources, which because of new discoveries since 1936, when the American share had been only 13 percent, had increased 5.8 times, or 1900 percent.[19]

But it should be stressed that at that time Arabian oil was *not* important to the American domestic economy. In 1948 the United States imported a mere 8 percent of the oil it needed for its domestic consumption, and only a small percentage of that came from Saudi Arabia or the Middle East.[20] With the end of World War II, however, and the spread of the Cold War, the Middle East in general, and its oil resources in particular, took on new significance in American strategic thinking. Bases in the Middle East along the Suez Canal (most of which were still British) were seen as springboards for an attack on vulnerable areas of the Soviet Union in the event of war. The Arab world was now regarded by the American defense establishment as "a key link in the defensive arc being built around the Soviet Union," and "[Ibn Saud's] economic well-being and good will became a matter of vital national interest to the Department of State, the Department of Defense, and the National Security Council."[21]

In July 1945 Secretary of the Navy James Forrestal (former president of Wall Street bankers Dillon, Read and Company) told Secretary of State James Byrnes that Saudi Arabia was "one of the three great [oil] puddles left in the world" and that although the United States was spending millions there the British, and not themselves, were gaining the benefits.[22]

Furthermore, even if Arabian oil was not essential to the American economy, it *was* seen as vital to *European* economic recovery and consequently to Europe's postwar ability to stand up to the threat of Communism, both internal and external. In addition there remained. entrenched anxieties concerning dwindling domestic reserves. Therefore, as put by Max Ball, director of the Oil and Gas Division at the Department of the Interior, Middle Eastern oil resources had to be developed as quickly as possible for "the supply of Europe, to prevent European industry from collapsing and falling to Communism or to the dogs. . . . Middle Eastern oil would release for U.S. consumption the Caribbean oil" that was currently going to Europe.[23]

It has been denied that an oil lobby worked against the administration's support for Zionism. Indeed, Evan Wilson, head of the Palestine desk at NEA from 1942 to 1947, published a book in 1979 in which he claimed that he remembered no oil lobby and could unearth no documents in the State Department archives proving the existence of one.[24]

The Arabian American Oil Company (Aramco), a conglomerate formed in 1936 by Standard Oil of California and the Texas Company, was concerned most directly with and involved in the American exploitation of Saudi Arabian oil.[25] The historian of Aramco, Irvine H. Anderson, has claimed that from as early as 1937 the companies had warned the administration that its continued support for Zionism might result in the loss of Aramco's oil concessions in Saudi Arabia and "the destruction of the U.S. political and economic position in the Middle East." By 1947 all the key people in the departments of State and Defense were quite aware of the risks to American interests. Thus, Anderson claims, no special advocacy of the oil companies' case against the Zionist cause was required. In any case, periodical Arab threats were reported more than adequately through the media and diplomatic channels. Therefore, Anderson concludes, the companies adopted a relatively low profile for two very good reasons: first, they feared a domestic backlash against the oil companies themselves; and second, they hoped that the Arabs would distinguish between the policies of the administration and "good business relations with the companies."[26]

The portrait of such enlightened behavior on the part of Aramco is in fact totally misleading. The oil lobby was by nature different from the Zionist lobby, yet it was none the less active, and was certainly more influential, in government circles. The lobby's efforts at the highest levels of the political and military establishment were critical in keeping alive fears of an Arab boycott. Where the Zionist lobby, public by nature, held as its trump card the political and financial influence of the large Jewish community, the oil lobby, discreet by nature, held as *its* trump card the ever-open doors and sympathetic ears of the Washington establishment.

The oil executives, frequently former State Department or government employees, moved in the same social circles as the heads of the Washington administration. Much of their contact was oral, over meals or by telephone. Therefore, as might be expected, written records of their concerns are sparse and not easy to track down, yet—contrary to the claims of Evan Wilson—they most certainly do exist.

State Department officials received the oil lobbyists with open arms. In its debates with the White House, the department at times deliberately exaggerated the risks of losing Arab goodwill and oil, knowing only too well how minimal that risk was. In

December 1947 Prince Sa'ud, the son of the Saudi ruler, Ibn Saud, told Ambassador J. Rives Childs that Iraq and Transjordan had asked the Saudis to break relations with the United States and cancel the oil concession because of American support for the UN partition resolution (passed on November 29). The Saudis had replied that they were "at one with other Arab States in opposition [to the] establishment [of a] Jewish state but saw no reason [to] run counter to [their] own interests by severing relations with [the] U.S."[27]

Fraser Wilkins, one of the officials at NEA at the time and its director from 1955 to 1957, later admitted that they had never received any concrete Arab threat to cut off their oil. Wilkins claimed that such threats in the press were not treated seriously, since the administration was well aware that the Arabs were dependent upon the export of their oil.[28]

A further argument of the lobby was that continued American support for the Zionists and for Israel would force the Arabs into the arms of the Soviets. In an informal conversation with correspondents early in 1948, Terry Duce, Aramco vice-president of operations, acknowledged that there was no danger of the Arabs canceling the oil concessions following American support for the UN partition resolution. But, he added, if the administration became involved in the implementation of the plan, the Arabs would "turn sooner or later against the United States" and would "facilitate the groundwork for Russian penetration in the Middle East."[29]

As noted already, Aramco endeavored to dissociate itself in Arab eyes from its own government. At times of crisis the company repeatedly warned the State Department that to save its investment it might be forced to convert itself into a foreign corporation. Presumably, the Arabs would have no problem exporting their oil to a pro-Zionist America, providing the company working the concession was not incorporated in the United States.

In November 1946 Duce called at the State Department to advise that Aramco was considering incorporating as a British company.[30] In June 1948 Ambassador Childs sent a telegram to the State Department warning of Ibn Saud's dismay at American policy and recommended that should American support for Israel continue "consideration should be given to allowing Britain to assume responsibility for the Dhahran air base, and to advising Aramco to shift its incorporation to Canada."[31]

At key points in the Palestine diplomatic drama Aramco sent its executives and agents on tours of the Middle East to gauge and report back on Arab reactions to the latest American moves. Upon their return they disseminated alarmist propaganda, both to government circles and through the company's public relations department to the media, in a campaign to stress the vital importance of the oil concessions to "American strategic and political interests."[32]

Perhaps the most critical period came between the UN decision on November 29, 1947, to partition Palestine and the de facto establishment of Israel in May 1948. During this time, the State Department, ably assisted by the Defense Department, the National Security Council, and the CIA, determined to reverse American support for partition. In this battle of minds waged in Washington the oil lobby helped to provide the administration with background material on real or alleged threats to American interests in the Arab world.

Following the UN resolution, Aramco vice-president Terry Duce together with Colonel William Eddy, a former State Department official turned Aramco executive, went to the Middle East on behalf of the company.[33] Aramco also sent another employee, Colonel Halford Hoskins, a Lebanese-educated American, who during the war had served Roosevelt twice on presidential missions to the Middle East. Their reports found their way to the highest echelons of the State and Defense departments and the military establishment.

Upon his return Colonel Eddy met with the Joint Chiefs of Staff at their invitation and followed this up with a memorandum (written on Aramco notepaper) to Major General Alfred W. Greunther, chairman of the Joint Chiefs.[34] Eddy issued a dire warning about the strategic implications in the Middle East of Truman's Palestine policy:

Overshadowing all other matters is the adverse effect on Aramco and Tapline of the Pro-Zionist Policy of the United States Government. . . . All Arabs resent the actions of the present United States Administration as unfriendly to them. . . . The prestige of the United States Government among the Arabs has practically vanished, while that of Great Britain has greatly increased. . . . Popular Arab resentment against the United States is at present greater than fear or dislike of the U.S.S.R.

Eddy added that the Arab states had evidence that the United States had exerted economic pressure on several small countries at the United Nations, causing them, "against their own better judgment and wishes," to vote for partition. Eddy claimed that this "hostile act" of the United States, publicized just as the Syrian Parliament was convening (on November 8, 1947), had caused the Syrian government to hold up the ratification of the Tapline Agreement (an agreement to lay a pipeline across Arabia to carry oil north through Syria to the Mediterranean).

He went on to warn that until now the Arab League had rejected the "proposals of fanatics" to cancel American commercial concessions but that should the United States now proceed to arm the Jewish state against the Arabs it would become "impossible for any Arab Government, including that of Saudi Arabia, to maintain the distinction between their American friends and partners on the one hand, and an unfriendly United States Government on the other."

In conclusion Eddy warned that should the administration arm or finance a "Zionist State" it should expect the following consequences: cancellation of commercial concessions, expropriation of property, closure of American schools and universities, physical attacks on American companies and individuals, attacks on Jews in Arab countries, and an Arab war aimed at "driving all Jews from Palestine." The American assets being placed at risk were nothing short of colossal: "The United States is jeopardising the good will of 30,000,000 Arabs and 220,000,000 Muslims, risking the loss of its cultural and educational leadership in that part of the world, the sacrifice of many hundreds of millions of dollars of investments . . . and the strategic loss of access to air and naval bases throughout the entire Moslem world."

Terry Duce's report, also sent to the Joint Chiefs, was a little more circumspect. Duce produced the sophisticated argument that even though the Arab rulers appreciated the benefits accruing to them from the company's operations, they might lose control of their own people and be forced by popular will to break off all relations with American institutions even if they had no direct connection with the home government. But Saudi Arabia was an exception to this rule, admitted Duce, presumably because its rulers were not in the habit of consulting or bending to the popular will. Furthermore, as noted recently by William Roger Louis, Duce believed that the Arabs would win the war in Palestine before Ibn Saud felt constrained to act against Aramco's concessions.[35]

Halford Hoskins, now also an Aramco director, added a new angle to the argument about pushing the Arabs into the arms of the Russians. In his report, obligingly forwarded to the State Department by the U.S. embassy in Baghdad, he warned of repercussions in the Northern Tier, where American interests had been defined by the Truman Doctrine in March 1947: "For the United States to spend money and effort in Greece and Turkey and, at the same time, to open the back door for Russian infiltration into Palestine seems to the Turks either incomprehensible inconsistency or a foolishly naive ignorance of Russian intentions."[36]

On May 14, 1948, at the time of President Truman's precipitate recognition of Israel, Loy Henderson, then director of NEA, was in constant telephone contact with Terry Duce. Duce was concerned about the continued suspension of permission to build an Aramco pipeline, and on May 15 he phoned from New York to ask if Henderson had any information about the Saudi reaction to Truman's recognition. Duce was concerned also for the safety of the company's personnel since he had been given no opportunity to warn them. Henderson regretted having been unable to give any advance warning and explained that this had been because the decision had been made just a few minutes before it was announced. The department had immediately notified its diplomatic and consular representatives and assumed they had taken necessary precautions. Duce felt that with a war brewing in Palestine it would be unwise for the company to continue construction of its oil pipeline for the present. Henderson tried to reassure him and advised Duce to postpone any decision for a couple of weeks while the situation clarified.[37]

On May 25, 1948, Duce rang up Secretary of State George C. Marshall to tell him of a telegraphic message he had just received from Mr. Davies, another vice-president of the company, then in Saudi Arabia. Duce was unable to explain everything over the telephone but would come to Washington in the next day or so. But the gist of the message was that Ibn Saud was now contemplating sanctions against the United States, especially if it lifted its arms embargo on Israel. Should Ibn Saud resort to such action "it would not be because of his desire to do so but because the pressure upon him of Arab public opinion was so great that he could no longer resist it."[38]

It is to be doubted whether the Truman White House was ever much impressed by alleged Arab threats to cut off their oil supplies. Clark Clifford was prepared with the counterargument that the Arabs needed American dollars much more than the United States needed Arab oil. But the argument drummed in by both the oil lobby and the State Department that American pro-Zionist policies might drive the Arabs into Russian arms did have a significant impact on the Truman White House.

The circumstances of the postwar period were not auspicious for a successful oil lobby. The United States was not yet as dependent on foreign oil as it would be in the 1970s; the Western world had never experienced either an oil embargo or even an oil-price inflationary spiral. And in any case, the military did not expect to be able to obtain access to Arab oil in an emergency.

But during the period under discussion here, it did seem to many in the Washington establishment that the pro-Zionist policies of the White House were placing American interests in the Middle East at unnecessary risk. For them the oil lobby was an invaluable resource. Traces of Aramco memoranda may be readily detected in those submitted by the State Department to the White House. That the Zionist cause ultimately prevailed in Washington should not lead to any underestimation of the oil lobby.

THE AMERICAN JEWISH
ESTABLISHMENT AND JEWISH
ANTI-ZIONISTS

By the 1930s the second and third generations of American-born Jews, descendants of Eastern European Jewish immigrants, were making their mark in American grass-root politics. The young Adlai Stevenson, a Washington lawyer in the 1930s, has been quoted as saying: "There is a little feeling that the Jews are getting too prominent and many of them are autocratic."[39]

President Roosevelt's close association with the Jews was in part because of widespread Jewish support for his New Deal and the large number of Jewish advisers in his brain trust. But those Jews who made their way to Washington and other power centers did not usually identify with Jewish issues and would have felt too embarrassed to promote specifically Jewish causes. That the influential Jewish elite failed to spur Roosevelt's administration to greater efforts to save European Jews during the war has provoked controversy ever since and provided a source of what has been called Jewish "self-flagellation." Even Henry L. Feingold, however, who has emphasized the limits to Jewish ethnic politics, has concluded, in reference to the Holocaust, that there *was* a real possibility of moving Roosevelt to do more—vide the success of Henry Morgenthau, Jr., in getting the War Refugee Board established in 1944.[40]

But in general the Jewish elite under Roosevelt did not use their power and influence "for the enhancement of Jewish corporate power." The same process of secularization that had facilitated their rise inhibited them from acting upon matters of specific Jewish interest. Even had they been so inclined, they were inhibited further by fears of domestic anti-Semitism, which might react against any overt "Jewish lobby."[41] Anti-Semitism was prevalent in the United States during the 1930s and 1940s. Opinion polls indicated that over half the population held images of the Jews as "greedy and dishonest" and about one-third considered them "overly aggressive."[42]

Truman did not retain many of Roosevelt's advisers—the significant exceptions being David Niles and Judge Sam Rosenman. Truman would not have felt comfortable in the intellectual circles in which Roosevelt mixed. Truman's Jewish entourage was made up of men like Eddie Jacobson, Abe Feinberg, and Dewey Stone, self-made business successes, rather than the Harvard-educated professional elite of the Jewish establishment. Although Max Lowenthal was perhaps the exception who proved the rule.

The most respected and prestigious Jewish communal organization was the American Jewish Committee (AJC). It had been organized in 1906 in the aftermath of the Kishinev pogroms "to prevent the infraction of civil and religious rights of Jews, in any part of the world . . . ; to secure for Jews equality of economic, social and educational opportunity; [and] to alleviate the consequences of persecution and to afford relief from calamities affecting Jews, wherever they may occur."[43]

The AJC was a small, oligarchic organization, representing the German Jewish elite in the United States. Its membership and adherents included a few wealthy and influential Jews, but in fact it exerted little influence on the American Jewish community at large. But despite the committee's lack of a popular base, it was treated by the administration as an important representative of the Jewish community.[44] Judge Joseph Proskauer, president of the AJC from 1943 to 1949, wrote later that during the war he had been involved in

endless delicate negotiations with governments and government officials of many countries, including our own . . . with unstinted endeavors to rescue European Jews . . . ; to consider the explosive problems that arose in Palestine and from the activities of certain extreme Zionist groups; and to combat the creeping menace of new forms of anti-Semitism which the example of Hitler seemed to have brought to our own America.[45]

Proskauer has been called "one of the important American Jewish obstructionists to the creation of Israel, who believed that a Jewish state would be catastrophic for the Jews."[46] In 1943 Proskauer, aided by New York judge Herbert Lehman and presidential adviser Sam Rosenman, drew up a "Statement of Views," which presented clearly the committee's opposition to the Zionist viewpoint: "In the United States as in all other countries Jews, like all others of their citizens are nationals of those nations and of no other[;] there can be no political identification of Jews outside Palestine with whatever government may there be instituted."[47]

In 1943 Proskauer and his committee walked out of an American Jewish conference that adopted the Zionists' (Biltmore) program advocating the establishment in Palestine of a Jewish commonwealth after the war. In vain, Proskauer delivered the State Department's warning that "efforts to press the claim for statehood would be a 'tragedy.'" Proskauer boasted later: "There is no Jew in America who has maintained closer rapport with our State Department than I have."[48] But the AJC became increasingly isolated since "Zionist political activities were too rambunctious and democratic for the discreet elite of German Jewry who . . . ruled the American Jewish Committee." As put acidly by one Jewish historian: "While the Zionists spoke to a growing Jewish majority, Proskauer spoke to the State Department."[49]

There developed between Proskauer and the State Department an affair of the heart and the mind. Proskauer felt privileged to be consulted by the department, whose officials were only too pleased to encourage any Jewish allies in its struggle against the Zionists.[50] The AJC performed useful services for the State Department, and its members were always assured of a warm welcome. The AJC's anti-Zionist position legitimized the State Department's own hostility and strengthened its claim that the Zionists represented neither the aspirations nor the votes of American Jewry. Jewish attacks on the Zionists, frequently more bitter and defamatory than its own, relieved the department of any trepidations that its own condemnations were possibly unfair or tainted with anti-Semitism.

The State Department also developed close ties with the anti-Zionist American Council for Judaism. The council had the dubious honor of being "the only American Jewish organization ever created to fight against Zionism and the establishment of a Jewish state in Palestine." Formed in 1942 soon after the Zionists passed the Biltmore resolution, the council was at first essentially an association of Reform rabbis. In the spring of 1943 it was transformed into a "secular anti-Zionist pressure group, whose membership consisted mainly of middle and upper class lay Reform Jews of German descent."[51]

The council vigorously opposed the Zionists' efforts to raise money for their cause or speak on behalf of the American Jewish community. It tried to establish and maintain a clear distinction between humanitarian efforts on behalf of its persecuted brethren and the Zionists' political goal of a Jewish state in Palestine.[52]

The executive head of the council was Elmer Berger, a young Reform rabbi from Flint, Michigan, who dedicated his life to fighting Zionism. Berger was convinced that "Zionism was a wicked movement with devious designs to foist Jewish nationalism on American Jews" and believed that the council "stood as the last barricade against a mighty flood of Jewish nationalism."[53]

The council's strength lay not so much in its membership, however, which was relatively small, but in the prestige and resources of some of its leaders, especially those of Lessing Rosenwald, chairman of Sears, Roebuck and Company, prominent philanthropist, and internationally renowned art and book collector. Thanks to his affluence and well-placed connections (which in particular provided the backing of the *New York Times*), council executives enjoyed easy access to the administration and Congress.[54] Thus, the State Department entertained hopes that the council might "neutralize the pro-Zionist lobby in Congress."[55]

As has been noted already, perhaps the biggest success of the American Council for Judaism was convincing many prominent non-Jews, including Truman, that the Zionists' goal was to establish "an exclusive, racial, theocratic state in Palestine," a notion that was anathema to most Americans.

Rosenwald became president of the council in 1943, but not before Under Secretary of State Sumner Welles had assured him that "organized Jewish anti-Zionism would serve the interests of the United States." Rosenwald was also a good friend of White House insider Sam Rosenman, a non-Zionist member of the American Jewish Committee.[56] From 1946 to 1948 the council's main liaison with the State Department was George L. Levison, a close friend of Dean Acheson, Loy Henderson, and Kermit Roosevelt. Levison had served in the State Department in the Middle East during the war and had worked for some time in Washington under Dean Acheson.[57]

The State Department hoped that the two anti-Zionist bodies would explode the myth of Jewish unity behind Zionism. On May 2, 1947, at the special meeting of the UN General Assembly requested by the British to discuss the Palestine problem, the American delegate, Warren Austin, stated: "It should be borne in mind that the Jewish Agency is not speaking for all the Jews of the world. My government is in receipt of numerous communications from various Jewish groups which make it clear that they do not recognize the Jewish Agency as their spokesman."[58]

At a private meeting on September 30, 1947, between Secretary of State Marshall, General Hilldring, and Rosenwald and Levison (a meeting that Marshall insisted be kept secret), Hilldring expressed his admiration for the council's arguments and spoke of the "vital importance of breaking the theory of 'Jewish unanimity' in the United States."[59]

Some of Proskauer's closest friends were members of the American Council for Judaism. But as he confessed to a close friend, their "God-awful" techniques and poor public relations made the council "abhorrent to the masses of American Jews."[60]

In effect, both organizations became somewhat eccentric and increasingly isolated within their own community. The Zionists successfully represented their Jewish opponents as "traitorous, irreligious and anti-Jewish." The backlash caused by the anti-Zionist committees may even have strengthened Jewish cohesion on the Zionist question.[61]

The AJC's opposition to a Jewish state in Palestine collapsed once it perceived that its own government was heading in that direction. When in August 1946 Under Secretary Dean Acheson hinted to Proskauer that the government would lend its support to partition, that is, a Jewish state in a part of Palestine, Proskauer's apparent acquiescence was so rapid that he took his own colleagues by surprise. In addition, Proskauer was persuaded by the Zionist diplomat Nahum Goldmann that his opposition to the Zionist cause was placing him in an intolerable position vis-à-vis his own community: "Look. I know you and the Committee are against the Jewish State, etc. [In] what posi-

tion will you be? You will fight the Jews in Palestine after Auschwitz because they want to have a Jewish State? You will be torn
to pieces between your loyalty to America and your loyalty to
the Jewish people."[62]

Dissension in public with his own government or with the obvious consensus within his own community was unthinkable for
Proskauer, even if he still hoped that partition "would be a ve-
hicle for nothing more than increased immigration." But he
continued, though henceforth in private, to oppose a Jewish
state.[63] But since his primary concern was with Jewish immigration into Palestine, if he could secure it without a Jewish state,
then so much the better; if he could not, then a Jewish state it
would have to be.[64] His public support for the Zionist cause was
politically faute de mieux.

The American Council for Judaism, in stark contrast to the
Zionists, who skillfully penetrated most American Jewish organizations during the 1940s, failed to win over even a single important Jewish organization to its own struggle against a Jewish
state. By 1948 the council had become "a marginal Jewish organization, hopelessly trapped by its unfavorable image among
American Jews." The council was forced to reconcile itself to
the Zionist state, but it resolved at the same time to "concentrate
more than ever on fighting Jewish nationalism" and reaffirmed
its "single, indivisible, and exclusive allegiance to the United
States."[65]

The State Department's hopes for an effective, anti-Zionist
working alliance with the two bodies never materialized. The
Zionist cause captured the hearts of the Jewish community at
large, and in the summer of 1946 with the defection of Judge
Proskauer to the Zionist camp, his committee's "special liaison"
with the State Department evaporated.

PART THREE

"Refugee Zionism"

SEVEN

The Problem of Jewish Displaced Persons

THE 100,000

The relocation of Jewish displaced persons (DPs) in Europe after the war became integral to the Palestine problem and to the Zionists' struggle in the United States. The Zionists argued that these refugees had no place other than Palestine in which to make their home. With 50,000 housed in Allied camps at the end of the war and well over 250,000 by summer 1946, Jewish DPs constituted one of the most emotionally charged postwar political issues.[1]

Non-Zionist Jews, in an alliance of convenience with the State Department, determined to neutralize the Zionists. By way of a counterbalance to the Zionist lobby the American Council for Judaism (ACJ) sought to reduce the number of potential Jewish immigrants to Palestine by improving their living conditions in Europe and by securing the swift passage of an international bill of human rights, still pending at the United Nations.[2] The ACJ organized its own lobby to secure the lifting of American immigration restrictions and thus facilitate the entry of Jewish DPs into the United States, which would thereby debilitate the Zionist case. Their lobby, well screened behind a facade of prominent Gentile personalities, was recognized subsequently as "one of the largest and best-run lobbying groups in the nation in 1947 and 1948."[3]

President Truman's first campaign on behalf of the Jews was

his demand of the British government to allow the immediate entry of 100,000 Jewish DPs into Palestine. This demand arose out of the recommendations of Earl G. Harrison, who in June 1945 was sent to Europe to examine the situation of displaced persons there.[4] (See chapter 8.)

Eddie Jacobson had only a minor influence in making Truman more sensitive to the urgent need to solve the Jewish DP problem. Once Truman succeeded to the presidency, the Zionists made several attempts to convert Jacobson to their cause but with little apparent success. Dr. Israel Goldstein, president of the Zionist Organization of America, even paid a personal visit to Kansas City but failed to persuade Jacobson to use his influence with Truman to secure the Zionists access to the White House.[5]

Jacobson's own Jewish community and friends were divided on the issue. His rabbi (Mayerberg) was closer in sentiment to the ACJ, which gave priority to the entry of Jewish refugees into the United States over entry into Palestine. Although Mayerberg was in favor of the admission of Jewish DPs into Palestine, his opposition to Zionism was "unalterable." In contrast, Irving Fane, the president of Jacobson's congregation, B'nai Jehudah, had become an outspoken Zionist. Although Fane made it clear that the Zionist question was beyond the functions of the synagogue, he visited Jacobson's new store, although in vain, in an attempt to convert him to Zionism.[6]

Jacobson's approach, therefore, was close to that of the ACJ; he wanted to work for an early solution of the refugee problem by securing the entry of Jewish DPs both into Palestine and into the United States. In early June 1945 Jacobson was received by President Truman at the White House, apparently for the first time. But as he wrote to his rabbi later: "We were in such a rush that I did not get to speak to him about the Jewish situation in Europe, but you can rest assured that when I see him in Kansas City next week, I will certainly appeal to him to get the British Government to relax their restrictions for those entering Palestine."[7]

During Truman's visit to Kansas City, he met Jacobson and Herman Rosenberg, a mutual friend from the days of Battery D. They spoke about the Jewish DP problem in Europe. Jacobson did *not* apparently refer to Palestine but did press for the admission of Jewish refugees into the United States. Truman apparently promised to secure the entry of 150,000 annually. Jacobson noted later in his diary, however, that "the congress refused."[8]

By the time Truman met Jacobson and Rosenberg he had already given his consent to the dispatch of the Harrison mission. Ironically, this mission, whose findings would significantly direct Truman's early Palestine policy, arose from a State Department initiative.

In May 1945 Secretary of the Treasury Henry Morgenthau, Jr., was approached by the Zionists to take an initiative on behalf of the Jewish DPs.[9] Morgenthau had appealed first to Truman to set up a cabinet-level committee to deal with the DP problem, but the latter dismissed the proposal out of hand. Truman's arrival at the White House coincided with "the height of antiforeign and antisemitic feelings" in the United States, and therefore he felt unable to make bold changes to the country's immigration policies.[10]

Morgenthau turned next to the State Department, where acting Secretary of State Joseph Grew took up the idea. Morgenthau's close associate John Pehle, who had been active in the rescue of Jews during the war, explained to Grew the difference between Morgenthau's primary concern—the welfare of the displaced persons—and the goal of the Zionists—the exclusivity of Palestine as a refuge.[11]

Grew was convinced, and on June 21, 1945, he wrote to Truman informing him that the department was sending Earl Harrison to Europe to inquire into the position of the displaced persons, "particularly the Jews." Grew added that the Supreme Command Allied Expeditionary Forces Europe had approved and advised that "an expression of [Truman's] interest [would] facilitate the mission and reassure interested groups concerned with the future of the refugees that positive measures are being undertaken on their behalf."[12] Truman signed the letter of appointment, and Harrison set off on his mission the next day. Truman was concerned that the U.S. military should be sensitive to the special nature of the DP population and that past abuses and some cases of ill treatment should not be repeated.

In addition, he was surely mindful of the domestic political dividends to be reaped.[13]

Harrison reported back in August 1945. He referred to the proposal made by the Jewish Agency to the British government that 100,000 additional immigration certificates be made available. Harrison suggested that although the precise number of certificates might need to be reconsidered the agency's request, if granted, "would contribute much to the sound solution for the future of the Jews still in Germany and Austria and even other displaced Jews who do not wish either to remain there or to return to their countries of nationality."[14] Truman forwarded Harrison's report to London on August 31, 1945, together with his own conclusion that "the main solution" to the problem of the DPs was "the quick evacuation of as many as possible of the non-repatriable Jews, who wish it, to Palestine."[15]

But the British blocked Truman's intention of announcing his conclusions in public. They threatened to declare in the House of Commons that they expected the Americans to provide four divisions to help quell the disorder that would result from any large-scale Jewish immigration into Palestine.[16]

On December 22, 1945, President Truman issued a directive, "a Christmas present," to the DPs. It mandated preferential treatment for all DPs within the existing immigration quotas with special preference for orphans. The directive resulted in part from American Jewish Committee appeals to the State Department "to designate the unused immigration slots that had accumulated during the war for DP utilization." The president also allowed nine hundred refugees who had been interned since August 1944 in a camp at Fort Ontario, Oswego, New York, to leave the country and reenter as immigrants.

The directive actually was of little help, since the entire annual DP quota for Eastern European nations was just 13,000 (in contrast to a quota of 26,000 reserved exclusively for Germans).[17] Even then the House of Representatives Immigration Committee, reflecting the national mood, opposed the Truman directive. There was little national desire to lower the barriers facing immigrants.[18]

By expediting the admission of displaced persons into the United States, the directive was intended to set an international example. For the first time since 1940 U.S. immigration quotas were made available for full use. In 1948 the directive would assume crucial significance as a demarcation line for the DP legislation of that year.

THE DP LOBBY

Truman recognized the DP problem from the outset as a potentially explosive domestic issue. The Jewish community was itself split between those who favored more Jewish immigration into the United States (the ACJ) and the Zionists, who sought to bolster their claim for a Jewish state by the accretion of refugees in Palestine. Truman had to take into account on the one hand the anti-immigration mood of the country as reflected in the Congress and on the other State Department opposition to Zionism. Truman groped for a solution along both avenues.

On August 16, 1946, he announced that he would seek congressional legislation to bring into the country an unspecified number of DPs. He contemplated as many as 300,000 but mentioned no figure in public. But national sentiment was against any easing of immigration restrictions. Richard Russell, the Democratic chairman of the Senate Committee on Immigration, castigated any possible changes in the current quota system as a "dangerous precedent." Texas Congressman Ed Gossett not only opposed any increase in current immigration quotas but hinted that he would introduce legislation to cut the quotas in half. In a national poll conducted in August, 72 percent of those asked disapproved of Truman's proposal to increase immigration.[19]

Truman's tentative proposal, coming at a critical juncture in Zionist diplomacy, when they were seeking presidential approval for a Jewish state in a part of Palestine (i.e., partition), increased the rift between Zionist and non-Zionist American organizations. Until that point all Jewish groups had supported Truman's demand for allowing 100,000 Jewish immigrants into Palestine.

The Zionists disapproved of the proposed DP legislation. They feared that the proposal reflected a "collapse on Palestine" by the administration and that the admission of more

DPs into the United States would weaken the pressure to establish a Jewish state in Palestine.[20] With Truman therefore having apparently abandoned hope of getting the 100,000 into Palestine, the non-Zionist establishment Jews, in particular the ACJ, seized upon his tentative proposal to plan a well-organized, well-financed lobby to get through Congress the necessary legislation to bring the 100,000 into the United States and empty the European DP centers.[21]

The decision to set up the lobby was made on November 5, 1946, at a luncheon of an ACJ subcommittee, which decided to set up "a broadly based national citizens committee, composed of prominent Christian, and perhaps a few Jewish, leaders from the ranks of the ministry, business, labor, education, and social welfare." Because of their fear of an anti-Jewish backlash and a reluctance to become too closely identified with any movement to bring in DPs, the ACJ's limited goal of helping the Jewish DPs was subsumed in the wider humanitarian goal of aiding all DPs, 80 percent of whom were in fact Gentile.[22]

The new lobby was named the Citizens Committee on Displaced Persons, and the ubiquitous Earl Harrison lent his name as chairman. The prime mover behind the establishment of the new lobby was Lessing Rosenwald (he and his family contributed more than $650,000 of the committee's $1 million budget), who was also instrumental in recruiting Harrison. Rosenwald kept his own role a closely guarded secret (quite apart from any political sensitivity, the ACJ had been established as a nonpolitical organization and therefore was not permitted to be a party to direct lobbying).[23]

Staff of the ACJ approached congressmen, alerted senators, distributed the committee's material to the media, and mobilized prominent persons to the cause. The committee relied heavily on contacts at the White House, especially David Niles. Niles kept them informed of the president's thinking and regularly attended the lobby's "strategy committee," headed by Irving M. Engel, a New York attorney.[24]

The committee was carefully balanced, politically and geographically. Although more than 90 percent of its financing came from Jewish sources, most of its members were non-Jewish, politically conservative, and representative of major national organizations. Among those who had their names on the committee's letterhead were Eleanor Roosevelt, Fiorello La Guardia, William Green, Edward R. Stettinius, Jr., and Charles B. Taft (president of the Federal Council of the Churches of Christ in America). Earl Harrison invited a distinguished group to an initial strategy session at the Waldorf Astoria Hotel in New York on December 20, 1946. The invitees included Owen Roberts, former Supreme Court justice, General William J. Donovan, former head of Strategic Services, and Senator Taft. Few of those attending knew of the ACJ's involvement.[25]

The ACJ's overriding concern to downplay any Jewish involvement or motivation ultimately backfired and worked to the Jews' detriment. The ACJ Immigration Committee opted for a target figure of 400,000 European DPs to be allowed entry into the United States over a four-year period. This was based on the calculation that since only 20 percent to 25 percent of the approximately 850,000 DPs were Jewish, the actual goal of securing the entry of 100,000 Jewish DPs could be reached. Anxious to avoid stereotypically "Jewish" occupations, the ACJ did not lobby for tailors, doctors, or lawyers but instead, and in line with American economic requirements, stressed agricultural and construction workers, which in fact discriminated against the Jews, only 2 percent of whom fell into those categories.[26]

On April 1, 1947, Representative William G. Stratton introduced a bill into the House to allow 400,000 DPs into the country over the next four years. Truman thought the idea preposterous and wrote to Niles: "The idea of getting 400,000 immigrants into this country is, of course, beyond our wildest dreams. If we could get 100,000 we would be doing remarkably well."[27]

Truman was keenly aware of the national sentiment against large-scale immigration. Mail to the White House and to Congress ran seven to one against allowing in the DPs. Among the most frequently mentioned objections were the housing shortage, insufficient job opportunities, opposition to the Jews, fears of "Communist infiltration," and the threat to the "American way of life." In view of all this, Truman urged Congress in his State of the Union address to turn its attention to the world problem of the DPs but restricted himself to the bland comment that "Congressional assistance in the form of new legislation is needed." [28]

A House subcommittee began hearings on the Stratton bill in June 1947 and was still debating it when Congress adjourned. A modified version of the bill was introduced into the Senate, but all action was postponed by the appointment of a special committee to study the issue and report on it in 1948. Truman neither endorsed the Stratton bill nor did he send any measures to Congress for its consideration. He maintained utter silence on the matter for the next six months. Niles sent word to Stratton that although the president would not endorse his bill publicly he nonetheless supported it. In the meantime Niles continued to meet with ACJ strategists. [29]

By the summer of 1947 the Citizens Committee on Displaced Persons was able to show some results. Numbers of prominent Americans began to respond from throughout the country—chief executives, mayors, and the major bodies of the Catholic, Protestant, and Jewish faiths all expressed support for the Stratton bill. [30]

But grass-roots opposition to any easing of immigration restrictions persisted. Hostility to the Jews exacerbated this sentiment, and many ascribed the proposed legislation to Jewish interests. One military official, who presumably met with the Senate subcommittee in Europe, claimed that several legislators thought that "if there were no Jews in the displaced persons camps, the problem would be solved in no time." [31]

This was also the period in which a UN special committee was recommending the partition of Palestine. The UN General Assembly began its debates on Palestine in September 1947. White House attention, and hopes, were by now focused on Palestine as the main solution to the Jewish DP problem.

But the State Department was now interested more than ever in some easing of U.S. immigration laws: first, to end the friction with the Germans and the Austrians that the handling of the DP centers in Europe was provoking; and second, to undermine the Zionists' cause and weaken their case at the United Nations. "Cold war considerations, and blocking the establishment of a Jewish Palestine . . . made the support of DP legislation almost mandatory." [32]

Assistant Secretary of State John Hilldring (regarded as a Zionist supporter) prepared two draft proposals for Truman to submit to Congress. The first would admit 150,000 DPs, or the American "fair share," and the other would allocate the accumulated unused certificates for 1942–1945, a total of 571,057, solely for the use of the DPs. Truman never took up either proposal.[33]

By the summer of 1947 the DP problem had been transformed. Most of the DPs had become the victims of *postwar* dislocation and persecution. About 50 percent of those Jews who had been in Germany in 1945 had left for Palestine or elsewhere. More than 100,000 of the Jewish DPs remaining in the assembly centers had either been released from Russia in the spring of 1946 or had fled from Polish anti-Semitism. A mere 10,000 of the Jews then in the camps had arrived there before December 22, 1945, the date of Truman's directive. In the fall of 1947 a subcommittee of the House Foreign Relations Committee declared: "If the Jewish facet of the problem could be cleared up, the solution of the remainder of the problem would be greatly facilitated. The opening up to [*sic*] Palestine to the resettlement of Jewish displaced persons would break the log jam."[34]

Following the passage of the UN resolution on Palestine on November 29, 1947, the ACJ was forced to reconsider its support for its lobby. Most of the Jewish DPs in the camps were probably to receive entry permits into the new Jewish state, thus eliminating the issue that had prompted the council to set up the lobby in the first place. Its dilemma was the more acute since the Stratton bill was likely to allow into the United States a considerable number of Eastern European anti-Semites and fascists: "The question has been raised as to whether, with the probable large movement of DPs to Palestine, support of the Stratton Bill should be discontinued, on the theory that there would be too few Jewish DPs coming to the U.S. to justify the known risk of admitting a large number of fascist-minded DPs of Polish and Baltic origin."[35]

Nonetheless, the council decided to continue its support of the lobby, since even with Jewish migration to Palestine a sizable number of DPs would remain, although only about 30 percent of them were Jewish. With its own brand of logic the council surmised that the objections of American anti-Semites might be removed once large numbers of Jews had chosen Israel. It was decided to stress the "humanitarian" and "American asset" aspects of the Stratton bill and that the DPs included 500,000 Catholics and 100,000 Protestants as well as 250,000 Jews.[36]

THE 1948 DP BILL

The new immigration bill was introduced into Congress in March 1948. It allowed the admission of 100,000 DPs over two years and confined eligibility to those who had been in Allied camps *prior* to December 22, 1945, the date of Truman's directive. Fifty percent of the visas were reserved for agricultural workers and 50 percent for former residents of the Baltic states and eastern Poland, annexed by Russia after the war. The bill thus recognized the country's economic need for agricultural workers and provided for those who had suffered longest or could not return to their homes for political reasons. But it also excluded automatically the more than 100,000 Jews who had fled Poland and Russia during the summer of 1946, and as such, the bill was regarded universally as a reflection of the legislators' desire to exclude Jews.[37]

The State Department, interested now in allowing Jewish immigrants into the United States (to allay Zionist pressures for Palestine), made known its objections. Under Secretary of State Robert Lovett wrote to one of the joint sponsors of the 1948 bill, Senator William Chapman Revercomb, pointing out that almost all the Jewish DPs still in the camps had arrived there *after* the December 22, 1945, cut-off date. Lovett also advocated doubling the 100,000 quota and lifting the priority for agricultural workers.[38] President Truman issued a stinging critique: "The bill discriminates in callous fashion against displaced persons of the Jewish faith. This brutal fact cannot be obscured by the maze of technicalities in the bill or by the protestations of some of its sponsors."[39]

Secretary of State Marshall later admitted to Ernest Bevin, the British foreign secretary, that Congress was "strongly anti-

Jewish" and had created great difficulties for him when he had tried to make immigration easier into the United States. Their actions had been based "entirely on anti-Jewish prejudice."[40]

As Max Lowenthal's private diary notes make clear, Truman's reactions, in an election year, were not entirely devoid of domestic political considerations, namely, that the final bill was the product of *Republican-managed* Senate and House committees. Therefore, Truman's critique would "help the Administration politically at the same time that it [would help] to prevent unsound compromises." When Lowenthal discussed the bill with Matt Connelly, the latter "talked about the merits, not the politics." Lowenthal retorted that it would also be useful on votes.[41]

The historian of the Eightieth Congress has concluded that Truman was well into his campaign of denouncing Congress and, "anticipating the use of the displaced-persons legislation as a campaign issue despite the significant number of Democratic restrictionists, preferred to emphasize the bill's shortcomings."[42]

Of the liberalizing amendments introduced into the Senate, only one, that doubling the number of DPs to 200,000, was accepted. The December 1945 cut-off date remained. The bill became law on July 1, 1948. Truman signed it reluctantly, while denouncing the measures "in a manner which suggested that his speech might have been drafted at the offices of the CCDP [Citizens Committee on Displaced Persons]."[43]

Many American Jews were outraged by the 1948 bill, and many castigated the ACJ strategy "of always getting up a non-Jewish front to press for Jewish causes." A majority of Jewish groups, especially the Zionists, wanted the bill vetoed. But the American Jewish Committee and the American Council for Judaism, the two organizations committed to bringing Jews into the United States, thought it best that the president sign, since it did bring some relief. They also appreciated that having supported the Citizens Committee on Displaced Persons, which all along had emphasized that 80 percent of DPs were Gentiles, it would now be politically unwise "to demand that no one receive any assistance because Jews were being discriminated against."[44]

Both Jewish organizations had fully recognized the discriminatory nature of the proposed bill. In a personal letter to the president on June 18, 1948, Proskauer had written: "We are certain that you regard the vicious features of this bill as a betrayal of the American spirit. Through ignorance or design the sponsors of this legislation have made it in effect an act not to permit Jewish immigration into this country from the DP camps, but rather to prevent it." [45]

Nonetheless, Proskauer had urged Truman to endorse the bill as it did "permit a moderate trickle of relief for non-Jews in the DP camps," and the American Jewish Committee did not believe that its "just resentment as Americans and as Jews" should lead it to any action that "would deny any measure of relief to the unfortunates in the DP camps." Proskauer had closed his letter with the pious hope that Truman would assert his leadership to promote additional legislation at the earliest possible moment that would secure relief for the Jewish DPs and "remove the stigma of this legislation from the fair name of our beloved country." [46]

Thus the final irony for the ACJ was that "those who had done the most, because they wanted to help Jewish DPs, ultimately wound up supporting a bill which circumscribed opportunities for Jews to emigrate to the United States." [47]

There was a marked nexus between the Zionist and the DP questions. When President Truman failed in his efforts to get the British to allow more Jewish DPs into Palestine, he tried to have American immigration laws modified. David Niles was the president's agent in both matters; he sat in on the weekly strategy meetings of the Citizens Committee on Displaced Persons; he let Stratton know that the president would support his bill; and he maintained regular contact with the ACJ (as he did with the Zionists). But why should Truman exert himself against the anti-Jewish legislation of 1948 when members of the American Jewish establishment urged him to support it, notwithstanding its discriminatory nature?

The DP problem was never a high national priority during the Truman administration, however, and the passage of the UN resolution on Palestine defused much of its combustible nature. More compelling domestic matters were paramount, and congressmen saw no urgent reason for departing from "traditional nativist attitudes."[48] Truman was a weak legislator and took no initiative with Congress on the DP issue.

The historian of the DP legislation has concluded that "strong national prejudices, procrastination in Congress, and less than dynamic leadership from the White House combined to prolong the miseries of those Jews who survived the Holocaust. . . . Passage of the DP acts helped non-Jews more than it did those who had suffered and survived the Holocaust . . . [and] failed to meet the needs of the majority of the Jewish DPs in Europe."[49]

EIGHT

Toward an Anglo-American Consensus

THE ANGLO-AMERICAN COMMITTEE ON PALESTINE

A mounting crescendo of anti-British agitation in the United States that dwelt on the humanitarian aspect of the Jewish DP problem, combined with Truman's pressure to grant 100,000 immigration certificates for Palestine, led the British to search for a consensus with the Americans.

On his return from the Potsdam Conference, Truman informed the press on August 16 that he had asked Churchill and Attlee to allow into Palestine as many Jews as possible. But he posited that any solution would have to be implemented peaceably, for "he had no desire to send half a million American soldiers to keep the peace in Palestine."[1] Dr. Weizmann thought Truman's statement was "phony": "He takes away with one hand what he gives with the other, and here again I see nothing but disappointment ahead of us. He will never jeopardize his oil concessions for the sake of the Jews, although he may need them when the time of election arrives."[2]

On October 2, 1945, both Republicans and Democrats spoke in a Senate debate of the need for speedy and effective relief for "the first victims of Hitler terrorism" and censured the British for their rigid implementation of the 1939 white paper immigration restrictions. Republican senator Robert Taft, prompted probably by Rabbi Silver, had even proposed making the $3.5 billion American loan to the British (still under negotiation) conditional on a change of British policy in Palestine.[3] Rabbi Silver, a Republican supporter, was organizing a Zionist campaign to block the loan. Upon a complaint from the State Department, David Niles secured statements in favor of the loan from moderate Zionists such as Rabbi Stephen Wise.[4]

By October 4, 1945, Foreign Secretary Ernest Bevin took his own cabinet by surprise in proposing a new Anglo-American committee to examine the DP problem and, almost incidentally, Palestine's capacity to help ease it. Bevin hoped thereby to involve the Americans "responsibly" and bring them to the inevitable conclusion that Palestine on its own was incapable of solving the Jewish DP problem. He believed that an international solution was needed, one to which the Americans too would have to contribute by relaxing their own immigration laws.

Bevin conveyed the cabinet's decision to the American administration through his ambassador in Washington. His message expressed his misgivings about Truman's "dishonesty" on the Palestine issue: "To play on racial feeling for the purpose of winning an election is to make a farce of their insistence on free elections in other countries." Repeating the apprehensions expressed by his own officials when first apprised of the proposed American involvement, Bevin concluded: "My only fear of bringing the United States into the picture at this stage is this: the propaganda in New York has destroyed what looked to me a few weeks ago as a reasonable atmosphere in which we could get Jews and Arabs together."[5]

The Americans wanted to alter significantly the terms of reference suggested by the British for the joint committee. The statement of purpose of the innocuous British draft, "to examine the position of the Jews in Europe," was expanded into:

To examine the position of the Jews in those countries in Europe where they have been victims of Nazi and Fascist persecution, and the practical measures taken or contemplated to be taken in those countries to enable them to live free from discrimination and oppression and *to make estimates of those who wish, or will be impelled by their conditions to migrate to Palestine or other countries outside Europe.*[6]

After prolonged haggling the British side conceded to the American terms.[7] But then the Americans confirmed Bevin's worst fears by asking to delay the announcement of the formation of the committee because of "intense and growing agitation about the Palestine problem in the New York electoral campaign," which was just about to reach its climax. Any public statement before election day (November 6) on the administration's agreement to take part with the British in yet another inquiry, which could only postpone further the immigration into Palestine of the Jewish DPs, would "inflame the million or so Jewish voters . . . and altogether destroy the prospects of the Democratic candidate whose Republican rival for Mayor was . . . a Jew."[8]

The political objections to the proposed joint committee may be traced to the White House itself, where Judge Sam Rosenman wrote for Truman the following blistering appraisal:

Why in the world there has to be a statement on October 25th, ten days before the election in New York, I cannot possibly imagine. There was no need to publish President Roosevelt's letter of April 5th, when it was published. The repercussions over it in New York are terrific, as Bob Hannegan can tell you. The effect of this action in the Commons will be bad enough, but if we participate in it, it will be terrible.

Apart from any politics, the whole scheme outlined in this proposal is merely one of temporizing, appeasing and seeking to delay the settlement of the issue. Seven-eighths of what this commission is supposed to do is wholly unnecessary, because the information can be obtained in a few days' notice. It seems to me the only valid purpose for a joint commission would be to determine just how many people could be absorbed into Palestine per month.[9]

The Democratic candidate for mayor of New York, William O'Dwyer, won the election, thus bringing to a close the three straight terms of Fiorello La Guardia. Three days later, on November 9, the Americans settled on the terms of reference for the joint committee, which were announced in Washington and London on November 13, 1945.

Truman's announcement in Washington was greeted with widespread dismay by the Zionists and their supporters in Congress. On November 15, 1945, Rabbis Wise and Silver sent a joint telegram to Truman, regretting American involvement in the joint committee and calling it "the withdrawal, at any rate for the time being, of your request for 100,000 immigration certificates." In the name of "millions of Americans" they asked him to reconsider the whole matter.[10]

An exchange of letters between Truman and Eleanor Roosevelt is also enlightening, in that it reflects once again the general sympathy for the Jewish DPs with opposition to the Zionist goal of a Jewish state in Palestine. Mrs. Roosevelt took exception to the appointment of the joint committee, not because she was committed to a Zionist solution to the Jewish DP problem but because she resented the British embroiling the United States in problems of their own making:

I am very much distressed that Great Britain has made us take a share in another investigation of the need of the few Jews remaining in Europe. If they are not to be allowed to enter Palestine, then certainly they could have been apportioned among the different United Nations and we would not have to continue to have on our consciences the death of at least fifty of these poor creatures daily.

The question between Palestine and the Arabs, of course, has always been complicated by the oil deposits, and I suppose it always will. I do not happen to be a Zionist, and I know what a difference there is among Jews as consider themselves nationals of other countries and not a separate nationality.

Great Britain is always anxious to have someone pull her chestnuts out of the fire. . . . I object very much to being used by them.[11]

Truman found nothing exceptionable in her letter: "I am very hopeful that we really shall be able to work out something in Palestine which will be of lasting benefit. At the same time we expect to continue to do what we can to get as many Jews as possible into Palestine as quickly as possible, pending any final settlement."[12]

When Truman received the committee in Washington, he again dwelt on the DP problem. He told the members that "never before in the history of the White House had there been such a tremendous volume of mail as that dealing with the displaced persons." Truman believed strongly that the democratic world had an obligation to resettle these people, who had wronged no one: "there was no problem which concerned him more deeply." [13]

The nominations of the American members of the Anglo-American committee were made by the president himself, evidently on the advice of David Niles. Truman apparently aimed at securing a "balanced" committee, one that would represent both State Department and Zionist views. [14] But one appointment provoked a clash between Niles and Loy Henderson of NEA, which the latter still remembered vividly thirty years later.

When one candidate, O. Max Gardner, former governor of California, withdrew because of ill health, Niles pressed for the appointment of Bartley Crum, a San Francisco lawyer of undisguised Zionist leanings. Niles had befriended Crum in 1944, when the latter had headed a Republicans for Roosevelt breakaway group. The State Department resisted the appointment on the grounds that Crum was "a shabby opportunist politically." [15]

Even the pro-Zionist Richard Crossman, a British member of the committee, wrote later: "[Crum] had a political career in front of him which could be made or marred by the attitude he adopted towards the Jewish question." [16] The State Department ran an FBI check on all candidates for the committee. That on Crum indicated that he was a member of "certain Communist front groups." Not only did Niles insist on Crum but, according to Henderson, he had even passed on the State Department materials on Crum directly over to the candidate himself. [17]

Crum was thus made aware that he owed his appointment to the White House, and he reported back to Niles directly and regularly and likewise received instructions. Like James MacDonald, another pro-Zionist member of the committee, Crum soon discovered that his colleagues on the committee refrained from open discussion in his presence. [18] The Niles-Crum liaison, kept up by transatlantic telephone while the committee wrote its report in Lausanne, Switzerland, was of crucial importance in securing Truman's goal of a recommended solution to the Jewish DP problem.

On April 16, 1946, Crum conveyed to the president through Niles that the committee had agreed on the abrogation of the 1939 white paper and the immediate move of the 100,000.

Niles urged the president to send a telegram to the committee chairman indicating his personal interest in the committee's report. The cable drafted by Niles, which stressed the humanitarian aspect of the DP problem, was apparently sent by Truman the same day:

I have followed reports of your inquiry and deliberations with great interest. The world expectantly awaits a report from the entire Commission which will be the basis of an affirmative program to relieve untold suffering and misery. In the deliberations now going on, and in the report which will evolve from them, it is my deep and sincere wish that the American delegation shall stand firm for a program that is in accord with the highest American tradition of generosity and justice.[19]

The joint committee's report was completed on April 20, 1946, and presented to the British and American governments.[20] Its first recommendation (of ten) was to allow the 100,000 Jewish DPs into Palestine by the end of 1946 if possible; recommendation seven advocated the abrogation of the 1940 land regulations. The report was clearly against the Zionist program of a Jewish state, however, and recommended the continuation of the British mandate in Palestine, pending the execution of a trusteeship agreement under the United Nations. Palestine was *not* to become either an Arab or a Jewish state. Recommendation ten called for the disbanding of all "underground" armed forces before the implementation of any political solution.[21]

    Although the report delivered a great blow to the white paper regime and placed at the head of its list the quick migration of the 100,000, it also delivered a potentially fatal blow to the main Zionist aspiration, the attainment of a sovereign Jewish state in Palestine. In a telegram sent to the American Zionist Emergency Council, Ben-Gurion inveighed against the report. The American committee members had been caught in a Foreign Office trap; instead of the Palestinian state proposed by the 1939 white paper, the joint committee now proposed a "British colonial-military state, which was no longer to be a homeland for the Jewish people, and which would never become a Jewish State." Ben-Gurion urged his American colleagues to press the president and the heads of the Democratic party not to endorse the report, making it clear that any attempt to do so would condemn Palestine to continuous disturbances, would exacerbate the position of the Jewish DPs in Europe, and upset American Jewry.[22]

But calmer, more calculating opinions prevailed in Zionist circles. David Horowitz, an economist acting as political adviser and liaison to the committee, concurred with Ben-Gurion on the long-term negative aspects of the report, but he saw overriding *tactical* reasons for expressing conditional support:

An uncompromising rejection and condemnation of the report in all its provisions would be a mistake. . . . America would be antagonised considering that the report is unanimous. The result may be a return to the White Paper policy in the worst case, lack of any active American assistance, both political and economic in the best case. The position would be a struggle against both British and American public opinion. It would deprive us of the great advantages of the short term policy [and] would bring the clash to a head before the great reinforcement of our position by the admission of the 100,000.[23]

The two pro-Zionist members of the committee, James MacDonald and Bartley Crum, believing they had secured the maximum possible for the Zionists, now worked to preempt a Zionist attack on their work, one that would anger Truman and possibly lead him to abandon the cause. Ben-Gurion raged in his diary about how the Americans had given their stamp of approval for "the elimination of Zionism": "Crum and MacDonald think they have achieved a brilliant triumph and done an historical service to the Jewish people! Now Crum demands the price—expressions of thanks to Truman. 'If there's no enthusiasm,' he says, 'that is ingratitude,' and 'Do not be Talmudic,' says MacDonald!"[24]

On his return to the United States, Bartley Crum showed the report to Zionist leaders Wise and Silver. On April 29 Crum and MacDonald met with Silver separately, entreating him not to make any public attacks on their report, attacks that might be taken by Truman as personal. Quite independently, Silver arrived at the same conclusion as David Horowitz, that the Zionists should first secure the 100,000 immigration certificates and only later tackle the long-term political solution. Emmanuel Neumann, Silver's colleague, proposed a deal whereby the president would give his public approval to the first recommendation in the report, dealing with the 100,000, and in their turn, the Zionists would praise his "humane and constructive approach." Neumann drafted the statement, and Crum took it to David Niles at the White House. With two additions, a clause about safeguarding the holy places and one about the Arabs, Truman approved Neumann's draft.[25]

Whatever the tactical wisdom in this move, the Zionists were in fact playing into Truman's hands, since the president was preoccupied exclusively with the DP problem and did not share the Zionists' belief in a Jewish state. He would be quite satisfied if the British allowed him to make good on his demand for the 100,000 immigration certificates into Palestine.

Truman would continue to believe, even in 1948, that the joint committee's report had offered the best prospect for a solution. He was encouraged in this view by no less than Justice Felix Frankfurter, pillar of the Jewish establishment, described by Niles as "the most prominent supporter of Palestine in public life today among the Jews" and an intimate friend of Justice Louis Brandeis, "the greatest Zionist leader in this country and in the world." On the very day that Truman made the statement drafted by Neumann, Niles met with Frankfurter, who launched into a tirade against Silver and other Zionists, who, Frankfurter said, "prefer a Jewish State on paper rather than doing something real for human beings." In reporting the conversation to Truman, Niles assured the president that he would "use this to the limit with our friends in New York the next couple of days."[26]

By May 1946 the figure of 100,000 DPs had become an anachronism. The 50,000 Jews who had been in the DP camps when Earl Harrison had visited them the previous summer would soon swell to more than 250,000 with new refugees from pogroms in Poland. Had some plan been agreed on between the British and the Americans that settled for Truman's figure of 100,000, the Zionists, not to mention the hundreds of thousands of Jewish DPs still stranded in Europe, would have been placed in an impossible position.

But the president's unilateral statement on April 30, expressing satisfaction that his request for the admission of the 100,000 Jews into Palestine had been endorsed unanimously by the committee, condemned from the outset any prospect of an Anglo-American consensus on Palestine. The State Department had made every effort to head off Truman's statement. Henderson and Under Secretary of State Acheson had both telegraphed Secretary of State Byrnes in Paris and had put all possible pressure on the White House, but to no avail.[27]

In a riposte in the House of Commons on May 1 Attlee announced that he wished to know to what extent the American government "would be prepared to share the resulting additional military and financial responsibilities" that would result from the immigration of the 100,000.[28]

Attlee's announcement solved a problem for the Zionists, notwithstanding their protests to the contrary at the time. It relieved them of the dilemma of whether to settle for the 100,000 immigration certificates while leaving the long-term solution on hold.[29] The Zionists' dilemma was the more complicated since their friends on the committee, MacDonald and Crum, were now committed to their own plan.

The British position was that a comprehensive political solution must be implemented and that to allow in the 100,000 Jewish DPs before such a framework was agreed on between Britain and the United States would provoke Arab disturbances, if not rebellion. In any case, Britain was still seeking a consensus with the Americans. The latter accepted the British stand, and talks between the two countries began in London.

THE MORRISON-GRADY PLAN

On May 22, 1946, the State Department was obliged to issue a statement denying that the London talks indicated any retreat from Truman's statement of April 30.[30] Truman insisted that early discussions in London on the immigration problem precede the main talks, primarily to "deflect American criticism of inaction." The State Department reassured London that any preliminary decisions on immigration would be integrated into the final comprehensive plan.[31]

The American team of experts to London was headed by Henry F. Grady, a career diplomat, just returned from leading the American section of an Allied mission to observe the elections in Greece. Truman's private briefing of Grady provides an accurate assessment of the president's views on Palestine in the summer of 1946. Truman stated categorically that the United States would *not* employ its armed forces in Palestine or take on or share any trusteeship of that country. Truman still opposed the transformation of Palestine into either a Jewish or an Arab state, but he *was* willing to help finance the immigration and resettlement of the 100,000.[32]

In London the American team was presented with a British scheme whereby Palestine would be given a federal government in which there would be semiautonomous Jewish and Arab provinces. The Americans accepted the scheme with alacrity. It provided for the migration of the 100,000, but it did not assume an American military involvement, and the British financial demands were well within the limits approved by Washington.[33] Truman inclined to accept the new plan, soon to be called the Morrison-Grady scheme for provincial autonomy. In private he told Grady repeatedly that he thought it "the best of all solutions proposed for Palestine."[34]

With the American and British teams in substantial agreement, all seemed set for the much sought after consensus. But the initial stumbling block proved to be the timing of the migration of the 100,000. Truman had made clear his interest in the immediate movement of the DPs. The United States would finance their transport to Palestine and living expenses for two months. Byrnes then learned from Grady that the migration was to start only after all sides had accepted the entire plan. On July 26 Byrnes told Grady over the telephone: "We feel we should be able to announce we have not, repeat not abandoned position taken by the President in this regard. I understand the British position, but feel that the President cannot recede from his position. The trouble with the British plan is that immigration never starts unless they get the acquiescence of Arabs and Jews."[35]

Truman had come under a great deal of lobbying pressure while the experts had been meeting in London. The new scheme appeared to the Zionists as a conspiracy by the British to perpetuate their mandate. Once details of the plan were leaked to the press, the Zionists countered with articles and massive ads condemning it. The White House was flooded with telegrams and letters demanding that the president repudiate it. Congress was also mobilized.[36]

Niles reported that he "had been staving off Rosenwald, Proskauer and Celler, all of whom were seeking appointments with the President." Truman finally received a Zionist delegation at the beginning of July (after two months of lobbying). Inevitably, he dwelt on his determination to press for the 100,000, but he left the Zionists none the wiser about Grady's terms.[37]

Truman was becoming irritated and weary of the Palestine problem. By the end of July he was threatening to "wash his hands" of the whole issue. In September 1948 he would tell General Julius Klein, head of the Jewish War Veterans of America, that he and Bevin "had agreed on the best possible solution for Palestine and it was the Zionists who killed that plan by their opposition." Truman did not seem to be clear as to which of the several plans he was referring to, but his visitor had the impression that he was discussing the Morrison-Grady plan.[38]

At the end of July 1946 Truman was prevailed upon to receive two separate deputations of congressmen, both from New York. The first, a delegation from New York state headed by Sol Bloom, had been turned down by Truman in June. Veteran New York congressman Emmanuel Celler had written at the end of June to Matt Connelly, the president's appointments secretary, advising against such a rebuff: "I am hesitant about telling this to the delegation. It certainly will give political ammunition to the upstate Republicans who wanted to attend and you remember New York faces a very crucial election. Frankly, it is my opinion that it is bad politics for the President not to meet with them—even if it is on the Palestine question."[39]

In the meantime on July 27 he met with James MacDonald of the joint committee, accompanied by two New York Democratic senators, James Mead and Robert Wagner. MacDonald came to protest the Morrison-Grady plan, rumors of which had been leaked by the Zionists to the press. MacDonald was preoccupied with the immigration of the 100,000, and he regarded the "federalization" plan as a euphemism for partition, discussion of which would hold up a solution to the DP problem.[40] Mac-Donald told Truman that the joint committee had discussed partition for weeks and had rejected it (ironically, the Zionists themselves were just about to adopt partition and to mount a diplomatic campaign to secure it).

MacDonald's meeting with Truman degenerated into an open clash. Truman was short-tempered and impatient. He rebuffed MacDonald's criticism of the new scheme, claiming that the latter did not even know what it was. MacDonald told the president bluntly that the Jews would rather not have the 100,000 than the new plan and that if that was the price they paid for it then Truman's name would go down in history as anathema. At that Truman exploded and insisted he would not underwrite anything as the price of the new plan. Visibly irritated, Truman grumbled: "Well, you can't satisfy these people. . . . The Jews aren't going to write the history of the United States or my history."[41]

MacDonald next pursued a dangerous line of argument by contrasting Truman with his predecessor. MacDonald said that Roosevelt had understood some of the imponderables and what the Balfour Declaration had meant, and he had known how the Jewish people felt. Truman retorted: "I am not Roosevelt. I am not from New York. I am from the Middle West." MacDonald accused Truman of having sent "green men" and stated that the Zionists had proved their moderation in asking him, Mac-Donald, to see the president. Truman replied that the Zionists knew he would not receive some of *them*. Grady was not "green," and Henderson of NEA had had nothing to do with the new plan: "It was all done by Byrnes, Acheson and myself."

MacDonald wrote for the Zionists an assessment of Truman's current disposition. The president was "hell-bent" on the 100,000. He had become convinced that the new plan would give him this and involve him in no further commitment, other than the $45 million financing. MacDonald concluded:

The President has a mind set which incapacitates him from understanding Jewish psychology. . . . I think one reason the President is friendly to me is that all my introductions have been via Kansas City and Missouri. . . . He referred only to the Jews generally and not to the Zionists. I don't think he distinguishes very much. . . .

. . . He is not a scholar and is not interested in following the thing through. . . . He is really at home only with his buddies from the old days. For this reason Hannegan is important, too.[42]

When the New York congressmen were received by the president three days later, they fared little better. Congressman Celler read out a three-minute prepared statement. Truman was again impatient, shuffled papers on his desk, and interrupted constantly. He interjected that he had heard all these arguments before. He was fighting with the British to get the 100,000 in, but they were imposing conditions, and there was nothing to do but agree to them. In exasperation Truman protested: "This is all political. You are all running for re-election." He added that he was tired of having Jews and Irishmen and Poles and Italians and Armenians come to him in their own interests and of never hearing anything from "Americans." At that point Truman rose, said there was nothing further to discuss, and dismissed the delegation.[43]

Celler drew the same conclusion as MacDonald. The president had already made up his mind to agree to the British proposal and was only irritated by attempts to change his mind. Even worse, Celler feared that Truman no longer cared about the political damage that a wrong decision might cause (in the upcoming congressional elections). Truman seemed like "a man who is sick and tired of his job, wants to get out of it, and doesn't care any more."[44]

Truman was indeed on the very point of endorsing the Morrison-Grady plan. On July 29 Secretary of State Byrnes had telegraphed from Paris a draft press release written by himself and Grady declaring Truman's support of the scheme. The Paris draft stated that the solution should be found within the framework of the joint committee report and concluded that the Morrison-Grady plan was "the best solution of this difficult problem that can now be secured."[45]

That same day, a Monday, Leo Kohn, a Zionist diplomat in Washington, received a cable from colleagues in Paris to the effect that Byrnes had now accepted the new plan and that Truman and Attlee were to issue simultaneous endorsements of it that Wednesday, July 31. Kohn telephoned immediately to

David Niles, who agreed to see him at once. Kohn met Niles with Robert Nathan, the economist, and explained to both of them the Zionists' objections. Nathan had already spoken to Judge Rosenman and would speak also to Secretary of War Robert Patterson. Kohn believed that Rosenman's opinion carried great weight with the president (it will be recalled that Rosenman was also a good friend of Lessing Rosenwald, of the American Council for Judaism, and a non-Zionist member of the American Jewish Committee).[46]

Niles promised to speak to Truman. Kohn also alerted Justice Frankfurter, who approached Acheson, Patterson, and Secretary of the Treasury John Snyder, warning them all against accepting the new plan. (Acheson, Patterson, and Snyder were the members of a cabinet committee on Palestine set up by Truman on June 11, 1946.)[47]

On July 30 Kohn phoned Niles several times during the day, but the latter was extremely busy and did not meet with him until 4:00 P.M. Niles reported that he had told Truman that on no account should he endorse the new plan but should recall the six American members of the joint committee and lock them up with the three members of Grady's team until they jointly found a way out of the impasse. Niles explained that Truman was in a difficult position. If he accepted the Grady report, he would be accused of having sacrificed everything else for the emigration of the 100,000; but if he rejected it, he would be accused of not having secured even that. Moreover, he was in an awkward position vis-à-vis Byrnes, who had already announced his acceptance to a press conference—it would be most difficult to disown Byrnes now, on the eve of the Paris peace conference. Niles told Kohn that the cabinet was meeting on the problem at that very moment.[48]

According to the record kept by Henry Wallace (secretary of commerce), the cabinet meeting that day was devoted entirely to Palestine and the question of whether to go along with the British in support of the Morrison-Grady plan.[49] Truman brought to the meeting "a sheaf of telegrams about four inches thick from various Jewish people." Under Secretary of State Acheson and Secretary of the Navy James Forrestal were all for going ahead with the British. But (in a telegram from Paris) Secretary of State Byrnes, "sensing the political hotness of the question," adopted a "strictly neutral attitude."

Wallace stated that "the whole matter was loaded with political dynamite" and that the Jews expected more than fifteen hundred square miles. He asked Truman to look into the matter further before supporting the British. Truman in evident exasperation finally told Acheson to wire Byrnes that he would not go along with Attlee. Truman stated that he was "put out" with the Jews: "Jesus Christ couldn't please them when he was here on earth, so how could anyone expect that I would have any luck? . . . he had no use for them and didn't care what happened to them." Wallace concluded his diary entry: "President Truman really thinks that the plan worked out by Henry Grady . . . is really fair." [50]

Truman phoned Niles to tell him of the cabinet's decision. Kohn was still with Niles and recalled how the latter "actually broke down." Niles stressed how nice it was of the president to have rung him up personally, knowing how he felt on the subject. He pleaded with Kohn not to tell a soul about his role, otherwise his position would become untenable. [51]

Acheson took the unusual step of informing the British ambassador, Lord Inverchapel, that the president could not for the present endorse the new plan since "intense Jewish hostility" had made it a domestic political liability. [52]

Byrnes later told Forrestal that Rosenman and Niles had turned the president against the Morrison-Grady plan by warning him "that the Republican candidate was about to come out with a statement in favor of Zionist claims on Palestine." They had insisted that unless the president anticipated Dewey the Democrats would lose New York. [53]

Acheson believed that the Grady report had in it the makings of a compromise. But when the two American teams met under his chairmanship, Judge Joseph Hutcheson, the American chairman of the joint committee, called the Grady plan "a sellout—very pretty, even grandiose—but a sellout nevertheless." Acheson concluded that the Hutcheson group's opposition derived from excessive pride in its own report. [54]

But as everyone was quite aware, the pending congressional

elections in November overshadowed all other considerations. Paul E. Fitzpatrick, chairman of the New York State Democratic Committee, cabled the president: "If this plan goes into effect it would be useless for the Democrats to nominate a state ticket this fall."[55]

Lord Inverchapel, the British ambassador, reported to London that

as at present advised, the Administration intend drastically to recast the recommendations jointly agreed upon in London, if not to reject them *in toto.*

This deplorable display of weakness is, I fear, solely attributable to reasons of domestic politics which, it will be recalled, caused the Administration last year to use every artifice to defer the announcement about the establishment of the Anglo-American Committee until after the New York elections. . . . The Director of the Near Eastern Division [Henderson] . . . frankly admitted as much in a talk with me this evening. But for the attitude of the Zionists, he declared, there was nothing in the joint committee recommendations which would not have been acceptable to the United States Government.[56]

Truman himself confirmed as much in a press conference he gave on September 5, 1946. When asked about the Palestine question, he replied: "All I was trying to do was to get a hundred thousand Jews into Palestine. Still trying to do that." When asked if he had rejected the Morrison-Grady plan or not, Truman stated: "It is still under consideration."[57]

THE YOM KIPPUR STATEMENT

By the summer of 1946 Zionist fortunes had dropped to a nadir. For the previous nine months the Yishuv had been revolting against the British in Palestine. Their efforts had brought meager results politically. At the end of June 1946 the British had mounted a nationwide counterattack, in which many Jewish Agency and Hagana leaders had been arrested and detained. In response the dissident Jewish terrorist group IZL on July 22 blew up a wing of the King David Hotel in Jerusalem, where British military and intelligence headquarters were located.

Nearly one hundred people were killed in the explosion, and the Yishuv was appalled at the scale of the tragedy. The erstwhile collaboration between the Hagana and the dissident paramilitary groups disintegrated abruptly.[58]

At the beginning of August the Jewish Agency Executive met in Paris to take stock. Although it had secured the deferral of the Morrison-Grady plan, it had been at the price of all but alienating President Truman. During the discussions, Nahum Goldmann received a transatlantic telephone call from Niles, warning that Truman would "wash his hands" of the Palestine problem unless the agency came up with a realistic alternative.[59] The Zionists were left with their now anachronistic demand for the 100,000, and it was plain that insistence on that single aspect was no alternative to a considered policy.

For all these reasons the Jewish Agency Executive altered course and made a historic decision in favor of partition, that is, for a viable Jewish state in part of Palestine. Goldmann was dispatched to Washington to try to secure the administration's support and to urge it to pressure London for that solution. Goldmann arrived in the American capital on August 6 and was received the next day by Dean Acheson, then acting secretary of state, and the senior State Department official dealing with Palestine.[60]

Goldmann reported back to his colleagues later that Acheson had been "sold" on partition, provided that Goldmann could also convince Niles and secretaries Snyder and Patterson. But Acheson's private note of their meeting indicates otherwise. The key point in their conversation, according to Acheson, came when Goldmann referred to the Morrison-Grady plan as being preferable to the joint committee one. Its main weaknesses, said Goldmann, were that the transition from autonomy to independence was far too indefinite and too prolonged and that the territory offered to the Jews was inadequate. Four days after his meeting with Goldman, Acheson reported to Averell Harriman, the American ambassador in London, that Goldmann's readiness to consider the Morrison-Grady plan now offered new hope for an agreement with the British: "Examination Goldmann plan indicates although [Jewish Agency] Executive states . . . it rejects Morrison plan as basis for discussion, *counter-proposals of Executive as elaborated upon by Goldmann might be regarded as certain alterations and extensions in various provisions Morrison plan rather than outlines of an entirely new plan.*"[61]

Goldmann evidently regarded the impasse as one given to solution by his own diplomatic virtuosity. For him the latest Anglo-American plan, the provincial autonomy scheme, could be used as a natural stepping-stone to the Zionists' own ultimate goal, partition. It was merely a question of using the right language with each audience to keep up the diplomatic momentum.

Goldmann next met David Niles and convinced him that partition was the only solution. They agreed that Goldmann would put down the agency plan on paper for Niles to present to the president.[62]

But first Goldmann had to persuade the other members of the cabinet committee on Palestine, secretaries Snyder and Patterson. Snyder was soon persuaded, but Goldmann could not secure an appointment with Secretary of War Patterson.[63] Goldmann learned that Judge Joseph Proskauer, president of the American Jewish Committee and close friend of Patterson, had broken off a vacation at Lake Placid to come to Washington to influence Patterson against partition. Goldmann interceded and met with Proskauer first, in the latter's hotel room on August 8, 1946.

Goldmann appreciated that he had no chance of convincing the administration to support a Jewish state unless he could first carry the AJC, the non-Zionist organization closest to the government. Goldmann told Proskauer that the immigration problem had become so urgent that the Jewish Agency was ready to consider partition. As noted already (see chapter 6), he soon persuaded Proskauer to support him and to procure him an interview with Secretary of War Patterson.[64]

Proskauer took Goldmann to the Pentagon, where they were received by Patterson. Goldmann explained the Jewish Agency position then left Proskauer and Patterson alone. Patterson is reported to have reacted sympathetically: "Joe, it makes sense. . . . I don't know what to do with these poor people any more. MacDonald's White Paper keeps them out of Israel [Palestine]. I can't get them into America because of our terrible immigration laws. I'm for it, but you've got to clear it with the State Department."[65]

Goldmann then went back for a second meeting with Acheson and informed him that secretaries Patterson and Snyder agreed to partition. Niles and Acheson told Truman of the cabinet committee's endorsement. That evening, August 9, Niles told the Zionists that Truman endorsed the partition scheme and had instructed Acheson to inform the British.[66]

These accounts, all resting on Jewish sources, present an oversanguine picture that owes more perhaps to wishful thinking than to a realistic appreciation of the situation. In fact, Truman had made a *tactical* adjustment, the long-term consequences of which he probably failed to appreciate. He now urged the British prime minister to give due consideration to the Jewish Agency proposals: "In view of the critical situation in Palestine and of desperate plight of homeless Jews in Europe, I believe search for a solution to this difficult problem should continue. I have therefore instructed our Embassy, London, to discuss with you or with appropriate members of British Government, certain suggestions which have been made to us and which, I understand, are also being made to you."[67]

Truman's overriding preoccupation was still the Jewish DPs. If the American administration now advocated British consideration of partition, it was probably because Goldmann had led it to believe that the Zionists would agree to the Morrison-Grady scheme as a first step to that goal. On August 14 Loy Henderson met with John Balfour, minister at the British embassy in Washington, D.C., and suggested that if the British and Zionists were unable to reach an agreement, the British might at least concede the immigration of the DPs—"thus the President would be able to escape from the corner in which he had put himself regarding the 100,000"; failing that, Henderson warned, the president might feel constrained to repeat his public demand for the 100,000.[68]

The American administration had agreed to bring the Jewish Agency's terms before the British as a *Zionist* proposal, not an American one. And that was all. Truman was *not* prepared to exert pressure on the British or to come out in unconditional support of the Zionists. Much less was he ever prepared to commit American forces to Palestine. Truman was also anxious lest the Jewish Agency plan not command unanimous Jewish support and that by supporting it he might lose Jewish electoral support.[69] Finally, important sections of the American Zionist movement, and Rabbi Silver in particular, resented Goldmann's solo initiative, however virtuoso, as a coup against their own status and authority.[70]

It should be remembered too that Truman (and Niles) was still contemplating the solution of the DP problem by increased immigration into the United States and other countries. On August 16, 1946, Truman stated in public that "the solution of the Palestine problem will not in itself solve the broader problem of the hundreds of thousands of displaced persons in Europe" and that he would be asking Congress to authorize the entry into the United States of "a fixed number" of DPs including Jews.[71]

On August 20 Truman's statement was endorsed by Proskauer. Proskauer, although being careful not to use the words "state" or "commonwealth," added that the Zionists were "striving to create a governmental unit to which Jews could legally immigrate." He stressed that this immigration was "the true, main and immediate objective." But when he asked Acheson to endorse his statement, even in private, Acheson declined.[72]

When Goldmann returned to Europe to negotiate with the British in a vain attempt to win them round to partition, the American Zionists, excluded by Goldmann and having little confidence in his diplomatic achievements with the administration, took the initiative. In view of the pending mid-term congressional and gubernatorial elections in November, they decided to employ to maximum advantage the influence of the Jewish electorate.

Concentrating on New York, a wide-scale propaganda campaign was mounted with mass meetings and giant ads in the press to remind the Democrats of their 1944 election pledges on Palestine and to urge an improvement in the situation in the DP camps. On October 1, 1946, at a meeting of the American Zionist Emergency Council, Judge Bernard Rosenblatt announced the formation of a Greater New York Zionist Action

Committee to be headed by himself.[73] The announcement appears to have been a formal courtesy, for the committee had already acted. Two days earlier, on September 30, a giant ad had appeared in the *New York Herald Tribune* reviewing the Democrats' past, unfulfilled pledges. The caption read:

WE DO NOT SEEK NEW PROMISES OR NEW PLANKS. THE OLD ONES ARE GOOD ENOUGH. WHAT WE ASK IS THAT OUR ADMINISTRATION FULFILL OLD PROMISES NOW.[74]

Judge Rosenblatt, head of the Keren Hayesod (a trust for Jewish settlement in Palestine) and a lifelong Democrat, had already in July sent a memorandum to New York party boss Ed Flynn. Flynn had forwarded the memo to Truman with his own note saying that he would not be doing so were he not certain he was writing in a just cause, and one in which the president himself believed. Apart from the "justness" of the cause, Flynn also promoted its pragmatic aspect: "I might add that what he [Rosenblatt] says about the reaction on the British position in New York State is very true. Conditions are very bad and I am sure if something is not done, the effects will be severely felt in November."[75]

Truman's reply to Flynn, written the day after Niles had headed off his acceptance of the Morrison-Grady plan, reflects his exasperation. After commenting that Rosenblatt's memo followed "the usual line," Truman wrote: "Of course, the British control Palestine and there is no way of getting One Hundred Thousand Jews in there unless they want them in. I have done my best to get them in but I don't believe there is any possible way of pleasing our Jewish friends."[76]

At the end of August, Goldmann wrote to Acheson from Europe asking that either he or Truman make a statement in support of partition to strengthen his hand in his negotiations with Bevin.[77]

In Acheson's absence from Washington, acting Secretary of State William I. Clayton advised Truman against issuing any statement lest it prejudice the negotiations then in progress in London. The State Department warned that yielding now to pressure from "highly organized Zionist groups" would only encourage them to press for more of the same in the future.[78]

Truman himself was extremely reluctant to speak out further on the Palestine question and informed the State Department that he hoped it would not prove necessary.[79]

Truman had singed his fingers more than enough on this thorny problem. As the British ambassador had suggested, Truman had possibly already given up on the Jewish vote. The president's outlook may be gauged from a letter he wrote to his wife on September 15, 1946:

Wallace now seems to have his eye on 1948. Hannegan is acting like a ten-year-old child and of course Byrnes has the pouts. Jim Mead came to see me about the New York campaign and then shot off his mouth as he went out the front door. The Jews and crackpots seem to be ready to go for Dewey. If they do, Jim's beaten and so he has to grasp at straws. There's no solution for the Jewish problem and I fear the crackpots would turn the country over to Stalin if they had half a chance.[80]

But nonetheless, at the end of September, Truman *was* prevailed upon to issue another public statement on Palestine. The key men responsible for Truman's volte-face were David Niles, Bartley Crum, and Robert Hannegan (Democratic party national chairman).

Niles told Truman that on October 6, in a speech to the United Palestine Appeal, Thomas Dewey (governor of New York State from 1942 to 1954) would make a strong statement in favor of Jewish immigration. Niles urged Truman to preempt Dewey, since "the Jewish vote in New York was going to be crucial." Crum convinced Hannegan of the need to obtain a statement from the president.[81]

The timing from the Jewish point of view was crucial. Abe Feinberg told Truman that if he spoke on the eve of Yom Kippur, the holiest day in the Jewish calendar, "every single Rabbi in every single synagogue will broadcast what you say. Forget the newspapers, forget any other media. You will have word directly to the Jewish people."[82]

Truman issued his statement on October 4, 1946, the eve of Yom Kippur. It may well have been Truman's desperate political straits that led him to such a blatantly political gambit.

Even so, the original Zionist draft of what would become

known as the Yom Kippur statement was amended significantly by the State Department. Eliahu Epstein and Judge Sam Rosenman had drafted a statement expressing American support for partition. Truman passed it on to Acheson, who with his officials inserted a key clause in support of a *compromise* between partition and the Morrison-Grady scheme.[83] The critical part of Truman's statement read:

The British Government presented to the [London] Conference the so-called Morrison Plan for provincial autonomy and stated that the Conference was open to other proposals. Meanwhile, the Jewish Agency proposed a solution of the Palestine problem by means of the creation of a viable Jewish state in control of its own immigration and economic policies in an adequate area of Palestine instead of in the whole of Palestine. It proposed, furthermore the immediate issuance of certificates for 100,000 Jewish immigrants. . . . it is my belief that a solution along these lines would command the support of public opinion in the United States. *I cannot believe that the gap between the proposals which have been put forward is too great to be bridged by men of reason and goodwill. To such a solution our Government could give its support.*[84]

Both Truman and Acheson later denied any ulterior political motivation. Truman stated in his memoirs that his timing was "nothing unusual" and just "happened" to be on the eve of Yom Kippur. Truman was upset by Foreign Secretary Bevin's criticism and claimed that he had simply restated his position, namely, that he wanted "to see one hundred thousand Jews admitted to Palestine."[85]

Dean Acheson's account, published twenty-three years later, is yet more interesting. Acheson, who admitted helping draft the statement, denies that it was an election ploy, even if with hindsight he concedes it may have been of "doubtful wisdom." He also makes the credulity-stretching statement that Truman "never took or refused to take a step in our foreign relations to benefit his or his party's fortunes."[86]

Acheson's memoirs may be compared with his own contemporary record. On October 3, 1946, it fell to Acheson to explain to the British ambassador the contents of and motives behind the president's statement. Acheson told him that for the past several weeks Truman had been trying to keep Palestine out of domestic politics but pressures had increased over the past ten days. The administration understood that Governor Dewey intended to make a major speech on the subject, and in view both of the public interest and of the adjournment of the Arab-British conference in London, Truman now felt it vital to make a statement.[87]

The Yom Kippur statement was interpreted universally as an expression of Truman's support for the Zionist position. When Epstein pointed out to Niles the emasculation of his original draft by the State Department, Niles retorted it did not make any real difference since the public would interpret it as presidential support for partition.[88] Epstein himself reported that "not a single newspaper had pointed up this part of the statement and all the headlines carried by the papers read 'Truman's support of a Jewish State.'"[89]

The Yom Kippur statement marked a watershed in the political and diplomatic struggle for the Jewish state. The British saw in the statement a demonstration of Jewish political power and gave up their quest for an Anglo-American consensus on Palestine. Bevin began issuing threats that the British would evacuate Palestine, and in February 1947 they did indeed refer the question with no recommendations to the United Nations.

The Yom Kippur statement also had a most sobering effect on Truman. He was undoubtedly embarrassed by accusations, both private and public, that he had exploited the Palestine question for domestic political gain. Thus his denial of the obvious in his memoirs, published ten years later. To make matters worse, this last political ploy had no apparent effect on the election results, which resulted in a Republican avalanche.

The Democratic defeat was particularly painful in New York, where Governor Dewey received 650,000 votes more than Senator Mead, and the Republican nominee for senator, Irving M. Ives, beat the popular former governor, Herbert H. Lehman, a Jew, by nearly 250,000 votes. For the first time since 1928 the Republicans gained a clear majority in New York City, a traditional Democratic stronghold. The results were seen as "a massive repudiation of the domestic policies of Truman and the Democratic party."[90]

The episode marked the end of Truman's refugee Zionism although he continued to view Palestine exclusively as a refuge for the Jewish DPs. At the end of October 1946 he officially re-turned the supervision of the Palestine issue to the State De-partment and rejected all further Zionist attempts to approach him. On December 8, 1946, Truman told Foreign Secretary Bevin how difficult it had been for him with the New York Jews but that with the elections now over he would be able to give the British a freer hand.[91]

The Yom Kippur statement was Truman's last public utter-ance on the Palestine issue and his last effort to press the British to permit a mass Jewish migration to Palestine. During the course of 1947, with the arrival of Max Lowenthal as adviser on Palestine to Clark Clifford, a new policy would emerge—one of White House support for a Jewish state.

Senator Harry S. Truman and Max Lowenthal, October 23, 1939.
(*Kansas City Journal*. Courtesy Harry S. Truman Library.)

Jacob Blaustein, executive secretary, and Judge Joseph M. Proskauer, president of the American Jewish Committee, leaving the White House after a conference with President Truman, September 29, 1945. They urged the continuation of U.S. efforts to open Palestine to substantial immigration of European Jews, survivors of more than a decade of Nazism. (Courtesy Harry S. Truman Library.)

Truman with his friend Eddie Jacobson, 1954. (Photo by Max Bengir.
Courtesy Harry S. Truman Library.)

Truman and friends in Abraham Granoff's home, February 22, 1956. *From left to right:* Granoff, Truman, Earl J. Tranin, A. D. "Doc" Jacobson (Eddie Jacobson's brother). (Courtesy Loeb H. Granoff.)

Truman and Abraham Granoff, February 22, 1956. (Courtesy Loeb H. Granoff.)

Truman in Key West in 1949. *Back row, from left:* Charles Murphy, General Landry, Admiral Dennison, General Vaughan, General Graham, David Niles, Donald Dawson. *Middle row:* Clark Clifford, William Hassett, John Snyder, President Truman, John Steelman, Charles Ross, Frank Pace. *Front row:* Phillip Maguire, unidentified, George Elsey, unidentified, David D. Lloyd, Stephen Spingarn. (U.S. Navy. Courtesy Harry S. Truman Library.)

Truman at the Little White House, Key West, April 4, 1950. *Front row, from left:* John Steelman, Mrs. Truman, President Truman, Margaret Truman, William Hassett. *Back row:* Stephen Spingarn, General Landry, Admiral Dennison, Mr. Woodward, Charles Ross, General Vaughan, General Graham, David Niles. (U.S. Navy. Courtesy Harry S. Truman Library.)

President Truman is met on his return from Wake Island, October 18, 1950, by George C. Marshall (*left*) and Averell Harriman. (National Park Service—Abbie Rowe. Courtesy Harry S. Truman Library.)

President Truman receives the Torah from Dr. Chaim Weizmann, president of the new State of Israel, May 25, 1948. (UPI/Bettmann Newsphotos.)

President Truman died in 1972. The United States Philatelic Service honored him in 1973 with a stamp issued on his birthday, May 8. The B'nai B'rith issued a cachet to complement the stamp, highlighting Truman's recognition of Israel on May 14, 1948. (American Jewish Archives, Cincinnati campus, Hebrew Union College, Jewish Institute of Religion.)

PART FOUR

Truman and Israel

NINE

The UN Partition Resolution
November 29, 1947

A last Arab-Zionist conference, convened in London by the British from January to February 1947, failed to yield a compromise solution that the British felt able to implement. Therefore, on February 18, 1947, Foreign Secretary Bevin announced in the House of Commons that the government was referring the Palestine question without recommendations to the United Nations.[1]

On May 13, 1947, a special session of the UN General Assembly appointed a thirteen-person special committee on Palestine (UNSCOP) to study the Palestine problem and report back to the assembly by September. On August 31 UNSCOP completed its report at Geneva. The committee recommended unanimously that the British terminate their mandate and grant Palestine independence at the earliest practicable date. A majority of eight states (Australia, Canada, Czechoslovakia, Guatemala, the Netherlands, Peru, Sweden, and Uruguay) recommended the partition of Palestine into Jewish, Arab, and Jerusalem states to be joined in an economic union. The Arabs and the Jews would be granted independence after a two-year transition period beginning September 1, 1947. Jerusalem would remain under an international trusteeship. A minority plan (signed by India, Iran, and Yugoslavia) recommended that Palestine become "an independent federal state" after a transition period of three years under a UN trusteeship.[2]

149

On September 20, 1947, the British cabinet decided to end its mandate over Palestine and to evacuate the country. The British were unwilling to enforce the partition of Palestine against the will of the Arabs and had despaired of reaching a consensus with the Americans.[3] On September 26 Colonial Secretary Arthur Creech-Jones made the following announcement before the UN General Assembly, sitting as an ad hoc committee on Palestine:

In order that there may be no misunderstanding of the attitude and policy of Britain I have been instructed by His Majesty's Government to announce, with all solemnity, that they have consequently decided that in the absence of a settlement they must plan for an early withdrawal of British forces and of the British Administration from Palestine.[4]

Because of the general skepticism about British intentions, Creech-Jones was instructed by Bevin and Attlee to repeat the announcement, which he did on October 16: "My government desire that it should be clear beyond all doubt and ambiguity that not only is it our decision to wind up the mandate but that within a limited period we shall withdraw."[5]

THE AMERICAN DECISION
TO SUPPORT PARTITION

President Truman had kept his silence on the Palestine issue since the previous October. He had developed something of an allergy toward Palestine and still nursed his old irritations. But the UNSCOP report, soon to be debated by the United Nations, forced the American administration to take a stand.

In the summer of 1947, prior to UNSCOP's majority finding in favor of partition, Truman still clung to the plan for a unitary Palestine as advocated first by the Anglo-American committee and revised later by the Morrison-Grady plan.[6] This concept had become, and would remain, an idée fixe with Truman.

At the beginning of August, Truman received a telegram from Rabbi Stephen Wise urging him to do something to break the cycle of terror and bloodshed in Palestine. Truman retorted: "I . . . appreciate your viewpoint but there seem to be two sides to this question. I am finding it rather difficult to decide which one is right and a great many other people in this country are beginning to feel just as I do."[7]

At a cabinet meeting two days later Truman made it clear that he would make no pronouncements on Palestine before UNSCOP issued its report; "he had stuck his neck out on this delicate question once, and he did not propose to do it again."[8]

On September 4, 1947, Robert Hannegan, postmaster general and retiring chairman of the Democratic National Committee, brought up the Palestine issue at a lunch held for the cabinet. Although the UNSCOP report had been published, Hannegan did *not* speak of partition. He suggested that if Truman again appealed to the British government before the UN discussions began, this time for 150,000 immigration certificates for Palestine, the party's chances of winning the elections would increase. Secretary of the Navy James Forrestal reacted violently. Referring evidently to the party's debacle the previous November, Forrestal commented acidly that the president's pro-Zionist policy had *not* helped the Democratic party but *had* harmed Anglo-American relations.

Truman was not present at the lunch, but Hannegan reported back to him the same day with Senator Howard McGrath, the incoming chairman of the Democratic National Committee, who had also attended. Both Hannegan and McGrath warned Truman that if his policy on Palestine was not consistent with his previous statements on the subject, the party was likely to lose two to three states in the presidential elections, which would swing the results against him.[9]

The Zionists, who were informed of these exchanges, were thus aware that Truman had yet to make up his mind on the vexatious Palestine question. In mid-September, Moshe Shertok reported that a reliable source had warned him that they should not take Truman for granted. When Shertok had replied that Truman had taken a helpful attitude in the past but had been thwarted repeatedly by the State Department, he was told not to take that as "the gospel truth."[10]

At the State Department, Loy Henderson, director of NEA, masterminded the attack on partition. Matters were complicated by the existence of the presidentially appointed delegation to the United Nations, where the UNSCOP report would be debated shortly. The delegation became a middle-ground arena in which State Department officials and White House aides fought their struggles.

As noted above (see chapter 6), when Loy Henderson and George Wadsworth (former agent and consul general to Lebanon and Syria during the war and ambassador to Iraq, Turkey, and Saudi Arabia after it) were appointed to the delegation, David Niles had persuaded Truman to appoint General John Hilldring also as a reliable liaison to the White House.[11] In addition to Hilldring, the president also appointed Eleanor Roosevelt, the venerated widow of the late president. She was a staunch supporter of the United Nations, and her inclusion in the American delegation was intended to symbolize the administration's determination that the new international body should succeed where the late League of Nations had failed.

Eleanor Roosevelt was *not* a Zionist and did not favor the establishment of a Jewish state in Palestine. Once UNSCOP recommended the partition of Palestine, however, she held it mandatory to support the UN committee's plan. Partition may not have been the best way to settle the Jewish problem, but no better way had been suggested, and once the UN endorsed it she came to regard the UNSCOP partition plan as "the first real test of the organization's capacity to take a position and make it stick."[12] She went so far as to telephone David Niles, asking him to tell the president of her anxiety for the good name of the United States should the American delegation not state clearly its support for the UNSCOP majority plan.[13]

Also on the American delegation was John Foster Dulles, an aspiring Republican and a supporter of Governor Dewey. Dulles knew that any reservations he expressed about UNSCOP's partition plan would be leaked to the Zionists—through Hilldring and Niles—which would affect adversely the Republicans' electoral chances.[14]

But the Republicans shared the State Department's concern that the UN delegation should maintain a low profile during the debates on partition. They agreed that the United States should not get itself into the position of sponsor of the Jewish state in Palestine. On October 8, 1947, Senator Arthur Vandenberg wrote to Senator Robert A. Taft that he had supported partition long before Rabbi Silver himself had come around to it. But he added:

We must refrain from urging any final action which logically involves primary *American* responsibility for *imposing* partition against armed resistance. . . . *This* is a matter which the President and his Secretary of State will have to handle. . . . We should not put ourselves in a position at the moment where we can be charged with responsibility for what happens though we do not have the authority to make things happen. In a word, I think the less said the better at the moment.[15]

The State Department resented outside "interference" and machinations, particularly the White House nomination of General Hilldring and the "alien" considerations brought to bear on the UN delegation:

Our main difficulty is that when New York puts a draft position to us, we don't know how much steam the suggested position has behind it. We are uncertain how high up that position has been cleared at your end, or what new policy line lies behind it. A further difficulty is that while we are collecting a few preliminary thoughts on the subject, we are informed by the radio or the press that the USUN [the U.S. delegation to the United Nations] has already spoken up in the meeting.[16]

But State Department officials also appreciated the complexity of the Palestine issue for the administration. They knew that the president had to consider the domestic as well as the international ramifications of the problem and that Truman's Yom Kippur statement had been taken universally as a commitment to partition. Any opposition to the UNSCOP majority report would be regarded as a politically suicidal reversal of presidential policy. In addition, there was widespread faith, as represented by Eleanor Roosevelt, that the United Nations would finally inaugurate an era of peaceful settlement of international conflicts.[17]

But it was still expected that the Communist bloc and a substantial bloc of other countries would oppose the establishment of a Jewish state in Palestine. The department's policy was therefore to be a sophisticated blend of passive support for the United Nations with a pronounced abstinence from pressuring fellow member-nations, which alone might procure the two-thirds majority required to make a UN resolution binding. As late as October 20, one week after the official American announcement in support of partition, Robert McClintock, a senior State Department official, wrote to Under Secretary Robert Lovett that the UN partition plan might pass the ad hoc committee on Palestine but it would fail to receive a two-thirds majority in the plenary session "unless a more active line [was] taken by the U.S. Delegation."[18]

On September 15, 1947, Secretary of State George C. Marshall called a meeting at his office to brief the American delegation to the United Nations. Henderson was called in to state the case against partition, but he had just returned from a trip abroad and was not really prepared. Marshall instructed the delegation not to "show [its] hand" until it became absolutely necessary. Hilldring, who had served under and retained great reverence for Marshall, agreed that although American reticence would greatly disappoint many Jews their disappointment did not "warrant a definite statement by the United States." The Jews would have to wait a little longer. Eleanor Roosevelt entered the sole reservation; she stated that support for the UNSCOP report, and thereby for the United Nations, was more important than pleasing American Jewry. Marshall warned that the British would not help in enforcing partition and should the United States take any initiative it would have to send its own troops to Palestine.[19]

On September 17, 1947, Marshall addressed the UN General Assembly, now constituted as an ad hoc committee on Palestine. Marshall commended UNSCOP on its report and stated: "While the final decision of the Assembly must properly await the detailed consideration of the report, the Government of the United States *gives great weight* not only to the recommendations which have met with the unanimous approval of the Special Committee, but also to those which have been approved by the majority of that Committee."[20]

A few days later Henderson was called to the White House to explain his views to the president and his aides, including Niles and Clifford. After stating his reasons for opposing a Jewish state, Henderson was cross-examined. What were the sources of his views? Were they merely opinions that might be based on prejudice or bias? Did he think that his judgment and that of his staff at NEA was superior to that of the group (i.e., UNSCOP) that the United Nations had selected to study the problem?[21]

Henderson recalled later how he had felt humiliated, as if the White House aides were trying to break him down in front of the president. He pointed out that the views he had just expressed were held not only by himself but by all American legations and consular offices in the Middle East and by all State Department officials who had responsibility for the area. According to Henderson, the cross-questioning became rougher and rougher, until finally Truman stood up and muttered: "Oh, hell, I'm leaving." Henderson deduced from Truman's bearing and facial expression that even at that stage, in late September 1947, the president had yet to decide finally to support the establishment of a Jewish state.[22]

As Henderson interpreted it retrospectively, Truman realized that Congress, the press, the Democratic party, and aroused public opinion would all turn against him should he withdraw his support for the Zionists. Therefore, he was hoping desperately that the State Department would tell him that the UNSCOP partition plan would be in the best interests of the United States. But this the State Department was unable to do.[23]

At another meeting between Marshall and the UN delegation on September 24, it was decided to support the UNSCOP partition plan but to work for amendments that would make it more palatable to the Arabs. But again the delegation was instructed not to make any statements during the opening stages of the debate to ensure that other delegations might decide free of American influence. The delegation also discussed the contingency that partition would *not* receive the necessary two-thirds majority and the need to have an alternative policy ready.[24] More than two weeks were to pass before the American decision was made public.

The Zionists were fully aware of the strategy behind State Department policy. Two days after the delegation's decision to support partition, Moshe Shertok and Rabbi Silver tried to draw out Marshall on the American position toward UNSCOP. Marshall burst out in anger that he was not ready to reply, and he could suggest only that Silver look up the part of his UN speech that had dealt with Palestine. For the present he was not ready to commit himself on what stand the American government would take.[25]

Eliahu Epstein told Judge Sam Rosenman of Shertok's and Silver's meeting with Marshall and their feeling that the State Department was intent on sabotaging partition. Rosenman replied that he had heard a similar view from Mrs. Roosevelt. He promised to talk with the heads of the Democratic party in New York and advise them to take urgent action. That same evening Epstein met Niles, who had been told by Hilldring of his difficulty in keeping track of the various members of the UN delegation.[26]

On September 29, 1947, the heads of the New York Democratic party met to discuss Palestine. Among those present were Paul E. Fitzpatrick, chairman of the New York State Democratic Committee; party boss Ed Flynn; William O'Dwyer, mayor of New York; and Karl Sherman, the New York party treasurer. After the discussion Ed Flynn was appointed to meet with Truman to explain the dangers to the party and to the president himself in next year's elections should it appear that he was not standing by his promises to support the Jews in Palestine. Flynn spoke with Truman over the telephone and received a favorable impression.[27]

Niles and Clifford mobilized three cabinet members—Robert Hannegan, Oscar Ewing, administrator of the Federal Security Agency (forerunner of the Department of Health and Human Services), and Tom Clark, attorney general—to persuade Truman that the UN delegation had to come out with a clear statement on Palestine. The three men visited Truman and impressed on him the international importance of the UN decision, on which rested the prestige of the United States and of the president.[28]

At the end of October, Shertok met with Henderson and told him that unless the Americans made their intentions clear it was doubtful that the Latin American states would vote for partition. Henderson replied that his government was anxious that the solution be a UN plan and not come to be regarded as an American one. Any attempt by the American delegation to "corral" votes for the majority plan, concluded Henderson, would inevitably leave that impression.[29]

The Zionists also organized an intensive White House lobby. During the month of September 1947, Truman received an estimated forty to fifty letters from members of Congress urging him to endorse the UNSCOP majority report. Truman was becoming the reluctant, bitter hostage of the Zionist lobby, which he now blamed for the current impasse. On October 20, 1947, one week after the official American statement in support of partition, Truman wrote the following to a U.S. senator: "Had it not been for the unwarranted interference of the Zionists, we would have had the matter settled a year and a half ago. I received about thirty-five thousand pieces of mail and propaganda from the Jews in this country while this matter was pending. I put it all in a pile and struck a match to it."[30]

At the beginning of October, Truman was still undecided, hoping he could keep out of the fray and leave the issue to Secretary of State Marshall. But the Democrats' losses in the congressional elections of the previous year had been sustained partly as the result of a defection of the Jewish vote. This evidently convinced the party managers and aides that Truman would have to try hard to recover the support of Jews in the 1948 elections for the presidency. Like it or not, Truman would be forced to fall in line with the Zionist lobby.

He then received an emotional appeal from Eddie Jacobson:

The future of one-half million Jews in Europe depends on what happens at the present meeting of the United Nations. . . . In all this world, there is only one place where they can go—and that is Palestine. . . . if it were possible for you, as leader and spokesman for our country, to express your support of this action, I think we can accomplish our aims before the United Nations Assembly. . . . Harry, my people need help and I am appealing to you to help them.[31]

On October 5 Truman had a short talk alone with Marshall. At this meeting the president apparently instructed Marshall to make public American support for partition.

On October 8, at a meeting at the White House attended by Lovett, Niles, and Clifford, Truman confirmed the speech prepared by the State Department, which clearly declared American support for a Jewish state.[32] In his instructions to Lovett, Truman stated that any American financial or economic aid was to be given exclusively through UN auspices and added that he was unwilling to "pick up the present United Kingdom responsibility for the maintenance of law and order in Palestine." Likewise, any American forces would be made available only as part of a UN force.[33]

On the same day, Truman replied to Eddie Jacobson, turning down his request to intervene in person:

The matter is now pending before the General Assembly of the United Nations and I don't think it would be right or proper for me to interfere at this stage, particularly as it requires a two-thirds vote to accomplish the purpose sought.

General Marshall is handling the thing, I think, as it should be and I hope it will work out all right.

I don't want to be quoted on the subject at all. When I see you I'll tell you just what the difficulties are.[34]

Niles later told Epstein that one of the reasons why Truman had not given explicit instructions to support partition at the beginning of the assembly had been his concern that American support would commit him to sending American troops.[35] Truman feared that the appearance of an American force in the Middle East, especially near the borders of the Soviet Union, would appear to the Soviets as provocative, spurring Stalin to send in troops, which might even lead to a full-scale conflict. This Truman was determined to prevent.

Niles also warned the Zionists that they should expect further difficulties until they convinced the president that the Palestine problem could be settled peacefully. All his military advisers were telling Truman that the Yishuv could not defend itself against an invasion by the Arab states or even against the Palestinian Arabs if supported by those states.[36]

The American announcement was made at the United Nations on October 11. A Zionist public relations expert assessed cynically the new demarche at a closed meeting of the American Zionist Emergency Council: "We had won a great victory, but under no circumstances should any of us believe or think we had won because of the devotion of the American Government to our cause. We had won because of the sheer pressure of political logistics that was applied by the Jewish leadership in the United States."[37]

THE ZIONIST LOBBY

On October 13, two days after the American announcement, the Soviets also announced their support for the UN partition plan. Given the Great Powers' endorsement of the plan, it seemed unlikely that any other plan would be accepted by the General Assembly, even if the UNSCOP plan failed to secure the required two-thirds majority vote. Therefore, the State Department now concentrated in the working committees on securing border adjustments favorable to the Arabs.

Two areas allotted by UNSCOP to the Jews came in for particular criticism: the town of Jaffa, whose "essentially Arab character" dictated its inclusion in the Arab state, and the Negev desert area, thought to be more suitable for "seasonal grazing by Arab herdsmen . . . than use by Jewish colonies."[38] On November 19, the day on which Subcommittee One was due to determine which state would have domain over the Negev, Lovett instructed Johnson and Hilldring not to yield to the Jewish demand for the area.[39]

At this point Zionist intervention at the White House brought an instant countermanding of the State Department's orders from the president. Shertok alerted Weizmann that Johnson had proposed the partition of the Negev, which would cut the future Jewish state off from the Red Sea. Weizmann foresaw the strategic import of the Red Sea outlet for Israel's trade with Africa and the Far East. On November 17 Eliahu Epstein rang up Niles at the White House, saying that it was urgent that Weizmann meet with the president within forty-eight hours, before the subcommittee on borders finished its work. One hour later Niles rang back and advised that an interview had been fixed for lunchtime on November 19. Weizmann was to enter by the East Gate, and the meeting was to be kept secret.[40]

Weizmann was provided with maps of the Negev, which he studied prior to his meeting with Truman. Weizmann later recounted how the president had understood the situation at once: "It is the first time in my life that I have met a president who can read and understand maps." He convinced Truman that the Negev could be made fertile by irrigation and spoke also of the Gulf of 'Aqaba as an alternative route to the Suez Canal.[41]

A little after 3:00 P.M. that same afternoon, Johnson and Hilldring summoned Shertok to tell him of Lovett's instructions to transfer the Negev to the Arab state. But as they began to talk, Hilldring was called to the phone and informed by Truman that he wanted the delegation to vote for the inclusion of the Negev in the Jewish state.[42] When Lovett telephoned Truman that evening, the president insisted that he had not meant to countermand the under secretary's directives. He had wanted to prevent the United States from standing out as a useless minority against the Zionists' demands.[43]

But notwithstanding the successes of the Zionists, their rejoicing was to be short-lived. The United States kept to its policy of not exerting pressure on smaller, dependent states, and despite both American and Soviet support the UNSCOP partition plan failed to receive the required majority on the ad hoc committee, as had been foreseen by the State Department. On November 25, 1947, an amended version of the UNSCOP plan was adopted, with twenty-five votes for the plan, thirteen against, and seventeen abstentions, but it was still a single vote short of the two-thirds majority required for a resolution to pass the General Assembly plenum.[44]

The decisive vote was to be on November 29, 1947. (The Zionists, needing to buy time, had by means of a filibuster at the plenary session on November 26 secured a further thirty-six-hour interval—for the next day began the Thanksgiving holiday.) The few days before the vote were the most critical and decisive in the diplomatic struggle for the State of Israel. Both sides concentrated on those states that had abstained on November 25. The British were informed that the delegates of the Philippines, Liberia, and Greece (all dependent on the United States) were "deliberately lying low to avoid pressure" but had promised their votes in the plenary to the Arabs.[45]

Until that point, as may be deduced from the Greek and

Philippine statements, the United States had not tried to influence other countries to follow its example in support of partition. On the contrary, when approached by the Greeks at the end of September, the State Department had advised them that it had no objections to their supporting the Arabs.[46] Truman had endorsed the State Department strategy of "non-intervention" lest the United States be maneuvered into the inheritance of Britain's Palestine legacy.

On November 24 Lovett had reported to the White House on a talk with the U.S. delegation at the United Nations. Its case was "being seriously impeded by high pressure being exerted by *Jewish* agencies." There had also been indications of "bribes and threats by Jewish groups." Liberia and Nicaragua were among the countries that had been threatened with American sanctions. Lovett evidently feared Zionist access to the White House and imminent presidential involvement or intervention. He asked Truman not to discuss the Palestine question with anyone and reassured him that "everything consistent with good taste and courtesy [was] being done by [the UN] delegation."[47]

Truman responded immediately that he did not wish "to use improper pressures of any kind on other Delegations to vote for the majority report." Accordingly, Lovett instructed the UN delegation not to coerce other delegates to follow its lead.[48]

THE QUEST FOR A
BIPARTISAN POLICY

James Forrestal, now defense secretary, mounted a lone, futile campaign to include Palestine in an informal bipartisan agreement between the Democrats and Republicans that domestic politics should not extend beyond the seaboard. In 1944 New York governor Thomas Dewey, on the advice of John Foster Dulles, had made an agreement with Secretary of State Cordell Hull to remove the issue of the future of the United Nations from that year's election campaign. This ad hoc agreement developed into a broader bipartisan approach to foreign policy after the war, culminating in Republican support for the Truman Doctrine and the Marshall Plan.[49]

On November 6, 1947, Forrestal buttonholed Senator Howard McGrath, chairman of the Democratic National Committee, and in reference to the Zionists told him: "No group in this country should be permitted to influence our policy to the point where it could endanger our national security."[50]

McGrath told Forrestal that Jewish sources were responsible for a major part of the contributions to the party and that much of the money was given "with a distinct idea on the part of the givers that they will have an opportunity to express their views and have them seriously considered on such questions as the present Palestine question."[51] At election time McGrath stated: "There were two or three pivotal states which could not be carried without the support of people who were deeply interested in the Palestine question."[52]

Forrestal replied that he would rather lose those states in a national election than run the risks that he felt might develop in the handling of the Palestine question. But Forrestal was also a Truman appointee and could hardly expect to enjoy the same politically neutral status as State Department officials.

Forrestal never enjoyed the influence he would have liked to have had with the Truman administration. His loyalty to the Democratic party was suspect. So far as anyone knew, he never made any substantial contributions to the party, and in 1948 he let it be known that he was ready to serve under Governor Dewey, who Forrestal was sure was going to win the election. Predictably, Forrestal was not included in Truman's second administration.[53]

In addition, Forrestal's personal relations with Truman were poor. He made pathetic attempts to break into Truman's White House stag circle, forcing himself to play poker, a game which he disliked and at which he regularly lost large sums of money. But despite Forrestal's efforts, he never gained Truman's confidence nor did the president ever feel able to relax in his presence.[54]

On top of all this, Bartley Crum attached an anti-Semitic slur to Forrestal in a speech made on March 10, 1948. In a demagogic attack Crum insinuated that Forrestal was at the center of an administration anti-Zionist conspiracy. This had its origins in Forrestal's personal interests, deriving from his former position as a partner and president of Dillon, Read and Company, a Wall Street investment firm that had been active in floating large loans for a number of oil companies.[55]

There was more than enough in Forrestal's background to arouse suspicions of anti-Semitism on his part. His family apparently were anti-Semitic; he was ambivalent toward Jews and had difficulty accepting them as social equals. Many of the Wall Street investment banking houses and law firms refused to employ Jews, and some of the Washington and New York clubs to which Forrestal belonged denied them admission. The Navy Department was notorious for its discrimination against Jews, although Forrestal to his credit broke with this tradition.[56]

For all the above reasons Forrestal's bipartisan campaign had little impact. When he tackled McGrath a second time, on November 26, this time showing him a secret CIA report on Palestine, McGrath prevaricated and said he would like time to study the documents.[57]

THE JACOBSON-GRANOFF CONNECTION

On November 27, the White House lobby in favor of partition moved into top gear. Truman's own later denials notwithstanding, there can be little doubt that he and his White House staff did intervene decisively after the partition plan had failed to obtain the necessary two-thirds majority on November 25. In March 1948, during another crisis in Palestine affairs, Clark Clifford in an internal memorandum reminded Truman of his crucial role the previous November: "We 'crossed the Rubicon' on this matter when the partition resolution was adopted by the Assembly—largely at your insistence."[58]

Several contemporary Zionist sources confirm Truman's decisive role. Michael Comay, at the time in charge of the Jewish Agency's New York office, analyzed the progression of events in a personal letter written three days after the final vote: "A number of delegations, normally very susceptible to American views, told us that they had been given to understand that Washington did not insist on their support on this particular issue. . . . in

Marshall's view this was a UN policy rather than a US one." The climax to the American "policy of indifference" had come on November 25:

Greece, the Philippines and Haiti—three countries completely dependent on Washington—suddenly came out one after another against its declared policy. We stalled off a decision, and over Thanksgiving Day, which was a holiday, an avalanche descended upon the White House while some newspapers openly accused officials in the State Department of sabotage. The President, we learned, became very upset and threw his personal weight behind the effort to get a decision. . . . It was only in the last 48 hours, i.e. on Friday and Saturday, that we really got the full backing of the United States.[59]

Rabbi Silver confirmed this train of events in his report to the American Zionist Emergency Council:

When the Philippines, Haiti and Greece fell away on the same day, this served notice to many wavering delegations that the American Government was not really concerned about the outcome. Fortunately, we were given a breathing spell of 36 hours. During this time, we marshalled our forces, Jewish and non-Jewish opinion, leaders and masses alike, converged on the Government and induced the President to assert the authority of his Administration to overcome the negative attitude of the State Department which persisted to the end, and persists today. The result was that our Government made its intense desire for the adoption of the partition plan known to the wavering governments.[60]

What led to Truman's eleventh-hour reversal? Historians have been at a loss to explain it, primarily because of the dearth of hard evidence. As has been noted already, the lobby within the White House was somewhat clandestine, and therefore many of its operations were never committed to paper. But more facts have come to light in recent years, especially on one important member of the lobby—Eddie Jacobson.

Jacobson's well-publicized role in the diplomatic struggle for Palestine has until now been related almost exclusively to the American trusteeship proposal of March 1948 (see chapter 10). In 1968 Ian Bickerton suggested that Jacobson had lobbied Truman on the Zionists' behalf prior to the November resolution.[61]

But in 1972 the Bickerton thesis was rejected by Frank Adler of Kansas City, a local Jewish historian and an acknowledged authority on the Truman-Jacobson relationship. Relying on presidential logbooks, Adler concluded that Jacobson had no meetings with Truman between April 30 and December 9, 1947.[62]

Truman's daughter, Margaret, in her biography of her father, has dismissed as "absurd myth" the idea that Jacobson was a frequent visitor to the Truman White House. She claims that after a single appeal to the president, the well-publicized one of March 1948, Jacobson "learned his lesson" and never approached Truman again.[63]

But using White House records, Adler also discovered that Jacobson was received by Truman no less than twenty-four times in the Oval Office. Thirteen of those meetings were marked "off the record." In addition, Jacobson met Truman several times outside the White House—in New York, in Key West, and in Kansas City; in 1948, during Truman's whistle-stop tour, Jacobson traveled for three days aboard the presidential train.[64]

Such was the frequency of Jacobson's visits to the White House that none other than Clark Clifford, the front advocate of the Zionist cause against the State Department line, protested in irritation. In June 1948, when David Niles reported to Clifford on a Jacobson visit to speak about the final boundaries of the State of Israel, Max Lowenthal noted: "Clifford blew up and said that Jacobson ought not to be coming in to see the President on these matters. Dave said to Clifford: 'I did not arrange it; Jacobson was seeing the President for years before we began seeing the President; the President will be seeing Jacobson for years after the present date and we can't stop it.'"[65]

In 1973, one year after Adler published his book, Jacobson's personal diary was discovered, tucked away at the bottom of a box of old letters and photographs in a Kansas City attic. Jacobson's diary entries indicate that he saw the president in February 1947 and that he was in frequent contact with him during November of that year.[66]

Another Kansas City personality influenced the Jacobson-Truman relationship during this period—Abraham Granoff, Jacobson's old friend and oracle. Granoff, a lawyer, had a trained mind and was intellectual mentor to the uneducated Jacobson.

During this period, they usually visited Truman at the White House together.

The two men had first met in the early 1930s when they were carpooling their children to the same school. When Jacobson bought his store, Granoff gave him legal advice, and in lieu of payment, which Granoff refused to accept, Jacobson gave him items of clothing.[67]

Granoff had already met Truman in 1924, when they both happened to be having their hair cut at Frank Spina's (of Battery D) barbershop. The acquaintance developed when they later began to play poker regularly at Eddie Jacobson's house. If Truman and Granoff happened to sit next to each other, Truman would look into his hand and quip: "I got you beat already." Neither politics nor Zionism was ever discussed. According to Granoff, Truman had liked to embarrass him with risqué stories, which he continued to do even in the White House, where Granoff's blushes had produced roars of laughter from Jacobson and the president.

Granoff could not have imagined "even two brothers being as close and affectionate as these two friends were."[68] Truman's attitude toward Jacobson never changed, but when Truman became president, Jacobson's respect amounted to awe. Jacobson never fixed up appointments in advance. He first made sure that Truman was in Washington, then flew up and telephoned Matt Connelly, the appointments secretary. After going through a regular, jocular cussing routine ("what the hell are you doing here without his permission"), Jacobson and Granoff would get in within a few hours with no limit on time. They were generally shown in through the back door to avoid the press and photographers.

Truman always had time for his two old friends from Kansas City. Undoubtedly, they provided a welcome break from more "official" business. And in contrast to most other visitors who came to promote the Zionist cause, they never lectured or hectored the president. The fifteen-minute appointments usually ran to half an hour. Truman would ask about their wives and children by name and sign a dollar bill for them. But Granoff was aware that Truman never took them fully into his confidence. Nor did he ever commit himself one way or another.

Granoff had joined the Zionist movement briefly in the 1920s. But he had soon left "due to their fanaticism." Jacobson never joined. Once Truman became president, the Zionists made repeated attempts to mobilize the two men but were rebuffed.[69] When Granoff and Jacobson visited the president, they were extremely sensitive about their position as American Jews and on their guard lest their appeals on behalf of their fellow Jews should be construed as conflicting with their patriotic duty as Americans. On one occasion Granoff stated that "neither he nor Jacobson would ever ask [Truman] to do anything against the best interests of the United States." Truman, grim, and apparently irritated by the remark, replied: "You guys wouldn't get to the front gate if I thought any differently. You needn't have said it."[70]

In June 1947 through Granoff, Jacobson was prevailed on to press Truman to act again to get the 100,000 DPs admitted into Palestine. In that month Granoff received a phone call from Maurice Bisgyer, one of the heads of B'nai B'rith. The national president, Frank Goldman, was on an extension. Bisgyer asked if Granoff knew of a man called "Jacobs, Jacobstein, or something," who was supposed to be a close friend of the president. Granoff replied: "Sure I know him, I ought to; I'm his friend and lawyer!" B'nai B'rith was concerned about the Jewish DPs still languishing in the European centers. Granoff helped arrange a meeting with Jacobson the next week in the Hotel Muehlbach in Kansas City.[71]

At their meeting Bisgyer asked Jacobson to intercede with the president to get the 100,000 into Palestine, adding: "We must overcome the State Department." Jacobson replied: "Harry Truman will do what's right if he knows all the facts. If I can help supply them I will. But I'm no Zionist so first I need the facts from you."[72]

Within a week Jacobson and Granoff flew to Washington, at their own expense. Their mission was to appeal for the 100,000 but *not* to urge partition. Backing them now was the powerful B'nai B'rith organization, which in contrast to the Zionists had not fallen out with Truman.[73] At their meeting with the president, Truman evidently insisted that he could not intervene while the problem was under UN consideration.

As noted, in October the administration had come out in favor of partition. Once it became official American policy to support the UN partition plan, many non-Zionist Jewish bodies, such as the American Jewish Committee and B'nai B'rith, followed the administration's lead. By November 1947 the problem was not to secure the administration's support for a Jewish state in Palestine but to get the administration to use its influence at the United Nations in that cause.

In November 1947 Jacobson was again mobilized to secure a more forward presidential promotion of the UN partition plan. He noted in his diary that the president was "fighting [the] entire Cabinet and State Department to put over Partition." On November 17 he wrote: "again to [the] White House." On Wednesday, November 26, he received a call from the White House—"everything O.K." The next day Jacobson sent a two-page wire to Truman. On November 28 he received a telephone call from Truman's secretary (presumably Matt Connelly), who told him "not to worry." On November 29 Jacobson noted enigmatically: "Mission accomplished."[74]

WHITE HOUSE INTERVENTION

Truman undoubtedly allowed his aides to lobby for partition, notwithstanding his assurance to Lovett to the contrary. Jacobson's was just one more voice emanating from Truman's close entourage, which included Niles, Clifford, and Lowenthal—not to mention the party managers, who at the end of November pressed the president to stop the rot at the United Nations.

Loy Henderson recalled later a telephone conversation in late November with Herschel Johnson, the State Department's deputy head of the American delegation to the United Nations. Henderson asked if American representatives had been engaged in any "arm-twisting." Johnson, evidently under considerable tension, actually burst into tears: "Loy, forgive me for breaking down like this, but Dave Niles called us here a couple of days ago and said that the President had instructed him to tell us that, by God, he wanted us to get busy and get all the votes that we possibly could; that there would be hell if the voting went the wrong way."[75]

Clark Clifford took an active part in the lobby. During a series of interviews given in 1949, he made the following graphic statement: "I was concerned that it might not go through and talked with the representatives of other nations about it. We went for it. It was because the White House was for it that it went through. I kept the ramrod up the State Department's butt."[76]

Clifford conferred with the Philippines ambassador in Washington on November 28.[77] The Philippine president, Carlos Rojas, had already come under considerable American pressure—a cable from two Supreme Court justices and one from ten senators, both warning him of the consequences in the United States if his country did not change its antipartition vote. By the end of the day the Philippine delegate was ready to vote for partition.[78]

Liberia, which had abstained on November 25, was another prime target for the Zionist lobby. Liberia was dependent upon its rubber exports, the major part of which were bought by Firestone Rubber. On Niles's suggestion the Liberian delegate to the United Nations was warned that if he did not change his vote to a positive one, former Secretary of State Stettinius would use his business connections to see that he did. Stettinius got Harvey Firestone, fearful of a Jewish boycott of his products, to advise Liberian president Tubman that if his country's vote were not revised the Firestone company would have to reconsider its plans to extend its holdings in his country. On November 29 Liberia voted for partition.[79]

Greece, though dependent on U.S. aid under the Truman Doctrine, was one country that did not change its vote. Some warnings were transmitted to the Greeks by Zionists and members of the administration in New York. David Niles tried to exert some pressure through a leading Boston businessman of Greek extraction. But apparently the pressure did not come from persons high up enough in the administration, or it came too late.[80]

The Central and Latin American countries were also prime targets for the lobby. The Cuban delegate, Guillermo Belt, informed State Department officials that one Latin American country had changed its vote in return for seventy-five thousand dollars; another delegation, believed to be that of Costa

Rica, had turned down forty thousand dollars, though it was ordered subsequently by its government to change its vote to positive.[81]

Cuba, Haiti, and even France all came under pressure to vote for partition. The French, fearful of adverse reaction by Arabs in their North African colonies, preferred not to commit themselves. Bernard Baruch, mobilized by David Niles, delivered a stiff warning to the French delegate that the United States would cut off its aid if France voted against partition. This, together with last-minute instructions from French premier Leon Blum (with whom Weizmann had spoken), led finally to a positive French vote.[82]

On Saturday afternoon, November 29, 1947, the UN General Assembly convened at Flushing Meadow for the decisive vote. The result, transmitted live on radio around the world, showed a comfortable majority for partition (map 1): thirty-three for, thirteen against, and ten abstentions.

Nine of the seventeen countries that had abstained on November 25 still abstained. Seven switched their votes in favor of partition. The Arabs had manged to persuade just one abstainer to switch to a negative vote—Greece. One former affirmative vote was lost to the Zionists when Chile switched to abstention.[83]

Truman might well have felt gratified that his efforts and, even more, those of his staff had produced the desired result. He probably took satisfaction in the congratulations that poured in. On December 3 Congressman Celler congratulated him for "the effective work you did with regard to the Palestine Resolution passed by the U.N. General Assembly."[84]

On December 8 Truman received a private visit from Eddie Jacobson and Abe Granoff. As Granoff recalled later, it had been *his* idea for once to call on the president, this time not to ask him for anything but simply to thank him. As usual they paid their own fares from Kansas City to Washington. "And we two poor guys dug into our little bank accounts and went there. We were ushered in and stayed quite a while. . . . we said, 'Mr. President, we came here once in our lives not asking you for anything. Just to say thank you and God bless you.'"[85]

Truman told them that he and he alone had been responsible for swinging the votes of several delegates.[86]

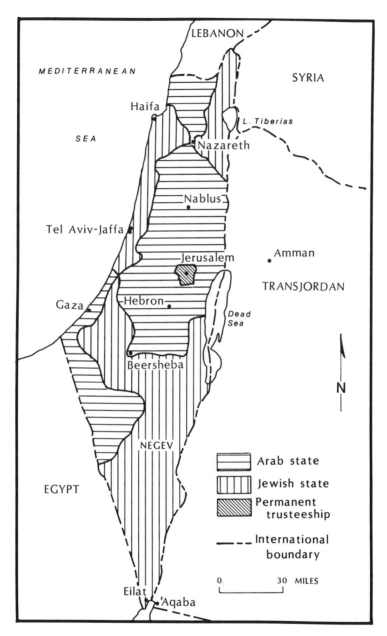

Map 1. The United Nations Partition Plan, November 1947

On December 12 Jacobson wrote Truman that he and Granoff had written an editorial for the January edition of the B'nai B'rith magazine, *National Jewish Monthly*, "to tell American Jews that it had been Truman's leadership which had secured the necessary two-thirds vote for partition." The magazine's editorial, unsigned, duly gave Truman personal credit for having instructed the American delegation to the United Nations to use its influence.[87]

But although Truman may have savored, if only ephemerally, the personal and political accolades of old friends and party members, it is highly unlikely that he foresaw the consequences of the UN partition vote. Truman could not have known that war would break out in Palestine on the morrow of the vote. Much less was he yet really persuaded that a Jewish state was necessary to solve the Jewish problem.

The UN partition resolution was a recommendation only with no machinery to enforce it. Those voting for partition had done so on the assumption that it could be effected peaceably and that the two successor states (and the internationalized "State of Jerusalem") would enter into an economic union. None of these assumptions were translated into reality. Furthermore, the civil war in Palestine would be fought during a period of grave and deepening crisis in Europe.

TEN

The Retreat from Partition

The day after the passage of the UN partition resolution, civil war erupted in Palestine. Until the end of March 1948 the Palestinian Arabs retained the upper hand and through their control of Palestine's arterial roads threatened to carve up the Jewish community into isolated islands. That month the Yishuv's military and political fortunes sank to their lowest. But in April 1948 the Hagana defense forces went on the offensive, and by May 14, the date designated for independence, the nascent State of Israel had established territorial contiguity between most Jewish settlements (including those in the Arab state) and secured most of the areas allotted to it by the United Nations.[1]

During the first three months of 1948, when the Yishuv seemed threatened with military disaster, the Cold War in Europe was escalating. On February 25 the legitimate government in Czechoslovakia was overthrown by a Communist coup; on March 5 General Lucius Clay, U.S. military governor of the American-occupied zone in Germany, cabled the director of intelligence of the U.S. Army in Washington to warn that war with the Soviets might come "with dramatic suddenness";[2] at the beginning of April the Soviets began to hinder the passage of Western convoys to West Berlin—the Berlin blockade had begun.

The American military establishment was ill-equipped to counter Soviet conventional forces in Europe. An army that had numbered 3.5 million men in May 1945 was by March 1946 reduced to 400,000, mostly new recruits.[3] Because of the tense situation in Europe, Truman reintroduced conscription in March 1948.

Against this background, Truman was called on by the State Department during the spring of 1948 to approve an American retreat from partition.

THE RETREAT FROM PARTITION

On November 14, 1947, that is, two weeks prior to the passage of the UN Palestine resolution, the State Department had imposed an arms embargo on Israel and its Arab neighbors. The Zionists felt that the American embargo worked primarily against them. Until the summer of 1948 the Arabs continued to receive arms shipments from the British under existing contracts. Israel was reduced to smuggling arms in from Eastern Europe. In addition, the Zionists claimed, it was they who had accepted the UN partition resolution and the Arabs who were opposing it with armed force.

The embargo was made public only on December 5, 1947. David Niles explained to the Zionists that he, Clifford, and even Truman had learned of the State Department move only *after* its publication. But Truman, being opposed to any American military intervention in Palestine and the use by either side of American arms, had agreed immediately.[4]

The Zionists appealed repeatedly to the State Department, and Weizmann directly to President Truman, to lift the embargo, but with no result. A letter from Weizmann to Truman in April 1948, at one of the bleakest moments for Israel in the war, expresses well the sentiment of the Zionists at that time:

Having recognized the right of our people to independence last November, the great powers now expose them to the risk of extermination and do not even grant them the arms to provide for their own defence. Arab aggression is now more confident than ever. . . . The practical question now is whether your Administration will proceed to leave our people unarmed in the face of an attack which it apparently feels unable to stop. . . . The choice of our people, Mr. President, is between Statehood and extermination.[5]

The arms embargo provided a lively topic for many domestic political debates and became an issue for which Truman was held to account. In June 1948 the Democratic party plank on Palestine included the resolution: "We favor the revision of the arms embargo to accord the State of Israel the right of self-defense." But Truman's administration did not lift the embargo. It even refused an Israeli request for armored plate to protect passenger buses against the Arabs' armed attacks.

During December 1947 and January 1948, a general consensus on Palestine developed within the American administration. This held that because of the war in Palestine partition could not be implemented except by force. But it was taken as axiomatic that American military involvement in support of a Jewish state would jeopardize the national interest in the entire Middle East. Not only would the Arabs impose sanctions against American businesses but the introduction of any UN force would probably provoke the Soviet Union to extend its influence (and the Cold War) into the area.[6]

Given the blatant discrepancies between American commitments overseas and the mobilized manpower available, military intervention in the Middle East, even as part of a UN force, was hardly even an option. On February 12, 1948, at a meeting of the National Security Council, the Joint Chiefs of Staff warned Truman that the dispatch of any sizable ground forces to Palestine would require partial mobilization.[7] One week later, Major General Alfred W. Greunther, head of the Joint Chiefs, told Truman that the implementation of the partition plan by force would require a minimum of 80,000 and a maximum of 160,000 American troops.[8]

Truman had declared his opposition to the dispatch of American troops to Palestine as early as August 1945. The deepening crisis in Europe served only to reinforce his position.

Because of American pressures and lobbying during the last stages of the General Assembly, it was now generally believed that the partition plan finally passed by the United Nations was an American one, for whose implementation the United States now bore a heavy responsibility. Therefore, the State Department concluded, it was incumbent upon the United States to announce that it had become convinced that partition was not a practical solution and to initiate a special session of the United Nations, at which the United States would propose a temporary trusteeship for Palestine, pending agreement between the two communities on a final solution.[9]

On February 9, 1948, Truman received Judge Joseph Proskauer of the American Jewish Committee. Proskauer received the impression that the president had no intention whatever of intervening in the Palestine issue: "He was satisfied with issuing general guidelines and leaving the practical initiatives in the hands of Marshall and his aides."[10]

Truman confirmed this on February 19, 1948, when he met with Secretary of State Marshall. Truman reassured Marshall that he would support whichever course the department believed was right and that it could disregard politics.[11] But the State Department remained skeptical of the will or ability of the Truman White House to ignore the heavy domestic overtones of the Palestine problem.

THE BIPARTISAN
APPROACH FAILS

Secretary of Defense Forrestal was still pursuing his lone campaign to include Palestine in the bipartisan agreement on foreign policy that generally held between the two parties, but he was not making much progress. On December 10, 1947, he had spoken with Senator Vandenburg, the Republican champion of bipartisanship, who reported the feeling in Republican circles that the Democrats had exploited the Palestine issue politically and that the Republicans were entitled to do the same. Three days later Forrestal approached Governor Dewey, the Republican candidate for the presidency. Dewey concurred in principle but doubted if agreement was in fact possible because of "the intemperate attitude of the Jewish people who had taken Palestine as the emotional symbol" and because he did not believe that the Democratic party would be willing to forego the advantages of the Jewish vote.[12]

Concerned by the Republican leaders' cynicism, in January 1948 Forrestal went to Truman. He secured the president's permission to make a demiofficial offer to the Republicans to include Palestine in the bipartisan agreement. On January 21 Forrestal reported back to the State Department that the majority of Republican leaders had accepted the agreement, with the exception of Dewey, who remained skeptical. Forrestal suggested that Secretary Marshall personally take up the issue with Truman.[13]

At the beginning of February, Forrestal met with Gale Sullivan, vice-chairman of the Democratic National Committee. He urged that the party "eat crow" on the UN partition resolution and warned that if American forces were drawn into any conflict in Palestine it would spark off in the United States "the biggest wave of anti-Semitism . . . that [had] ever been imagined."[14]

Forrestal's efforts did not go unnoticed, or apparently unmonitored, by the Zionists. During his last months in office, he suspected he was under continuous surveillance by Zionist agents. In part his suspicions reflected the severe mental illness that would consume him. But they were also not entirely unfounded. Close associates recalled that at the height of the Palestine controversy Forrestal had had police follow him. The police had apprehended two photographers employed by the Zionists in the hope of securing shots of Forrestal visiting Arab embassies.[15]

On February 6, 1948, Forrestal was warned off by none other than Bernard Baruch, not exactly an ardent Zionist himself. Baruch warned Forrestal that he was already identified with the opposition to the UN policy on Palestine to a degree not in his best interests. Although Baruch did not approve of the Zionists' actions, he believed that the Democratic party could only lose by trying to get the government's policy reversed. Forrestal made two further approaches to Secretary of State Marshall, on February 12 and 18, 1948, and then apparently gave up.[16]

For the present a political standoff was maintained. While the State Department was preparing an orderly retreat from the UN partition plan, no event of significance on the domestic political calendar required the intervention of the White House.

At a meeting on February 12, 1948, attended by Dean Rusk (director of the Department of Special Political Affairs, soon to be renamed Office of the United Nations), Marshall, and George Kennan (director of the newly formed Policy Planning Staff), it was agreed to mark time in the hope that events in Palestine would force the Security Council to take matters in hand by itself instituting a UN trusteeship. Bearing in mind the ever-present risk of a domestic public opinion backlash, Marshall preferred *not* to put forward trusteeship as an American initiative.[17]

DOMESTIC POLITICAL
CONSIDERATIONS

On February 17 the delicate political balance was upset by a Democratic defeat of traumatic proportions in a congressional by-election. The special election, which took place in the Bronx, was the first test of strength for the secessionist Wallace movement. The Democrats' candidate, the relatively unknown Karl Propper, was defeated by the American Labor party's Leo Isaacson, a Wallace supporter. The defeat was by a two-to-one margin in a district normally controlled by Democratic party boss Ed Flynn.

Some analysts predicted that in the presidential elections, Wallace's candidacy would split the Democratic vote and thereby throw New York, California, Michigan, Illinois, and Pennsylvania to the Republicans, ensuring their victory. Even though the election result did not in fact reflect the true strength of the Wallace movement, it did serve as a tonic and almost sent Democrats into fits of hysteria.[18]

Truman's popularity had begun declining since the fall of 1947, and he now faced further defections. On February 20, fifty-two southern congressmen condemned a vigorous message on civil rights that Truman had sent to the Congress earlier that month. The Democrats began to look for an alternative candidate for president.

On March 15 *Time* magazine commented that only "a political miracle, or extraordinary stupidity on the part of the Republicans can save the Democratic party, after 16 years of power, from a debacle in November."[19]

The Bronx electoral district was 55 percent Jewish, and the vote was seen also as a protest against Truman's vacillating Palestine policy and the arms embargo. During the campaign, both Isaacson and Wallace had played up the Palestine issue. Wallace had charged: "Truman talks like a Jew and acts like an

Arab." It was taken as a warning by Truman that "Palestine would rival the Cold War as an election issue in 1948."[20]

But notwithstanding the Bronx result, the State Department believed that the American public as a whole opposed any American military involvement in the Middle East. Its immediate objective was to defuse the situation in Palestine and to prevent the conflict there from spreading, thereby creating a situation in which the United States would be forced to intervene, perhaps even against Soviet forces.

At the end of February the department commissioned its own series of opinion polls designed to test the readiness of the public to send American troops to Palestine to implement partition. The poll found that general support for partition had dropped to 38 percent from a high of 65 percent the previous November; 83 percent of all those questioned and 61 percent of the Jews asked were *against* a unilateral American intervention. But in a separate poll 91 percent of the Jews favored the dispatch of American troops within the framework of a UN force, compared with 50 percent in favor in the general poll.[21]

Which Palestine strategy should the Truman White House therefore adopt in 1948? Would a more vigorous pro-Zionist policy recoup the Jewish vote, or should Truman write them off? Or did the State Department polls prove that promotion of the Zionist cause would cost Truman far more non-Jewish votes than he could hope to win from the Jews? One astute British observer commented on the polls: "The pro-Zionist voters could be appeased only by a policy which would alienate the larger number of voters who would object to the shedding of American blood in a Jewish cause."[22]

TRUMAN APPROVES
THE TRUSTEESHIP

While the Bronx election result was still being analyzed and digested by the Democratic party, the State Department took the next step to resolve the Palestine imbroglio at the United Nations. On February 21 it submitted a position paper to Truman stating that once it became apparent that the UN Security Council was unable to implement the November partition plan, "due to insufficient acquiescence on the part of the people of Palestine," the problem would be submitted to a special session of the General Assembly. It would then be self-evident that the peoples of Palestine were not ready for independence and that a trusteeship for an additional period was necessary.[23]

Truman approved the department's proposal, provided "that nothing should be presented to [the] Security Council that could be interpreted as a recession on our part from the position we took in the General Assembly."[24]

On February 24, 1948, Warren Austin, the American ambassador to the United Nations, in a speech that had Truman's stamp of approval told the Security Council: "The Security Council is authorized to take forceful measures with respect to Palestine to remove a threat to international peace. The Charter of the United Nations does not empower the Security Council to enforce a political settlement. . . . The Security Council's action, in other words, *is directed to keeping the peace and not to enforcing partition*."[25]

In a column headlined "The Wriggling President" in the *Washington Post*, the Alsop brothers complained about the lack of resolution in Truman's policy and stated the need "for a very necessary briefing of the press on the legal niceties" of Austin's speech.[26] The British Foreign Office saw clearly through the American subterfuge:

I think that Mr. Austin is in effect saying "For [internal U.S.] political reasons we cannot go back on our view that partition is the right course. But we have come to realise that it will produce a God-awful mess in solving which we shall have to take a major part. Therefore, it is now convenient for us to argue legally that that part of the Assembly resolution which in effect told the Security Council to enforce partition was wrong because it conflicted with the Council's powers under the Charter."[27]

The administration was giving due warning, even if wrapped in legal jargon, of its refusal to enforce the UN partition plan against Arab resistance. At the end of January 1948 Eleanor Roosevelt had warned Truman precisely against just such reticence:

If the United Nations does not put through and enforce the partition and protection of people in general in Palestine, we are facing a very serious situation in which its position for the future is at stake. . . .

If we do not take some stand to strengthen the UN organization at the present time, I shall not be surprised if Russia does, which will put us in a difficult position to say the least.

If the United Nations is going to be the instrument for peace, now is the crucial time to strengthen it.[28]

But Truman had been led to believe what the State Department still hoped—that given the state of war raging in Palestine, the UN Security Council would itself suspend the partition plan and set up a trusteeship in the country. So long as the United States took no initiative against partition, the White House need not fear any adverse Jewish reaction. But although Austin's February speech produced no domestic backlash, the tactical retreat on Palestine did not go entirely unnoticed.

Senator Francis Myers of Pennsylvania warned Truman that a few lower-level Democratic party leaders in his state had resigned and that many Jews in his constituency were bitter about the president and the party.[29] Conversely, William Philips, former under secretary of state and a member of the 1946 joint committee, gave Loy Henderson a message heartening to the State Department and duly passed on to Truman: "I believe the whole country, except the fanatical New York Zionists is sighing with relief this morning with the news that we are not committed to enforce the decision with respect to Palestine."[30]

At the end of February, Kermit Roosevelt and Virginia Gildersleeve (dean emeritus of Barnard College) set up in Washington the Committee for Justice and Peace in the Holy Land, a pressure group committed to the reversal of partition. The committee had a 100-member national council, which included well-known Protestant churchmen and educators who had once lived in the Middle East. The committee collaborated closely with the American Council for Judaism.[31]

Under political siege at home and confronted with grave threats and decisions abroad, President Truman was as usual weary of and perplexed by the Palestine problem. The UN partition plan had ignited a war in Palestine, one which the Jews were currently losing. If the State Department could manage a UN suspension of partition while avoiding any direct American responsibility or blame, then he might yet escape adverse domestic repercussions. In the meantime he was determined at all costs to evade Zionist pressures.

EDDIE JACOBSON AGAIN

The Zionists had been monitoring events in Washington and at Lake Success, New York, headquarters of the United Nations. As early as January 1948 they had arrived at an accurate prognosis. The State Department officials, once more in full control of Palestine policy, were determined to "slow down the implementation and eventually go back on the decision of the United Nations Assembly." Many Zionist leaders were convinced that "the mass pressure of public opinion" was required immediately to induce President Truman to reassume control of policy, "as he [had] on several occasions before and during the meetings of the United Nations Assembly."[32]

The Zionists were fully aware of the differences of opinion between the State Department and the White House on the question of the Jewish vote. They were told by party officials that "the top people in State and Defense don't care a thing about the elections. They are telling the President that if he has any courage at all, he will be willing to lose next Fall if that is the way to safeguard American security. . . . all this comes down to bases and oil and the whole problem of building up our position vis-à-vis Russia."[33]

In London, Dr. Chaim Weizmann, Zionist elder statesman (albeit recently deposed from the presidency of the World Zionist Organization), was besieged by phone calls and telegrams from New York, urging him to come to the United States to exert his personal influence at the White House (the previous November, Weizmann's intervention had persuaded Truman to issue instructions to the UN delegation to work for the inclusion of the Negev in the Jewish state). Weizmann changed his plans to travel to Palestine and booked passage on the *Queen Mary* for New York.[34]

On February 3 the Jewish Agency staff consulted in Washington with a galaxy of advisers to assess the situation. They decided on a two-tiered strategy: to stress the merits and justice of the UN decision and its "coincidence with long-term American national interests" and to lobby leading figures in both political parties, stressing that "it would be most unwise, from a strictly electioneering point of view, to jettison the UN decision." Among those to be lobbied were Democrats General William Donovan (founder of the Office of Strategic Services), Eleanor Roosevelt, Adlai Stevenson (alternate U.S. delegate to the United Nations), General Hilldring, and leaders of the Republican party, including Governor Dewey, John Foster Dulles, and Senator Vandenberg. Appointments were to be sought for Weizmann as soon as possible with both the president and Secretary of State Marshall.[35]

Weizmann arrived in New York on February 4. David Niles was asked to use his connections to secure him an interview with Truman. Niles agreed with the assessment of Felix Frankfurter that Weizmann was the only one who could influence Truman to remain true to his previous promises. But Niles did not think the president would be willing to receive Weizmann before the completion of general discussions on Palestine within the global context.[36]

Weizmann would wait for nearly one and a half months before Truman met with him. On March 12 Truman told Eddie Jacobson why he had closed the White House to the Zionist lobby. Truman complained "how disrespectful and how mean certain Jewish leaders had been to him" and how they had "slandered and libeled" him. Truman had instructed his appointments secretary, Matt Connelly, to admit no more Zionists, especially not Abba Hillel Silver, "who had more than once raged into the office of the President of the United States and pounded his fist on his desk and shouted at him."[37]

It was Frank Goldman, president of B'nai B'rith, who thought of asking Eddie Jacobson to persuade his old friend Truman to receive Weizmann.

In fact, Jacobson had already approached Truman at the end of January to ask him for a public statement reaffirming his support for partition—but to no avail. On February 2 Jacobson wrote to Truman to inform him that Meir Steinbrink, a justice of the New York Supreme Court and national chairman of B'nai B'rith's Anti-Defamation League, was about to publish a "blistering letter on Palestine," attacking the "sabotaging" of the partition plan by government officials. Jacobson and Granoff had evidently visited the White House just a few days before and had been told "off the record" of the president's efforts on behalf of Palestine. In his letter Jacobson now asked for some general, public statement from the president to let Jews know what was "really going on."[38]

In his reply Truman returned to what was by now a recurrent theme of his—that he could have had the Palestine problem cleared up long ago had it not been for outside (i.e., Jewish) meddling:

I think he [Steinbrink] would make a mistake in issuing a statement of that sort because progress is being made along the lines about which I spoke to you the other day but nearly every time we get to the point of an agreement in this matter somebody upsets the applecart and it wouldn't surprise me a bit if they didn't upset this one before we can get it working. I sincerely hope that doesn't take place.[39]

Jacobson was prepared to be stubborn in defense of a cause that, as he saw it, had UN and presidential support. So when Frank Goldman called him, well past midnight on February 21, 1948, asking him to get Weizmann an interview with the president, Jacobson telegraphed the president immediately. He knew Truman was on a vacation cruise so he addressed his telegram to Matt Connelly, asking him to forward it to Truman on board the presidential yacht: "I have asked very little in the way of favors during all our years of friendship, but I am begging you to see Dr. Weizmann as soon as possible. I assure you I would not plead to you for any other of our leaders."[40]

But Truman refused to become embroiled again with Palestine, preferring still to leave the State Department a free hand. In a private reply to Jacobson written from Key West, Truman insisted that there was nothing new that Weizmann could possibly tell him and explained why:

The situation has been a headache to me for two and a half years. The Jews are so emotional, and the Arabs are so difficult to talk with that it is almost impossible to get anything done. The British have, of course, been exceedingly noncooperative. The Zionists, of course, have expected a big stick approach on our part, and naturally have been disappointed when we can't do that. I hope it will work out all right, but *I have about come to the conclusion that the situation is not solvable as presently set up.*[41]

Truman evidently concurred with the State Department view that the UN partition plan had to be placed on hold to avert the spread of hostilities in Palestine and possibly beyond its borders.

The Zionists tried all possible avenues to gain Weizmann access to the White House. On March 8 Eliahu Epstein wrote to Judge Sam Rosenman:

Failure of the partition plan will be the seemingly inevitable end-result if the American delegation hews to the State Department line. . . . It is clear now that *only the President* can countermand this obstruction of the implementation of the General Assembly recommendation.

I am aware of how important a factor you have been, in the past, in influencing the President to a right attitude on the Palestine issue. There has never been so great a need for persuasion as now.[42]

On that same day John M. Redding, publicity director for the Democratic National Committee, reported to Truman that since Austin's statement of February 24, "we have Zionist Jews in the office every day . . . and the pressure is building up a terrific head of steam." Truman replied: "It's no use putting pressure on the committee, the Palestine issue will be handled here and there'll be no politics."[43]

The Zionists were seemingly at a dead end. Nothing could apparently move Truman. What made matters worse was that throughout this critical month of March 1948 David Niles was indisposed because of illness. This meant that Truman failed to receive his regular assessment of the reactions in the Jewish community—particularly to Austin's statement of February 24.[44] It meant also that the one man inside the White House who might have secured Weizmann an audience was absent.

But now came Eddie Jacobson's chance to enter the pages of Zionist mythology. Rebuffed by Truman's letter at the end of February, Jacobson determined to see the president in person when Truman returned to Washington. On March 12 Jacobson flew to Washington and as usual got in to see the president immediately and without an appointment.[45]

On his way in Jacobson was warned by Matt Connelly *not* to discuss Palestine. But that was precisely why he had come. As soon as Jacobson broached the subject, Truman turned "tense and grim." Jacobson recalled later that he had thought that his "dear friend, the President of the United States, was at that moment as close to being an Anti-Semite as a man could possibly be."[46]

Truman was in a bitter mood and told Jacobson how the Jews had slandered and libeled him when he had been in the Senate and from the moment he had entered the White House. Truman cut him short and made it almost impossible for Jacobson to pursue his theme: "he didn't want to discuss Palestine or the Jews or the Arabs or the British. . . . he was satisfied to let these subjects take their course through the United Nations."[47] Truman noted later in his memoirs: "I do not believe that in all our thirty years of friendship a sharp word had ever passed between Eddie and me, and I was sorry that Eddie had brought up the subject."[48]

Jacobson was later surprised at his own temerity in continuing to press his case. He reminded the president of his feelings for Weizmann, but Truman remained immovable. Jacobson felt crushed. Twenty-five years later Truman related that Jacobson had spent most of the interview with big tears rolling down his cheeks.[49] Then Jacobson noticed a miniature reproduction of a life-size statue of General Andrew Jackson that Truman had had erected in front of the Kansas City County courthouse. The figure of Jackson, Truman's lifelong hero, gave Jacobson his cue:

Well, Harry, I too have a hero, a man I never met but who is, I think, the greatest Jew who ever lived . . . Chaim Weizmann; [who] is a very sick man, almost broken in health, but he travelled thousands of miles just to see you and plead the cause of my people. Now you refuse to see him because you were insulted by some of our American Jewish leaders, even though you know that Weizmann had absolutely nothing to do with these insults, and would be the last man to be a party to them. It doesn't sound like you, Harry, because I thought that you could take this stuff they have been handing out.[50]

Jacobson's switch to the personal, invoking their respective heroes, was sheer inspiration. (Granoff later poked fun at this move, seeing that Eddie had yet even to meet Weizmann and had barely heard of him, though he conceded that the gambit had worked.)[51] As Jacobson finished, he noticed Truman drumming his fingers on his desk, a sign that he was changing his mind. Truman blurted out: "You win, you bald-headed s.o.b. . . . I will see him. Tell Matt to arrange this meeting as soon as possible after I return from New York on March 17."[52]

On the next day, March 13, Jacobson went to New York and met Weizmann for the first time. He was overwhelmed by the charisma of the Zionist leader. They formed a close working relationship, based on mutual recognition of each other's standing. On March 15 Jacobson called Matt Connelly at the White House, who set up a meeting between Weizmann and the president for March 18, with strict orders that it was to be "off the record." Weizmann invited Jacobson to accompany him, but it was decided that as a figure familiar to White House reporters he would attract unwanted attention.

Weizmann was ushered in through the side East Gate. Truman explained why he had put off seeing the Zionist leader until now. Next he told Weizmann what the basis of his interest in the Jewish problem was (presumably still the solution of the Jewish DP problem) and that his *"primary concern was to see justice done without bloodshed."*[53] Weizmann recalled that Truman had told him he was still resolved "to press forward with partition." Truman's recollection was slightly, perhaps significantly, different: "I felt that he had reached a full understanding of my policy and that I knew what it was he wanted."[54] Truman's version of their meeting is not identical to Weizmann's, and no official record was kept.

The Zionists' achievement—Weizmann's audience with the president—must be seen in its proper perspective. In making an exceptional gesture to his old friend Jacobson and to Weizmann, the aging Zionist statesman, Truman was not in fact making any concrete concessions. During the months of February and March 1948, Truman was privy to developments in Palestine and at the United Nations, and was in full agreement with the State Department prognosis that partition should not be enforced militarily. This issue quite obviously preoccupied him when he talked with Weizmann, and he hinted as much. But Truman did not apprise Weizmann of the trusteeship option then under consideration by his administration.

ELEVEN

The American Trusteeship
Proposal

THE WHITE HOUSE–
STATE DEPARTMENT DEBATE

On the day after Truman's interview with Weizmann, Warren
Austin, the American delegate to the UN Security Council, proposed that partition be suspended since it could not be implemented by peaceful means. Austin asked to convene a special
session of the General Assembly to consider the establishment
of a temporary trusteeship over Palestine "to maintain the peace
and to afford the Jews and Arabs . . . further opportunity to
reach an agreement regarding the future government of that
country . . . without prejudice to the character of the eventual
political settlement."[1]

The great rift that was to open up between the White House
and the State Department the next day was caused not by any
differences over essentials but by the department's poor sense
of timing and lack of coordination with the White House. It was
a difference over tactics, not strategy.

It will be recalled that on February 22 Truman had approved
Austin's statement at the United Nations that the Security Council was not empowered to implement partition by force. Truman's only proviso had been that, for understandable domestic
reasons, the United States itself should not initiate any move
against partition.

But at the beginning of March as conditions in Palestine deteriorated, State Department officials urged the suspension of partition in favor of trusteeship. On March 5 Secretary of State Marshall, with cabinet approval, deferred to Austin's advice that within a week to ten days the situation would mature, showing the irreconcilability of the Arab and Jewish positions. On March 9 Marshall instructed Austin that in the event of a special assembly on Palestine the American government would support a UN trusteeship for Palestine.[2] Austin was informed of the president's approval of the draft statement on the retreat from partition.[3]

The State Department demarche during the first week of March provoked a last-ditch counter by Clark Clifford. Clifford suggested to Eliahu Epstein that he send over Max Lowenthal, his assistant on Palestine, to gather background material for his memoranda on Palestine to the president. Lowenthal spent several hours in the Zionists' Washington office and returned to the White House with a stack of material.[4]

Lowenthal proceeded to draft Clifford's memoranda.[5] The line he proposed was that American support for partition was consistent with American interests in the Middle East and in accord with traditional policy in the area. If partition was not implemented, Russia might intervene "in the guise of preserving world peace and defending the UN Charter." In response to State Department warnings of Arab sanctions or possible defections to the Soviet camp, Clifford's reply was that the Arabs needed American dollars more than the United States needed Arab oil and that it would be suicidal for the Arabs to align themselves with the Soviets. Finally, the defeat of a UN resolution at American instigation would constitute a grave blow to the new international body. In the final draft of the memorandum sent to the president, Clifford commented acidly on Austin's speech of February 24: "In large part, it seemed to be the sophistries of a lawyer attempting to tell what we *could not* do to support the United Nations—in direct contradiction to your numerous statements that we meant to do everything possible to *support* the United Nations."[6]

Truman claimed in his memoirs that he was never convinced by the Arabist arguments of the diplomats.[7] He *was* concerned, however, about possible Soviet exploitation of the Palestine conflict and was *not* prepared to have partition imposed by outside force—as seemed to be necessary in March 1948. On March 12 a commission to monitor events in Palestine, composed of the UN Security Council's five permanent members, reported back: "Present indications point to the inescapable conclusion that when the Mandate is terminated Palestine is likely to suffer severely from administrative chaos and widespread strife and bloodshed."[8]

On March 16 Marshall instituted the plan he had held up for tactical reasons on March 5. At the Security Council the Soviet representative, Andrei Gromyko, had challenged the American interpretation of the Security Council's authority to deal with the Palestine problem. Marshall feared a Soviet initiative to persist with partition in Palestine might provoke a further military deterioration there, necessitating outside intervention.[9]

Primarily because of his fears of this Soviet initiative, Marshall instructed Austin on March 16 to ask the Security Council to divest itself of responsibility for Palestine and consider the security problem there distinct from the UN partition resolution. Once the Security Council suspended partition, the Americans could introduce trusteeship, to which Truman had already given his backing on March 5.[10]

On March 18, the same day that Truman received Weizmann, the Palestine commission reported its failure to arrange any compromise between Arabs and Jews. It concluded that steps should be taken immediately to restore peace to Palestine and to "reach an agreement between the interested parties regarding the future government of Palestine. . . . [to which end] a temporary trusteeship for Palestine should be established under the Trusteeship Council of the United Nations."[11]

The State Department considered the commission's recommendations to have met the president's proviso that the Security Council itself should first suspend partition before any American initiative on trusteeship was made. Therefore, on March 19, without further consultation with or confirmation from the White House, Austin announced at the United Nations what would become the notorious American trusteeship proposal.

THE DOMESTIC BACKLASH

The domestic political backlash was immediate and severe. It took the White House completely by surprise because there had been no prior indications of opposition, not even after Austin's first speech of February 24. The presence of David Niles was now sorely missed by Truman.

Rabbi Silver castigated the trusteeship proposal as "a shocking reversal" and "a fatal capitulation" to Arab threats. In Palestine, in a similar vein, David Ben-Gurion called it "a surrender to Arab terror." A *New York Times* editorial stated that the White House was "utterly at sea" on Palestine. A subheading cried out: "Bewilderment Follows Austin's Palestine Bombshell." [12]

In Kansas City, Eddie Jacobson, informed of the proposal by Abe Granoff by phone at 5:30 P.M., was completely bewildered. He received messages from all over the United States telling him how untrustworthy his friend the president had turned out to be and what a "traitor" Truman was to the Jewish people. The one exception was Weizmann.

On the afternoon of Austin's speech, Sam Rosenman visited Truman, who asked Rosenman to contact Weizmann as soon as possible and tell him that the policy they had talked about the day before still stood and that Weizmann should not attach any importance to the Austin statement. Rosenman went to Weizmann's hotel, the Shoreham Washington, told him of Truman's distress at the Austin statement, and reassured him that Truman would remain faithful to his word. [13]

Weizmann then rang up Jacobson to tell him not to be disappointed and that he did not believe Truman had known about the State Department initiative when they had met on March 18. But more important, Weizmann reminded Jacobson of his own still-vital role: "Don't forget for a single moment that Harry S. Truman is the most powerful single man in the world. You have a job to do so keep the White House doors open." [14]

Weizmann was evidently trying to boost Jacobson's morale. His own private thoughts were a little less sanguine. He wrote a private note to his secretary in London: "I need hardly tell you that the trip here was not very successful. The unexpected and sudden let down by the American Government will, I am afraid, have tragic effects, and the only thing which is left for me to do is to go on with our work and await better times."[15]

With Austin's announced change in U.S. policy, the American Jewish Committee found itself in a peculiarly sensitive position. The committee had originally proposed its own trusteeship plan to UNSCOP, but following the administration's support for partition it had given the UN resolution its blessing. After nine days of internal debate the committee passed a resolution confirming its continuing support for partition. It also stated: "No reasons have been advanced to the American people to alter their belief that these objectives can be attained consistently with the security of the United States which we, together with all other American citizens, will always regard as paramount."[16]

The American Jewish Committee's continuing support for partition was crucial in maintaining a united Jewish front against trusteeship.

The American Council for Judaism was the only Jewish organization to support trusteeship. Loy Henderson, the council, and the recently formed Committee for Justice and Peace in the Holy Land all coordinated activities. On March 20, 1948, George Levison reported to Elmer Berger that he had spoken to Henderson, Kermit Roosevelt, and Lessing Rosenwald. Henderson had urged that the council send a strong letter of support to Secretary of State Marshall and give it wide publicity. He thought that the battle in Washington had only just begun and stated that terrific pressures were being brought to bear. Henderson wanted them to do all they could "to put over the fact that there [were] Jews who [were] not Zionists." Levison also told Berger: "Kim [Kermit Roosevelt] says he is going to try to get his group to send wires too. He and Loy both feel that the new policy took great courage on Truman's part, as it is a tough move from the domestic political side, and was made only because the President was finally convinced (mainly by Forrestal) that the thing is too serious to play politics with."[17]

But the support offered by the anti-Zionist groups was of little consequence amidst the internal political conflict in Washington. Truman took personal offense at what he considered to be the machinations of the State Department bureaucrats, Henderson in particular. The backing of the splinter American Council for Judaism was meager compensation.

Given the importance Truman set on his word, it appears that what irked him most was that he had reassured Weizmann just the day before of his support for partition uninformed that the trusteeship option was about to be announced. Although Truman had told Weizmann that his primary concern was to avert further bloodshed, he still felt that the State Department, by not consulting him in advance of the Austin speech, had left him looking like "a liar and a double-crosser." With both Marshall and Under Secretary Lovett absent from Washington, Truman laid the blame on "the third and fourth levels of the State Depart[ment,] who have always wanted to cut my throat." [18]

On Saturday, March 20, when Truman read the morning headlines concerning Austin's announcement, he became furious. He called Clark Clifford to come over to the White House "right away"; it was 7:30 A.M. As Clifford recalled later, Truman was preoccupied with what Weizmann would think. Clifford's recollection is even more lurid than Truman's diary entries. According to him, Truman had raged: "How could this have happened? I assured Chaim Weitzmann [*sic*] I would stick to it. He must think I am a shitass." [19]

Clifford phoned Lovett, on holiday in Florida, to ask what had happened. Lovett professed surprise and explained that there had been an understanding in the top echelons of the department that they would try to get partition through but if they failed they would try trusteeship in order not to leave a vacuum. When Clifford called over two other State Department officials, they both claimed that Marshall had authorized the Austin speech in advance.[20] Clifford too was furious at the political setback suffered by Truman and also blamed the lower ranks at the State Department, who, he believed, had played havoc with policy under an ignorant secretary of state: "Marshall didn't know his ass from a hole in the ground. Marshall left every one of those who had done this thing to the President in power. Not a hair singed. . . . But every Jew thought that Truman was a no good son-of-a-bitch." [21]

Further trouble came from a different quarter: Eleanor Roosevelt wrote to Marshall stating her intention to resign from the

UN delegation. Although she felt the United States had a moral obligation to the Jews under the Balfour Declaration, her primary concern was the harm being done to the United Nations: "I feel at the present time that we have more or less buried the UN." The disagreement over Palestine also reflected Mrs. Roosevelt's reservations about Truman's alleged "increased deference to military considerations" in the formulation of foreign policy. She advised that she would have to state her feelings in public and reply honestly to those asking her about her position.[22] She sent a copy of the letter to Truman under cover of "a very frank and unpleasant letter": "I am afraid that the Democratic Party is, for the moment, in a very weak position, with the Southern revolt and the big cities and many liberals appalled by our latest moves. . . . I realise that I am an entirely unimportant cog in the wheel of our work in the United Nations, but I have offered my resignation to the Secretary."[23]

Truman knew that Eleanor Roosevelt's withdrawal from the UN delegation would be a disaster for the administration and that without her endorsement he had little chance of clinching the election in November.[24] He hastily reassured her that the trusteeship proposal was but a temporary measure to fill the vacuum that would be created in Palestine at the end of the mandate and was not meant to be a substitute for partition. He appealed to her not to resign: "I would deplore as calamitous your withdrawal from the work of the United Nations at this critical time. Such a step is unthinkable. . . . May I appeal to you with the utmost sincerity to abandon any thought of relinquishing the post which you hold for which you have unique qualifications."[25] After much hesitation, she agreed to stay on with the UN delegation. It was a decision she would live to regret.

On March 23 Oscar Ewing's brain trust discussed the Palestine issue and heard an analysis by economist Robert Nathan of the critical effect it would have on the elections that fall. Ewing reported to Truman on the meeting and explained also that the critical military position of the Yishuv required the lifting of the arms embargo. Truman did not respond.[26]

The next day Truman summoned the senior State Department officials responsible to a "clarification" at the White House. Secretary of State Marshall, Loy Henderson, Dean Rusk, and

Charles Bohlen were confronted by President Truman, Clark Clifford, David Niles (who had returned to work on March 23), Max Lowenthal, Matt Connelly, Oscar Ewing, and Howard McGrath.

Truman told the meeting that he would give a press conference the next day at which he would explain the temporary nature of the trusteeship and announce that he still supported partition. The atmosphere was charged with tension, especially between Henderson and Niles.[27] Henderson elaborated on the damage that would be caused to American interests in the Arab world if they supported partition. Truman cut him short, saying it was not the United States that had proposed partition, and he had not yet heard a new or convincing argument from Henderson. Ewing argued how much the trusteeship announcement had impaired faith in the American government, especially among the small states, which would in the future hesitate before relying on the United States.[28]

The State Department officials argued that they were trying to secure a truce in Palestine and claimed that they could get both the Jews and the Arabs to agree to a truce and trusteeship. The department was given the chance to try to establish a truce. But if an agreement could not be obtained, "United States support for immediate implementation of the Partition Plan would be reinstated."[29]

At the close of the meeting Truman asked Clifford to prepare the statement for the next day. The State Department was effectively shut out. Clifford claimed later that he and his assistants worked all night on the draft, which was not ready until 9:00 A.M. the morning of the press conference. The hand that drafted the president's announcement was Max Lowenthal's.[30] Truman's press statement went as follows:

Unfortunately, it has become clear that the partition plan cannot be carried out at this time by peaceful means. We could not undertake to impose this solution on the people of Palestine by the use of American troops, both on Charter grounds and as a matter of national policy. . . .

Trusteeship is not proposed as a substitute for the partition plan but as an effort to fill the vacuum soon to be created by the termination of the mandate on May 15. The trusteeship does not prejudice the character of the final political settlement. It would establish the conditions of order which are essential to a peaceful solution.[31]

When asked about the considerable criticism of American support for partition in the first place and whether the difficulties could not have been foreseen at the time, Truman ad-libbed: "Did I ever tell you that any schoolboy's hindsight is worth all the President's foresight?"[32] The journalists were amused, but it is doubtful whether the Zionists appreciated the president's sense of humor.

A STATE DEPARTMENT COUP?

The trusteeship episode caused a severe crisis of confidence between the White House and the State Department and plunged their relations to an all-time low. The incident has since provoked much historical controversy over whether there was a State Department "conspiracy" against White House policy. The conspiracy theory originated with Truman and has been adopted by several historians since.[33]

In effect the crisis of confidence was primarily because of the State Department's attempts to exclude domestic political considerations. Truman had been kept advised on all the major steps that had led to the trusteeship proposal. He had approved in advance Austin's speech of February 24, itself a clear indication that the United States would not help impose partition by force; the State Department draft of March 5 that announced the abandonment of partition had been approved by Truman's cabinet; Under Secretary Lovett claimed later that on March 8 the president had given definite authorization to proceed with trusteeship if they failed to get approval of the UN resolution; and on March 16 Marshall's instructions to Austin, authorizing his speech of March 19, had been shown to the president.[34]

The problem was that the State Department had not advised Truman *when* the trusteeship announcement was to be made. As Truman himself later told Marshall, had he only known the date in advance he could have taken measures to avoid "the political blast of the press."[35] Charlie Ross, Truman's press secretary, confirmed this essential point in an internal, handwritten memorandum dated March 29:

What caused all the trouble? The cause lay in the fact that no final check had been made with the President before Austin spoke. He had assumed that the alternative plan would not be urged till after a *vote in the Security Council* had demonstrated the impossibility of putting over the partition plan. At the least, the whole business had been handled with singular maladroitness by State. No pronouncement of the momentous nature of Austin's should have been made without prior consultation with the President or someone on his staff. . . . As it was, the reversal was without warning to the public and the President was placed in the most embarrassing position of his presidential career.[36]

It is possible, as has been suggested, that the officials deliberately refrained from obtaining a final clearance because of fears that the White House would abort the new move. But Professor Philip Jessup, of the staff of the UN delegation at the time, has claimed that it was *not* usual practice to seek presidential approval for statements once the general lines of policy had been laid down and cleared.[37]

It had been as clear to President Truman as to the State Department that the hostilities in Palestine ruled out the peaceful partition the United Nations had envisaged in November 1947. Truman's sole concern, for domestic reasons, was that the United States, and he personally, should not be saddled with the blame for the abandonment of the UN resolution. But it was a moot point apparently whether or not by March 19 the conciliatory machinery of the Security Council had been exhausted. On March 16 Marshall had instituted the American initiative to preempt and forestall a feared Soviet demarche and possible intervention. Perhaps Austin did jump the gun by not waiting on the Security Council's formal rejection of partition. But the Big Five's report of March 18 made it quite clear that the Security Council would suspend the partition plan, even with an American positive vote.[38]

Truman did *not* in fact oppose the trusteeship initiative per se. Even in retrospect he wrote: "My policy with regard to Palestine was not a commitment to any set of dates or circumstances; it was a dedication to the twin deal of international obligations and the relieving of human misery. In this sense, the State Department's trusteeship proposal was not contrary to my policy."[39] But he *did* blame the department for the electoral damage he sustained: "Anybody in the State Department should have known—and I am sure that some individual officers actually expected—that the Jews would read this proposal as a complete abandonment of the partition plan on which they so heavily counted."[40]

The State Department never reconciled itself to the subordination of policy making in Palestine to Truman's and the Democratic party's domestic political interests. Whether they *should* have, when they believed that the result would be harmful to the national interest in the Middle East, is a point that will continue to excite controversy.

Truman quite evidently believed that the officials in his administration should be subordinate in every sense. As recalled thirty-five years later by Clark Clifford: "We finally got it straightened out but from that time on, he [Truman] knew of attempts to undermine his policy."[41]

Truman never forgave the State Department for the domestic debacle aroused by the trusteeship announcement. In his memoirs one can detect the bitter resentment and desire for personal vendetta. With his administration undermined both at home and abroad and even his own party turning against him, the trusteeship episode dealt Truman another political blow as painful as it was unexpected. In a sense the State Department became the scapegoat for Truman's political woes. The White House advisers were again given control of Palestine policy. They would have their day, and a revenge of sorts, when Truman granted immediate recognition to Israel on May 14, 1948.

TWELVE

Truman Recognizes Israel

TRUSTEESHIP: A LAME DUCK

The State Department's trusteeship proposal proved a non-starter for two fundamental reasons. First, it failed to receive the endorsement of either the Arabs or Zionists or of any major UN power; and second, because of the resistance expected from Arabs and Jews in Palestine, the American military commitment to enforcing a trusteeship was calculated at no less than that which the State Department had feared would be required to enforce partition itself.

On April 13, 1948, the American administration invited the British and the French to present a joint trusteeship proposal to the United Nations and, if it should prove necessary, to join in raising the military forces with which to impose it. The State Department told the British that if they did not intervene to halt the fighting in Palestine hostilities might spread, which would place at risk the continued supply of oil from the area, jeopardize the Anglo-American position in the Middle East, and invite Soviet penetration.[1]

But Britain, along with other powers at the United Nations, was already skeptical of the ability of the American administration to conduct any consistent policy in Palestine. Truman's press conference on March 25, at which he had stressed that trusteeship was but a temporary measure to prevent further bloodshed in Palestine and not intended to prejudice the final settlement, had prompted the comment from Foreign Secretary Bevin that any Arabs who may have been ready to discuss trusteeship had now been convinced by the president himself that the plan was but a new ruse to secure the immigration of the 100,000 immediately and partition later on.[2]

Since announcing their intention to quit Palestine the previous September, the British had been preoccupied with making an orderly, peaceful withdrawal without becoming embroiled in the forceful imposition of any political solutions of foreign origin. They were not entirely above gloating over the American predicament and not at all inclined to use their leverage to help the United States. Britain, like many other nations represented at the United Nations, felt that the trusteeship initiative was a pathetic and futile atten.pt by the Americans to extricate themselves from the consequences of their efforts the previous November to promote the UN partition plan.

The British evacuation was by now irreversible. The British believed that events in Palestine had removed the problem from the realms of Great Power diplomacy and that only a bloodletting could generate a solution.[3] Furthermore, since Palestine was in effect being partitioned, the deployment of an army to impose trusteeship would have meant the use of force against a UN resolution, that is, partition, a course that made even the State Department flinch.[4]

Ambassador Lewis Douglas in London believed that the British government was handicapped by the same rift between the permanent officials and the politicians as that which hampered the formulation of policy in Washington. He reported that whereas British officials might be sympathetic to trusteeship and saw the logic in the State Department's position they were "faced with the problem of getting a hearing from British politicians who now [had] a popular and firm Palestine policy which they [would] not abandon easily."[5]

But the ambassador was making false analogies, based to some extent on wishful thinking. The British officials, old hands in Palestine and the Middle East, regarded the Americans as inexperienced amateurs who had failed to comprehend the nature of the problem, the scale of force needed, and the likely reaction of the Arabs to the appearance of allied troops in Palestine sent to impose trusteeship:

The Palestine question is at present by far the most important political question in the minds of practically all Arabs. If British and American forces took serious action against Arab forces or prevented the achievement of Arab aspirations, the results on the relationship between the Arab states, and the United States and the United Kingdom would be disastrous, and in their turn open the way for Communist penetration.[6]

At the United Nations many delegations were reluctant to support the U.S. initiative until convinced that the Americans were ready to commit their own forces.[7] Some delegations, the French, for instance, were openly cynical that the Americans might reverse their policy yet again, leaving other countries high and dry.[8]

The cynics at the United Nations had good reason to doubt whether the United States would in fact commit the military forces needed. On April 4 the American Joint Chiefs of Staff told Truman that it would take more than one hundred thousand ground troops, six destroyers, and considerable air support to impose and supervise trusteeship. If Britain and France agreed to help, providing forty-seven thousand and ten thousand troops, respectively, the Americans would still have to dispatch forty-seven thousand men. Such a commitment, the Joint Chiefs of Staff warned, would necessitate at least partial mobilization, would overextend the army by increasing its dispersion abroad, and would require a supplementary budget. In addition, the United States would be unable to deploy its share of such a force prior to May 15, 1948, the date scheduled by the United Nations for Arab and Jewish independence.[9]

Both the Zionists and the Arabs rejected trusteeship. As Moshe Shertok told Marshall on March 26, trusteeship would in effect mean a continuation of British rule in Palestine.[10] Nahum Goldmann, known for his moderate views and readiness to compromise, told the Americans that the trusteeship scheme was meaningless without the troops to enforce it and that he did not believe that either the United States or the British would send their men.[11] In mid-April the Arab League rejected trusteeship formally, stating that it would "create a new regime, bring about a phase of trouble between Jews and Arabs, [and] cause trouble between Arabs and trustee powers."[12]

THE ZIONIST LOBBY:
HILLDRING AGAIN

The weeks following the trusteeship proposal saw Truman's popularity ratings sink steadily and domestic political pressures on the White House rise to a crescendo. Clifford kept in touch with leading Democrats, who advised him that if the administration adhered to trusteeship it would cost Truman the presidency. The disenchantment was widespread.

On March 27 Truman's first secretary of the interior, Harold Ickes (who had resigned in 1946 in protest at Truman's support for the appointment of oil magnate Edwin Pauley as assistant secretary of state for the navy),[13] wrote Truman a stinging "open letter," suggesting that Truman announce that under no circumstance would he run again for the presidency: "Even the party Democrats have been breaking up under you. . . . Candidates for senator and representative, and even for governor and county offices, appreciating the handicap that your candidacy would constitute, are openly saying that you ought to give way to someone who might have a chance to win."[14]

During the month of April, the anti-Truman movement gathered force. Mayor William O'Dwyer of New York City attacked Truman harshly for his retreat on partition.[15] The New York State Democratic Committee refused to commit itself to Truman for the presidency, and a movement developed inside the party to draft Eisenhower as an alternative candidate.[16]

Jacob Arvey, a Jew, a Chicago party boss, and one of the most important men in the Democratic party in Chicago, was among those who opted for the Eisenhower candidacy in protest at Truman's Palestine policy.[17] Arvey warned that Truman's statements on Palestine were liable to lose them not only the Jewish vote but also that of the masses. William L. Batt, head of the Democratic National Committee's research department, warned that an American retreat from partition might be interpreted at large as a sign that the word of the United States could not be relied on and it would not stand by its commitments.[18]

Through private channels Truman tried to reassure the

Zionists that he still supported partition. On April 11 Eddie Jacobson flew to New York City to confer with Chaim Weizmann. The next day Jacobson visited Truman at the White House, entering unnoticed by the East Gate, something he had never done before. Truman reaffirmed in strong terms the promises he had made to him and to Weizmann and gave Jacobson permission to communicate his assurances to the Zionist leader.[19]

At the White House, Truman's assistants wanted to prevent being upstaged again on the Palestine issue as they had been in March. To that end, they determined to place someone sympathetic inside the State Department. Their candidate was General John Hilldring. Back in February, they had engineered Hilldring's appointment as special assistant to the secretary of state, with a ranking superior to that of Loy Henderson and responsibility both to the president and the secretary (see also chapter 6).

The manner in which the appointment was pushed through was unusual to say the least. The brain trust chaired by Oscar Ewing (see chapter 5), at a meeting attended by Clifford, Niles, and Oscar Chapman, had decided to press Truman to appoint Hilldring and have Henderson sent abroad, where he would have no further contact with Palestine. Ewing and Chapman brought the suggestion to Truman. He concurred with the Hilldring appointment, though not yet with the proposal to "promote" Henderson out of Washington.[20]

But Hilldring himself was extremely reluctant to take up the position, and with good reason. As he explained to Henry Morgenthau, he appreciated only too well the difference between his temporary appointment to the U.S. delegation to the United Nations the previous fall and his being "infiltrated" as "the Zionists' man at State":

I certainly could not insinuate myself into the State Department between NEA and the Secretary, unless he were to ask me to advise him on the Palestine matter. If I were to attempt to do so, I would completely lose any influence I may have. I have seen it happen to better men than I am. I know the Secretary and I know therefore that I would ruin myself with him, and not help the cause of Palestine in the slightest.

This doesn't mean I may not be able to help. I think I can in my own way, but my efforts must be completely devoid of any involvement as intruder or protagonist.

In any case, without meaning to be immodest, I doubt the value of feeding me into a meat grinder that would produce no results and that would leave me impotent for any future usefulness.[21]

After six long-distance phone calls from Chaim Weizmann, one from Eleanor Roosevelt, and a telegram from Morgenthau, Hilldring was persuaded to take the appointment, but against his better instincts.[22]

The Zionists had found out about the pending appointment of Hilldring, which they regarded as a minor triumph, through Judge Sam Rosenman. Rosenman, a member of the Democratic party committee on presidential campaign strategy, was preparing the forthcoming party convention. He approached Weizmann to offer his mediatory services, on condition this was kept strictly secret. Weizmann agreed, and Rosenman now became a key figure in the White House attempts to heal the breach with the Zionists (and thus reclaim the Jewish vote).[23]

On April 23, the eve of the Jewish Passover, Weizmann was called suddenly to Essex House, where Rosenman lay incapacitated with an injured leg. According to Weizmann, Rosenman told him that the president still had him on his conscience and wanted to reassure him that he would not desert the Zionists. When they had last met, Truman had not realized that the State Department was about to abandon partition. Truman wanted Weizmann to know that he had given instructions that the direction of Palestine policy was to be transferred from Henderson to Hilldring. Truman also wanted Weizmann to know that if the UN partition plan was not revised by the special General Assembly and a Jewish state was declared, he would recognize it. Truman's message ended with two provisos; first, he would deal only with Weizmann and have nothing to do with Silver; and second, the substance of this message must be kept absolutely secret.[24]

Evidently at the Zionists' prompting since he could hardly

have known who Hilldring was, Eddie Jacobson wrote a personal letter of thanks to Truman the next day:

It naturally was a terrible shock when I was informed of your request for reversal on the Partition of Palestine. I have always realized what a task you have, and have always had confidence, and always felt that you did what you thought was best for our whole country.

I have been very worried about what is going to happen in Palestine, but I really feel that your appointment of GENERAL HILLDRING is going to help solve this whole situation.

Have been doing a lot of thinking about the attitude of my people in this coming election, and hope there is some way or some place that I can help change the situation.[25]

Meanwhile, with domestic political pressures building, Loy Henderson had become apprehensive about possible White House "back-sliding." On April 22 he had urged Under Secretary Lovett to return as soon as possible from the conference of foreign secretaries he was attending in Bogota so he could "devote a major portion of his time and energy to the Palestine problem." Henderson proposed "a series of conferences with leaders of Congress and the two political parties in order to remove Palestine from domestic politics and to give it its rightful place as a dangerous and difficult international problem." Henderson suggested also that they call a conference of "outstanding leaders of the Jewish Community in the United States in order to obtain their support for our policy as developed by the National Security Council."[26] In addition, Henderson evidently placed the department on the alert to give Hilldring an appropriate reception.

Hilldring's first visit to the State Department confirmed his worst premonitions. Marshall and Lovett were "too busy" to see him, and no office had been prepared for him. State Department officials made it clear that they already knew Hilldring's views on Palestine, that they resented the method of his appointment, and that they would do all they could to obstruct his involvement in policy making. Hilldring feared that even if they allowed him in on meetings of senior members of the department, they might hide from him documents they did not want him to see.[27]

Niles tried to persuade Hilldring not to draw hasty conclusions and promised he would get the president to speak with Secretary of State Marshall and persuade him to cooperate. Hilldring insisted that he would not return to the department until he had received a clear, positive report on Truman's discussion with the secretary. In the meantime, he would inform Marshall that he could not begin work because of illness.[28]

Niles phoned Hilldring repeatedly at his home in Arizona to try to encourage him to come back to Washington. But Hilldring begged off, with laryngitis and a weak heart, and said that his doctor had forbidden him to move for another week. Lowenthal meanwhile lamented: "There is no adviser on Palestine in State who has the necessary imagination and sympathetic understanding, and who is not taken in by the Arabist State officials."[29]

The second week of May 1948 was *the* critical period, when American policy toward the fledgling State of Israel was hanging in balance. Perhaps for this reason Hilldring also received phone calls from old friends at the State Department—who tried to ensure that he stayed at home. These friends informed him that Marshall was "on the spot" and intimated that it would help the secretary if Hilldring resigned. Hilldring revered Marshall and felt that he had been placed in an intolerable position. There was now no way left to retrieve the appointment.[30]

On May 26 Marshall brought to the White House a handwritten note from Hilldring that said that he was making no progress toward better health. The State Department suggested that the prospect of his new job was holding up his recovery. Clifford and Charlie Ross tried to persuade the president not to make the resignation public, but Truman thought this would be be unfair to Hilldring, and the news was posted in the evening papers.[31]

Lowenthal told Clifford philosophically: "We'll have to try to find someone else."[32] Niles took the episode to heart and told Lowenthal that it represented a "double-cross" by both the president and Marshall. Niles said he would tell the president so and try to have him reestablish Hilldring's position. He thought that Hilldring would be willing to become the first American ambassador to Israel, but Lowenthal thought it more important for him to be in Washington.[33] Clifford agreed: "I cannot keep up the State Department work all the time. If Hilldring had gone there, I could have phoned him, when a paper came over from State, and asked: are you for this? If he said no, I could go to the President and tell him that."[34]

The Hilldring fiasco reflected poor judgment, even delusions of grandeur, on the part of the White House aides. They were naive to expect that they could coerce the State Department bureaucracy to cooperate with a White House watchdog or accept passively what was a crude and blatant exercise in arm-twisting.

Furthermore, the aides did not perhaps take into full account the extent of Truman's (not to mention Hilldring's) reverence for Marshall. Marshall's presence in a lame administration at a period of acute international crisis was an asset that Truman could not afford to dispense with. A man of Marshall's military background and national prestige was bound to take bitter exception to what he considered the intrusion of domestic politics, manipulated by the president's political aides, in his prerogative of setting foreign policy.

THE DEBATE OVER RECOGNITION

In the meantime, events were working to the benefit of the White House. While State Department promotion of trusteeship met with universal cynicism, in Palestine the Yishuv's armed forces were turning partition into reality.

The State Department made one last maneuver. On April 30 Dean Rusk informed Truman of the difficulties he was encountering in securing a truce in Palestine. The Zionists had rejected the terms proposed since they would have barred further Jewish immigration and imposed a political standstill, that is, statehood would be deferred indefinitely. Truman told Rusk that he would do whatever Marshall thought necessary to bring about a truce. When asked by Rusk what they were to do if the Jews refused, Truman replied: "If the Jews refuse to accept a truce on reasonable grounds they need not expect anything from us. . . . go and get a truce. There is no other answer to this situation."[35]

A new proposal, approved by the president, was to transport the principal parties to the dispute to the Middle East on the "Sacred Cow" (the presidential plane) to pursue direct negotiations. To facilitate this, the British mandate was to be extended for ten days, and the UN special assembly was to be recessed for the same period. But the British refused to delay their own withdrawal, and the Zionists refused to defer their declaration of statehood beyond May 14, 1948.[36]

But given that no one seemed to want or to be able to impose either a trusteeship or a truce, good political sense was beginning to dictate the recognition of the new reality in Palestine, that is, the de facto existence of a Jewish state, enjoying the support of a UN resolution. Indeed, an additional, major consideration now intruded itself—the desirability of recognizing the Jewish state before the Soviets did.

By early May 1948, with the State Department's previous initiative on the rocks, it seemed to White House aides that at long last American national interests coincided with Truman's political fortunes.

On May 5 Dean Alfange, chairman of the American Christian Palestine Committee of New York, sent a "confidential letter" to Major General Harry Vaughan, Truman's military aide and friend of his since 1917. The letter, written by one "interested in the President's political fortunes," is worth quoting at length since many of his arguments would be used by Max Lowenthal in the briefs he prepared for Clark Clifford on the eve of a White House–State Department showdown on May 12, 1948.

Frankly, the President could not carry the State of New York in the present circumstances. The Jewish vote against him would be overwhelming.

Only a dramatic move on the President's part that would electrify the Jewish people could change the situation.

Such a move might well be the recognition of the Jewish State which will come into being on May 16 [*sic*], and the nomination of an American Minister to the new State. . . . recent events have knocked the props from under the Trusteeship proposal . . . [which] is no longer tenable, not because either side accepts it, but because the Jewish military forces have since demonstrated by their decisive victories over the Arabs that they can implement partition singlehanded.

The President, therefore, can logically take the position that events and not he have reversed the Trusteeship plan and that the UN decision can be best carried out by recognizing the new Jewish State.[37]

Although Max Lowenthal, and consequently Clark Clifford, would use identical arguments to persuade Truman to recognize Israel, Truman's own reply, written *after* he had already recognized Israel, indicates an inability to reconcile himself with the new state and a curiously anachronistic nostalgia for the "solutions" tabled in 1946:

My soul [*sic*] objective in the Palestine procedure has been to prevent bloodshed. . . . In 1946 when the British-American Commission on Palestine was appointed and Mr. Bevin made an agreement with me that he would accept the findings of that Commission I thought we had the problem solved but the emotional Jews of the United States and the equally emotional Arabs in Egypt and Syria [?] prevented that settlement from taking place, principally because of the immigration clause in that settlement.[38]

On May 11, 1948, David Niles showed Truman a public opinion poll on the recognition of Israel. According to it, some 80 percent of the press now favored recognition with the establishment of the state, and a majority of both parties in the Congress and a majority of state governors supported immediate recognition. During the last few days before Israel was to declare its independence, Truman was deluged by appeals for recognition from prominent Jewish figures, including Judge Herbert Lehman, Bernard Baruch, and Judge Joseph Proskauer.[39]

During the first week of May, Max Lowenthal had begun composing the case for an early recognition of the Jewish state, that is, by Friday, May 14, at the latest. During the week prior to May 11, Lowenthal had drafted half a dozen memoranda, checked them over with Matt Connelly, and passed them on to Clark Clifford. Connelly and Clifford were all for it, but when Clifford mentioned early recognition to Under Secretary of State Lovett, the latter "hit the ceiling."[40]

Whereas the State Department had argued for trusteeship

on the grounds that partition was impossible, Lowenthal emphasized that recent Jewish military victories had transformed
the situation in Palestine:

The Jews in Palestine, by showing unexpected strength in relation to
the Arabs, succeeded in achieving that objective. . . . it is clear that
partition is an accomplished fact. Everyone realizes this except the
State Department. . . .

It is now only a question whether it can be reversed. To reverse the
reality of partition would require military force, threats, sanctions or
persuasion. None would be effective. If we could not muster military
support to implement the UN resolution, or our trusteeship proposal,
surely we could not muster it to dislodge the Jews from the areas assigned to them by the UN. . . .

Since we cannot, and would not want to, reverse the reality of partition, we should derive the maximum advantage for the President and
for the U.S. government from the existing situation. This can best be
done by an immediate statement that he intends to recognize the Jewish State when it is proclaimed.[41]

Lowenthal dealt also with the domestic political implications.
But because the White House case for recognition was to be argued purely on "national interests," Lowenthal's involvement
and the political issues he raised were to be given the lowest of
profiles. Lowenthal's final draft, to be found also in the Clifford
papers at the Truman Library, has no identification on it and
is marked: "This is for the protection of the Administration,
not to be shown, in written form, to anyone else, *under any
circumstances.*"[42]

Lowenthal argued that as soon as the Jewish state was proclaimed there would be tremendous pressure at home for its
recognition, including from the Republicans. He pushed for
early recognition: "Nothing would be accomplished by waiting
for everybody to climb on the bandwagon, while we insist on
getting some sort of agreement between Jews and Arabs." If the
United States granted early recognition, it would retrieve its
own prestige and that of the United Nations. Lowenthal agreed
that if the national interest required a certain policy then that
course should be taken, "whatever the political damage." But,
he continued, this must be clearly established, before making
the president "hold the bag." Furthermore, he argued: "The

truism that a reasonably clear case for a policy must be made out before the Administration is required to pay a high political price for it is especially important in an election year in which the Administration's opponents are dangerous to the country's interests, foreign and domestic alike."[43]

In evident reference to the political setback suffered by Truman because of the State Department's trusteeship coup, Lowenthal argued that if the United States, like other major nations in the United Nations, accepted the realities in Palestine the president would no longer be subjected to "unjust and unjustified losses and sacrifices." But "the opportunity to undo the damage to the President" would "fade out" if the administration "continue[d] to retrieve the reputations, or to satisfy the *amour propre* of a few State Department officials."[44]

In conclusion, Lowenthal argued that recognition of the Jewish state was the only policy consistent with American national interests. The "conciliation of the Jews would line up on the side of the United States a far abler fighting force." In any case, as the British experience in Palestine had shown, the Arabs were not to be relied on. Recognition would also strengthen the American position in the Near East vis-à-vis the Soviets, eliminate or reduce bloodshed and violence in Palestine, and strengthen the United Nations.[45]

In a memorandum dated May 9, 1948, Clifford recited Lowenthal's brief. The president should exact maximum advantage from the new situation in Palestine and in the process rescue the United Nations from the "terrible morass in which it was floundering," forestall the Soviets, and defuse the domestic political pressures that in any case would build up.[46]

The need to preempt Soviet recognition was stressed also by Eleanor Roosevelt in a letter written to the president on May 11. Mrs. Roosevelt had been prompted by the Zionists, who had warned her that the Soviets were going to recognize the Jewish state as soon as it was declared, which was to be at midnight on Friday.[47] She informed Truman that she had no idea what the administration's position on recognition was going to be but: "If we are going to recognize it, I think it would be a mistake to lag behind Russia." In a handwritten postscript she added: "I personally believe in the Jewish State."[48]

CLASH AT THE WHITE HOUSE—
MAY 12, 1948

At 4:00 P.M. on Wednesday, May 12, exactly forty-eight hours before Israel was due to declare its independence, Truman convened a meeting between his aides and the State Department at the White House. Present were Truman and his aides, Clark Clifford, David Niles, and Matt Connelly, and from the State Department, Secretary of State Marshall, Under Secretary of State Lovett, Fraser Wilkins of NEA, and Robert McClintock of the UN office.[49] Significantly, Loy Henderson was *not* in the State Department delegation.

Clifford recalled later that Truman had instructed him before the meeting: "Now I want you to prepare for this meeting. General Marshall is opposed to our recognizing Israel. He'll bring his assistants with him. But I want you to prepare the case supporting the independence of Israel just as though you were going to make an argument before the Supreme Court. . . . I think that between the two of us maybe we can convince Marshall of the rightness of our cause."[50]

That morning Clifford had conferred with Niles and Lowenthal. Clifford was evidently taking it for granted that a positive decision on recognition would be made. He even asked Lowenthal to draft a press release stating as much, which would be issued the next day. Lowenthal also gave Clifford the background memoranda he had been working on for the past week so Clifford could study them prior to the afternoon conference.[51]

Just before Matt Connelly's departure for the meeting, Lowenthal and Niles had made a "warm plea" to him to "get something done," perhaps have the arms embargo lifted. Connelly had replied: "No, that is not enough, nothing will do that is less than the recognition of the Jewish State."[52]

The White House conference proceeded under the all-pervasive atmosphere of domestic politics and the ongoing feud between the State Department and Truman's aides. As Marshall entered the meeting, he glared at Clifford. Marshall said that he had been working on the assumption that as secretary of state Palestine was within *his* sphere of responsibility; therefore, he did not even understand why Clifford was present. Truman replied curtly that Clifford was present because he had invited him.[53] Marshall was not to be put off; he argued that they were about to consider a serious question of policy, which should be decided on its merits. He for one had no need of Clifford's assistance. And, as Clifford recalled it in 1949: "He said it all with a righteous God-damned Baptist tone."[54]

Marshall and Lovett were skeptical of the Jewish military successes. They feared that the Jews, believing they could make a behind-the-scenes deal with King Abdullah of Transjordan to partition Palestine, now believed they could establish their state without reaching a truce with Palestine's Arabs. This was a course that Marshall had warned the Jews against. On May 8 he had told them that the military tide could easily turn against them, serving notice that in that event they should expect no help from the United States.[55]

Truman invited Clifford to respond. As George Elsey noted in his diary: "Clifford read the Lowenthal-Elsey statement." Marshall apparently reacted violently. "This is straight politics. . . . CMC [Clark M. Clifford] was enraged—& Marshall glared at CMC. State had no policy except to 'wait.'"[56]

Clifford said that the State Department policy of seeking a truce in Palestine was unrealistic and suggested that President Truman recognize the Jewish state at his press conference the next day (May 13), thus preempting a likely Soviet recognition. But Clifford really aroused the department's contingent when he referred to the presidential elections and said that an early recognition would restore the president's position with his Jewish voters.[57]

Lovett rebutted Clifford's arguments. It would be "highly injurious" to the United Nations to announce the recognition of the Jewish state before it had even come into existence and when the special assembly was still considering the question of the future government of Palestine. It would also be highly injurious to the prestige of the president and would be regarded as a "transparent attempt to win the Jewish vote," which would lose more votes than it would gain.[58] Marshall added jocularly, although perhaps not without some serious intent, that if Truman followed Clifford's advice then he, Marshall, would not vote for Truman in the November elections.[59]

Clifford protested that he was not conscious that he had in any way touched upon politics; he had only tried to speak on the merits of the case.[60] But the degeneration of the conversation to the level of Truman's electoral prospects plus Marshall's implied threats were enough for Truman, who abruptly called a halt to the conference. Clifford recalled in 1949: "Truman raised his hand as peacemaker. 'I think I understand the question involved and I think we need no further discussion of it. I think we must follow the position General Marshall has advocated.'"[61]

According to Clifford, as they left the meeting Truman said to him: "I'm sorry Clark, how this turned out. I didn't have any idea it would turn out this way." Clifford replied philosophically: "Mr. President, this isn't the first case I've lost, nor will it be the last."[62] But Clifford had not given up; he was not about to pass up a historic opportunity. And, as he confided to Jonathan Daniels one year later: "I was enraged by the terrible fu--ing the Boss had gotten in April [*sic*]."[63]

After the meeting Connelly told Lowenthal that the department had won the argument because there were no precedents for granting recognition before an application for such had even been made. But Connelly felt two things had been gained: first, the president, he thought, now saw the advisability of discussing State Department proposals instead of simply "signing on the dotted line" whatever they submitted to him; and second, the department had not taken the position that recognition should be refused after an application was made.[64]

This assessment provides the key to White House strategy over the next two days. If the State Department would not consider recognition before an application was made by the new Jewish state, then the White House aides would see to it that such an application *was* made posthaste.

The next day, May 13, Truman gave a press conference. As they were going in, Truman said to Niles: "I was sorry to have to decide against you fellows yesterday." A reporter asked Truman if the United States would recognize the Jewish state when it was proclaimed. He replied: "We will cross that bridge when we come to it."

After the conference Niles said that he was sorry Marshall and Lovett had claimed that the Jewish state would be Communist. Truman replied: "Don't pay any attention to the communism charge, they are always making it. . . . those two men [Marshall and Lovett] mean well, but they follow their subordinates." Niles said that that was the trouble and that the real point was that they should recognize the new Jewish state before the Soviets or any of their satellites did. Truman agreed that Western recognition should precede that of the Soviet bloc "to give it the right slant from the beginning."[65]

THE RECOGNITION

On May 13 pro-Zionist pressures on the White House intensified. A telegram from Judge Herbert Lehman of New York urged recognition "as promptly as possible."[66] David Niles reported to Truman on a phone call from Jacob Arvey, political leader of Cook County, Chicago, and a Jew. Arvey was organizing a series of mass meetings to celebrate the establishment of the Jewish state, which would provide "a great opportunity for acclaim for the President" if Truman could grant recognition before those meetings. Truman received a phone call from Ed Flynn, political boss of New York, to the same effect. Flynn reported that three hundred mass meetings were to be held around the country. Niles told Truman that he and Lowenthal were trying to forestall any adverse references to him at those meetings. Truman replied that some day he would show Niles and Lowenthal his appreciation for all their efforts.[67]

John A. Kennedy, a longtime personal friend of Truman's, later recalled a visit he had paid to Truman "sometime in April or May, 1948." On his way into the Oval Office, he noticed waiting "all the heads of Jewish organizations, who were urging the President to recognize Israel." Kennedy "kiddingly" called Truman's attention to the group of Jewish leaders, who were scheduled to see the president after himself: "Well, Mr. President, are you going to recognize Israel as, of course, that is what this group who are following me in here are going to ask you." Truman replied: "Well, how many Arabs are there as registered voters in the United States?" Kennedy laughed, and so did Truman.[68]

Clifford was keenly sensitive to domestic politics, and he now determined to break down State Department resistance to early recognition. He chose to tackle Under Secretary of State Lovett. Once again Clifford's recollections are at some variance with those of both Lovett and Lowenthal.

According to Clifford, Lovett had approached him that evening after the White House conference. Lovett was feeling "uneasy" about the decision and about the attitude of the State Department. Lovett indicated that "some of his boys were swinging round."[69]

But according to Lowenthal, it was *Clifford* who contacted *Lovett,* the day after the conference, to tackle him on the question of the correct procedure for recognizing the new state. Lowenthal recorded in his diary that Clifford had told Lovett: "Yesterday there was a decision. I am a great believer in abiding by decisions. You won the decision. That decision was that recognition should not be announced, and intention to recognize should not be announced, before application for recognition has been made. There still remains the question whether and when we should recognize after application is made."[70]

Lovett replied that the State Department was considering this question. The next morning, Friday, May 14, Clifford phoned Lovett again, suggesting a new formula, which would not make it appear that the administration were merely succumbing to pressure. Clifford said that if they were going to recognize the Jewish state, they should do so before the weekend—"recognition a week later would be too late to do the President any good." Lovett said that the department was working on a draft statement and invited Clifford to discuss it over lunch.[71]

Lovett and Clifford lunched privately at the 1925 F Street Club. Lovett showed Clifford the draft statement, which announced that Truman was considering the subject of recognition. Clifford said: "That won't do. Let's talk plainly; while you and Secretary Marshall were away [i.e., in March], your staff placed the president in a very unfair position. It was not of his making in any way. It was unnecessary to place him in that position."[72]

According to Lovett, Clifford then told him that the president had come under "unbearable pressure to recognize the Jewish State promptly." On May 12 Truman had been persuaded by State Department arguments that recognition in advance of any request would place the United States in the position of a sponsor, thereby increasing its responsibility, and that such an act while the United Nations was still sitting in special session would be "a grave breach of propriety and would be labelled a doublecross." But now, Clifford stated, that same Friday night, "there would be no government or authority of any kind in Palestine. Title would be lying around for anyone to seize and a number of people had advised the President that this should not be permitted."[73]

Lovett replied that legally there was no bar to recognition, but "indecent haste in recognizing the state would be very unfortunate." He therefore urged delay for a day or two until they could confirm details of the new state's proclamation of independence. Lovett feared that otherwise they "might lose the effect of many years of hard work in the Middle East with the Arabs." Lovett added that he would need time to inform Warren Austin, head of their delegation to the United Nations, and the British and French governments, as "it was manifestly impossible to time messages to arrive in a distant capital" when they did not know when the decision would be made. Clifford replied that "the President could not afford to have any such action leak" and that they should "try to insure against it." Clifford was sure the formal request for recognition would be received soon and hoped to be able to give the State Department a final answer late that afternoon.[74]

At this point Clifford's and Lovett's versions again diverge. According to Clifford, he agreed with Lovett that they would "split the job"; Lovett would inform the French and the British, and he would obtain the request for recognition from Israel.[75] At 3:00 P.M., straight after his lunch with Lovett, Clifford went to Truman and told him that Lovett now agreed to recognition. Truman was pleased that the State Department had changed its position, and he agreed to Clifford's procedure.[76]

Clifford could well afford to be confident of receiving the Jewish Agency's request for recognition, since that same morning he had in fact already commissioned it. At 9:30 A.M. David Niles, working in close conjunction with Clifford, had phoned Eliahu Epstein, the Jewish Agency representative in Washington, to tell him to expect a phone call from Clifford between 10:00 and 11:00 A.M. At the same time, Clifford had phoned Ben Cohen and told him that if the Jewish Agency sent in an appropriate request to the president and the State Department the United States would grant recognition to the new Jewish state on its establishment. Clifford phoned Epstein at exactly ten o'clock (4:00 P.M. Palestine time, at which hour in Tel Aviv's museum David Ben-Gurion was reading out Israel's proclamation of independence). Clifford asked Epstein to send in his request by noon to the White House and to the State Department.[77]

Epstein's official letter of request had just been dispatched by taxi with an aide, Zvi Zinder, when an office worker rushed in and said she had heard on the radio that Ben-Gurion had proclaimed the new state of "Israel." Epstein sent the woman clerk off after Zinder, whom she intercepted at the very gates of the White House. So that the request would not be delayed, it was not brought back for retyping; the new name, "Israel," was written in with pen.[78] All this had been completed *before* Clifford lunched with Lovett.

Perhaps the critical factor in Truman's final decision to recognize Israel was the attitude of General Marshall. According to one of Clifford's post hoc versions, it was *Lovett* who had brought Marshall round to a neutral stance. In 1948 Clifford told Congress that on the morning of May 14 Marshall had called the president and said: "Mr. President, I cannot support your action in recognition but I will not oppose it. I will say nothing at all." Truman had replied: "Thank you, General Marshall. That is all that I need."[79]

During the latter part of Friday afternoon, telephone conversations continued between the White House and the State Department until at about 5:30 P.M. they had arrived at the text of the White House statement of recognition. Lovett told Clifford that the UN special session was expected to finish at about ten o'clock that evening. Could the White House not delay its statement? Clifford did not feel that the president could, but he agreed to discuss it with him.[80]

As with the trusteeship proposal in March, the key problem was one of timing. Whereas Clifford's accounts describe how Lovett and, consequently, Marshall were eventually convinced by his (i.e., the Zionists' and Lowenthal's) arguments, Lovett's own contemporary record does not corroborate this: "My protests against the precipitate action and warnings as to consequences with the Arab world appear to have been outweighed by considerations unknown to me, but I can only conclude that the President's political advisers, having failed last Wednesday afternoon to make the President a father of the new state, have determined at least to make him the midwife."[81]

At 5:45 P.M., Clifford phoned back to the State Department. Dean Rusk answered, and Clifford informed him that the president would announce his recognition of Israel shortly after 6:00 P.M. (eastern standard time, which would be midnight in Palestine). When Rusk protested that Truman's action was in conflict with the American delegation's efforts at the United Nations to secure a truce in Palestine—which Rusk claimed now enjoyed majority support—Clifford insisted that this nevertheless was what the president had decided to do.[82]

Truman made his declaration in Washington, D.C., at 6:11 P.M. on May 14, 1948 (12:11 A.M., May 15, in Israel). Just as there had been loud domestic repercussions after the trusteeship episode in March, so now there were astounded reactions among America's allies at the UN special assembly, where even the American delegation was taken unaware by the president's recognition of Israel.

Dean Rusk had telephoned from Washington to Warren Austin at Lake Success. When informed of the president's decision to grant recognition, Austin had been so disgusted that he had refused to return to the assembly to tell his colleagues but drove straight home. Rusk surmised that Austin had wanted the assembly to know clearly that the decision had been Truman's and that the American delegation at the United Nations had not been deceiving the other delegations.[83]

At about 6:15 P.M., as he recalled later, Rusk received a telephone call from Marshall asking him to "get up to New York and prevent the U.S. Delegation from resigning en masse." But by the time Rusk arrived, tempers had apparently cooled, and his mission proved unnecessary.[84]

In the assembly Philip Jessup and Francis B. Sayre, the only members of the U.S. delegation in the plenum, had been left in the dark. The first clue they had of Truman's action was when Alberto Gonzales Fernandez of Colombia asked from the rostrum if the rumors about American recognition of Israel were true. The Cuban delegate, Guillermo Belt, mocked the Americans: "It seemed that the Polish and Soviet Governments were better informed than they regarding events in Washington."[85]

Shortly after 6:00 P.M., a member of the American delegation, John Ross, had picked up the news that Truman's recognition had appeared on the UN ticker tape. Jessup told a staff member to procure him a copy, which she found in the wastepaper basket of Trygve Lie (the United Nations' first secretary-general). Jessup took the rostrum and read out Truman's statement of recognition from the crumpled ticker tape. Porter McKeever, a staffer on the American delegation, physically restrained Belt in his seat to prevent him from returning to the rostrum to announce Cuba's withdrawal from the United Nations in protest of American duplicity.[86]

On May 17, 1948, Marshall discussed the episode with Truman and told him what had happened at the Security Council in Austin's absence. Marshall reported back to Lovett: "[he] treated it somewhat as a joke as I had done but I think we both privately thought it was a hell of a mess." Marshall believed that the United States "had hit its all-time low before the UN."[87] A story circulated that some of Marshall's friends had advised him to resign because of this incident. Marshall is reported to have replied to them: "No, gentlemen, you do not accept a post of this sort and then resign when the man who has the Constitutional authority to make a decision makes one. You may resign at any time for any other reason but not for that one."[88]

Two days later Austin reported from Lake Success the general feeling that the United States by its immediate recognition of the new state had endorsed Israel's sabotage of the truce efforts and violated the terms of the Security Council truce resolution. The failure of the Americans to consult or inform other delegations before recognition had deeply offended those who had collaborated most closely with them and had left a "lack of confidence in the integrity of US intentions and disbelief of further statements of future US intentions and policies." Other delegations, such as those of Canada, China, and a number of Latin American states, stated frankly that they felt "double-crossed."[89]

Eleanor Roosevelt also wrote to Truman, telling him of the "complete consternation" created at the United Nations by his precipitate recognition. Although Mrs. Roosevelt had opposed the March reversal of American support for partition, she could not agree with the fashion in which Truman had recognized the new state—without the knowledge of his own representatives at the United Nations and without a "very clear understanding beforehand with such nations as we expected would follow our lead." Several delegates had since told her that they did not see how they could ever support American intentions again, "because the United States changed so often without any consultation." Referring to the low morale of the UN delegation, she concluded: "I have seldom seen a more bitter, puzzled, discouraged group of people than some of those I saw on Saturday. Some of them I know are favorable to the rights of the Jews in Palestine, but they are just nonplused by the way in which we do things."[90]

As usual, Truman wrote a placatory, euphemistic letter:

There was not much else to be done. Since there was a vacuum in Palestine and since the Russians were anxious to be the first to do the recognizing, Gen. Marshall, Secretary Lovett, Dr. Rusk and myself worked the matter out and decided that the proper thing to do was to recognize the Jewish Government promptly. Senator Austin was notified of what was taking place but he didn't have the chance to talk with other members of the delegation until afterward.[91]

It appeared that Truman was unruffled by all the shock waves transmitted by the State Department and the UN delegation. He did not even react when Ambassador Douglas in London, who had just been lectured in dire terms by Foreign Secretary Bevin, reported that the president's act had delivered the "worst shock so far to the general Anglo-American concert of policy."[92]

It is true, as many commentators have noted already (perhaps with some of the wisdom that comes with hindsight), that
Truman's recognition proved to be a wise acceptance of the inevitable. Once he was reasonably certain of Marshall's loyalty,
Truman was able to take the path pressed on him by his White
House advisers, thereby, not coincidentally, also giving a boost
to his own sagging political fortunes.

Yet doubts must remain whether, on May 14, Truman intended to make any long-term commitment to the State of
Israel. On the next day he wrote the following letter to Bartley
Crum, the pro-Zionist lobbyist: "You, of course, are familiar
with all the effort put forth by me to get a peaceable and satisfactory settlement of the Palestine question. I am still hoping
for just that. I think the report of the British American Commission on Palestine was the correct solution and, I think, eventually we are going to get it worked out just that way."[93]

THIRTEEN

The First Arab-Israeli War
Truman and the Bernadotte Plan

The diplomatic jockeying over the future of Israel did not end with Truman's recognition on May 14, 1948. It merely moved on to a different plane. As before, the attempts by the State Department to reach a consensus with the British were destined to be foiled by the White House. But this time, with Truman's political survival imminently at stake—in elections that had hung like a pall over the Palestine problem for the previous two years—even the State Department reconciled itself to the exigencies of domestic politics.

On May 14, 1948, the General Assembly of the United Nations (at the same session at which Truman's recognition of Israel had been "leaked") decided to appoint a mediator to "promote a peaceful adjustment of the future situation of Palestine."[1] On May 20 Count Folke Bernadotte, vice-president of the Swedish Red Cross, was appointed to the position by the United Nations.

Just as immediately after the UN partition resolution of November 29, 1947, a civil war had erupted in Palestine, so on the night that Israel declared its independence, and following the British evacuation, the armed forces of five Arab countries invaded the infant Jewish state. The war in Israel was fought in three main phases: (1) from May 15 until the first truce, which lasted from June 11 to July 9; (2) the so-called ten-days war, from July 9 to 18; and (3) the campaigns in October and December 1948, in which the Israelis conquered the Negev and

Galilee. This first Arab-Israeli war was brought to an end by a cease-fire signed on January 7, 1949.[2]

Bernadotte's principal task would be to bring about a permanent cease-fire in Israel and, as Bernadotte himself saw it, to negotiate a new political settlement that would be acceptable to all sides. In this latter, self-appointed task Bernadotte would stray far from the 1947 partition resolution.

The State Department had never reconciled itself to the UN partition resolution. It will be recalled that only the intervention of Chaim Weizmann with President Truman in November 1947 had at the last minute prevented the American delegation from moving that the Negev be transferred to the Arab state.[3]

The Negev would become the focus of a new diplomatic struggle during the summer and fall of 1948. For this southern desert also constituted a key strategic land bridge between Britain's two allies, Egypt and Transjordan. The British convinced the State Department of the importance of keeping the Negev in "friendly" Arab hands. On June 6, 1948, Harold Beeley, Ernest Bevin's principal adviser on Palestine, told State Department officials that the Arabs would agree to a Jewish state, provided they were given the Negev, the territorial link between their capitals. As a quid pro quo, the British would support the transfer of Galilee to the Jews (which in fact constituted a return to the partition plan proposed in 1937 by the Royal Commission on Palestine headed by Lord Peel).[4]

In addition, the British relentlessly impressed on the Americans the dangers of Israel becoming a Soviet satellite, thus driving a Jewish wedge between Egypt and the rest of the Arab world. The British, and thus the Allies', entire strategic infrastructure in the Middle East would be at risk.[5]

FURTHER SKIRMISHES IN WASHINGTON: THE "FIRING" OF HENDERSON

But quite apart from the new military reality in Palestine itself and the logic in preempting the Soviets, the ongoing feud between the White House and State Department officials had to be played out. It is quite evident from the private papers that personal account-settling was never far from the minds of those involved; Clark Clifford and Loy Henderson were to be particularly affected by the domestic hostilities.

Clifford's campaign for immediate recognition of Israel was a virtuoso performance, even if he was ably backed by Niles and Lowenthal. Clifford was the able court lawyer who had squared off with the State Department, and it was he who had finally closed the deal over lunch with Lovett. No one was more aware of Clifford's role than Lowenthal and Niles. On the morning of May 16, 1948, Niles jested over the phone to Clifford: "I have just received a cable from Palestine; they are going to change the name of their new state, they are going to call it Cliffordville."[6]

In June 1948, Lowenthal told Clifford:

In all the Truman administration, the most dramatic affair of all, as history looks back on it, will be the Palestine affair. . . . And in this dramatic affair, your part is so dramatic—more than anything I have seen in the 30 years or more I have been coming to Washington. If the time ever comes when you and the President decide to permit the story to be written, from the memories of men who know about it, and you tell me to release what I have, I shall open secret notes I have, locked away. . . .

. . . don't forget that when the time comes to write up this whole Palestine story, let me know if there is a writer you approve of, and you want my secret notes on what took place.

Clifford replied: "All right, old man."[7]

Clifford went from the Truman White House to a successful private law practice in Washington. In the 1960s he served as Lyndon Johnson's secretary of defense.

In stark contrast, the career of Loy Henderson was marred permanently, and he carried the personal scars for the rest of his life. The watershed of Henderson's career at NEA came with the trusteeship episode in March 1948. When Truman referred in his memoirs to the "second and third ranks" having pulled off a coup behind their superiors' backs, he had been referring primarily to Henderson. Following the White House investigation of the episode, Eben Ayers, a White House staffer, noted in his diary: "Ross and others have been suspicious of Henderson and some others in the State Department who are regarded as 'Anglophiles.' Henderson's position was made pretty clear to Secretary Marshall through the discussion and there is indication that his stay in the Department, or in his present position at least, may not be long."[8]

In an interview given in 1968, Matt Connelly remembered that Truman had given him specific instructions to call Secretary Marshall and to see to it that Henderson was dismissed. Connelly recalled that this had occurred after the May 12 meeting although, as noted already, Henderson had not in fact been present at that meeting. Truman believed that Henderson had deliberately lied to him about the ability of the Israelis to win the war although the State Department had had access to the same intelligence sources as the White House. Truman said to Connelly: "He lied to me. . . . I want you to tell Secretary Marshall and have him fired."

When Connelly met with Marshall to pass on Truman's instruction, Marshall asked: "Is that an order?" Connelly replied: "That's an order." Marshall called back later and said that he had better come round and see the president, as Henderson was protected by the career service and could only be transferred. Truman had asked: "How far . . . ?"[9]

But prior to his departure Henderson was involved in one further, curious episode, which perhaps may have just provided the White House with the final provocation for his removal from the State Department.

On May 15, 1948, Henderson telephoned Eliahu Epstein, the Israeli envoy in Washington, to ask him if the Jews wanted any territories other than those allotted in the UN partition resolution. Epstein replied in the negative and added that any additional territories taken by the Israeli army were being held only to protect adjacent Jewish settlements and would be returned to the Arabs once peace was achieved.[10]

On May 27 Henderson gave Epstein a letter that stated that the United States would "be prepared to exchange Envoys Extraordinary and Ministers Plenipotentiary with Israel when the situation in Palestine is such as to cause the Government of the United States to decide that it would be appropriate for it to accord de jure recognition to the Provisional Government of Israel."[11]

When handing over the letter, Henderson explained that

originally he had wanted a prompt exchange of ministers. But this had been found to be impossible, since the department lawyers had advised that such an exchange would constitute full de jure recognition whereas de facto recognition did not involve the acceptance of any particular frontiers. He then asked, apparently quite casually and incidentally, whether Israel would agree to make some "frontier adjustments in order to accelerate de jure recognition." [12]

When Epstein replied that the UN resolution had settled the frontier question, Henderson retorted that "American recognition was not based on November Twentynine but rather on a de facto situation in Palestine and the desire to avoid a vacuum." When asked by Epstein to be specific, Henderson dropped the matter hastily. When Epstein warned that his government would regard Henderson's position as a reversal of the administration's earlier one and expressed concern about the universal reaction, Henderson was taken aback and asked Epstein to withhold transmission of the letter to Israel until Epstein had seen Under Secretary Lovett. [13]

Epstein met Henderson and Lovett on May 29. When he stated that his lawyers had advised that American practice did *not* preclude the exchange of ministers with a de facto recognized government, Lovett admitted that the difference between de facto and de jure was "very thin." Lovett quite obviously wanted to extricate Henderson and to avoid yet another embarrassing incident with the White House, where Max Lowenthal had actually been kept apprised of developments all along. Lovett now suddenly produced a new letter, the changed text of which stated that the United States was "giving careful consideration to the exchange of legations and envoys extraordinary and ministers plenipotentiary . . . and will communicate later with the Provisional government of Israel." [14]

The whole episode was reported through Lowenthal to David Niles and also to Clark Clifford, who wrote a memorandum for the president on it on June 17, 1948. Clifford suggested that de jure recognition was being withheld by the State Department to conciliate the British and the Arabs and would encourage the Arabs to believe that they might secure better terms if they could only hold out. [15]

In a 1976 interview with State Department historians, Henderson denied having substituted letters or having suggested that Israel give up territory in exchange for full recognition.[16] But in a private correspondence some months before, after initially denying the episode "flatly," Henderson conceded that he "may have asked [Epstein], on a personal basis, if his government would be prepared to make boundary adjustments" and "may have intimated that a realistic solution of the boundary problem might contribute to the facilitation of the granting of *de jure* recognition."[17]

The question of the de jure recognition of Israel would continue to be a debating point between the State Department and the White House. Henderson's apparently private initiative with Epstein would be his last on the Palestine/Israel issue. His days in Washington were now numbered.

Henderson had come under considerable public criticism, both in the press and in Congress. In January 1948 the *New York Post* had run a series of articles accusing him of working with "frantic zeal" for a "backward and decayed policy" based on "such deep-seated prejudices and biases that he functions as a virtual propagandist for feudalism and imperialism in the Middle East, in conflict with progressive principles and democratic interests of the United States."[18]

In the wake of the trusteeship episode Representative Arthur Klein of New York called for a congressional investigation "of the administrative inefficiency and unbalance in the structure of the State Department, and of the grasp for power in the National Security Council by the representatives of the armed services."[19]

Klein named Henderson as personally responsible for "many of the most flagrant reversals of policy." But, he added, Henderson would have been unable to exert such control had it not been for an "antiquated and cumbersome system of administration." Klein asked also that the investigating committee examine the relations between Aramco and its Washington vice-president, Terry Duce, and the National Security Council.[20]

Klein's proposals languished for a month or so. But then in mid-May 1948 Jacob Javits, the Republican congressman from New York, an "ambitious and self-pushing" lawyer according to Lowenthal, apparently persuaded the chairman of the House

Foreign Relations Committee to agree to hearings on the State Department's handling of the Palestine question.

Still savoring their recent triumph over the State Department, however, the White House advisers could afford to take a more forebearing, even generous, attitude. Even some political ground might be gained if they intervened to shield the State Department. Niles also saw possibilities for restoring Clifford's badly impaired relations with the department. He therefore proposed that Clifford inform the department of the congressional initiative and that he had succeeded in having it shelved. Thus on May 17, when Javits informed Niles of his initiative, Niles advised the congressman to "lay [his] resolution on the table, [but] keep it alive for possible use later."[21] When Secretary of State Marshall heard about the proposed legislation, he exclaimed, with his face "very red," that it was "outrageous."[22]

A congressional investigation of NEA would have provoked a direct clash between Marshall and the White House, which was to be avoided at all costs. White House purposes would best be served by the removal of Henderson as NEA's director.

Toward the end of June 1948 Clifford told Niles that he had given up hope of having Henderson moved out. Niles replied that he remained hopeful and reported that Henderson had had a nervous breakdown and had been out of circulation for three weeks. Lowenthal interjected that although that might be good for Israel "only Loy's removal . . . would be helpful to the President."[23]

White House pressure on the State Department eventually paid off. At first Henderson was asked to be ambassador to Turkey. But when the Zionists objected, on the grounds of his proximity to the Middle East, his posting was switched to India. The appointment was announced officially on July 14, 1948.[24]

In the twilight years of his life Henderson still remembered his clashes with the Zionist lobby and the White House staff with chagrin and bitterness. He recalled that during the latter part of 1947 and the first six months of 1948, he had been attacked on the floors of Congress, and thousands of letters had poured into the State Department demanding his dismissal. He assumed that similar numbers had arrived at the White House. He obviously felt that he had been made a scapegoat. His feelings were still evidently overpowering in 1976, when he granted an interview to Allen Podet (Podet consequently published an article that exonerated Henderson of charges of anti-Semitism).[25] Shortly after, Henderson wrote to Podet, asking him not to publish parts of the interview:

In my criticism of Niles, Crum and MacDonald I had made comments that I would never make publicly and must ask you in your writings not to quote them. Although I shall bear the scars as long as I live from the attacks that they and others have made upon me and although I shall be remembered in Zionist history as a minor villain, I do not wish to be the author of public attacks upon them, particularly since they are dead and are not in a position to defend themselves.[26]

THE MacDONALD APPOINTMENT

The White House staff were still jockeying for closer supervision of Palestine policy. Having failed in their efforts the previous spring to place General Hilldring inside the State Department, they now asserted the president's prerogative by appointing the United States' first diplomatic representative to Israel.

On June 15, 1948, Under Secretary of State Lovett forwarded to the White House the name of the State Department nominee, Charles F. Knox, Jr., an American Foreign Service officer, who was appointed special representative, pending the appointment of an ambassador.[27]

On June 24 Niles asked Hilldring about Knox, without telling him about Lovett's proposal. Hilldring said that Knox had been on his staff at the United Nations the previous fall and that he was "pro-Arab and no damn good." Niles rushed back to the White House and told Matt Connelly that it was urgent that he see the president immediately—before Lovett's appointment with the President later that afternoon. Niles had a "long, pleasant talk" with Truman, whose response to the story was that "the underlings of the State Department" were doing to Marshall what they had done to him. Truman asked Niles for alternative names, and Niles produced a list he had brought with him.[28]

All the State Department nominees were rejected; the White House wanted its own man in Tel Aviv.[29] Truman picked out

James MacDonald, a member of the Anglo-American committee on Palestine from 1945 to 1946 who had firmly established his pro-Zionist credentials. Truman wanted only to satisfy himself first whether MacDonald was a Democrat and whether he was tied in in any way with "the John Foster Dulles crowd" or the peace movement. Niles had Clifford check this.[30] Clifford rang up MacDonald from the White House and after he had satisfied himself that MacDonald was indeed a Democrat told him that the president wanted him to be the first U.S. ambassador to Israel. Clifford brushed aside MacDonald's misgivings, about coming out of retirement, about salary, and missing his golf. Truman wanted to announce the appointment that same evening.[31]

Secretary of State Marshall was hospitalized at the time, so Under Secretary Lovett was informed. Lovett asked for time in which to find out if MacDonald was acceptable to Israel. According to Lovett's record written that same afternoon, when he had asked Clifford who MacDonald was, Clifford had answered that he knew only that MacDonald had been a member of the Anglo-American committee and he assumed that "this meant that Mr. MacDonald was recognized as a proponent of the Zionist cause." Lovett asked whether the president had considered the possible repercussions of such an appointment during the current truce period in the war in Israel. Clifford replied that he knew none of the background but "the President was positive, had made up his mind, and . . . there was obviously no room for argument." When Lovett asked if the department could have time to consider the matter, Clifford said that the president's directive was affirmative and the decision had already been made.[32]

The White House aides, Clifford, Connelly, and Niles, derided Lovett's apparent concern whether Israel would agree to MacDonald as sheer "nonsense." Clifford phoned Israel's ambassador-elect, Eliahu Epstein, to find out if he had the authority to approve MacDonald and whether he would be in favor. Epstein replied to both queries in the affirmative. Clifford next informed Lovett, who was left with no choice but to contact Epstein and inform him officially of MacDonald's appointment.[33]

MacDonald later told State Department officials about the

president's desire to have "his own independent means of communication and of information to and from the State of Israel."[34] On July 21, when Marshall eventually received MacDonald for an interview prior to his departure for Israel, the secretary of state reassured the new ambassador that he had not opposed his appointment on personal grounds but that he had resented it being made without any "opportunity for consultation or comment."[35]

Marshall had been so upset by the White House's "precipitate action" and its failure to give the department "an opportunity to put the President in possession of any pertinent facts" that he had written Truman a letter from Walter Reed Hospital. He was persuaded not to send it, but he was still determined to discuss the issue in person with the president.[36]

Marshall and Truman evidently did meet, though no protocol of any such meeting has been found. Marshall elicited from the president a promise "that no more off-the-cuff statements on Palestine would be forthcoming from the White House without Marshall's consent."[37] Whether Marshall went so far as to lay down an ultimatum or not, Truman dared not alienate his secretary of state in an election year. The White House was aware that if it again overruled Marshall on Palestine, it would be open to Republican charges of playing politics with the national interest against the advice of the official primarily responsible for the direction of foreign policy.[38]

THE ANGLO-AMERICAN "ENTENTE CORDIALE"

In the meantime, war had raged in Israel for nearly a month. Following negotiations with the belligerents, the UN mediator, Count Bernadotte, was able to secure a precarious truce, which held from June 11 to July 9, 1948. On June 28, after conferences with both Arabs and Jews, Bernadotte produced his first plan for a solution to the problem.

The plan constituted a drastic departure from the UN partition resolution. It proposed a union of Israel and Transjordan, with Israel to cede all of the Negev and Jerusalem to Abdullah. In return, the Jews would receive a part, or the whole of, western Galilee.[39]

Bernadotte's plan reflected what he saw as a military stalemate and his opinion that a binational, unitary state was now preferable to partition. In this he was trying to turn back the clock from the UN resolution to the now-defunct proposals of the Anglo-American committee.

The only party that took any satisfaction in the plan was Abdullah, whose desert kingdom was to receive between 50 percent to 80 percent of mandatory Palestine. Ben-Gurion was convinced from the outset that Bernadotte was Bevin's "cat's-paw."[40] But the plan was perhaps tilted too overtly in Abdullah's favor for even the British to stomach. They thought that the mediator's proposal had "given dangerous encouragement to the extremists of both sides" and that the proposal to hand over Jerusalem (where the "bulk of population and nearly all the brains [were] Jewish") to the Arabs was not a claim the Arabs themselves would have made.[41]

Even so, through the agency of Abdullah, their faithful ally, the British stood to retain control over large parts of Palestine, including the strategically important Negev and several military bases. This outraged not only the Zionists—who would now accept nothing short of full sovereignty, as resolved by the United Nations the previous November—but also the other Arab states and the dominant Husayni faction of the Palestinian Arabs, who saw in the plan a conspiracy to divide up Palestine between the Zionists and Abdullah.

Bernadotte's first plan was greeted with universal derision. Even Abdullah dared not support it in public. On July 9 fighting broke out again, and during the "ten-days war" that followed, Israeli victories brought under Israel's control three times as much territory as it had won during the first month's fighting. The second cease-fire, imposed on July 18 under threat of UN sanctions, had none of the virtues of the military stalemate that had pertained at the time of the first truce. The Israelis had greatly increased their military capacity, and their victories inspired confidence. In contrast, the Arab states, having committed themselves publicly to a jihad against the Jewish state, were unable either to concede military defeat or to back down.

It became obvious that any further attempt by Count Bernadotte to formulate a solution would require the determined support of the Great Powers, primarily of the patrons of the warring parties, Britain and the United States. Britain in particular wanted to prevent Bernadotte from repeating the mistakes of his first plan. That plan had contained important strategic dividends for Britain, but it had been discredited because of its undue bias in favor of Abdullah, universally regarded as a British stooge.

The State Department was all in favor of close collaboration with the British on the Israel question. On June 25, Secretary of State Marshall had cabled Ambassador Lewis Douglas in London: "We hope, now that the 'entente cordiale' has been reestablished, that both govts will be able to pull in tandem to assist in the constructive working out of this onerous Palestine problem."[42]

Marshall agreed readily that Douglas, who enjoyed "direct and influential access to Bevin," should be the main channel of communication between the two governments.[43] In effect, Douglas slavishly advocated the British viewpoint. On August 2 he conveyed to Marshall London's opinion that once Britain and the United States could "agree that a new hand has been dealt in Palestine and that cards now available must be played to secure a lasting settlement" they might make it clear to Bernadotte, either in the Middle East or during his Swedish visit, that in general they approved of his first plan, which recognized the new military reality after the fighting. In that event the two countries would then be able to go to the United Nations in joint support of the mediator's new report.[44]

Two days later Bevin sent to Washington his ideas for a permanent settlement. He now conceded that the State of Israel had proved itself on the field of battle and was securely established. It was now up to the Atlantic allies to bring an end to the war and promote a permanent solution along the "lines-of-force frontier." The British warned that the disruption of work at the Haifa oil refinery was posing a "grave threat" to Europe's oil supplies and that the West was now confronted with bitter Arab resentment, exacerbated by the recent imposition of the truce under threat of sanctions.[45]

The Foreign Office was well aware of the "special difficulties" (i.e., the presidential elections) confronting the U.S. government at the time but hoped that even if the Americans were unable openly to support the British position they would not oppose a British resolution at the United Nations, like the truce which might need to be imposed. The British favored a solution along the lines of Bernadotte's plan, minus the idea of a union between the two states while retaining some form of international responsibility for Jerusalem, though not necessarily under Arab sovereignty.[46] With the Negev in Abdullah's hands and Haifa a free port or under some form of international regime, British strategic interests would be assured.

If they did not cooperate on this, warned Bevin, "Arab revulsion for West would help spread Soviet influence," and the West would be unable any longer to count on the Arabs for their strategic requirements.[47]

Two days after this dispatch was sent, Douglas informed the State Department that Bevin thought "the Palestine situation [was] just as serious as Berlin" and that in Palestine also, if the two allies went "slack" they would "lose."[48]

On August 12 Count Bernadotte returned to Europe, where he chaired an international conference of the Red Cross for nearly a month. On August 9, his deputy, Ralph Bunche, called on Marshall in Washington. Bernadotte was only too ready to cooperate with the British and Americans. He now believed that if he could bring about a joint Anglo-American consensus with him, then both Jews and Arabs, although protesting, would arrive eventually and quietly at a settlement. Bernadotte, like the British, still adhered to the basic ideas of his first plan; western Galilee (which the Jews had just conquered) should be given to Israel, in return for which it should give up most of the Negev. Marshall made no comment to Bunche, but as he reported to Douglas, they had yet to receive clearance for any stand on the mediator's proposals from the White House.[49]

Three days later Marshall warned Truman they were running grave risks in the Middle East. Should Israel renew hostilities against Transjordan, the British might feel obliged to honor their commitments to that country under their existing treaty. If that came to pass, there would be an outcry in the United States for lifting its arms embargo on Israel. The result would be that "the two great Anglo-Saxon partners would be supplying and aiding two little states on the opposite sides of a serious war, from which only the Soviet Union could profit."[50]

Bernadotte's mission had now undergone a significant transformation, one which was to be well hidden from the public
eye. From a mission to seek a solution through negotiation with
the belligerents, Bernadotte now became the willing instrument
wherewith the Great Powers would try to impose a settlement
on both sides.[51]

President Truman was kept fully apprised of the new policy
in its general outline, if not in its specific details. Truman approved in advance a State Department policy instruction sent
September 1 to Ambassador MacDonald in Tel Aviv. The intention to propose territorial amendments to the UN partition
resolution was explained as follows:

> The US feels that the new State of Israel should have boundaries
> which will make it more homogeneous and well integrated than the
> hourglass frontiers drawn on the map of the November 29 Resolu-
> tion. . . . Specifically, it would appear to us that Israel might expand
> into the rich area of Galilee, which it now holds in military occupation,
> in return for relinquishing a large portion of the Negev to Transjor-
> dan. This would leave the new State with materially improved fron-
> tiers and considerably enriched in terms of natural resources by ac-
> quisition of Galilee in return for the desert Negev.[52]

Truman also approved Marshall's intention to coordinate
U.S. policy with Britain and his suggestion that the two governments "concert a line of policy with the United Nations Mediator, Count Bernadotte." Truman was informed that Bernadotte's views were similar to those of the department, save for
its suggestion that Jerusalem be placed under Arab sovereignty
with the Jews being guaranteed local autonomy. The department was "still inclined to believe that internationalization of
this holy city would be the wisest course."[53]

On the same day, September 1, Douglas telegraphed to Washington the Foreign Office "tactical plan." After Anglo-American
agreement on the substance of the Bernadotte plan, the United
States and Britain should jointly present their views to the mediator, who might wish to amend it. This consultation was regarded by the British as being of "cardinal importance," as the
final product "must appear to be entirely [the] Mediator's own
and must have behind it [the] full weight of [the] Mediator's

conviction."[54] The Foreign Office felt it essential that from the moment that Bernadotte's proposals became known they should be labeled "Mediator—made in Sweden." Douglas's telegram read further: "If through leaks a Jewish-American label should become attached to US-UK thinking this would stiffen Arab resistance to proposals when US and UK voice support for Mediator and ask Arab States to acquiesce in them."[55]

On September 10 Robert McClintock, of the State Department's Office of UN Affairs, was directed to proceed to Rhodes to consult with Bernadotte, who had returned there on September 3. McClintock was to present the Anglo-American plan, which essentially followed Marshall's directive of September 1. McClintock's mission was to be shrouded in secrecy—the ostensible purpose of his visit was to study the Arab refugee problem.[56]

McClintock traveled to Egypt and thence to Rhodes with Sir John Troutbeck of the British Middle East Office, Cairo. The two men arrived on Rhodes on September 13. After two days of talks they reached agreement with Bernadotte on the exchange of the Negev for Galilee and on the internationalization of Jerusalem. There was but a single American reservation. Although McClintock supported the transfer of the Negev to the Arabs, he warned that Jewish pressure might force his government to question this. As a sop to the Zionist lobby, the State Department was considering offering the Jews a "token salient" in the northern Negev, down to the Beersheba-Gaza road.[57]

THE BERNADOTTE PLAN

Bernadotte completed his second plan on September 16. It followed the Anglo-American desiderata. The Jewish state was to receive Galilee but was to cede to the Arabs the Negev from Majdal (today's Ashkelon) south. The United Nations would guarantee the new borders; Haifa, including the oil refineries and terminals in the bay area, was to become a free port and Lydda a free airport. Jerusalem was to remain under UN control, with full safeguards for the holy places. The right of the Arab refugees to return was declared inalienable.[58]

On September 17, the day after completing his report, Bernadotte was assassinated in Jerusalem by Jewish terrorists. His plan was published posthumously on September 20.

Ambassador Douglas telegraphed Marshall an important message, "Personal for eyes Secretary and Lovett only," enclosing what he believed might become "the keystone of the arch" that they had been trying to build. Bevin had handed him a draft statement in support of the new report with the "greatest trepidation" since it would "once and for all put His Majesty's Government flatly on record as favoring partition as a permanent solution for Palestine and thus burn His Majesty's Government's boats with the Arabs."[59]

Bevin was due to make his endorsement public in the House of Commons on September 22, and he wanted Marshall to publicize his support the day before if possible. Making simultaneous statements would strengthen the idea that the Bernadotte plan was in fact an Anglo-American deal, and if the British "were to speak first, and be echoed by [a] later US statement, this would strengthen [the] idea which [the] Zionists have been propagating that US foreign policy is formulated in Whitehall." Bevin asked Marshall to state that the new plan was in his opinion fair and constituted an equitable basis for negotiation.[60]

Inevitably, fears of Zionist influences at the White House were never far from the minds of the diplomats. Douglas warned: "If we should become the prey of Zionist forces, which will cause the UK to become the protector of the Arabs, this will only prolong that dangerous sore in Palestine, and possibly spread the infection."[61]

The annual General Assembly of the United Nations opened in Paris on September 21, 1948. (John Foster Dulles, a Republican member of the U.S. delegation to the United Nations, told the Zionists that the assembly was convened in Paris to "reduce to a minimum" the influence of the Jews and of President Truman. Dulles and Marshall saw "eye to eye" on this.)[62] At 4:00 P.M. local time on the opening day of the assembly, Secretary Marshall issued the following statement: "The US considers that the conclusions contained in the final report of Count Bernadotte offer a generally fair basis for settlement of the Palestine question. My government is of the opinion that the conclusions are sound and strongly urges the parties and the General Assembly to accept them in their entirety as the best possible basis for bringing peace to a distracted land."[63] On the next day, September 22, Foreign Secretary Bevin issued a similar statement in the British House of Commons.

History rarely repeats itself, but events from here on begin to resemble those of the previous spring. Marshall's September 21 statement may be compared in many respects to Austin's trusteeship statement of March 19. Both statements, which enjoyed the general endorsement of the president, ignited domestic political storms in the United States, where the Zionist lobby would manage to engineer a reversal of policy. In each case domestic pressures would bring the reassertion of direct control by the White House. In each case also subsequent Israeli victories on the battlefield would significantly help to nullify the efforts of the diplomats and their officials.

FOURTEEN

The 1948 Elections

THE ZIONIST LOBBY IN ACTION

After his precipitate recognition of Israel in May, the president had promised Secretary of State Marshall not to intervene unilaterally in the Palestine question. There are several indications that Truman did his best to honor this promise even as domestic pressures built up. Indeed, this time it would take a politically inept statement by his rival for the presidency, governor of New York Thomas Dewey, to provoke Truman once more to countermand the actions of his secretary of state. In an election year, it was perhaps inevitable.

The White House aides were concerned that Truman would suffer a setback at the November polls for not having imposed his will on the State Department. At the beginning of August, Max Lowenthal told David Niles that many Jews would abstain in the elections: "All intelligent Jews know there have been two opposing Palestine policies in this government and hold that against Truman." Lowenthal "assumed that it would not be possible for the President to change his method with Marshall, and take the Palestine situation out of [the] State Department altogether." Niles replied that a few days before the president had sent over to Marshall "a lot of stuff showing how Dewey is trying to sidle up to the Jews re Palestine, promising them everything." But Niles did not expect to learn what Marshall had said to Truman, if anything.[1]

The key development during the summer months, the Anglo-

American consultations with Count Bernadotte, was successfully kept a secret from the public. During those same months, however, Democratic politicians continued to pressure Truman on what were for the Zionists two other urgent issues: the promised $100 million loan for Israel and de jure recognition.

Israel's minister in Washington, Eliahu Epstein, complained about Washington's procrastination: "Quite frankly, the Administration has done nothing to implement its promises of financial assistance for our settlement and development requirements. Instead, we have been put off by empty words from week to week, and from month to month. I can hardly imagine that the President has known what a run-around we are being given on this question."[2]

Pressure on the White House was stepped up after August 23, when Henry Wallace released a statement urging full recognition of and a large loan to Israel. Senatorial candidate Hubert Humphrey, Congress of Industrial Organizations president Philip Murray, and the entire New York City congressional delegation, led by Emmanuel Celler, all urged Truman to "implement the Democratic party platform pledges for assistance to Israel."[3]

In early September, following Zionist pressure, Clark Clifford drew up for Truman's signature a memorandum addressed to Marshall stating the president's "desire to see an independent Jewish state flourish in Palestine" and instructing Marshall to authorize the pending loan, extend de jure recognition, and "take active steps to assist Israel in gaining admission to the United Nations." Democratic party chairman Howard McGrath claimed that the president's "sincere intentions have been sabotaged by the State Department." But Truman refused to sign the Clifford draft and acceded to Marshall's advice to hold up full recognition until after the elections in Israel, scheduled for early November.[4] (Because of the renewal of the war in Israel, the elections were delayed until January 1949.)

Truman's aides took great pains to remain tuned in to the trends of opinion prevalent within the American Jewish establishment.

On September 8 Truman received a delegation of the Jewish War Veterans of America, headed by General Julius Klein.

Truman stated that he was "the best friend the Jews had in America." Klein did not respond. Truman lamented that "he and Bevin had agreed on the best possible solution for Palestine and it was the Zionists who killed that plan by their opposition." It was Klein's impression that Truman was not quite clear as to which plan he was referring to but that he had in fact meant the Morrison-Grady plan. On the question of the American arms embargo, Klein told Truman that Israel was now forced to get its arms from Czechoslovakia and that he was driving Israel, against its wishes, into the hands of the Russians. Truman appeared worried by this line of argument. Upon leaving the White House, Klein told correspondents curtly that he had no comment, creating the impression he was dissatisfied with the interview.[5]

At their fifth convention, in November 1945, the Jewish War Veterans had resolved to call on Truman to urge the British to open Palestine to free Jewish immigration and to establish there a "Jewish National State." Although the veterans as a rule were not prominent in the American Jewish community, the White House apparently considered General Klein too important a figure to leave disenchanted. Shortly after the first interview, Klein received a telephone call, asking him to return to the White House alone to see the president again.

During their second talk, the general told Truman that even though he himself was a Republican most of the members of his organization were Democrats. Klein stated that the question of Palestine ought to be removed from domestic politics and dealt with on its own merits. The president's friendly intentions were known, but it appeared that the State Department was able to block any action favorable to the Jews. According to Klein, Truman was not at all displeased by the distinction drawn between himself and the State Department.[6]

Truman promised to get in touch with the State Department immediately, and that same afternoon Klein was invited over to see Secretary of State Marshall. Klein told Marshall that he objected strongly to the president describing himself as "the best friend" of the Jews, when such statements were not followed by any action. These statements did only harm, making the whole issue appear as one of racial relations. Klein wanted the issue judged on merit: "If justice and American interests required them to take favorable action on Israel, such action should be taken without regard to their feelings towards the Jews."[7]

Marshall, due to leave shortly for the UN General Assembly at Paris to promote Bernadotte's second plan, told Klein that "the present situation in Palestine gave more promise of a satisfactory solution than at any time since the problem had arisen" but warned that "an effective solution would probably please neither the Arab nor Israel governments."[8]

Klein was invited later by Governor Dewey to become his chief campaign adviser on Jewish affairs. But on Epstein's advice, Klein refused to take the offer "as long as the Republicans maintained their silence on Palestine."[9]

During the second week of September, Jacob Blaustein of the American Jewish Committee was called to the White House twice. On September 16 he talked alone with Truman for more than half an hour. Blaustein pressed for the full de jure recognition of Israel *before* the Israeli elections, support for an application to join the United Nations, the appointment of a full minister, an early loan, and the appointment of General Hilldring to the State Department. Blaustein was given grounds for optimism that some of his requests would be granted, in particular the loan and the appointment of Hilldring. But in a letter to Joseph Proskauer, he speculated whether the assassination of Count Bernadotte on the day after his visit to the White House might not have an adverse affect.[10]

The floodgates of domestic protest really burst with Marshall's public endorsement of Bernadotte's second plan on September 21. The American Zionist Emergency Council took out full-page ads in the press headed: "Mr. Truman: Where do you stand on this issue?" If the White House reaction was slower than that of the previous March, it was because the president was out of town, already campaigning on his whistle-stop tour. It took a week for the reports, and the pile of protest mail, to catch up with him.[11]

On September 22 a *Washington Star* column reported that New York State Democratic Committee chairman Paul Fitzpatrick had told national party leaders that the Marshall statement would prevent the party from carrying any large city in the country.[12]

Chester Bowles, Democratic candidate for governor in Connecticut, wrote a personal letter to Clark Clifford, urging him to have the president extend de jure recognition to Israel at the end of the month, the time of the Jewish high holy days. Bowles reported that Dewey was to make an important statement at the beginning of October:

If [the president] loses the opportunity of making some such statement on the occasion of the Jewish Holidays, and if action is delayed until later in October, we will get no help as far as registration is concerned and the opposition will charge him with playing politics with our foreign policy.

I really believe some action along this line is vital. I know how important it is in Connecticut; and if we are up against it here, it must be infinitely tougher in New York.[13]

Clifford, who had been Truman's special counsel at the time of the Yom Kippur statement in October 1946, must have had a feeling of déjà vu. But there was to be no Yom Kippur statement in 1948.

The State Department tried to head off the Zionist lobby. Officials were no doubt apprehensive that as in the previous March they might now fall victims to accusations of having pulled off a coup. On September 24, acting Secretary of State Lovett cabled to Truman a message informing him that Rabbi Silver had tried to plant an item in a newspaper to the effect that the Bernadotte report "was written in the State Department . . . [and] taken to Bernadotte by a State Department official after coordination with the British, and that Bernadotte used it with a few minor changes." Lovett claimed that there was no truth in Silver's story and that his department had had no part in the preparation of the report, though he did concede that it had had an opportunity to exchange views with the mediator and had been informed confidentially about the report's conclusions on the political future of Palestine.[14]

True, Truman had not been informed about McClintock's and Troutbeck's visit to Bernadotte on Rhodes, and for this the

State Department has been accused of duplicity. Yet it should be recalled that Truman had approved in advance State Department ideas about consulting with the British and about exchanging the Negev for Galilee.

Toward the end of September, Eddie Jacobson was mobilized again. Shortly after the Marshall statement Maurice Bisgyer of B'nai B'rith, who was attending the UN General Assembly, telephoned Jacobson from Paris and asked him to speak with Truman. Jacobson then rang up the president and reminded him of his promise to adhere to the November 29 borders. Truman refused to talk about the Negev although he spoke with Jacobson for one hour and twenty minutes. Truman reaffirmed his desire to help the Jews but said that he had yet to decide on any public statement.[15]

On September 27 Jacobson received a lengthy cable from Chaim Weizmann: "Only intervention of your friend, who has done so much for us, can avert the worst dangers. Please go and see him without delay, reminding him of Democratic Party pledges that no change boundaries would take place without consent Government of Israel."[16]

Jacobson left immediately for Oklahoma City to intercept the presidential train. He arrived at the same time as Brooklyn congressman Abraham J. Multer, who had flown there to advise the president of the rising storm over the Israel issue.[17] Jacobson was allowed to sit in on a meeting of White House staff aboard the train, which included Truman, Clark Clifford, Jonathan Daniels, Matt Connelly, and Charlie Ross.[18]

Jacobson was convinced by "the entire White House staff" that not only were they the Zionists' friends "but [they] were going all out for Palestine." Truman stated that he would not budge from the UN partition resolution, regardless of what Marshall, Lovett, or anyone else said; the United States would not endorse the Bernadotte proposal as written but "wanted very much to bring about peace in Palestine." Truman claimed that Marshall had acted without consulting him and that he had had nothing to do with the approval of the Bernadotte plan by the American delegation at the United Nations.

Jacobson spoke bluntly about Truman's own political future. After reminding Truman of how many times he had promised

Weizmann and himself that he would stand by the UN resolution (as recently as in August in Kansas City), Jacobson fanned the embers of Truman's animosity toward the State Department:

Now as on March 19th. your State Dept. has again acted without authority from you, but you are the man taking the blame.

You are out here shaking the bushes for a few votes while you are losing millions of them in N.Y. and Penn by the actions of a State Dept. who are tied body and soul to the British Foreign Office. To me it doesn't make sense.[19]

Jonathan Daniels drew up a pro-Zionist statement, which he insisted the president sign. But his criticism of Marshall notwithstanding, Truman refused until he had first consulted with Marshall himself.[20] Although Truman may have given the impression that as in the previous March the State Department had again embarrassed him with a public statement that he had not cleared previously, this was not apparently the case in September.

The next day, September 29, Clifford telephoned from the presidential train in Tulsa, Oklahoma, to Lovett in Washington.[21] Lovett claimed that the State Department had sent the president a copy of the Marshall statement on September 18, asking for instructions if he was not in agreement. The message had been sent via the White House Signal Center, and the department had later checked twice with the center, on the evening of September 20 and the morning of September 21, but it had not received any reply from the president. With Truman on his whistle-stop tour, communications with the White House had evidently been less than perfect. Clifford claimed that "this was all news to him" and promised to investigate.

During the one-and-a-half-hour telephone conversation between Tulsa and Washington, heated at times, and punctuated by the whistles of passing trains, Clifford returned to the by now well-worn theme: "The pressure from the Jewish groups on the President was mounting and . . . it was as bad as the time of the trusteeship suggestion."[22]

Clifford told Lovett that Truman was "deeply concerned by an apparent over-emphasis by the Secretary on the necessity for accepting the Bernadotte Plan *in its entirety*," which would contravene the "Democratic National Platform," and had ordered him to send a telegram to Marshall in Paris "completely disavowing" the secretary of state's endorsement of the Bernadotte plan.[23]

Lovett replied that any presidential rebuttal of Marshall's statement "indicating a reversal of the president's clear approval of a program discussed with him by the Secretary on September 1 and formally signed by the President on that date would put the Secretary in an intolerable position," leading to "absolutely disastrous" consequences at the United Nations, where the U.S. delegation had made agreements with others on the basis of the policy. Lovett then read to Clifford the memorandum of September 1, which referred specifically to the exchange of western Galilee for parts of the Negev.[24]

Clifford promised to put these arguments to the president. That same evening Truman personally spoke with Lovett and was finally dissuaded from sending his original message to Marshall. He compromised on a draft message to send that week to the Zionist leader Rabbi Stephen Wise, to which the State Department had no objections. In fact, it repeated the secretary of state's own language, endorsing the Bernadotte plan as offering "a basis for continuing efforts to secure a just settlement."[25]

Truman's record of these events is confusing and incomplete. He writes that at the end of September he prepared a statement reaffirming the Democratic party platform but that he waited to confer with Marshall, which he did on October 9, and then deferred to Marshall's advice to hold up the statement.[26]

Truman was still resisting domestic pressures, but barely. At the end of September, Ed Flynn was apparently authorized by the White House to inform Ben-Gurion that Truman promised to grant de jure recognition and support the loan as early as in mid-October—if he could overcome State Department opposition. If he did, he would invite Ben-Gurion to the White House for the announcement.[27]

Bearing in mind his promise to Marshall, Truman waited first for the Republicans to give their greetings on the occasion of the Jewish New Year. On September 29 Dewey issued a routine message, instead of the anticipated denunciation of the Bernadotte plan.[28]

At the State Department, Under Secretary Lovett prepared for the worst and forewarned the British:

[The State Department] and the White House are under very heavy pressure from Jewish organizations, who were very critical of American acceptance Bernadotte report, pressing strenuously through full page adverts in the newspapers and every other means for its modification in their favour. The nearness of the elections, the fact that the President had to make an election speech in New York very soon, and imminence Jewish New Year all complicating factors.[29]

But on October 2 Truman followed Dewey's lead and sent his own innocuous "personal greetings and congratulations" to Israel's first president, Chaim Weizmann. The message, drafted by Lovett, made no mention of recognition, boundaries, or the Bernadotte report.[30] In some contrast with 1946, Dewey's supreme confidence had led him to forgo playing up to the Zionists on Yom Kippur 1948.

But domestic pressure on the White House did not subside. On October 5 James B. C. Howe, a White House administrative assistant dealing with industrial affairs, sent Clifford a private memorandum recording a visit by C. T. Anderson of the Railway Political League, Washington. Anderson described the political damage done by Marshall's statement. Whereas Truman's de facto recognition had committed the United States to the boundaries recommended by the United Nations and agreed to by Israel, the Bernadotte plan had now cut that area by 50 percent. Anderson said that as a result: "The Democratic representatives in New York are being booed and heckled. For instance, such stalwarts as Congressman Celler and Congressman Sol Bloom are being given this sort of treatment when they appear in public to make speeches."[31]

Anderson, who stated that he was "not a Jew or a religious fanatic but . . . a practical politician," demanded that something had to be done "to lessen the tension over [the] situation in New York City, if the Democratic party [was] to get anywhere in the coming election in the state."[32]

As pressures for a presidential pro-Zionist statement built up in Washington, so did tensions within the American delegation to the United Nations in Paris. Eleanor Roosevelt and Ben

Cohen, the two "pro-Zionist" members of the UN delegation, were demoralized, having experienced the same discouragement from State Department officials that earlier in the year had persuaded General Hilldring to decline the White House posting to the State Department.

On October 3 Mrs. Roosevelt wrote to her friend Bernard Baruch, asking him to organize resistance to Marshall so that the Bernadotte plan would not be regarded as sacrosanct but merely as a basis for negotiation. She regarded the transfer of the Negev to the Arabs as "highly unfair" and lamented the way that she and Ben Cohen were being treated: "I have only one real backer and that is Ben Cohen. Neither of us was consulted before the Secretary made his announcement to the Press of the acceptance of the Bernadotte report."[33]

Ben Cohen poured out his own heart in a private letter to Justice Felix Frankfurter. He believed that he had been placed on the delegation "to try to help [the United States] out of hot water in the Palestine problem." But like Mrs. Roosevelt, Cohen felt a "deep sense of humiliation" over the handling of the Palestine problem and still had no idea of the delegation's real position. He went on to describe the lynch-mob atmosphere on the State Department–dominated delegation:

Marshall has been led to believe that the Department's position whatever it is is beyond reproach, that all criticism is unfair and based on ignorance and political motives or rank special pleading. Everyone who talks to the President against the Department's position is assumed to fall in one or the other of the above categories. . . . I feel only embarrassed and compromised by the piece-meal knowledge that is grudgingly accorded to us. (By us I mean generally Mrs. R and myself)—the others are generally content to be relieved of responsibility and to follow the inside click [*sic*]. . . . I don't think a public row would help particularly as my position would be ascribed to the fact that I am a Jew. My thought is therefore to try and find at an early opportunity a colorless excuse for quietly going home. . . . I have hesitated to write to Dave Niles for fear in some way the matter would get out that we were trying to upset the relations between the President and the Secretary. . . .

. . . if I remain there is always the danger that I may be unable to restrain myself and may explode in a more explosive way than I have exploded already.[34]

BIPARTISAN AND PARTISAN
POLITICS

The efforts of Secretary of Defense Forrestal the previous winter to secure a bipartisan agreement on Palestine had failed (see chapter 10). One of the reasons was that the Republicans felt that the Democrats had played politics with the issue unfairly. The Republicans, confident of winning the presidency, saw no reason to help the administration in its Palestine predicament and undoubtedly took satisfaction from the discomfort and political damage caused Truman by the clashes between the White House and the State Department. Moreover, the Republicans were not above trying to seek their own political gain from the issue. For their part the Zionists were not above playing the parties against each other. Obviously, a bipartisan agreement was the last thing they wanted. During the summer of 1948, rumors and speculation of concessions to the Zionists or of a bipartisan agreement were rife.

At the end of July 1948 a representative of John Foster Dulles and Governor Dewey called on four prominent Zionists at the suite of Dewey Stone in the Waldorf Astoria in New York City. The Republicans proposed that in return for the Zionists' support, they would "guarantee the complete recognition of a free and independent Jewish State of Palestine," the lifting of the American arms embargo, and a substantial American loan.[35]

In August Eliahu Epstein heard from "a responsible source" about a "deal" between the two major parties on Israel. Lovett, Dulles, and Vandenberg had apparently met at the beginning of August and had agreed that "they should not express views on the problems of Palestine and that U.S. Government policy on Palestine should be developed in close consultation with the British Government." Epstein wondered if party leaders knew about this agreement and what the Zionists could do to prevent "a direct betrayal of both Party platforms."[36]

All rumors notwithstanding, Dulles, who had been appointed by Truman as a member of the American delegation to the UN General Assembly in Paris, reached an understanding with the State Department that Palestine would be excluded from the area of bipartisan agreement within the delegation.[37]

Marshall's endorsement on September 21 of the second Bernadotte plan presented the Republicans with obvious political opportunities. Dulles had not been consulted by Marshall before issuing his statement, and the domestic uproar in the United States further strengthened Republican confidence. Rabbi Silver cabled directly to Dulles in Paris, protesting the Marshall endorsement of the new plan. Dulles advised Governor Dewey that should he feel constrained to dissociate himself from the administration on the Marshall statement, he "should avoid implying any position on merits," as he, Dulles, had no clear opinion as yet.[38]

Dewey, who complained that "constant travel and campaigning" were preventing him from keeping himself fully informed, replied to Dulles that he did not believe any public statement at that juncture would be wise.[39]

At the beginning of October, Dean Rusk had a talk with Dulles about the advisability of holding to a bipartisan line on Israel. Rusk, "speaking as a non-political civil servant," told Dulles that he believed that both parties agreed on the fundamentals of the Israeli issue. Differences had appeared because the administration had been in charge of negotiations between the Jews and Arabs and because the "Jews [had] succeeded in playing one party leadership off against the other in a contest for votes—votes which obviously [could not] be delivered to both parties."[40]

According to Rusk, Dulles had claimed that earlier in the year Dewey had supported a bipartisan position but the Democrats had not. Dulles was not ready to make any commitment but promised to do what he could to influence his party toward moderation. He had added that "since the Republicans felt quite confident, it might be possible for them to take a broader view on this specific issue than they might be able to do if the contest for votes were very close and bitter."[41] Rusk concluded: "If the Department of State is able to hold our line on the Bernadotte Report and to persuade Democratic leaders not to start a fresh round of new bids for Jewish support, there is a good chance that the Republicans will take a moderate view and assist in keeping the matter from flaring up again."[42]

Dulles had then discussed the matter at length with Dewey by transatlantic telephone and reported back to Rusk that the Republican leader was determined not to stir up the issue again, although he was under strong pressure to do so. Dewey's conduct would be conditioned by the president's.[43]

But Dulles was not being altogether frank with Rusk. As noted already, following Silver's protest at the end of September, Dulles had suggested to Dewey that he consider cashing in on the Zionists' anger at Marshall's endorsement of the Bernadotte report. Thus, it was to be Dewey, not Truman, who violated the domestic political status quo on Israel.

On October 22 Governor Dewey published a letter he had written to Dean Alfange, chairman of the American Christian Palestine Committee of New York, which in effect repudiated the administration's support for the Bernadotte plan and impugned Truman's personal integrity. Dewey reaffirmed the plank of the Republican platform granting "full recognition to Israel with its boundaries sanctioned by the UN and aid in developing its economy."[44]

There was an almost audible sigh of relief from the White House. Clifford wrote to Truman: "I consider Dewey's action as a serious error on his part and the best thing that has happened to us to date."[45] Lovett reported to Marshall in Paris that Dewey's statement had been "obviously designed to take advantage of [the] widely publicized criticism of [the] President for abandoning [the] Palestine plank in [the] Democratic platform and timed specifically to embarrass [the] President during his windup trip to Chicago, New York and Brooklyn next week."[46] He warned Marshall that the president's reaction was likely to be "immediate and aggressive" since Truman's adherence to the Democratic platform had been challenged.[47] Lovett had good reason to expect such a reaction, as he had just spent the morning with Clark Clifford. When Clifford had explained that the president's integrity had been impugned, Lovett had agreed that Truman now had no alternative but to reaffirm his support for his party's platform.[48]

Lovett expressed the hope that Truman would confine himself to such a reaffirmation and stress the importance of UN efforts in Paris to find an acceptable solution.[49]

ELECTION TIME:
TRUMAN REASSERTS DIRECT CONTROL

On Monday, October 25, 1948, Truman issued a press release blaming the Republicans for the renewed political outburst on Israel: "I had hoped that our foreign affairs could continue to be handled on non-partisan basis without being injected into the presidential campaign. The Republican candidate's statement, however, makes it necessary for me to reiterate my own position with respect to Palestine." [50]

Truman's statement went on to reaffirm his support for his party's platform, which had endorsed the UN partition plan, and added that "modifications thereof should be made only if fully acceptable to the State of Israel." Truman concluded by making reference to the Bernadotte plan: "A plan has been submitted which provides a basis for a renewed effort to bring about a peaceful adjustment of differences. It is hoped that by using this plan as a basis of negotiation, the conflicting claims of the parties can be settled." [51]

The contradictions in Truman's statement were exposed the next day by Senator Taft. He accused Truman of following an "uncertain and wavering" course on Palestine: "In one sentence he says that he still adheres to the Democratic platform pledge that no changes shall be made in the boundaries fixed in the UN partition resolution. In the next he says the Bernadotte Plan, changing the boundaries, cutting the State of Israel in half, and wholly unacceptable to the State of Israel, should be used as a basis for negotiations." [52]

But Truman did not restrict himself to a simple rebuff in the press.On the eve of his arrival in the critically important city of New York, Dewey had provided him with the pretext to waive all the restraints that he had hitherto observed. Truman arrived in New York City on October 27, for the climax of his whistle-stop election campaign. He was due to speak the next evening at Madison Square Garden. As early as October 25, he had informed Eddie Jacobson that he would make a statement on Palestine at the garden. Jacobson joined the Truman entourage in New York City, toured Harlem, Queens, and Brooklyn with the president and then returned with him to Kansas City on the presidential train.[53]

In the meantime, the military situation in Israel had been transformed significantly. On October 15 Israeli forces had attacked Egyptian positions in the Negev. Between October 15 and 20 the Israelis inflicted heavy losses on the Egyptian army and lifted the siege on twenty of their own beleaguered settlements. The new situation thus created threatened to render obsolete the Bernadotte plan, which rested on the "lines of force" before October 15. Yet Britain was still determined that the strategically critical Negev should go to its own client-state, Transjordan. At the United Nations in Paris, Britain and China introduced into the Security Council a joint resolution threatening sanctions if the Israelis did not withdraw behind the lines from which the recent fighting had begun.

Truman was greeted in New York by screaming headlines declaring that Britain and China had asked the United States to join them in asking for sanctions against Israel and that Marshall had agreed.[54] That evening Truman led a torchlight parade to Madison Square Garden, where labor leader Dave Dubinsky had been forced to fill empty seats with members of the band and the drill teams that were accompanying the president. In the part of his speech that dealt with Israel (drafted by Sam Rosenman), Truman boasted of his support for partition and the instant recognition of Israel. He concluded: "It is my desire to help build in Palestine a strong, prosperous, free, and independent democratic state. . . . It must be large enough, free enough and strong enough to make its people self-supporting and secure."[55]

During his stop in New York City, Truman was confronted by heavy pressure from local Democrats, especially Governor Herbert Lehman and Mayor William O'Dwyer, to reverse Marshall's support for sanctions against Israel.[56]

After intensive consultations on October 28 Clark Clifford and Oscar Ewing were deputed by Truman to draw up new instructions to Marshall. Both men missed the Madison Square Garden rally to prepare Truman's directive. Upon his return from the rally, Truman went over their draft and changed just one minor detail—the word "directed" was amended to "requested." Truman told his aides: "I don't have to direct Marshall."[57]

Truman's directive made the secretary of state's every move in Paris subject to prior White House permission. At around midnight Clifford dictated the following message in the president's name to Lovett with instructions to forward it immediately to Marshall in Paris: "I am deeply concerned over reports here of action taken in [the] Security Council on [the] Palestine question. I hope that before this nation takes any position or any statement is made by our delegation that I be advised of such contemplated action and the implications thereof."[58]

In a personal, "eyes only" telegram from Paris, Marshall asked Lovett: "To what do you think the President is referring? If you do not know, ask him direct for me."[59] Even before receiving Truman's clarification, Lovett reassured Marshall the next day: "Am told removal restrictions on normal procedures may be expected next week when silly season terminates."[60]

Lovett finally located Truman in St. Louis. The president's reply to Marshall's query came with the order that "utmost precautions be taken to maintain its personal and top secret character":

(1) President again directs every effort be made to avoid taking position on Palestine prior to Wednesday [November 3, the day after the elections]. If by any chance it appears certain vote would have to be taken on Monday or Tuesday he directs USDel to abstain. (2) On Wednesday or thereafter proceed on understanding of American position previously taken as regards truce in May and July resolutions.

Any other matters relating Palestine should be reported and cleared until present restrictions removed.[61]

On November 2 Lovett explained that Truman's latest instructions had been provoked by a headline story in the *New York Star* reporting a "serious rift in US Del to UN," according to which Mrs. Roosevelt, Ben Cohen, and Dulles had opposed any resolution that threatened sanctions. The president wished to avert any major split within the bipartisan delegation, especially as the results of the UN vote would not be known until after the results of the presidential election, at around midnight on November 2.[62]

Marshall had no choice but to withdraw American support

for the sanctions resolution, after which the British and Chinese withdrew also.

It is to be doubted if there has ever been, before or since, such a direct interplay between domestic politics and foreign affairs. The White House's interventions also prompted an unprecedented interest by State Department heads in Truman's political fortunes (which for some reason have been published in the *Foreign Relations of the United States* series of diplomatic documents). On October 30 Under Secretary Lovett sent an "Eyes only personal for Secretary" official telegram to Paris, conveying to Marshall the latest "Expert election predictions": "[they] forecast substantial Dewey majority of electoral votes by States but considerable improvement in Truman's position in popular votes, Dewey getting about fifty percent, Truman about forty-five percent. Senate race very close with probable Republican control by very slim margin."[63]

Lovett, like all the political pundits, regarded Dewey's victory as a foregone conclusion. The point of his letter was to express the pious hope that they could arrive at some "firmly agreed course of action between any succeeding Administration and [the] present one." Lovett feared the actions taken over the next few days might set a pattern that, "if subsequently reversed, could have disastrous consequences not only in [the] Middle East itself but with [America's] European associates in other vital affairs." Lovett suggested that Marshall try to arrive at an agreement with Dulles and concluded:

I am sure you agree that our past experience with formally approved positions and instructions which are subsequently and suddenly altered or revoked is increasingly dangerous and intolerable. I can imagine what you have been through in Paris. It has been absolutely hell here. As I see it, the national election itself, regardless of its outcome, gives us a new chance to review our Palestine policy, agree on a bipartisan approach and plan a consistent course of action which we can stick to honorably and resolutely.[64]

FIFTEEN

Reaching a Consensus
Israel as a Strategic Asset

Truman's victory in the presidential elections of 1948 was one of the greatest political upsets of the century, confounding all the pundits and embarrassing some newspaper editors who had rushed to press prematurely with headlines heralding Dewey's triumph.

The reasons for Truman's success have already been detailed competently by several political analysts. He won thanks to a combination of his own whistle-stop "take-it-to-the-people" politics ("oversimplification, exaggeration, stereotyping, and scapegoating") and the lackluster campaign of an overconfident Republican rival. Even so, Governor Dewey received a hundred more electoral votes than he had in 1944, and Truman's popular vote margin of 4.5 percent, in a light turnout election, was the lowest since 1916 and well below Roosevelt's average of 14.75 percent. In contrast to Roosevelt, it has been noted that Truman ran behind his own party in congressional and state races and that he "rode to victory on the coattails of Democratic governors and congressmen."[1]

On November 5 Chaim Weizmann, president of Israel, sent Truman a letter of congratulations on his electoral victory. Weizmann took the occasion to remind Truman of their meeting nearly one year before, when he had successfully persuaded Truman to intervene in person to ensure that the U.S. delegation did not work for the detachment of the Negev from the area allotted to Israel by the UN resolution. Weizmann appealed to Truman to intervene again now to prevent a forced exchange of the Negev for the Galilee.[2]

Truman's reply, not sent until November 29, is notable not so much for any political significance—for he did not in fact share Weizmann's views on the Negev and continued to believe that Israel should give it up if it wished to hold on to the new territories it had conquered, such as the Galilee—but for its sense of history and Truman's expression of a certain emotional affinity with Weizmann and the cause for which he was chief tribune. Truman's reply therefore bears quotation at some length:

> Today—the first anniversary of the Partition Resolution—is a most appropriate time for me to answer your last letter, dated November 5th.
>
> As I read your letter, I was struck by the common experience you and I have recently shared. We had both been abandoned by the so-called realistic experts to our supposedly forlorn lost causes. Yet we both kept pressing for what we were sure was right—and we were both proven to be right. My feeling of elation on the morning of November 3rd must have approximated your own feelings one year ago today, and on May 14th, and on several occasions since then.
>
> However, it does not take long for bitter and resourceful opponents to regroup their forces after they have been shattered. You in Israel have already been confronted with that situation; and I expect to be all too soon. So I understand very well your concern to prevent the undermining of your well-earned victories.[3]

One of the greatest ironies of the election, though not perhaps a surprise, was the falloff in Jewish support for Truman. Despite all his public rhetoric, and perhaps because of the sporadic nature of his interventions, Truman failed to persuade the mass of Jewish voters that his administration was pursuing a pro-Zionist policy in Israel. Secretary of State Marshall, who had expressed support for the Bernadotte plan, was still directing policy (with the president's apparent approval); and despite pious promises, Truman had yet to lift the arms embargo, or grant Israel de jure recognition, or ratify the $100 million loan he had promised Weizmann back in May. (The last two would be granted in January 1949.)

Despite strenuous efforts, Truman won only 75 percent of the Jewish vote, compared with Roosevelt's 90 percent. Because of a heavy vote for Wallace, Truman lost New York State, thus earning the dubious distinction of becoming the first president to be elected without taking that state since Wilson in 1916. He also lost Pennsylvania and Michigan, though he did win in three key states where the Jewish vote tipped the scales—California, Ohio, and Illinois.[4]

The question that will occupy us in this chapter is what became of Truman's policy on Israel once he was freed of electoral exigencies. If his support for Zionism was closely determined by electoral considerations, as I have maintained so far, then why didn't Truman fall naturally in line with State Department policy after November 3, 1948? Furthermore, it might be asked whether Truman did not feel that the defection of so many Jews from the Democratic party in 1948 had released him from any previous commitments.

Whatever the case, it should be stressed here that regardless of the plans well laid in Washington and London, Israeli military successes would ultimately determine the political outcome in Israel, as they had the previous spring.

This had been foreseen by the British well in advance. Toward the end of October 1948 the head of the Foreign Office had predicted presciently that by the time the American administration was ready to act to restrain Israel, that is, after the presidential elections, the Israelis would have ejected the Egyptians out of all of the Negev and would be "far too cock-a-hoop to be willing to retreat to the frontiers contemplated in the Bernadotte report." Once it became apparent that the report was no longer enforceable, securing a two-thirds majority for it in the General Assembly would become impossible.[5]

TRUMAN'S POSTELECTION POLICY

Truman was well informed about and gave his approval to State Department policy toward Israel during the weeks prior to the election. Both before and after the election he remained in agreement with the central thesis that guided the Foreign Office, the State Department, and Count Bernadotte: if Israel wanted to hold on to its conquests in the Galilee, it would have to give up part of the Negev. In other words, Truman adhered in principle to the 1947 UN partition plan. Any territorial revisions in Israel's favor would have to be balanced by Israeli territorial concessions elsewhere.

Shortly after the presidential elections Truman consulted on Israel with his State Department advisers and with Ambassador Douglas, who flew in from London.

The president was in general agreement with the Bernadotte plan, except for wishing to cede to the Jews a strip in the northern Negev, where most of the Israelis' twenty-three settlements were situated. But since on November 4 (the day after the presidential elections) the Security Council had finally passed a resolution threatening sanctions against Israel if it did not withdraw to the lines of October 14, it was suggested that to save face in Washington Israel should make at least a token withdrawal.[6]

On November 6 Truman met with Under Secretary Lovett and Ambassador Douglas to discuss Israel. Once again, all seemed to augur well for an Anglo-American entente on this thorny issue. Douglas reported that Bevin, in his efforts to arrive at an Anglo-American consensus, now accepted partition and was prepared to concede part of the northern Negev to Israel, provided compensation was made to the Arabs in Galilee.[7]

In a telegram approved personally by the president, Lovett reported to Marshall in Paris that Truman had reaffirmed his adherence to the Democratic party platform on Israel but he was *not* prepared to support Israel's claim to Jaffa and western Galilee (now occupied by the Israeli army) as recommended by Bernadotte unless the Israelis ceded part of the Negev as a quid pro quo. If the Israelis insisted on holding on to the Negev, as provided for in the UN plan, then Truman would insist on the UN plan in its entirety, that is, the Israelis would have to relinquish Galilee and Jaffa, and the Egyptians would have to evacuate the Israeli portion of the Negev.[8]

But there was one proviso attached to Truman's demands for a territorial compromise. On November 6, while Lovett was at the White House, Truman called in Clark Clifford. In front of Clifford, Truman told Lovett that he stood by his party's platform and did not want the boundaries of Israel, as fixed by the

UN resolution, to be changed without Israel's consent. Truman then asked Clifford to brief Lovett in detail on what he meant. The two met for half an hour. Abe Feinberg, whose financial contributions had made Truman's triumphant whistle-stop tour possible, was also at the White House that day and was shown the utmost courtesy by Clifford, who asked him to keep the White House briefed on anything he deemed important.[9]

Predictably, Truman did not wish his administration to be seen as pressuring Israel. He believed that Israel and the Arabs should be left to settle the matter between themselves or be made to adhere to the November 29 boundaries.[10] But there was a certain inner contradiction in Truman's logic. He repeated, tirelessly, that he would not support any changes in Israel's borders without its assent.[11] Yet at the same time, he refused to support any increase in the territory allotted to Israel by the UN resolution unless Israel gave up areas elsewhere, that is, in the Negev. But what was supposed to happen if Israel determined to hold on both to newly conquered Galilee and to the Negev?

James MacDonald, the American special representative in Tel Aviv, warned precisely against that contingency. His was the only discordant voice in the policy-making elite. In a telegram sent to the State Department at midday on November 4, he warned that it was "unrealistic politically and militarily" to imagine that Israel would now return to the October 14 lines, and he predicted that the UN resolution to enforce sanctions (to be passed that same afternoon) would split Israel and the West, leaving the Soviets to supply enough aid to render sanctions ineffective. In direct contradistinction to the views put by Ambassador Douglas from London, MacDonald warned against the dangers of American subordinance to the British line on Israel. In a telegram that was automatically copied to the White House, he did not fail to evoke Truman's past differences with Foreign Secretary Bevin.

The danger I fear most is that in its understandable desire to keep in step with Britain—despite HMG's record of a decade of mistakes and humiliations in this area and the British Foreign Minister's personal inclination [to] blame President Truman for HMG's failures in Palestine since [the] Anglo-American Committee report—the Department may yield to Bevin's intransigency. To do that would delay peace, weaken the US's influence and gratuitously enlarge the influence of the USSR in this strategic area.[12]

But if MacDonald's view was a singular one inside the administration, Truman's continuing reluctance to be politically aggressive toward Israel would provide the new state with the time in which to establish political facts by that branch of diplomacy known as war. The Truman administration's consistent refusal to back up its policy in the Middle East with force proved an invaluable asset to Israel.

This was well appreciated by Ambassador Douglas. Back in London by mid-November after his talks at the White House, Douglas warned against the consequences of the administration's reticence. He asked, almost rhetorically, what the administration was prepared to do if the Arabs and Jews failed to negotiate a settlement on their own: "Here, it seems to me, is the crux of the problem. Are we prepared, if necessary, to take measures against PGI [Provisional Government of Israel] to expel it from Galilee and Jaffa? If we are not prepared to do so; i.e., apply sanctions under Chapter 7, it seems to me the US position is somewhat unrealistic, since the Jews already hold Galilee and most important part of Negev by conquest."[13]

Once again, the British felt that the Americans had failed to grasp the realities of the situation in the Middle East. On November 13 Douglas was summoned to Chequers (the official country residence of British prime ministers) to be confronted by Prime Minister Attlee and Lord Tedder, chief of the Imperial General Staff. Attlee opened the forty-five-minute interview by stating that his government felt the situation in Palestine "present[ed] dangers as great and immediate to world peace and to Anglo-American cooperation as Berlin or any other present problem."[14]

The British chiefs of staff warned that Israeli advances deep into the Negev presaged an Israeli threat to 'Aqaba, the southern port of Transjordan. Bevin told Marshall that if the Jews attacked Transjordanian territory the British would be bound to come to the defense of its ally. The same applied to Egypt. But even worse, if the British now stood aside and allowed Transjordanian forces to be driven back across the Jordan (Bevin reminded Marshall that the Transjordanians had not occupied any territory that was allotted to the Jews under the UN resolution), then it might be too late to come to their aid, for the British airfield at Amman was "virtually defenseless at present." If that was allowed to happen, other countries might cease to believe in the value of a treaty with Britain, and "the whole British and perhaps Western position in the Middle East might be lost." [15]

The British also warned that if the Israelis refused to comply with the UN demands to withdraw their forces the way would be open for further unlimited breaches. The future of the UN itself was at stake ("Failure of League of Nations to take action on a similar issue was beginning of its downfall"),[16] but Washington remained unmoved by British entreaties.

On November 18 the Israelis received information about a meeting between Truman and the head of U.S. intelligence held two days before. Secretary of State Marshall had already advised Truman that to avoid sanctions the Israelis would accept the Security Council resolution (calling for a withdrawal to the October 14 lines). But the head of American intelligence held a contrary view: to the best of his knowledge, the Israelis would not give in. Truman replied that in that case his orders were not to impose sanctions on Israel. The head of intelligence warned Truman that Marshall would resign. Truman concluded enigmatically that he hoped his previous orders would be followed.[17]

On November 16 the passage of a Canadian-sponsored resolution at the United Nations calling on the Israelis and the Egyptians to negotiate took much of the sting out of the earlier sanctions resolution even if it did not abrogate it.

Three days later Philip Jessup announced in Paris that the United States would oppose any reduction in Israeli territory without Israel's consent, but if Israel wanted territory outside of that allotted by the UN resolution, it would have to negotiate an exchange with the Arabs.[18]

THE ISRAELI INVASION OF EGYPT AND TRUMAN'S ULTIMATUM

By the end of November the Egyptian expeditionary force to Palestine was tied up in what would become known as the Faluja pocket. On December 9 Israel announced that if Egypt agreed to talks Israel would allow the beginning of the evacuation of Faluja as a token of goodwill. But the Egyptian counter-condition—that the Israelis evacuate Beersheba—was rejected out of hand. Once it became apparent that the Egyptians refused to negotiate, the Israelis planned a final campaign to cut off their southern retreat, thus trapping the entire Egyptian force in Palestine.

The operation, planned by General Yigal Allon, involved crossing the Egyptian border at Abu Ageila to make diversionary attacks on Al-'Arīsh, with the main effort against the Gaza-Rafa (Gaza Strip) line. The Israeli operation was set initially for December 15 but had to be postponed because of heavy rains. It began finally on the evening of December 22 with Israeli bombing of Egyptian airfields along the coast to force the Egyptians to defend Gaza.[19]

The Israelis had taken into account the possibility of a British military intervention, in which case they would return their army across the international border. The Israeli military hierachy was not united behind Allon's plans. When Israeli forces crossed the international border on December 28, the Israeli deputy chief of staff, General Yigal Yadin, demanded that they be returned at once or, if it was impossible to stop them, that they be returned immediately after the action.[20]

Naturally, Israeli military plans were not known in advance or entirely clear to the West. The Israeli move appeared to be the materialization of the "worst-option" scenario that the British had been warning about for months. The Israeli invasion of Egypt was likely to precipitate British military action against Israel in defense of Britain's treaty ally. The consequences for the Anglo-American entente were potentially disastrous. And peace in the Middle East as a whole appeared at the brink of a precipice.

These considerations and apprehensions finally exhausted Truman's reticence and tolerance. Following representations to the State Department by Sir Oliver Franks, the British ambassador in Washington, on December 30 Truman directed James MacDonald in Tel Aviv to communicate immediately with Israeli Foreign Minister Moshe Shertok and Prime Minister David Ben-Gurion.[21] MacDonald was to inform the Israelis that the

United States was "deeply disturbed" by reports of the Israeli invasion of Egyptian territory and by the notification from the British government that unless Israeli forces withdrew the British would be bound to take steps to fulfill their obligations to Egypt under their treaty of 1936.[22]

Truman warned that his government, the first to recognize Israel and "a sponsor of Israel's application for admission to [the] UN as a 'peace-loving state,'" might be forced to reconsider its sponsorship as a result of Israel's "ill-advised action." Israel's immediate withdrawal from Egyptian territory would be the minimum required of Israel as proof of its peaceful intent.[23]

Finally, Truman stated that if reports of Israel's "threatening attitude" toward Transjordan were confirmed, the United States "would have no other course than to undertake a substantial review of its attitude toward Israel."[24]

MacDonald met Shertok first, in Tel Aviv on December 31. According to MacDonald, when the Israeli foreign minister heard the American warning, "his fingers tightened around his pen and his face [became] white with tension."[25] Ben-Gurion was holidaying at Tiberias on Lake Galilee in northern Israel. So urgently was the issue regarded that MacDonald traveled to Tiberias that same evening (New Year's Eve); he and Ben-Gurion talked for two hours, in the first hours of the new year.

When Ben-Gurion heard the American warning, he explained away the border crossing as a "tactical operation." He claimed that Israel had no intention of invading Egypt and that the Israeli forces had already been ordered to return to the Negev frontier. (Earlier, on December 31 at 6:45 P.M., Ben-Gurion had ordered his chief of staff to withdraw[26]—perhaps because he had already received a telephone report from Shertok on his meeting with MacDonald in Tel Aviv.) Ben-Gurion insisted further that Israel was on the best of terms with Transjordan and that no threats had been issued from either side. MacDonald returned to Tel Aviv by 3:15 A.M. on January 1 and cabled his report to Washington immediately.[27]

In a private part of their conversation, not reported back to Washington by MacDonald, Ben-Gurion had said that he was surprised at the tone of Truman's note, coming as it did from a friendly power. MacDonald admitted his own surprise and said he was sure that the British had dictated it.[28]

The Israeli administration was profoundly shocked by the American warning, which was interpreted universally as yet another American reversal, a return to toeing the British line. The Israeli attorney general asked MacDonald what was the legal difference between the Israeli attack on Al-'Arīsh and repeated Egyptian bomb attacks on Tel Aviv. President Weizmann asked why the Egyptian invasion of Israel had not been condemned and complained that Al-'Arīsh was a forward Egyptian air base that the Israelis had intended merely to neutralize, not to occupy.[29]

On January 2, 1949, Weizmann addressed a personal letter to Truman in which he deprecated the inequitable treatment received by Israel, in contrast to that of Egypt: "It cannot possibly be denied that Egyptian forces invaded Palestine with the object of destroying the State of Israel, while Israeli forces have not invaded Egypt with the intention of destroying the kingdom of Egypt." With "candour and frankness" he continued: "[When] Israel pursued the aggressive invader back to his base, the United States threaten[ed] to review its relations with Israel. . . . Yet at a time when Egypt was invading, attacking and bombarding Israel, the United States not only refrained from questioning Egypt's membership in the United Nations, it positively encouraged and sponsored Egypt's membership in the Security Council." Weizmann protested to Truman: "I am forced to remark that it is wholly disproportionate and out of place for Israel's right of membership to be questioned merely because the momentum of its defence temporarily took its forces into Egyptian territory."[30]

But the American warning, perceived by the Israeli government, and by some historians since, as an ultimatum, was not in fact as grave a step as it seemed at the time, and it certainly did not mark any departure from official policy. The Americans were concerned most with eliminating what might become a pretext for British military intervention, which could easily escalate into an Anglo-Israeli conflict. The American concerns were actually not unfounded. Ironically, the Israeli crossing into Sinai, as its military denouement, would finally undermine the anti-Israel forces in both the State Department and the British Foreign Office.

The last Israeli forces were supposed to have pulled out of Sinai by 5:00 A.M. on January 2, 1949. But they were still in Rafa on January 7, when between six to eight British Spitfires flew over on a reconnaissance flight. The Israelis, suspecting hostile intentions, shot down four of the British planes and, when a second flight returned later on, brought down another Spitfire. The Israelis claimed that the planes had been carrying bombs and had been shot down over Israeli territory.[31]

One plane *was* shot down over Israeli territory, and the British pilot was taken captive by the Israelis. Four other Spitfires were shot down over Egyptian territory. Ben-Gurion issued orders for the wrecks to be dragged back into Israeli territory, but this proved impossible before other British planes had photographed them.[32]

The British reconnaissance flights were in fact part of a top-secret British plan ("Operation Clatter") for military action against Israel in the event that Israel crossed the international border into Egypt. The two flights, protected by armed fighters, had been sent to determine the strength of the Israeli air force and locate its forward bases. Attlee and Bevin, both reluctant to become involved in the war, had bowed to military pressure.[33]

The Spitfires incident was a mistake, born of mutual suspicion and mistrust. (In a conversation on April 25, 1988, Ezer Weizmann, an Israeli pilot who had shot down one of the British planes, recalled that he had been sure that the planes were Egyptian. When asked if the pilots had not checked markings first, he replied, "Who ever had the time to start checking markings?")

The initial British impulse was to place the Royal Navy on the highest alert, reinforce the Royal Air Force in the Middle East, and advise British citizens resident in Israel to leave. But Foreign Secretary Bevin, mindful of American opposition and the reticence of British public opinion, recoiled from the prospect of outright war against Israel.[34]

The military option was in any case rendered academic by the cessation of hostilities between Israel and Egypt that same day, January 7. (On January 6 Ralph Bunche, acting UN mediator, had announced at Lake Success that Egypt and Israel had accepted an unconditional cease-fire, to be followed immediately by direct negotiations. Fighting stopped the next day.) As Bevin himself appreciated, the British public would not have understood, much less supported, a war against the valiant and victorious new State of Israel (map 2) in aid of a dubious, discredited, and somewhat reluctant ally, Egypt.

The Foreign Office began to reconcile itself to political defeat in Israel and drew the conclusion that it would be best to "cut [its] losses in the face of an unbreakable Israeli-American combination, though one that had begun to test American indulgence." [35] Any frontier rectifications henceforth would have to be achieved by diplomatic rather than by military moves.

The Spitfires incident, coinciding as it did with the end of hostilities between Israel and Egypt, marked a watershed in the Middle Eastern policies of Britain and the United States. The indisputable Israeli military triumph against the combined forces of the Arab world now led to a strategic reassessment of the new geopolitical reality in the area. Ironically, Truman's support for Israel, condemned so frequently as reflecting sheer political self-interest, would now be sanctified by the State Department with the halo of Western realpolitik.

STRATEGIC REASSESSMENT: ISRAEL AS A MILITARY ASSET

The British still regarded the Negev, especially the Gaza-Beersheba-Hebron-Jerusalem road, as a vital geostrategic requirement for Western interests in the Middle East. This view was pressed on London by, among others, the British military and civil authorities in Cairo: "If we believe outbreak of war with Russia in near future to be almost inevitable . . . we shall no doubt need Transjordan and Negeb [Negev] immediately for military purposes, while the other Arab countries except Egypt will be of secondary importance." [36]

After the diplomatic and military tensions of the previous months (or even years), the British were incapable of coming to terms overnight with the new Israeli state and were unable to brush aside the mutual suspicions nurtured so intensively. The

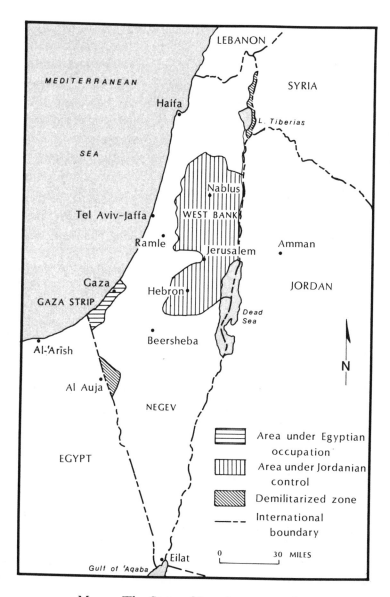

LEBANON

MEDITERRANEAN

SYRIA

Haifa

L. Tiberias

SEA

Nablus

WEST BANK

Tel Aviv-Jaffa

Ramle

Jerusalem

Amman

Gaza

Hebron

JORDAN

GAZA STRIP

Dead
Sea

Beersheba

Al-'Arish

Al Auja

N

NEGEV

Area under Egyptian
occupation

EGYPT

Area under Jordanian
control

Demilitarized zone

International
boundary

0   30 MILES

Eilat

Gulf of 'Aqaba

Map 2. The State of Israel, 1949–1967

British determined on one final, last-ditch effort to persuade the Americans of the vital need for the Negev to come under British control.

Sir Ronald Campbell, the British ambassador to Egypt, even contemplated a unilateral British action to drive the Israelis back to the October 14 lines. On January 10, 1949, he wrote to London in apocalyptic terms:

Nothing to my mind is more certain than that if the Jews are permitted to seize and hold the whole of the Negeb not only will our strategic position in the whole region be hamstrung but politically we shall be pretty well bankrupt in this part of the world.

. . . it will take force other than Egyptian or Arab to keep Jews out of Negeb, at least to keep line clear of Beersheba-Hebron-Jerusalem road:

British and American interests identical in keeping this road open in event another war—but United States too preoccupied with other issues to see this, so we might have to do it alone. . . .

. . . since our vital interests are so closely involved and our forces are on the scene, it will . . . almost certainly be up to us to take necessary action, preferably with American backing, but possibly alone, if the Middle East is, in fact, to be saved.[37]

On January 12, 1949, Ambassador Franks was received by President Truman. The British were of course preoccupied with the Negev. But Truman told Franks that he failed to comprehend British anxieties over "a small area not worth differing over." Truman saw no possibility of dividing up the Negev.[38] He apparently refused to bother himself with such "minor" questions as its strategic importance.

It had always been Truman's preference to secure a settlement without external intervention, and now he evidently believed that the armistice talks provided just such an option.

At a meeting the same day at the State Department (where Dean Acheson had replaced Marshall as secretary of state in Truman's new administration), Franks was confronted by a well-argued viewpoint that constituted no less than a revolution in the department's attitude toward Israel.

Franks told Under Secretary Lovett that the British had no confidence in the future disposition of Israel, and therefore it was "vitally necessary that [the] southern boundaries of Israel should be north of [the] Gaza, Beersheba, Jericho road." Lovett said to Franks that the British were pursuing an unrealistic policy "of containing the Israelis even at the risk of permanently estranging them." Lovett asserted that

the best way of securing Anglo-American strategic requirements in the Middle East was to win the Israelis over into the Anglo-American camp and not to alienate them permanently.[39]

The State Department was quicker than the British to draw fresh conclusions from Israel's recent military triumphs. As Lovett now saw it, Western interests in the future would lay in ensuring that Israel developed a Western orientation. If Israel was confined in a straitjacket, surrounded "with a circle of weak Arab enemies kept in a ring only by British armed assistance," it would inevitably turn hostile to the West and grow closer to the Soviets.

It is interesting to note that on December 13, 1948, *before* Israel's last offensive in the Negev, John Foster Dulles had told James MacDonald (who had duly relayed Dulles's views back to the Israelis) that he had discovered three things that past year: first, the true nature of the balance of forces in the Middle East had emerged—the impotence of the Arabs and the strength of the Jews; second, the Americans could not rely on the British, who had been proven wrong in all their estimates and prophecies; and third, whereas they must work together with the British, the Americans had to lead.[40]

But the Foreign Office was not ready yet to forget old prejudices and preconceptions and was disillusioned with what was perceived initially as President Truman's obtuseness. Taking scant encouragement from the president's swift reaction to recent events, the head of the Foreign Office wrote:

The fact is that the President has so deeply committed himself that nothing but [events] are going to move him from the position he has taken up. That he is susceptible to new events is clear from the way in which he immediately reacted to the Jewish invasion of Egypt. . . .

For instance the Jewish elections to be held on 25th Jan. may possibly produce results which will open his eyes to the Russian danger in the M.E.[41]

The continued American refusal to back Britain in ousting Israel from the Negev was still seen as a symptom of Truman's narrow-minded support for the Jews. But a proposal that either Bevin or Attlee travel to Washington to persuade the president in person was dismissed out of hand:

A weak, obstinate and suspicious man as is the President would I am certain bitterly resent such an attempt to influence him unduly. . . .

. . . we cannot achieve this cooperation at the present time by nagging at Mr. Truman either directly or by employing a neutral to do it for us. . . . there is . . . always the danger that the Jews, flushed with success, may force the issue so rapidly that events will get completely out of control before Mr. Truman has had time to react to them. Or else they may proceed so cautiously and cunningly that no "events" will happen to shock Truman out of his complacency before the whole position is lost as a result of clever diplomatic manoevering. . . . we must do our best to hold the position single-handed until President Truman begins to see straight and free himself from the Jewish pressure to which he has succumbed.[42]

But the new State Department logic filtered through gradually to the British establishment, even if the importance of Jewish influence on White House policy was never entirely discounted.

Sir Oliver Franks, in reporting back to London on the meager results of his recent talks at the White House and the State Department, explained American policy as follows: "Their attitude, at its firmest in the White House, is not due solely or mainly to Zionist pressure, though that is always there and is a powerful force. It is due chiefly to the fact that the Americans feel that their intervention with the Jews over the incursion into Egypt or the pressure they have put on the King of Egypt have together produced a situation in which agreement is likely."[43]

Franks believed also that with the recent diplomatic defeats in China and Indonesia (where Communist regimes had taken over) the Americans now believed they were in sight of a diplomatic success in the Middle East that would reverse their losses.[44]

The Foreign Office also took note of the views of its consul at Jerusalem, Sir Hugh Dow. He believed that the American attitude was based not only on internal political considerations but on a logical line of reasoning (whether mistaken or not) to the effect that a Jewish State in the Middle East is likely to prove a stronger bulwark against communism than can be formed by the Arab States. The American outlook on this pioneer immigrant State is bound to be different from the British, in view of recent American experience in assimilating large numbers of immigrants.[45]

From London the recently appointed (mid-1948) chargé at the U.S. embassy, Julius C. Holmes, reported on a fresh approach in some British circles:

Fact that US has reasoned point of view on Middle East problems as whole has begun to make its appearance in thoughtful British publications and conversations for first time without the overworked, and tendentious implications that US views re Palestine slavishly follow dictates of American Zionist pressure groups. It is source of surprise to some that underlying US policy there is hardboiled appraisal of elements of Middle East power and prospects for making best use of them in US-UK defense planning.[46]

As surmised by Holmes, Bevin had made his last attempt "to sell [the] US on UK Palestine policy." At the highest levels of the British Foreign Office, the Jewish factor was still considered paramount in White House calculations. And given the postwar reality of Britain's subordinance to its American ally, all further pursuit of a pro-Arab policy in Palestine was regarded as futile: "As long as America is a major power, and as long as she is free of major war, anyone taking on the Jews will be indirectly taking on America."[47]

Bevin did make one further effort to bind Washington to what he saw as their mutual interests in the Middle East. On his instructions Ambassador Franks sought an American public statement declaring that the two allies had a common policy in the Middle East and that both governments would recognize Israel and Transjordan. The State Department tended to accede to the British request, and on January 24 Truman approved a departmental draft that included the following passage: "While at times there may have been differences of opinion in London and Washington as how best to deal with the Palestine problem, there has been no difference whatever in our main objective."[48]

The American statement was made contingent on British recognition of Israel. Bevin had been expected to grant recognition during a debate in the House of Commons on January 26. But when the British put off their announcement (until January 29), the State Department suspended its own.[49]

On January 31 Truman granted de jure recognition to both Israel and Transjordan. Eddie Jacobson was invited to the ceremony, together with Frank Goldman and Maurice Bisgyer of B'nai B'rith.

The State Department draft statement was apparently never issued. It may be surmised that Truman's grant of de jure recognition to Transjordan, Britain's main client in the Middle East, met the British desiderata in full. The *New York Times* asserted that the timing of the American joint recognition had been suggested by the British government but added that "if the arrangement implied an Anglo–United States approach to the problem of the Middle East, there was no other evidence of it."[50]

But once forced by the Americans to shed their prejudices and entrenched stereotypes about the Jews, the British too, like their counterparts at the State Department, soon came to reassess the extent of the Israeli military triumph in 1948 and its significance for future Middle East strategic planning. Once Britain realized Israel's value as a potential ally, the domestic political underpinning of American support for the Jews was no longer relevant.

Conclusion

In the post-Watergate era public interest in "honest Harry" Truman revived. His simple, down-to-earth virtues were contrasted favorably with the double-talk and dubious machinations of some of his more polished, sophisticated successors. Yet Truman was arguably one of the most unpopular presidents during his first term in office, considered a certain loser for reelection in the presidential campaign of 1948. He then became an instant folk hero when, as underdog, he went out, "gave 'em hell," and pulled off the political surprise of the century.

It is well to bear in mind Truman's basic character traits when summarizing his record on Zionism and Israel. The straitlaced son of a small southern border town was completely at sea in the White House, as he readily confessed to reporters upon his unexpected arrival there. Determined to live down his party machine past, but browbeaten by the "striped-pants boys" (his term) of the State Department, Truman became the more dependent on his immediate, familiar entourage at the White House.

Unlike many Americans who grew up in the Midwest, Truman *did* have Jewish friends. But those few with whom Truman associated were Jews by religious conviction only. Their religion was a matter of private conscience, and they were hypersensitive about anything that might cast any doubt upon their undivided loyalty to their adopted country. The United States, not Palestine, was their "promised land."

Truman's attitude toward Jews was always ambivalent, and at times it seemed even schizophrenic. His childhood predilections for Passover matzo balls did not alter his ingrained bigotry against foreigners, whether "Rooshans" or "kikes." His business associations and enduring friendship with Eddie Jacobson did not inhibit him from writing to his fiancée, Bess Wallace, about his "smart Hebrew." Truman would undoubtedly have been surprised had anyone found this attitude sufficiently strange even to comment upon. He was a product of his parochial environment. Notwithstanding the boisterous poker games with Jewish friends and the picnics with the Jacobsons and cozy meals at their home (never reciprocated, because of Truman's snobbish mother-in-law), Truman never entirely shook off the prejudices he grew up with. Naturally, he did not air them in public, and he learned circumspection once in Washington. But well into the 1940s his private papers are replete with barbed, gratuitous comments.

Truman's Jewish acquaintances were mainly Reform Jews. Neither religion nor Zionism was ever discussed, and Truman learned nothing from them about any Jewish concerns. He could not ignore the Jewish tragedy during the 1930s or during the war, if only because many of his constituents appealed to him for help in getting their relatives out of Europe. But even so, "Jewish problems" were never brought up on social occasions.

It is impossible now for anyone to gauge Truman's feelings about the Holocaust or about those Jews who survived it, the displaced persons. But his correspondence and activity during the war do *not* indicate any deep, lasting concern with the Jewish tragedy. Like his contemporaries, he had no apparent appreciation of the historical significance of the Holocaust.

Neither Truman nor his Jewish acquaintances ever drew the same conclusions from the Holocaust as did the Zionists. Eddie Jacobson and Alex Sachs, at the local level, and the American Jewish Committee, at the national level, all agreed on Palestine as a suitable refuge for the Jewish DPs. The influential American Council for Judaism did not even agree on Palestine as the optimal shelter for the Jewish DPs. But none of the above agreed with the Zionists on the need for a Jewish state in Palestine. Their whole weltanschauung posited a pluralistic society, whether in the United States or in Palestine. Furthermore, they suffered the traditional anxieties of large sections of Diaspora Jewry, who feared that the establishment of a Jewish state elsewhere would affect their status in their adopted countries.

These were the views that Truman heard from his Jewish acquaintances and that guided him when he became president. Truman too opposed the establishment of a Jewish state, which Alex Sachs and members of the American Jewish establishment warned him would become a theocratic, even racist entity.

President Truman's record on the Zionist question is inconsistent, hallmarked by ad hoc, impromptu statements and sudden reversals of policy. The truth is that he never really knew his own mind on the issue and was therefore prone to be influenced, at times against his own inclination, by whichever issue or crisis threatened or assumed paramount importance at any particular juncture.

Truman's was basically a humanitarian approach, summed up appropriately as "refugee Zionism." After the war he was undoubtedly moved by the predicament of the DPs, languishing in makeshift camps during harsh European winters. Following the critique by Earl Harrison in August 1945, Truman ordered General Eisenhower to improve conditions in the camps. But there is little indication that Truman suffered any pangs of conscience at the failure of the West to have intervened during the war to stop the killings. But whatever his personal feelings, as president he could not have failed to appreciate the political repercussions on polling day if he did not demonstrate to five million American Jews his due concern and take vigorous action on behalf of the Jewish refugees.

Refugee Zionism, the quick dispatch of the Jewish DPs to Palestine, was Truman's solution. But it must be stressed that this *never* led him to support the Zionist goal of a Jewish state. His aides in the White House and the march of events in Israel itself, not conviction, influenced his decisions on Palestine.

It was Truman's concern to get the DPs into Palestine that led him to agree to the British proposal to set up a joint committee of inquiry. That committee's report, urging the migration of the 100,000 to Palestine but not the establishment of Jewish or Arab states, was the apogee of refugee Zionism. Truman adhered almost religiously to the report and was furious at the Zionists for rejecting it and its progeny, the Morrison-Grady plan for provincial autonomy.

Truman never ceased to believe that the joint committee's report had been the ideal solution. He referred back to it frequently, even after his own recognition of the State of Israel. In May 1948, at a meeting with Judah Magnes, the pacifist president of the Hebrew University at Jerusalem, Truman called the report a "great document" and told his interlocutor that he looked at it often and knew it almost by heart. He showed Magnes a copy of the report that he kept in his drawer, complete with a large number of tabs marking off certain sections.[1]

Why didn't the policy of refugee Zionism work? As I have shown above, Truman (and David Niles) pursued a two-track policy of trying to resettle the Jewish DPs in Palestine and, at the same time, ease American immigration laws to enable the Jewish refugees, alternatively, to find shelter in the United States. Those involved in the lobby to relax U.S. immigration restrictions—Truman, Niles, the American Council for Judaism, and the State Department—all appreciated perfectly well that large-scale Jewish immigration into the United States would deflate the Zionist campaign for a Jewish state in Israel. But, as has been seen, the new immigration bill was not passed until June 1948, *after* Israel's declaration of independence and Truman's recognition. Even then, the law passed by Congress actually discriminated against Jewish refugees.

Second, and perhaps most important, refugee Zionism did not work because the British would not agree to a unilateral gesture allowing 100,000 Jews into Palestine. And Truman was not prepared to overrule them, much less share in, or take over, their obligations in Palestine. Once Britain abdicated its mandate and the United Nations became involved, events in Palestine assumed a dynamic of their own. Once the United Nations opted for a Jewish state, it became impossible for Truman to oppose it without causing fatal harm to the new international body.

And third, from 1947, when Clark Clifford assumed control of policy making at the White House (and appointed Max Lowenthal as his adviser on Palestine), Truman was persuaded that support for a Jewish state was the most pragmatic course, one that would be not only politically rewarding but also consistent with the national interest. In particular, American support was needed to prevent the new Jewish state from becoming oriented toward the Soviets.

There can be no gainsaying the obvious fact that the Jewish vote was of considerable, potentially decisive importance in the American political system, especially during the "silly season," that is, election time. Added to this were Jewish donations to the Democratic party. For their part, the Jews worked under the conviction that they were exercising their legitimate rights as an ethnic minority, and as patriotic citizens.

But it should also be stressed that no number of Jewish votes or sum of Jewish money could have persuaded Truman to adopt a policy that he believed ran counter to the national interest. Here the White House aides turned the issue. As Truman himself believed, the unsung hero of the campaign was Max Lowenthal. He was the "back-room boy" who supplied the argumentation to Clark Clifford, the "court-house lawyer."

It should be remembered also that the Zionists did not have a monopoly on lobbying. The Arab states threatened repeatedly that they would go over to the Soviets; the State Department deliberately inflated the Arabs' threat that they would cut off their supply of oil to the West or cancel concessions; and the American oil magnates (who employed several former State Department officials) had convenient access to the highest echelons of the civil and military bureaucracy. The department also aided and encouraged the anti-Zionist Jewish organizations in their campaign to claim exclusive representation of American Jewry and coordinated efforts with the American Council for Judaism (and with David Niles) to solve the Jewish DP problem by securing them entry into the United States.

It is difficult to determine who irritated Truman more—the Zionists or the State Department. In the summer of 1946 Truman lost his patience with the Zionists and closed the White

House doors to all but Chaim Weizmann. In March 1948 it required the special mobilization of Eddie Jacobson to open them even for Weizmann.

But the State Department establishment was social anathema to Truman, too "bossy," and too transparent in its self-perceived sophistication and superiority over the small-town provincial. Truman became convinced that State Department officials were trying to subvert his presidential prerogatives and that they did not balk at withholding facts or even at telling him outright lies.

But the clashes between the White House and the State Department over Palestine not only pitted national against domestic political interests, as claimed by the department, but also jeopardized the continued tenure of Truman's revered secretary of state, General George Catlett Marshall. This was a weighty factor, one that inhibited Truman from dismissing State Department arguments outright.

But above all, two elements of force majeure defeated the attempts by Foreign Office and State Department officials to abort the establishment of Israel. First was the impact of the Holocaust on American Jewry. Following the liberation of the death camps and the publicizing of what had taken place inside them, most American Jews were converted to the Zionist thesis that Jews needed a sovereign state of their own, where those Jews who wished to might find shelter.

Even then none of the Zionist campaigns in the United States would have succeeded if the Israeli defense forces had not established Israel by the force of arms, thereby convincing the world that the Jewish community there was able and mature enough to stand on its own. The State Department was reduced to impotence in the face of Israeli military successes. By May 1948 the department's trusteeship plan would have had to have been imposed by force, against a Jewish state that enjoyed the legal and moral sanction of a UN resolution.

By the end of 1948, when against all the experts' prognoses Israel defeated the armies of five Arab states and extended its control to territories beyond those allotted to it by the UN resolution, the State Department itself changed tack. Israel's military performance in contrast to that of the Arabs led to a strategic reassessment of the Middle East. With the signing of the cease-fire agreements between Israel and its Arab neighbors in January 1949, the White House and the State Department, if only ephemerally, came to a consensus on Israel's vital importance to the West as a strategic asset.

Inherent in the Truman presidency was a unique set of circumstances that converged to determine the fate of Palestine: Truman's enduring friendships with Jews from Kansas City; a bankrupt party machine—baled out in part by significant Jewish contributions; Zionist supporters at Truman's elbow in the White House; and a stunning military triumph by Israel over the Arab states. Obviously, the same set of circumstances do not pertain today, and like history itself, they should not be expected ever to repeat themselves.

Truman's motives for supporting the rise of Israel were certainly mixed. But when the initial struggles were over and Israel was an established fact, Truman was evidently pleased with what he had done. We have no reason to doubt the sincerity of his sentiments when he wrote the following to Chaim Weizmann, the first president of Israel, on November 29, 1948, the first anniversary of the UN resolution on Palestine:

In closing, I want to tell you how happy and impressed I have been at the remarkable progress made by the new State of Israel. What you have received at the hands of the world has been far less than was your due. But you have made the most of what you have received, and I admire you for it.[2]

Notes

Chapter 1

1. Mary Paxton Keeley (childhood friend of Truman and Bess [Wallace] Truman), interview, July 12, 1966, pp. 23–24, Oral History Collection, Harry S. Truman Library (hereafter HSTL).

2. Ibid., p. 27.

3. Robert H. Ferrell, ed., *Dear Bess: The Letters from Harry to Bess Truman, 1910–1959* (New York: W. W. Norton, 1983), p. 3 (hereafter *Dear Bess*).

4. Merlin Gustafson, "Harry Truman as a Man of Faith," *Christian Century* 90 (January 1973).

5. Keeley, interview, pp. 43–44, HSTL.

6. Edgar C. "Bud" Faris, interview, March 8, 1971, p. 113, Oral History Collection, HSTL.

7. Jonathan Daniels, *The Man of Independence* (Philadelphia: Lippincott, 1950), p. 49.

8. Keeley, interview, p. 32.

9. Ibid., p. 33.

10. *Dear Bess*, p. 188.

11. Richard Lawrence Miller, *Truman: The Rise to Power* (New York: McGraw-Hill, 1986), p. 155.

12. Ibid., p. 157.

13. Daniels, *Man of Independence*, p. 49.

14. Merlin Gustafson, "Truman and Religion: The Religion of a President," *Journal of Church and State* 10, no. 3 (Autumn 1968): 380.

15. Andrew J. Dunar, *The Truman Scandals and the Politics of Morality* (Columbia: University of Missouri Press, 1984), p. 3.

16. Merle Miller, *Plain Speaking: An Oral Biography of Harry S. Truman* (New York: Berkley, 1974), p. 214.

17. Ibid., pp. 380–81; and Gustafson, "Harry Truman as a Man of Faith."

18. Louis L. Gerson, *The Hyphenate in Recent American Politics and Diplomacy* (Lawrence: University of Kansas Press, 1964), p. 95.

19. Truman, personal memorandum written in longhand, June 1, 1945, President's Secretary's Files, HSTL (hereafter PSF); this part of the memorandum has been edited out in William Hillman, ed., *Mr. President* (New York: Farrar, Strauss, and Young, 1952), p. 118.

20. Following the death of Bess Truman in 1982, the collection of Truman's letters to her was opened in March 1983 at the Truman Library. One month later, extracts were published in the *Kansas City Star;* extracts have since been published in book form; see *Dear Bess.*

21. M. Miller, *Plain Speaking,* p. 183; Brent Schondelmeyer and William D. Tammeus, article in *Kansas City Star,* April 10, 1983.

22. Harry to Bess, June 22, 1911, *Dear Bess,* p. 39; reprinted in the *Kansas City Star,* April 10, 1983.

23. Harry to Bess, June 22, 1911, *Dear Bess,* p. 52.

24. Harry to Bess, February 3, 1918, ibid., p. 242; my emphasis.

25. Ibid., pp. 227, 230.

26. Harry to Bess, February 23, 1918, ibid., p. 246.

27. Harry to Bess, March 27, 1918, ibid., p. 254.

28. Truman to Mary Ethel Noland, March 26, 1918, Mary Ethel Noland Papers, HSTL.

29. *Kansas City Star,* April 10, 1983.

30. Harry to Bess, June 30, 1935, *Dear Bess,* p. 366.

31. Harry to Bess, August 30, 1940, ibid., p. 443.

32. Carla L. Klausner, "The Zionist Spectrum," in *Mid-America's Promise: A Profile of Kansas City Jewry,* ed. Joseph P. Schultz (Kansas City, Mo.: Jewish Community Foundation of Greater Kansas City, 1982), pp. 115–16.

33. Sarah Peltzman, interview, January 15, 1973, Miscellaneous Historical Document File, HSTL. Mrs. Peltzman, matriarch of the local Orthodox and Conservative Jewish community, was a classmate of Mary Jane Truman, Harry's sister.

34. Frank J. Adler, *Roots in a Moving Stream* (Kansas City, Mo.: Congregation B'nai Jehudah, 1972), p. 199; and Richard Dean Burns, comp., *Harry S. Truman: A Bibliography of His Times and Presidency* (Wilmington, Del.: Scholarly Resources, 1984), p. xxviii.

35. Daniels, *Man of Independence,* p. 72.

36. Harry S. Truman, *Memoirs* (New York: Doubleday, 1955), vol. 1, *Year of Decisions,* p. 128; Adler, *Roots,* p. 199.

37. Truman, *Memoirs* 1 : 128.

38. Richard S. Kirkendall, "Truman's Path to Power," *Social Science* 43, no. 2 (1968): 68–69.

39. R. L. Miller, *Truman: The Rise to Power*, p. 156.

40. Kirkendall, "Truman's Path," pp. 68–69.

41. Harold F. Gosnell, *Truman's Crises: A Political Biography of Harry S. Truman* (Westport, Conn.: Greenwood Press, 1980), p. 126.

42. Jhan Robbins, *Bess and Harry: An American Love Story* (New York: G. P. Putnam's Sons, 1980), pp. 131–32.

43. Truman, *Memoirs* 1 : 128; Adler, *Roots,* p. 200; Jacobson, interview with Jonathan Daniels, September 28, 1949, no. 3466, Jonathan Daniels Papers, Southern Historical Collection, University of North Carolina, Chapel Hill.

44. Ferrell, *Dear Bess,* p. 220.

45. Truman, *Memoirs* 1 : 128.

46. Harry to Bess, December 14, 1917, *Dear Bess,* p. 238.

47. Jacobson, interview with his rabbi, Samuel S. Mayerberg, June 1945, in *Liberal Judaism* (August 1945); reprinted in *Kansas City Jewish Chronicle,* December 2, 1955, as part of the tribute paid to the recently deceased Jacobson.

48. Harry to Bess, October 28, 1917, *Dear Bess,* p. 233.

49. Harry to Bess, March 10, 1918, ibid., p. 248.

50. Truman, *Memoirs* 1 : 133.

51. Daniels, *Man of Independence,* p. 115ff; *Dear Bess,* p. 301.

52. R. L. Miller, *Truman: The Rise to Power*, p. 155.

53. Daniels, *Man of Independence,* p. 116.

54. *Dear Bess,* p. 301.

55. Gosnell, *Truman's Crises,* p. 47; Truman, *Memoirs* 1 : 134. The depression caused their stock to drop in value from thirty-five thousand dollars in January 1921 to under ten thousand dollars in January 1922.

56. R. L. Miller, *Truman: The Rise to Power*, p. 160.

57. Truman, *Memoirs* 1 : 133–34.

58. Ibid., p. 134.

59. R. L. Miller, *Truman: The Rise to Power*, p. 163; Gosnell, *Truman's Crises,* p. 47; *Dear Bess,* p. 301.

60. R. L. Miller, *Truman: The Rise to Power*, p. 159.

61. Adler, *Roots,* p. 200.

62. Jacobson, interview, September 27–28, 1949, Daniels Papers.

63. Truman, *Memoirs* 1 : 135; also Hillman, *Mr. President,* p. 173.

64. Truman, *Memoirs* 1 : 135.

65. Jacobson, interview, Daniels Papers.

66. *Kansas City Jewish Chronicle,* December 2, 1955.

67. M. Miller, *Plain Speaking,* p. 104. The Trumans lived with Bess's mother, Madge Wallace.

68. Ibid., p. 93.

69. Ibid., p. 184.

70. Paul R. Mendes-Flohr and Jehuda Reinharz, eds., *The Jew in the Modern World* (New York: Oxford University Press, 1980), p. 355.

71. Adler, *Roots,* p. 223.

72. Abraham J. Granoff, interview, April 9, 1969, pp. 23–24, Oral History Collection, HSTL.

73. Adler, *Roots,* p. 223; and Jacobson, interview, *Kansas City Star,* April 2, 1950.

74. Zvi Ganin, "Truman, American Jewry, and the Creation of Israel," in *Truman and the American Commitment to Israel,* ed. A. Weinstein and M. Maoz (Jerusalem: Magnes, 1981), p. 112.

Chapter 2

1. Truman, *Memoirs* 1:137; *Dear Bess,* pp. 303–4.

2. Truman, *Memoirs* 1:137.

3. Lyle W. Dorsett, "Truman and the Pendergast Machine," *Mid-Continent Studies Journal* 7, special section (Fall 1966): 16–17.

4. Daniels, *Man of Independence,* p. 113.

5. Ibid.

6. Ibid., and Dorsett, "Truman and the Pendergast Machine," pp. 16–17.

7. Truman, *Memoirs* 1:136.

8. Dorsett, "Truman and the Pendergast Machine," pp. 16–17.

9. Daniels, *Man of Independence,* p. 122.

10. Maurice M. Milligan, *Missouri Waltz* (New York: Scribner's, 1948), p. 223; also Truman, *Memoirs* 1:136.

11. Dorsett, "Truman and the Pendergast Machine," p. 24.

12. *Dear Bess,* p. 304.

13. Milligan, *Missouri Waltz,* pp. 97, 158, 161, 165–66; Milligan was U.S. attorney for the Western District of Missouri; following the demise of Boss Tom Pendergast in 1939, Milligan stood against Truman in the 1940 elections to the Senate.

14. Gosnell, *Truman's Crises,* p. 92.

15. *Dear Bess,* p. 304.

16. Dunar, *Truman Scandals,* p. 7.

17. Gosnell, *Truman's Crises,* pp. 122–23.

18. Dunar, *Truman Scandals,* p. 7.

19. Dorsett, "Truman and the Pendergast Machine," p. 18.

20. Dunar, *Truman Scandals,* p. 10.

21. Truman received a statewide plurality of forty-one thousand, when it was estimated that Pendergast had sixty thousand "ghost" votes at his disposal; Milligan, *Missouri Waltz*, p. 228.

22. *Dear Bess*, p. 362.

23. Dunar, *Truman Scandals*, p. 14.

24. Faris (secretary to Senator Truman, 1935–1938), interview.

25. Dunar, *Truman Scandals*, p. 14.

26. Milligan, *Missouri Waltz*, p. 191.

27. Truman, *Memoirs* 1 : 159; Milligan, *Missouri Waltz*, pp. 231–32.

28. Harry to Bess, September 15, 1940, *Dear Bess*, p. 446.

29. William E. Leuchtenberg, *In the Shadow of FDR* (Ithaca and London: Cornell University Press, 1983), p. 4.

30. Daniels, *Man of Independence*, p. 144.

31. *Washington Evening Star*, July 11, 1947, quoted in Milligan, *Missouri Waltz*, p. 260.

32. For Truman's views on the prerogatives of elected officials over civil servants, see Harry S. Truman, *Memoirs* (New York: Doubleday, 1956), vol. 2, *Years of Trial and Hope*, p. 165.

Chapter 3

1. Truman was an interventionist and spoke up frequently in favor of an all-out war effort against the Germans. He was chairman of an important Senate committee that monitored and checked military spending; his work on this committee brought Truman to national prominence and, in many senses, prepared him for the presidency.

2. Howard Sachs, memorandum, January 1978, Miscellaneous Historical Document File, HSTL. The Truman archives contain some 150 folders with files on people on whose behalf Senator Truman approached the State Department for entry visas.

3. Jacobson to Truman, January 24, 1937, box 64, Senatorial and Vice-Presidential files 71, HSTL (hereafter SVP).

4. Truman to Douglas Jenkins (U.S. consul general, Berlin), February 11, 1937, and reply, March 13, 1937, ibid.

5. Lee Erb to Truman, June 18, 1937, box 65, SVP.

6. Truman to Jenkins, June 24, 1937, ibid.

7. Truman to Jacobson, June 29, 1937, ibid.

8. Erb to Truman, July 9, 1937, ibid.

9. Erb to Truman, July 13, 1937, ibid.

10. Truman to Jenkins, July 16, 1937, ibid.

11. Truman to Erb, July 16, 1937 (enclosing a copy of his letter of the same date to Jenkins in Berlin), ibid.

12. For a critique of the Roosevelt administration's immigration

policies during World War II, see Henry L. Feingold, *The Politics of Rescue: The Roosevelt Administration and the Holocaust, 1938–1945* (New Brunswick, N.J.: Rutgers University Press, 1970); and David Wyman, *The Abandonment of the Jews* (New York: Pantheon, 1984).

13. Correspondence of February and October 1940, box 64, SVP 71.

14. Levy to Truman, June 28, 1941, and Vaughan to Levy, July 1 and September 17, 1941, box 65, ibid.

15. C. W. Evans to Truman, June 30, 1941, ibid.

16. Truman to Evans, August 7, 1942, ibid.

17. Cf. M. Marrus and R. Paxton, *Vichy France and the Jews* (New York: Basic Books, 1981).

18. William Friedman to Truman, September 28, 1942, box 66, SVP 71.

19. Correspondence between Truman and H. K. Travers, chief of the Visa Division, U.S. State Department, October–November 1942, ibid. With the Allied landings in North Africa on November 11, 1942, the Germans had occupied Southern (Vichy) France.

20. William Rosenwald, Rabbi A. H. Silver, Jonah B. Wise (national chairmen, United Jewish Appeal) to Truman, April 20, 1942, SVP 71.

21. Truman to Rosenwald, April 24, 1942, ibid.

22. Truman to Arthur Karbank, March 4, 1943, ibid.

23. David Wyman, "The American Jewish Leadership and the Holocaust," in *Jewish Leadership during the Nazi Era: Patterns of Behavior in the Free World,* ed. R. L. Braham (New York: City University of New York, 1985), p. 12.

24. Text in SVP 71; also in the records of the Senate National Defense Committee, RE 46, National Archives, Washington, D.C. (hereafter NA).

25. James H. Becker to Truman, April 16, 1943, SVP.

26. Cf. Mendes-Flohr and Reinharz, *Jew in the Modern World,* pp. 386–87.

27. Rabbi Phineas Smoller to Truman, December 2, 1943, SVP 71.

28. Truman to Smoller, December 12, 1943, ibid.

29. Cf. Zvi Ganin, *Truman, American Jewry, and Israel, 1945–1948* (New York: Holmes and Meier, 1979), p. 5; and Monty Noam Penkower, *The Jews Were Expendable: Free World Diplomacy and the Holocaust* (Urbana and Chicago: University of Illinois Press, 1983), p. 134.

30. Ganin, *Truman, American Jewry,* p. 22.

31. Wyman, "American Jewish Leadership," p. 11.

32. Andrew L. Somers to Truman, January 26, 1942, SVP 71.

33. Cf. Michael J. Cohen, *Palestine: Retreat from the Mandate, 1936–1945* (New York: Holmes and Meier, 1978), ch. 6.

34. Truman to Somers, January 28, 1942, SVP.

35. Ganin, *Truman, American Jewry*, p. 21.

36. On the Bermuda conference, see B. Wasserstein, *Britain and the Jews of Europe, 1939–1945* (Oxford: Oxford University Press, 1979), and Wyman, *Abandonment*, ch. 6.

37. Wyman, "American Jewish Leadership," p. 14.

38. Feingold, *Politics of Rescue*, p. 211.

39. Truman to Bergson, May 6, 1943, SVP 71.

40. Ibid.

41. Saul S. Friedmann, *No Haven for the Oppressed: United States Policy toward Jewish Refugees, 1938–1945* (Detroit: Wayne State University Press, 1973), p. 183; Feingold, *Politics of Rescue*, p. 211.

42. Friedmann, *No Haven*, p. 183.

43. Truman to Bergson, May 7, 1943, SVP 71.

44. Friedmann, *No Haven*, p. 184.

45. Wise to Truman, May 20, 1943, SVP 71.

46. Truman to Wise, June 1, 1943, ibid; my emphasis. The battle for North Africa was in fact already won. On May 12, 1943, the German army in Tunisia had surrendered to the Allies, and all effective German military action in North Africa had ended.

47. Ganin, *Truman, American Jewry*, p. 22.

48. Phillip Baram, *The Department of State in the Middle East, 1919–1945* (Philadelphia: University of Pennsylvania Press, 1978), p. 296.

Chapter 4

1. Abba Eban, "Dewey David Stone: Prototype of an American Zionist," in *Solidarity and Kinship: Essays on American Zionism, in Memory of Dewey David Stone*, ed. Nathan M. Kaganoff (Waltham, Mass.: American Jewish Historical Society, 1980), p. 30.

2. Cf. M. J. Cohen, *Palestine: Retreat*, ch. 5.

3. Cf. Adler, *Roots*, pp. 201–2, and Ganin, *Truman, American Jewry*, p. 21.

4. *Congressional Record*, 76th Cong., 1st sess., 1939, vol. 84, pt. 13, appendix, pp. 2231–32. I'm grateful to Dr. Benedict K. Zobrist, director of the Harry S. Truman Library, for information on this point.

5. Klausner, "Zionist Spectrum," p. 11.

6. Rabbi Stephen S. Wise to Truman, February 25, 1941, SVP 226; also Ganin, *Truman, American Jewry*, p. 21.

7. The British did not in fact stop Jewish immigration in March

1944 as feared. The Colonial Office had so carefully nursed the seventy-five thousand immigration quota allowed by the white paper that the quota was not reached until December 1945.

8. A. M. Levin to Truman, February 7, 1944, and Truman to Levin, February 16, 1944, SVP 71; my emphasis.

9. Ganin, *Truman, American Jewry*, p. 113.

10. M. J. Slonim to Truman, February 22, 1944, SVP 71; my emphasis.

11. Cf. Ganin, *Truman, American Jewry*, pp. 13–14.

12. Truman speech of March 28, 1944, and text of resolution in Reuben Fink, *America and Palestine* (New York: Herald Square Press, 1945), p. 153.

13. Ganin, *Truman, American Jewry*, p. 14.

14. Ibid; Ganin's emphasis.

15. Ibid., pp. 14–15, and Baram, *Department of State*, p. 294.

16. Ganin, *Truman, American Jewry*, p. 15.

17. Adler, *Roots*, pp. 204–6.

18. Alex F. Sachs to Truman, September 17, 1945, Post-Presidential Files 1296, HSTL (hereafter PPF).

19. Truman to Sachs, October 2, 1945, ibid.

20. Text in Ganin, *Truman, American Jewry*, p. 44.

21. Michael J. Cohen, *Palestine and the Great Powers, 1945–1948* (Princeton: Princeton University Press, 1982), p. 55; my emphasis.

22. Truman to Senator Joseph H. Ball, November 24, 1945, box 184, PSF.

23. Rabbi A. H. Silver to Senator Robert Wagner, September 6, 1945, Wagner Papers, Georgetown University, Washington, D.C., quoted in Dan Tschirgi, *The Politics of Indecision* (New York: Praeger, 1983), p. 159.

24. Proskauer to Truman, July 6, 1945, box 19 II, American Jewish Archives. My thanks to Dr. Menahem Kaufmann for showing me these documents.

25. Menahem Kaufmann, "An Ambiguous Partnership: Non-Zionists in America and the Struggle for Jewish Statehood, 1939–1948," typescript, Institute for Contemporary Jewry, Jerusalem, 1985, pp. 246–47. My thanks to Dr. Kaufmann for allowing me to see his book (forthcoming from Magnes Press, Jerusalem) before publication.

26. Ganin, *Truman, American Jewry*, p. 40.

27. Blaustein notes, September 29, 1945, Blaustein Papers, quoted in Ganin, *Truman, American Jewry*, p. 197, n. 40; see also Kaufmann, *Ambiguous Partnership*, p. 247.

28. Ganin, *Truman, American Jewry*, p. 44.

29. M. J. Cohen, *Palestine and the Great Powers,* p. 64; see also chapter 7 of this book.

30. On the joint committee of inquiry on Palestine, see Michael J. Cohen, *Palestine and the Great Powers,* pp. 60–67.

31. Vandenberg to Slomowitz, November 23, 1945, Vandenberg Papers, quoted in Ganin, *Truman, American Jewry,* p. 46.

32. Report in *Baltimore Sun,* December 9, 1945, enclosed in Halifax (British ambassador, Washington) to Foreign Office, December 9, 1945, E9614, FO 371/45403, Public Record Office (hereafter PRO).

33. Halifax to Foreign Office, December 5, 1945, E9490, FO 371/45403, PRO.

34. *New York Times,* December 5, 1945, quoted in Ganin, *Truman, American Jewry,* pp. 46–47; and Halifax to Foreign Office, December 6, 1945, E9542, FO 371/45403, PRO.

35. Halifax to Foreign Office, December 6, 1945, E9542, FO 371/45403, PRO.

36. Thomas A. Kolsky, "Jews against Zionism: The American Council for Judaism, 1942–1948," Ph.D. diss., George Washington University, 1986, p. 334.

37. Norman A. Rose, *Chaim Weizmann: A Biography* (New York: Viking, 1986), p. 407.

38. Halifax to Foreign Office, December 4, 1945, E9437, FO 371/45403, PRO.

39. Ganin, *Truman, American Jewry,* p. 47.

Chapter 5

1. Clifford, memorandum, November 19, 1947, Clifford Papers, HSTL, quoted in M. J. Cohen, *Palestine and the Great Powers,* p. 47.

2. M. J. Cohen, *Palestine and the Great Powers,* p. 48.

3. Stephen D. Isaacs, *Jews and American Politics* (New York: Doubleday, 1974), p. 6.

4. Ganin, *Truman, American Jewry,* p. 100.

5. As recalled by Emmanuel Neumann, Zionist leader, quoted in Ganin, *Truman, American Jewry,* p. 101.

6. Isaacs, *Jews and American Politics,* pp. 10–11, 16.

7. Ibid., p. 156.

8. Ibid., p. 125.

9. Peter Grose, *Israel in the Mind of America* (New York: Alfred A. Knopf, 1983), p. 187.

10. For this and following, see Marcus Cohn to John Slawson (executive vice-president, American Jewish Committee), April 19, 1945,

box 19/II, American Jewish Committee Archives, New York (here-after AJCA).

11. Ibid.

12. Cf. Jerold S. Auerbach, "Joseph M. Proskauer: American Court Jew," *American Jewish History* 69, no. 1 (September 1979): 103–16.

13. Ganin, *Truman, American Jewry,* pp. 99–100.

14. Ibid., p. 101.

15. Walter Eytan, memorandum, September 1946, Weizmann Archives, Rehovot (hereafter WA). Eytan was director of the Jewish Agency Civil Service and Diplomatic College, Jerusalem, and went on to become first director-general of the Israeli Foreign Office.

16. Silver to Ben-Gurion, October 9, 1946, WA; my emphasis.

17. MSS collection 17, 2/2, American Council for Judaism Files, American Jewish Archives; emphasis in original.

18. See Lionel Gelber to Eliahu Epstein (Jewish Agency representative in Washington), October 15, 1946, box 30, David Niles Papers, HSTL. For many years the Niles papers were held by Abram Sachar, former president of Brandeis University.

19. Ibid.

20. Ibid.

21. Eliahu Elath [formerly Eliahu Epstein], *The Struggle for Statehood: Washington, 1945–1948* (in Hebrew), vol. 2A, *January 1947–May 15, 1948* (Tel Aviv: Am Oved, 1982), p. 342.

22. Ibid., p. 81.

23. John M. Redding, *Inside the Democratic Party* (Indianapolis: Bobbs-Merrill, 1958), p. 149.

24. Truman to General Arthur G. Klein, May 5, 1948, OF 205 Misc., HSTL.

25. Bevin's record of conversation, in Fo 800/513, PRO.

26. Cf. M. J. Cohen, *Palestine and the Great Powers,* p. 135; Robert J. Donovan, *Conflict and Crisis: The Presidency of Harry S. Truman, 1945–1948* (New York: Norton, 1977), p. 320; and Nahum Goldmann, *Sixty Years of Jewish Life* (New York: Holt, Rinehart, and Winston, 1969), p. 232.

27. Donovan, *Conflict,* p. 319.

28. John Morton Blum, ed., *The Price of Vision: The Diary of Henry A. Wallace, 1942–1946* (Boston: Houghton Mifflin, 1973), pp. 189–90, 370–71.

29. M. J. Cohen, *Palestine and the Great Powers,* p. 293.

30. Quoted in Margaret Truman, *Harry S. Truman* (New York: William Morrow, 1973), pp. 384–85.

31. Joseph P. Lash, *Eleanor: The Years Alone* (New York: Norton, 1972), p. 124.

32. Leonard Dinnerstein, *America and the Survivors of the Holocaust* (New York: Columbia University Press, 1982), p. 37.

33. Eban, "Dewey David Stone," p. 34.

34. Ibid., p. 35.

35. Abraham Feinberg, interview, August 23, 1973, pp. 7–8, Oral History Collection, HSTL.

36. Ibid.

37. Ibid.

38. Ibid.

39. Alfred Steinberg, *The Man from Missouri: The Life and Times of Harry S. Truman* (New York: Putnam's, 1962), pp. 320–21.

40. Feinberg, interview (see n. 35).

41. Ibid.

42. Ed Kaufmann to David Niles, November 13, 1948, box 35, Niles Papers.

43. Feinberg, interview (see n. 35).

44. Isaacs, *Jews and American Politics*, p. 121.

45. Eban, "Dewey David Stone," p. 35.

46. Ibid., and Feinberg, memorandum, August 28, 1952, box 31, Niles Papers.

47. Gosnell, *Truman's Crises*, p. 200.

48. M. Miller, *Plain Speaking*, pp. 183–84.

49. Steinberg, *Man from Missouri*, p. 326.

50. Series of interviews with Tom L. Evans, August 8, 1962–December 19, 1963, Oral History Collection, HSTL.

51. Steinberg, *Man from Missouri*, p. 326.

52. Feinberg, interview (see n. 35).

53. Ganin, *Truman, American Jewry*, pp. 24–25.

54. Philleo Nash, untitled article, in *The Truman White House: The Administration of the Presidency, 1945–1953*, ed. Francis H. Heller (Lawrence, Kans.: Regents Press, 1980), pp. 52–56.

55. Ganin, *Truman, American Jewry*, p. 24.

56. Nash, in *Truman White House*, pp. 52–55.

57. Matt Connelly (White House press secretary), interview, November 1967 and August 1968, p. 197, Oral History Collection, HSTL.

58. Nash, in *Truman White House*.

59. Ibid.

60. Cf. M. J. Cohen, *Palestine and the Great Powers*, p. 49.

61. Henderson, interview with Allen Podet, August 5, 1975, box 2, Loy Henderson Papers, Manuscripts Division, Library of Congress.

62. Cf. *Dear Bess*, and Truman, *Memoirs;* there is no entry for Lowenthal in Burns, *Harry S. Truman: A Bibliography*, published under the auspices of the Truman Library.

63. Max Lowenthal, interviews, September 29 and November 29, 1967, Oral History Collection, HSTL; emphasis in transcript.

64. Cf. Eliahu Elath [formerly Eliahu Epstein], *The Struggle for Statehood: Washington, 1945–1948* (in Hebrew), vol. 2B, *January 1947–May 15, 1948* (Tel Aviv: Am Oved, 1982), pp. 558, 748.

65. Communication from Dr. Benedict K. Zobrist, director of the Truman Library, April 21, 1988.

66. Steinberg, *Man from Missouri*, p. 148.

67. Truman, *Memoirs* 1 : 157.

68. Daniels, *Man of Independence*, p. 184.

69. Ibid.

70. Steinberg, *Man from Missouri*, p. 148.

71. *Dear Bess*, p. 307.

72. Gosnell, *Truman's Crises*, p. 128.

73. Steinberg, *Man from Missouri*, p. 148; also Daniels, *Man of Independence*, pp. 185–87.

74. Daniels, *Man of Independence*, p. 186.

75. Harry to Bess, December 13, 1937, *Dear Bess*, p. 409.

76. Philippa Strum, *Louis D. Brandeis: Justice for the People* (Cambridge: Harvard University Press, 1984), p. 389; the other president influenced by Brandeis was Wilson.

77. Ibid.

78. Truman to Lowenthal, April 23, 1952, Post-Presidential Name File, HSTL; my emphasis.

79. Unsigned, undated memorandum, Palestine folder 1, box 12, Clark Clifford Papers, HSTL.

80. Oscar Ewing, interview, April 29–30 and May 1–2, 1969, Oral History Collection, HSTL; quoted also in Ganin, *Truman, American Jewry*, p. 157.

81. Grose, *Israel*, p. 177.

82. Ganin, *Truman, American Jewry*, pp. 157–58; and Eliahu Elath, *The Struggle for Statehood: Washington, 1945–1948* (in Hebrew), vol. 1, *1945–1946* (Tel Aviv: Am Oved, 1979), pp. 206–207.

83. Sam Rosenman, interviews, October 15, 1968, and April 23, 1969, Oral History Collection, HSTL.

84. Cf. Samuel Halperin, *The Political World of American Zionism* (Detroit: Wayne State University, 1961), p. 188.

85. Ibid., p. 187.

86. Ibid., p. 178.

87. Tschirgi, *Politics of Indecision*, pp. 47–50; Halperin, *Political World*, p. 182; Grose, *Israel*, p. 173.

88. Tschirgi, *Politics of Indecision*, p. 50.

89. Ibid.

90. Grose, *Israel,* p. 173.

91. Halperin, *Political World,* p. 184; Tschirgi, *Politics of Indecision,* p. 50.

Chapter 6

1. Baram, *Department of State,* p. 320.

2. Ibid., p. 328.

3. Ibid., p. 322.

4. Grose, *Israel,* p. 100.

5. Ibid., and Baram, *Department of State,* p. 322.

6. Some 90 percent of *Foreign Relations of the United States,* vol. 8, *1945* (Washington, D.C.: Government Printing Office, 1969) (hereafter *FRUS*), is taken up with these warnings.

7. Dean Acheson, *Present at the Creation* (New York: Norton, 1969), p. 169.

8. Baram, *Department of State,* p. 327.

9. William A. Eddy, *FDR Meets Ibn Saud* (New York: American Friends of the Middle East, 1954), p. 37. This quotation does *not* appear in the official State Department record of the meeting.

10. Eben A. Ayers diary, vol. 2, March 25, 1948, HSTL.

11. Loy Henderson to Dean Rusk, November 20, 1977, box 11, Henderson Papers.

12. Niles, memorandum to Truman, July 8, 1946, and Truman, handwritten comment, July 8, 1946, Niles Papers; Abram Sachar, *The Redemption of the Unwanted: The Post-Holocaust Years* (New York: St. Martin's/Marek, 1983), Appendix H, p. 319.

13. Elath, *Struggle for Statehood,* 2A: 36–37.

14. Max Lowenthal diary, May 26, 1948, box 27-2, Max Lowenthal Papers, University of Minnesota, Minneapolis (hereafter MLP).

15. Lowenthal diary, June 8, 1948, box 27-2, MLP.

16. Ganin, *Truman, American Jewry,* p. 127.

17. Niles to Truman, July 29, 1947 (submitted by Truman to Under Secretary of State Robert Lovett on August 6, 1947), box 184, PSF.

18. Cordell Hull, *Memoirs,* vol. 2 (London: Hodder and Stoughton, 1948), p. 1517.

19. Cf. M. J. Cohen, *Palestine: Retreat,* pp. 153–54; and George Kirk, *The Middle East in the War: Survey of International Affairs, 1939–1946* (London: Oxford University Press, 1952), p. 25, n. 1.

20. Aaron David Miller, *Search for Security: Saudi Arabian Oil and*

American Foreign Policy, 1939–1949 (Chapel Hill: University of North Carolina Press, 1980), p. 200.

21. Irvine H. Anderson, *Aramco: The United States and Saudi Arabia, a Study of the Dynamics of Foreign Oil Policy, 1933–1950* (Princeton: Princeton University Press, 1981), p. 202.

22. Lash, *Eleanor*, p. 123.

23. Epstein interview with Max Ball, February 18, 1948, in *Israel Documents, December 1947–May 1948*, ed. Gedalia Yogev (Jerusalem: Israel Government Printing Office, 1979) (hereafter *ID*), p. 355.

24. Evan M. Wilson, *Decision on Palestine* (Stanford: Hoover Institution Press, 1979), p. 152.

25. Anderson, *Aramco*, p. ix.

26. Ibid., pp. 169–70.

27. *FRUS, 1947:* 1340–41, quoted in Anderson, *Aramco*, p. 170, n. 34.

28. Fraser Wilkins, interview, June 20, 1975, Oral History Collection, HSTL.

29. Undated, unsigned memorandum, circa February or March 1948, box 30, Niles Papers.

30. 867N.01/11–446, NA.

31. Anderson, *Aramco*, p. 169, n. 29.

32. Unsigned memorandum, February or March 1948, box 30, Niles Papers.

33. Colonel Eddy left the State Department at the end of 1947 and was hired by Aramco to organize its anti-Zionist lobby in Washington. Cf. Benjamin Shwadran, *The Middle East, Oil, and the Great Powers* (New York: Transaction, 1973), p. 366, n. 43.

34. See William Eddy, memorandum, January 5, 1948, CCS 092, NA.

35. Duce report, January 1948, ibid. A copy of the memorandum was passed on to the State Department, 867N.01/1–2948, box 6762, NA; cf. William Roger Louis, *The British Empire in the Middle East, 1945–1951* (Oxford: Clarendon Press, 1984), pp. 202–3.

36. Hoskins to William Head (senior editor, *Reader's Digest*), January 26, 1948, forwarded by U.S. Embassy, Baghdad, to State Department, February 13, 1948, 867N.01/2–1348, NA.

37. Note of Henderson-Duce telephone conversation, May 15, 1948, 867N.01/5–1548, NA.

38. Marshall to Henderson, May 26, 1948, box 12, Henderson Papers.

39. Jerold S. Auerbach, *Unequal Justice: Lawyers and Social Change in Modern America* (New York: Oxford University Press, 1976), p. 188.

40. Cf. Henry L. Feingold, "Courage First and Intelligence Sec-

ond: The American Jewish Secular Elite, Roosevelt, and the Failure to Rescue," *American Jewish History* 72, no. 4 (June 1983): 424–60.

41. Ibid.

42. Cf. Wyman, *Abandonment*, p. 14.

43. Joseph M. Proskauer, *A Segment of My Times* (New York: Farrar Strauss, 1950), pp. 196–97.

44. Kaufmann, *Ambiguous Partnership*, pp. 315–16.

45. Proskauer, *Segment of My Times*, p. 198.

46. Auerbach, "Joseph M. Proskauer," p. 110.

47. Proskauer, *Segment of My Times*, p. 199.

48. Proskauer to Henry J. Kaufmann, December 13, 1948, Joseph Proskauer Palestine Correspondence File, 1948, AJCA.

49. Auerbach, "Joseph M. Proskauer," pp. 111, 115.

50. Auerbach, "Joseph M. Proskauer," p. 110.

51. Kolsky, "Jews against Zionism," p. 1.

52. Ganin, *Truman, American Jewry*, p. 11.

53. Kolsky, "Jews against Zionism," p. 10.

54. Ganin, *Truman, American Jewry*, p. 11.

55. Baram, *Department of State*, pp. 284–85.

56. Kolsky, "Jews against Zionism," pp. 9–10, 281.

57. Ibid., p. 10.

58. *New York Times*, May 3, 1947.

59. Kolsky, "Jews against Zionism," p. 429.

60. Proskauer to Kaufmann, December 13, 1948 (see n. 48).

61. Halperin, *Political World*, p. 315.

62. Goldmann, meeting with Proskauer, August 7, 1946, from the Hadassa Archives, quoted in Ganin, *Truman, American Jewry*, p. 92.

63. Auerbach, "Joseph M. Proskauer," p. 112.

64. Proskauer to Kaufmann.

65. Kolsky, "Jews against Zionism," pp. 15, 444.

Chapter 7

1. Yehuda Bauer, *Flight and Rescue: Brichah* (New York: Random House, 1970), pp. 78ff.

2. Kaufmann, "Ambiguous Partnership," p. 269.

3. Dinnerstein, *America and the Survivors*, pp. 126–27.

4. Cf. M. J. Cohen, *Palestine and the Great Powers*, pp. 55–57.

5. Adler, *Roots*, p. 203.

6. Ibid.

7. Jacobson to Mayerberg, June 18, 1945, Eddie Jacobson Papers, HSTL.

8. Notes found at the bottom of a pile of old letters and photo-

graphs in a Kansas City attic, Jacobson Holograph Chronology, HSTL. First published in the *Washington Post,* May 6, 1973; reprinted in the *Kansas City Times,* May 11, 1973.

9. Bauer, *Flight and Rescue,* p. 76.
10. Dinnerstein, *America and the Survivors,* p. 263.
11. Ibid., pp. 34–35.
12. Ibid., p. 36.
13. Ibid.
14. The report is reprinted in J. C. Hurewitz, *Diplomacy in the Near and Middle East,* vol. 2, *1914–1956* (New York: Van Nostrand, 1956), p. 253; see also Truman, *Memoirs,* 2:137–38.
15. M. J. Cohen, *Palestine and the Great Powers,* p. 57.
16. Ibid.
17. Dinnerstein, *America and the Survivors,* pp. 112–113.
18. Ibid., p. 114.
19. Ibid., p. 115.
20. Ibid.
21. Ibid., p. 116.
22. Ibid., p. 122.
23. Kolsky, "Jews against Zionism," p. 342.
24. Dinnerstein, *America and the Survivors,* pp. 121–22.
25. Ibid., pp. 123–26.
26. Ibid., pp. 123, 127, 131.
27. Ibid., p. 132.
28. Ibid., pp. 132–34.
29. Ibid., p. 135.
30. Ibid., pp. 146–47.
31. Ibid., p. 152.
32. Ibid., p. 135.
33. Ibid.
34. Ibid., p. 158.
35. Undated memorandum, MSS collection 270, 1/1 American Council for Judaism Files, American Jewish Archives.
36. Ibid.
37. Dinnerstein, *America and the Survivors,* p. 166.
38. Ibid., pp. 168–69.
39. Naomi W. Cohen, *Not Free to Desist: The American Jewish Committee, 1906–1966* (Philadelphia: Jewish Publication Society of America, 1972), p. 290.
40. Marshall-Bevin conversation, September 24, 1948, E12523, FO 371/68589, PRO.
41. Lowenthal diary, May 18, 1948, box 27-2, MLP.

42. Susan M. Hartmann, *Truman and the Eightieth Congress* (New York: Columbia University Press, 1971), p. 179.

43. Dinnerstein, *America and the Survivors*, pp. 174–75.

44. Ibid., pp. 176, 180.

45. Proskauer to Truman, June 18, 1948, Proskauer Files, Displaced Persons/Immigration, 1946–1953, AJCA.

46. Ibid.

47. Dinnerstein, *America and the Survivors*, p. 181.

48. Hartmann, *Truman and the Eightieth Congress*, pp. 184–85.

49. Dinnerstein, *America and the Survivors*, p. 271.

Chapter 8

1. *FRUS, 1945* 8:722.

2. Weizmann to Moshe Shertok, August 23, 1945, *The Letters and Papers of Chaim Weizmann*, vol. 22, *1945–1947*, ed. Joseph Heller (Jerusalem: Israel Universities Press, 1979), pp. 37–38.

3. Cf. M. J. Cohen, *Palestine and the Great Powers*, pp. 60–61.

4. Cf. John Snetsinger, *Truman, the Jewish Vote, and the Creation of Israel* (Stanford: Hoover Institution Press, 1974), p. 38.

5. Bevin to Ambassador Halifax, October 12, 1945, E7757, FO 371/45381, PRO.

6. Halifax to Bevin, October 24, 1945, E8060, FO 371/45382, PRO; my emphasis.

7. Cf. Michael J. Cohen, "The Genesis of the Anglo-American Committee on Palestine: A Case Study in the Assertion of American Hegemony," *Historical Journal* 22, no. 1 (March 1979): 185–207.

8. Halifax to Bevin, October 27, 1945, E8160, FO 371/45382, PRO.

9. Rosenman to Truman, October 23, 1945, Rosenman Subject File, Palestine, no. 3, HSTL. On April 5, 1945, Roosevelt had pledged to King Ibn Saud that no fundamental changes would be made in Palestine without consulting the Arabs.

10. Tschirgi, *Politics of Indecision*, p. 170.

11. Eleanor Roosevelt to Truman, November 20, 1945, Bernard M. Baruch Papers (a copy was mailed to Baruch the same day), Seeley G. Mudd Manuscript Library, Princeton University Library.

12. Truman to Eleanor Roosevelt, November 26, 1945, Baruch Papers.

13. Bartley Crum, *Behind the Silken Curtain* (Port Washington, N.Y.: Kennikat, 1969), p. 7.

14. Amikam Nachmani, *Great Power Discord in Palestine: The Anglo-*

American Committee of Inquiry into the Problems of European Jewry and Palestine, 1945–1946 (London: Frank Cass, 1987), p. 68.

15. Henderson, interview with Podet, August 5, 1975, box 11, Henderson Papers.

16. Richard Crossman, *Palestine Mission* (London: Harper and Brothers, 1947), p. 22.

17. Henderson, interview (see n. 15).

18. Nachmani, *Great Power Discord*, p. 75.

19. Niles Papers, quoted in Ganin, *Truman, American Jewry*, pp. 60–61; also Martin Jones, *Failure in Palestine* (London: Mansell, 1986), p. 80.

20. Cmd. 6808, April 1946, "Recommendations of the Anglo-American Committee on Palestine and Related Problems," HMSO.

21. Cf. M. J. Cohen, *Palestine and the Great Powers*, p. 105.

22. Ben-Gurion to American Zionist Emergency Council, April 22, 1946, David Ben-Gurion Archives, Sde Boker (hereafter BGA).

23. David Horowitz, memorandum, May 1946, BGA.

24. Ben-Gurion diary, April 22–23, 1946 (Paris), quoted in Nachmani, *Great Power Discord*, p. 211.

25. M. J. Cohen, *Palestine and the Great Powers*, p. 109, and Ganin, *Truman, American Jewry*, p. 63.

26. Niles to Matt Connelly, May 1, 1946, Niles Papers, HSTL.

27. Halifax to Foreign Office, May 7, 1946, in CO 537/1759, PRO.

28. M. J. Cohen, *Palestine and the Great Powers*, p. 113.

29. David Horowitz, *State in the Making* (New York: Knopf, 1953), p. 94.

30. 867N.01/5–2246, NA.

31. Attlee to Truman, June 10, 1946, and Lord Inverchapel (the new ambassador in Washington) to Bevin, June 10, 1946, E5400, E5401, FO 371/52528, PRO.

32. Undated memorandum (used by Truman at interview with Grady on July 9, 1946), *FRUS, 1946* 7:644–45, quoted in M. J. Cohen, *Palestine and the Great Powers*, p. 122.

33. Cf. Henry F. Grady, unpublished manuscript, "Adventures in Diplomacy," p. 159, HSTL; also Harriman (London) to Byrnes, July 19, 1946, *FRUS, 1946* 7:646–47.

34. Grady, manuscript, and Donovan, *Conflict*, p. 319.

35. Byrnes to Grady, teletype conference, July 26, 1946, 867N.01/7–2646, NA.

36. Ganin, *Truman, American Jewry*, p. 82.

37. Ibid., p. 75.

38. Benjamin Akzin to Rabbi Silver, September 10, 1948, Benjamin Akzin Files, 70/9, Israel State Archives (hereafter ISA).

39. Celler to Connelly, June 28, 1946, OF 204 Misc., HSTL.

40. Ganin, *Truman, American Jewry*, p. 77.

41. Reports of meeting in Z5/1175, Z4/20276, Central Zionist Archives (hereafter CZA) and in BGA.

42. Report in Z5/1175, CZA.

43. Harry Spiro to Benjamin Akzin, Z5/1175, CZA. The delegation included congressmen Celler, Marcatonio, Lynch, O'Toole, Rooney, Buckley, Rayfiel, and Klein, all Democrats, and Leonard Hall, a Republican.

44. Ibid.

45. Ganin, *Truman, American Jewry*, p. 79.

46. Kolsky, "Jews against Zionism," p. 281.

47. Leo Kohn diary, July 29, 1946, 576/P, ISA.

48. Ibid., July 30, 1946.

49. See Henry Wallace diary entry for July 30, in Blum, *Price of Vision*, pp. 606–7.

50. Ibid.

51. Kohn diary, July 30, 1946, 576/P, ISA.

52. Ganin, *Truman, American Jewry*, p. 83.

53. *The Forrestal Diaries*, ed. Walter Millis, in collaboration with E. S. Duffield (New York: Viking, 1951), p. 347.

54. Acheson, *Present at the Creation*, pp. 175–76, and Ganin, *Truman, American Jewry*, pp. 92–93.

55. Donovan, *Conflict*, p. 319.

56. Inverchapel to Foreign Office, July 31, 1946, E7325, FO 371/52548, PRO.

57. Press conference, September 5, 1946, p. 424, *Public Papers of the Presidents of the United States: Harry S. Truman, 1946* (Washington, D.C.: Government Printing Office, 1962).

58. On the Jewish revolt, cf. M. J. Cohen, *Palestine and the Great Powers*, ch. 4.

59. Goldmann, *Sixty Years*, p. 232.

60. For this and the following, cf. Ganin, *Truman, American Jewry*, pp. 90–91, and M. J. Cohen, *Palestine and the Great Powers*, pp. 147–51.

61. Acheson to Harriman, August 12, 1946, *FRUS, 1946* 7:679–82; draft in 867N.01/8–1246, NA; my emphasis.

62. Nahum Goldmann, "On the Road to Statehood: How American Support for Partition Was Achieved" (in Hebrew) *Ha'aretz* (April 4, 1958); Kohn diary, 68/34, ISA.

63. Goldmann, *Sixty Years*, pp. 234–35.

64. Kohn diary, 68/34, ISA; Proskauer, *Segment of My Times*, p. 243; Ganin, *Truman, American Jewry*, pp. 91–92.

65. John Slawson (executive of AJC), interview, Institute of Contemporary Jewry, Oral History Collection, Hebrew University, Jerusalem.

66. Kohn diary, 63/84 and Kohn Files, 576/P, ISA; Goldmann, *Sixty Years*, p. 235.

67. Truman to Attlee, August 13, 1946, E8050, FO 371/52552, PRO.

68. Balfour report, August 14, 1946, E7998, ibid.

69. Kohn (New York) to Goldmann (Paris), August 16, 1946, Kohn Files, 576/P, ISA.

70. Ganin, *Truman, American Jewry*, pp. 95–96.

71. Truman statement, *FRUS, 1946* 7:684–85.

72. Proskauer statement, box 1/19, AJCA; see also Kaufmann, "Ambiguous Partnership," p. 280.

73. Ganin, *Truman, American Jewry*, p. 102.

74. Quoted in ibid., and Jones, *Failure in Palestine*, p. 174.

75. Flynn to Truman, July 30, 1946, box 184, PSF.

76. Truman to Flynn, August 2, 1946, ibid.

77. Goldmann to Acheson, August 30, and Epstein to Goldmann, October 9, 1946, WA.

78. Clayton to Truman, September 12, 1946, *FRUS, 1946* 7: 693–94.

79. Copy of Truman to Clayton, undated, to Niles, quoted in Ganin, *Truman, American Jewry*, p. 104.

80. Harry to Bess, September 15, 1946, *Dear Bess*, p. 537.

81. Ganin, *Truman, American Jewry*, p. 105.

82. Abraham Feinberg, interview, New York, August 23, 1973, Oral History Collection, HSTL.

83. Elath, *Struggle for Statehood* 1:424–25.

84. *FRUS, 1946* 7:703; E10160, FO 371/152560, PRO; my emphasis.

85. Truman, *Memoirs* 2:153–54. In fact, Truman did *not* mention the figure 100,000 in his statement.

86. Acheson, *Present at the Creation*, p. 176.

87. Acheson-Inverchapel conversation, October 3, 1946, in 867N.01/10–346, NA. On the Arab-Jewish conference, see M. J. Cohen, *Palestine and the Great Powers*, pp. 197–202.

88. Elath, *Struggle for Statehood*, 2A:424–25.

89. Epstein to Goldmann, October 9, 1946, WA.

90. Ganin, *Truman, American Jewry*, pp. 107–8.

91. Note of Blevin-Truman meeting, December 8, 1946, FO 800/513, PRO.

Chapter 9

1. On the conference and the implications of the British reference to the United Nations, see M. J. Cohen, *Palestine and the Great Powers*, ch. 9 and pp. 266–76.

2. Ibid., p. 267.

3. Cabinet meeting, September 20, 1947, Cab 128/10, PRO.

4. Creech-Jones, September 26, 1947, E8917, FO 371/61789, ibid.

5. British UN delegation to Foreign Office, October 16, 1947, E9666, FO 371/61882, ibid.

6. Truman to Judge Robert G. Simmons, June 16, 1947: quoted in Ganin, *Truman, American Jewry*, p. 125.

7. Truman to Wise, August 6, 1947: quoted in Ganin, *Truman, American Jewry*, p. 125.

8. Cabinet meeting on August 8, 1947, reported in Millis, *Forrestal Diaries*, pp. 303–4.

9. Elath, *Struggle for Statehood* 2A:199.

10. Shertok report to American section of the Jewish Agency, September 18, 1947, 93.03/64/9, ISA. Moshe Shertok (who later took the name Sharett) was secretary of the Jewish Agency at the time. He went on to become the first foreign secretary of Israel and eventually prime minister.

11. M. J. Cohen, *Palestine and the Great Powers*, p. 279.

12. Lash, *Eleanor,* pp. 124–25.

13. Elath, *Struggle for Statehood* 2A:255.

14. See Loy Henderson, interview, June 14, 1973, p. 127, Oral History Collection, HSTL.

15. Vandenberg to Taft, October 8, 1947, box 735, Robert A. Taft Papers, Manuscripts Division, Library of Congress; emphasis in original.

16. Gordon Merriam to Fraser Wilkins, November 5, 1947, 501.BB Pal/10–2547, box 2182, NA.

17. Cf. Policy Planning Staff memorandum, January 19, 1948, *FRUS, 1948* 5:548.

18. *FRUS, 1947* 5:1190.

19. Minutes, September 15, 1947, ibid., pp. 1147–51.

20. Marshall, speech, ibid., p. 1151; my emphasis.

21. Henderson, interview (see n. 14).

22. Ibid., pp. 132–34.

23. Ibid., p. 134.

24. Hilldring, memorandum, September 24, 1947, *FRUS, 1947* 5:1162–63.

25. Elath, *Struggle for Statehood* 2A:253–54.

26. Ibid., pp. 254–55.

27. Ibid., p. 255.

28. Ibid., p. 256.

29. Meeting, October 22, 1947, 501.BB Pal/10–2247, box 2182, NA.

30. Truman to Claude Pepper (member of Senate Committee on Agriculture and Forestry), October 20, 1947, box 59, Confidential File, HSTL.

31. Jacobson to Truman, October 3, 1947, box 184, PSF, HSTL.

32. Elath, *Struggle for Statehood* 2A:256.

33. Hilldring, memorandum, October 9, 1947, *FRUS, 1947* 5: 1177–78.

34. Truman to Jacobson, October 8, 1947, box 184, PSF, HSTL.

35. Elath, *Struggle for Statehood* 2A:257.

36. Ibid., pp. 256–57.

37. Report by Leo Sack to American Zionist Emergency Council (AZEC), October 13, 1947, 2266/10, ISA.

38. State Department to UN delegation, September 23, 1947, 501.BB Pal/9–2347, box 2182, NA.

39. Lovett to Johnson, Hilldring, November 19, 1947, ibid.

40. Elath, *Struggle for Statehood* 2A:402.

41. Vera Weizmann, as told to David Tutaev, *The Impossible Takes Longer: The Memoirs of Vera Weizmann* (New York: Harper and Row, 1967), p. 219; and Chaim Weizmann, *Trial and Error* (New York: Schocken, 1966), pp. 458–59.

42. C. Weizmann, *Trial and Error*, p. 459; and Charles E. Bohlen (counselor at State Department) to Lovett, November 19, 1947, 867N.01/11–1947, box 6761, NA.

43. Donovan, *Conflict*, pp. 327–28.

44. M. J. Cohen, *Palestine and the Great Powers*, p. 292.

45. Ibid., p. 294.

46. Foreign Office to British UN delegation, September 27, 1947, E9051, FO 371/61880, PRO.

47. Matt Connelly to Truman, memorandum November 25, 1947, box 184, PSF, HSTL.

48. Lovett-Johnson-Hilldring telephone conversation, November 24, 1947 *FRUS, 1947* 5:1283–84.

49. Cf. Robert A. Divine, "The Cold War and the Election of 1948," *Journal of American History* 59 (June 1972–March 1973): 90–110. Forrestal served as secretary of defense from September 1947 to March 1949.

50. Millis, *Forrestal Diaries,* p. 344.

51. Ibid., p. 345.

52. Ibid., p. 344.

53. Arnold A. Rogow, *James Forrestal: A Study of Personality, Politics, and Policy* (New York: Macmillan, 1963), p. 276.

54. Ibid., pp. 272–73.

55. Ibid., pp. 187–88.

56. Ibid., pp. 191–92.

57. Millis, *Forrestal Diaries,* p. 344.

58. Clifford to Truman, March 8, 1948, box 14, Clifford Papers, HSTL.

59. Comay to Gering (chairman, South African Zionist Federation), December 3, 1947, 2266/15, ISA.

60. Minutes of AZEC meeting, December 11, 1947, quoted in Ganin, *Truman, American Jewry,* p. 145.

61. Ian J. Bickerton, "President Truman's Recognition of Israel," *American Jewish Historical Quarterly* 58, no. 2 (December 1968): 173–240.

62. Adler, *Roots,* p. 432, n. 59.

63. M. Truman, *Harry S. Truman,* p. 387.

64. Frank J. Adler, review of *Harry S. Truman,* by Margaret Truman, *American Jewish Historical Quarterly* 62, no. 4 (June 1973): 414–25.

65. Lowenthal diary, June 25, 1948, box 27-2, MLP.

66. Jacobson diary, Jacobson Papers, HSTL. Extracts from the diary were published first in the *Washington Post,* May 6, 1973.

67. See Granoff, interview, April 9, 1969, Oral History Collection, HSTL.

68. Ibid.

69. Ibid.

70. Ibid.

71. "Eddie Jacobson: Unofficial Envoy," *Kansas City Star,* May 13, 1965; Granoff, interview; and Maurice Bisgyer, *Challenge and Encounter* (New York: Crown, 1967), p. 188.

72. "Eddie Jacobson: Unofficial Envoy."

73. Granoff, interview (see n. 67); Abe Feinberg, interview.

74. Jacobson diary, November 1947, Jacobson Papers.

75. Henderson, interview, pp. 137–38 (see n. 14); also Donovan, *Conflict,* pp. 329–30.

76. Clifford, interview with Daniels, August 27–28 and October 10, 1949, Daniels Papers.

77. Ayers diary, November 29, 1947, HSTL. Ayers was assistant press secretary and special assistant at the White House.

78. M. J. Cohen, *Palestine and the Great Powers,* pp. 296–97.

79. Ibid., p. 297.

80. Henderson, interview (see n. 14); and D. B. Sachar, "David Niles and American Policy," senior honors thesis, Harvard University, 1959, p. 54.

81. Donovan, *Conflict,* p. 331.

82. D. B. Sachar, "David Niles," p. 73; M. J. Cohen, *Palestine and the Great Powers,* p. 298.

83. M. J. Cohen, *Palestine and the Great Powers,* p. 299.

84. Quoted in Ganin, *Truman, American Jewry,* p. 145.

85. Granoff, interview (see n. 67).

86. Jacobson diary, December 8, 1947, Jacobson Papers.

87. Adler, *Roots,* p. 207.

Chapter 10

1. M. J. Cohen, *Palestine and the Great Powers,* ch. 12.

2. Millis, *Forrestal Diaries,* p. 387.

3. J. Spanier, *American Foreign Policy since World War II* (New York: Holt, Rinehart, Winston, 1977), p. 33.

4. Elath, *Struggle for Statehood* 2B : 500.

5. Weizmann to Truman, April 9, 1948, *ID,* p. 590.

6. NEA, memorandum, December 17, 1947, 501.BB Pal/12–1747, NA; and George Kennan (director of Policy Planning Staff), memorandum, January 19, 1948, *FRUS, 1948* 5:546–54.

7. Donovan, *Conflict,* p. 370.

8. Greunther to departments of State and Defense, February 18, 1948, *FRUS, 1948* 5:631–33.

9. NEA, memorandum, December 17, 1947 (see n. 6).

10. Kaufmann, "Ambiguous Partnership," p. 382.

11. *FRUS, 1948* 5:648–49.

12. Millis, *Forrestal Diaries,* pp. 347–48.

13. Ibid., pp. 359–60.

14. Report of conversation between G. Sullivan and Freda Kirchway, February 2, 1948, *ID,* pp. 297–98.

15. Rogow, *James Forrestal,* p. 181, n. 44.

16. Millis, *Forrestal Diaries,* pp. 364–65.

17. Ibid., pp. 371–72, and Policy Planning Staff Files, lot 64 D, 543, NA.

18. Cf. Robert A. Divine, *Foreign Policy and U.S. Presidential Elections,* vol. 1, *1940–1948* (New York: New Viewpoints, 1974), p. 174, and Alonzo L. Hamby, *Beyond the New Deal: Harry S. Truman and*

American Liberalism (New York: Columbia University Press, 1973), pp. 218–19.

19. Divine, "Cold War," pp. 90–110.

20. Divine, *Foreign Policy*, 1:174.

21. Menahem Kaufmann, "Non-Zionists in American Jewry, 1939–1948," Ph.D. diss., Hebrew University, Jerusalem, 1978, pp. 567–68.

22. Harold Beeley, minute, March 21, 1948, E4008, FO 371/68540, PRO.

23. Leonard C. Meeker to Ernest A. Gross (Legal Department), November 11, 1948, 711.67N/11–548, NA, and Department of State to Truman, February 21, 1948, *FRUS, 1948* 5:637–40.

24. Truman to Marshall, February 22, 1948, *FRUS, 1948* 5:645.

25. Draft in McClintock to Lovett, February 19, 1948, 501.BB Pal/2–2348, NA; text of speech in *FRUS, 1948* 5:651–54; my emphasis.

26. Joseph and Stewart Alsop, *Washington Post*, February 27, 1948, quoted in Jones, *Failure in Palestine*, p. 334.

27. P. Mason, minute, March 4, 1948, E2937, FO 371/68535, PRO. Austin's legalistic definition of the Security Council's authority was in fact refuted by the State Department's own legal adviser, Ernest Gross; see Gross to Lovett, March 5, 1948, 501.BB Pal/3–548, NA.

28. Eleanor Roosevelt to Truman, January 29, 1948, folder 2, box 322, PSF personal file.

29. Senator F. J. Myers (Pennsylvania) to Truman, March 4, 1943, PSF.

30. William Philips to Loy Henderson, February 25, 1948, PSF.

31. Kolsky, "Jews against Zionism," p. 454.

32. Assessment by Israel Goldstein, January 19, 1948, *ID*, p. 191.

33. Gale Sullivan (vice-chairman, Democratic National Committee), interview with Freda Kirchway, February 4, 1948, *ID*, pp. 297–98.

34. C. Weizmann, *Trial and Error*, p. 471. On Weizmann's November 1947 interview, see M. J. Cohen, *Palestine and the Great Powers*, p. 289.

35. Memorandum, February 4, 1948, *ID*, pp. 294–96; among those present were Moshe Shertok, Eliahu Epstein, Ben Cohen, David Ginsburg, Robert Nathan, Oscar Gass, and Harold Leventhal.

36. Elath, *Struggle for Statehood* 2B:536.

37. Elinore Borenstine (Jacobson's daughter) to William B. Silverman, July 1968, Silverman Papers, B'nai Jehudah Archive, quoted in Adler, *Roots*, pp. 208–9.

38. Jacobson to Truman, February 2, 1948, box 184, PSF.

39. Truman to Jacobson, February 5, 1948, box 184, PSF.

40. Jacobson to Connelly, February 21, 1948, Jacobson Papers, HSTL.

41. Truman to Jacobson, February 27, 1948, Jacobson Papers, HSTL; my emphasis.

42. Epstein to Rosenman, March 8, 1948, *ID*, p. 440.

43. Redding, *Inside the Democratic Party*, p. 149.

44. Elath, *Struggle for Statehood* 2B: 629, n. 13.

45. Jacobson to Josef Cohn, March 27, 1952, reprinted in *American Jewish Archives* 20, no. 1 (April 1968): 4–15; also Adler, *Roots*, p. 210; M. Miller, *Plain Speaking*, p. 217; Truman, *Memoirs* 2: 160–61.

46. Jacobson to Cohn, March 27, 1952.

47. Ibid.

48. Truman, *Memoirs* 2: 160.

49. M. Miller, *Plain Speaking*, p. 217.

50. Jacobson to Cohn, March 27, 1952.

51. Granoff, interview, Oral History Collection, HSTL.

52. Jacobson to Cohn, March 27, 1952, and Donovan, *Conflict*, p. 375.

53. Truman, *Memoirs* 2: 161; my emphasis.

54. C. Weizmann, *Trial and Error*, p. 472, and Truman, *Memoirs* 2: 161.

Chapter 11

1. Text of Austin, statement, *FRUS, 1948* 5: 742–44.

2. Marshall to Austin, March 9, 1948, 501.BB Pal/3–948, NA; also M. J. Cohen, *Palestine and the Great Powers*, p. 354.

3. Ganin, *Truman, American Jewry*, p. 166.

4. Elath, *Struggle for Statehood* 2B: 558.

5. Lowenthal's drafts are in box 41b, MLP; the final memoranda of March 6 and 8, 1948, can be found in box 14, Clifford Papers, HSTL, and *FRUS, 1948* 5: 687–96.

6. Clifford to Truman, March 8, 1948, box 14, Clifford Papers, HSTL; emphasis in original.

7. Truman, *Memoirs* 2: 162.

8. Report of March 12, circulated on March 15, 1948, *FRUS, 1948* 5: 711.

9. McClintock to Humelsine, March 17, 1948, ibid., pp. 731–32.

10. Marshall to Austin, March 16, 1948, ibid., pp. 728–29.

11. Thorp to British Embassy, Washington, D.C., March 18, 1948, ibid., pp. 739–41.

12. *ID*, pp. 475–78; David Ben-Gurion, *Israel: A Personal History* (New York: Funk and Wagnalls, 1949), p. 72, and Donovan, *Conflict*, p. 375; *New York Times*, March 20, 1948.

13. Elath, *Struggle for Statehood* 2B: 625.

14. Jacobson to Cohn, March 27, 1952 (see chapter 10, n. 45), and Adler, *Roots*, p. 211.

15. Weizmann to Doris May, March 23, 1948, *The Letters and Papers of Chaim Weizmann*, vol. 23, *1947–1952*, ed. Aaron Klieman (Jerusalem: Israel Universities Press, 1980), p. 91.

16. Kaufmann, "Ambiguous Partnership," p. 417, and text of AJC statement of March 29, 1948, box I/2, AJCA.

17. Kolsky, "Jews against Zionism," p. 459.

18. Diary entries for Saturday, March 20, 1948, quoted in M. Truman, *Harry S. Truman*, p. 388.

19. Clifford, interview with Daniels, Daniels Papers.

20. Ibid.

21. Ibid.

22. Eleanor Roosevelt to Secretary Marshall, March 22, 1948, folder 2, box 322, PSF personal file.

23. Ibid.

24. Lash, *Eleanor*, p. 130; and Leuchtenberg, *In the Shadow of FDR*, p. 32.

25. Truman to Eleanor Roosevelt, March 25, 1948, PSF personal file.

26. Elath, *Struggle for Statehood* 2B : 632.

27. Charlie Ross, memorandum, March 29, 1948, box 6, Ross Papers, HSTL.

28. Elath, *Struggle for Statehood* 2B : 633–34.

29. L. C. Meeker to Ernest Gross (Legal Department), November 5, 1948, 711.67N/11–548, NA.

30. Elath, *Struggle for Statehood* 2B : 634; and various drafts in box 41b, MLP.

31. Press conference, March 25, 1948, *Public Papers of the Presidents of the United States: Harry S. Truman, 1948* (Washington, D.C.: Government Printing Office, 1964), pp. 190–95.

32. Ibid.

33. Cf. Truman, *Memoirs* 2 : 164–65, and Ganin, *Truman, American Jewry*, pp. 162–63.

34. M. J. Cohen, *Palestine and the Great Powers*, p. 361.

35. Marshall to Bohlen, March 22, 1948, *FRUS, 1948* 5 : 750, n. 3.

36. Memorandum, March 29, 1948, box 6, Ross Papers, HSTL; emphasis in original.

37. Ganin, *Truman, American Jewry*, p. 163; Philip Jessup, *The Birth of Nations* (New York: Columbia University Press, 1974), p. 266.

38. Charles Murphy (Truman's administrative assistant), memorandum, March 22, 1948, *FRUS, 1948* 5 : 745.

39. Truman, *Memoirs* 2 : 163.

40. Ibid.

41. Clark Clifford, "The Unique and Inspiring Leadership of President Truman," in *Harry S. Truman: The Man from Independence,* ed. William F. Levantrosser (New York: Greenwood Press, 1986). (Proceedings of Hofstra University International Conference on Harry S. Truman, April 1983.)

Chapter 12

1. E4796, FO 371/68649, PRO.

2. U.S. Embassy, London, to Secretary Marshall, March 27, 1948, 501.BB Pal/3–2748, box 2184, NA.

3. Cf. M. J. Cohen, *Palestine and the Great Powers,* pp. 299–300, 364–65.

4. Cf. Evan M. Wilson, *Decision on Palestine* (Stanford: Hoover Institution Press, 1979), p. 137.

5. Douglas to Marshall, March 24, 1948, 501.BB Pal/3–2448, NA.

6. E4796, FO 371/68649, PRO.

7. Austin to Marshall, March 29, 1948, 501.BB Pal/3–2448, box 2184, NA.

8. Ross to Rusk, April 17, 1948, ibid.

9. Memorandum, *FRUS, 1948* 5:798–800.

10. Meeting between Shertok, Epstein, Marshall, and Lovett, March 26, 1948, *ID,* pp. 509–21.

11. Gallman (London) to Marshall, March 31, 1948, 867N.01/3–3148, NA.

12. U.S. Ambassador Tuck (Cairo) to Marshall, April 18, 1948, 501.BB Pal/4–1848, box 2184, NA.

13. Cf. Gosnell, *Truman's Crises,* p. 287, and Dunar, *Truman Scandals,* p. 33.

14. Harold Ickes to Truman, March 27, 1948, folder 4, box 90, Harold Ickes Papers, Library of Congress.

15. Kaufmann, "Non-Zionists," pp. 657–58.

16. Tschirgi, *Politics of Indecision,* p. 252.

17. Divine, *Foreign Policy,* p. 194.

18. Elath, *Struggle for Statehood* 2B:681.

19. Jacobson diary, cited in the *Washington Post,* May 6, 1973.

20. Elath, *Struggle for Statehood* 2B:682.

21. Hilldring to Morgenthau, February 6, 1948, Henry Morgenthau Papers, 84/6, ISA.

22. Cf. V. Weizmann, *The Impossible Takes Longer,* p. 230; and Hilldring to Morgenthau, February 6, 1948, Henry Morgenthau Papers, 84/6, ISA.

23. *Letters and Papers of Chaim Weizmann* 23 : 109, n. 3.

24. Abba Eban, "Tragedy and Triumph," in *Chaim Weizmann: A Biography by Several Hands,* ed. Meyer Weisgal and Joel Carmichael (London: Weidenfeld and Nicolson, 1962), pp. 249–313.

25. Jacobson to Truman, April 29, 1948, PPF 1656.

26. Henderson to Lovett, April 22, 1948, Rusk/McClintock Palestine reference files, microfilm, reel 10, M1175, NA.

27. Elath, *Struggle for Statehood* 2B : 710.

28. Ibid.

29. Lowenthal diary, May 11, 1948, box 27-2, MLP.

30. Ibid., June 24, 1948.

31. Ibid., May 26, 1948.

32. Ibid., June 1, 1948.

33. Ibid., June 15, 1948.

34. Ibid., June 1, 1948.

35. Truman, meeting with Rusk, April 30, 1948, *FRUS, 1948* 5 : 877–79.

36. M. J. Cohen, *Palestine and the Great Powers,* pp. 371–74.

37. Dean Alfange to Harry Vaughan, May 5, 1948, box 184, PSF. Alfange's letter, in the form of an unheaded memorandum, can be found in box 27-2, MLP.

38. Truman to Alfange, May 18, 1948, box 184, PSF.

39. Elath, *Struggle for Statehood* 2B : 758.

40. Lowenthal diary, May 11, 1948, box 27-2, MLP.

41. Lowenthal, memorandum, May 9, 1948, box 41b, ibid.

42. Lowenthal, undated, fifteen-page memorandum, ibid., and box 13, Clifford Papers; emphasis in original.

43. Ibid.

44. Ibid.

45. Ibid.

46. Clifford, memorandum, May 9, 1948, ibid.

47. Lash, *Eleanor,* p. 132.

48. Eleanor Roosevelt to Truman, May 11, 1948, folder 2, box 322, PSF personal.

49. Based mainly on memorandum by Robert McClintock (UN Affairs division of State Department), May 12, 1948, *FRUS, 1948* 5 : 972–76; George Elsey, undated note, box 60, Elsey Papers, reprinted in *FRUS, 1948* 5 : 976; and Lowenthal's diary notes.

50. Clifford, "Unique and Inspiring," p. 386.

51. Lowenthal diary, May 12, 1948, box 27-2, MLP.

52. Lowenthal diary, May 14, 1948, ibid.

53. Ibid.

54. Clifford, interview with Daniels, October 26, 1949, Daniels

Papers; and Clifford, interview, April 13, 1971, Oral History Collection, HSTL.

55. McClintock, memorandum, May 12, 1948, *FRUS, 1948* 5: 972–76; also M. J. Cohen, *Palestine and the Great Powers*, p. 375.

56. Elsey, diary notes, May 12, 1948, box 60, Elsey Papers.

57. Cf. Snetsinger, *Truman, the Jewish Vote*, p. 139.

58. McClintock, memorandum, May 12, 1948, *FRUS, 1948* 5: 972–76.

59. Ibid., and Fraser Wilkins, interview, June 20, 1975, Oral History Collection, HSTL.

60. Clifford, interview with Daniels (see n. 54).

61. Ibid., internal quotation marks added.

62. Clifford, interview, April 13, 1971, HSTL.

63. Clifford, interview with Daniels (see n. 54). Clifford means March, not April.

64. Lowenthal diary, May 12, 1948, box 27-2, MLP.

65. Lowenthal diary note, May 13, 1948, ibid.

66. May 13, 1948, PPF 553.

67. Lowenthal diary, 11:00 A.M., May 13, 1948, box 27-2, MLP.

68. John A. Kennedy, interview by James R. Fuchs, April 13, 1974, pp. 69–70, HSTL. During World War II, Kennedy had been naval liaison to Truman's committee on wartime spending; after the war he was Forrestal's personal assistant.

69. Clifford, interview, HSTL, and Clifford, interview with Daniels (see n. 54).

70. Lowenthal diary, May 15, 1948, box 27-2, MLP.

71. Ibid.

72. Lowenthal diary, May 15, 1948, ibid.

73. Lovett, memorandum, May 17, 1948, 867N.01/5–1748, NA; reprinted in *FRUS, 1948* 5:1005–7.

74. Ibid.

75. Clifford, interview with Daniels (see n. 54).

76. Ibid.

77. Elath, *Struggle for Statehood* 2B:772.

78. Ibid., p. 773.

79. Address of May 8, 1984, *Congressional Record*, vol. 130, pt. 58. On Truman's reluctance to overrule Marshall, see also Lowenthal diary, May 14, 1948, box 27-2, MLP.

80. Lovett, memorandum, May 17, 1948 (see n. 73).

81. Ibid.

82. Rusk to Jessup, April 19, 1973, box B.42, Philip Jessup Papers, Manuscripts Division, Library of Congress; copied essentially in Mem-

orandum by State Department Historical Office, June 13, 1974, *FRUS, 1948* 5:993.

83. Ibid.

84. Ibid.

85. Jessup, *Birth of Nations*, pp. 279ff., and Jorge Garcia-Granados, *The Birth of Israel* (New York: Alfred A. Knopf, 1949), pp. 287ff.

86. Jessup, *Birth of Nations*, pp. 279ff; Garcia-Granados, *Birth of Israel*, pp. 287ff; Jessup to Rusk, April 23, 1973, Jessup Papers.

87. Marshall to Lovett, May 17, 1948, *FRUS, 1948* 5:1007–8.

88. Rusk to Jessup, April 19, 1973, box B.42, Jessup Papers.

89. Austin to Marshall, May 19, 1948, *FRUS, 1948* 5:1013–15.

90. Eleanor Roosevelt to Marshall (copy to Truman), May 16, 1948, folder 2, box 322, PSF personal.

91. Truman to Eleanor Roosevelt, May 20, 1948, ibid.

92. Douglas to Marshall, May 25, 1948, *FRUS, 1948* 5:1047–50, cited in M. J. Cohen, *Palestine and the Great Powers*, pp. 388–89.

93. Truman to Crum, May 15, 1948, OF 204 Misc.

Chapter 13

1. UN Resolution 186(5-2), May 14, 1948, reprinted in *FRUS, 1948:* 5:994–95.

2. Cf. Netanel Lorch, *Israel's War of Independence, 1947–1949* (Hartford: Hartmore House, 1968).

3. See chapter 9.

4. Memorandum of conversation by Loy Henderson, June 6, 1948, *FRUS, 1948* 5:1099–1101.

5. Cf. Louis, *British Empire*, pp. 557–58.

6. Lowenthal diary, May 16, 1948, box 27-2, MLP.

7. Lowenthal diary, June 1, 1948, ibid.

8. Ayers diary, vol. 2, March 25, 1948, Ayers Papers.

9. Matt Connelly, interviews, November 1967, August 1968, Oral History Collection, HSTL.

10. Lowenthal diary, May 15, 1948, box 27-2, MLP.

11. Epstein to Shertok, May 29, 1948, *ID*, p. 94: a copy can be found in box 41b, MLP.

12. Ibid.

13. Ibid.

14. Ibid.

15. Clifford, memorandum, June 17, 1948, *FRUS, 1948* 5:1117–19.

16. Ibid., n. 1.

17. Henderson to Adler, December 31, 1975, and February 23, 1976, box 11, Henderson Papers.

18. The article was read into the *Congressional Record,* 80th Cong., 2d sess., on January 26, 1948, by Representative Arthur G. Klein of New York.

19. Ibid.

20. Ibid.

21. Lowenthal diary, May 18, 1948, box 27-2, MLP.

22. Lowenthal diary, May 1948, ibid.

23. Lowenthal diary, June 24, 1948, ibid.

24. Henderson, interview, HSTL, and *FRUS, 1948* 5: 1217, n. 1.

25. Allen Podet, "Anti-Zionism in a Key U.S. Diplomat: Loy Henderson at the End of World War II," *American Jewish Archives* 30 (1978): 155–87.

26. Henderson to Podet, March 29, 1976, box 2, Henderson Papers.

27. *FRUS, 1948* 5: 1060, n. 1; Lowenthal diary, June 24, 1948, box 27-2, MLP.

28. Lowenthal diary, June 24, 1948, box 27-2, MLP.

29. James G. MacDonald, *My Mission in Israel* (New York: Simon and Schuster, 1951), pp. 6–7.

30. Ibid.

31. Ibid., pp. 4–5; Lowenthal diary, June 24, 1948, box 27-2, MLP. Lowenthal's contemporary diary note is presumably the more reliable.

32. Lovett, memorandum, June 22, 1948, *FRUS, 1948* 5: 1131–32.

33. Lowenthal diary, June 24, 1948; MacDonald, *My Mission,* pp. 4–5.

34. Lovett, memorandum, June 28, 1948, *FRUS, 1948* 5: 1151–52.

35. MacDonald, *My Mission,* p. 8.

36. Lovett, memorandum, June 24, 1948, FW 867N.01/6–2248, NA.

37. State Department, memorandum, late October 1948, Rusk/McClintock files, microfilm, reel 12, M1175, NA.

38. Confidential, unsigned memorandum, July 28, 1948, box 30, Niles Papers, HSTL.

39. Cf. Joseph Heller, "Failure of a Mission: Bernadotte and Palestine, 1948," *Journal of Contemporary History* 14, no. 3 (July 1979): 515–34; Sune Persson, *Mediation and Assassination: Count Bernadotte's Mission to Palestine* (Lowell: Ithaca Press, 1979).

40. Heller, "Failure of a Mission," p. 522.

41. Sir Hugh Dow (Jerusalem) to Harold Beeley (Foreign Office), July 31, 1948, E10476, FO 371/68578, PRO.

42. Marshall to Douglas, June 25, 1948, *FRUS, 1948* 5: 1148.

43. Ibid.

44. Douglas to Marshall, August 2, 1948, ibid., pp. 1268–70.

45. See Foreign Office (drafted by Bevin and Michael Wright, under secretary of state) to Washington, August 4, 1948, E10396, FO 371/68577, PRO.

46. Ibid.

47. Ibid.

48. Douglas to Marshall, August 6, 1948, *FRUS, 1948* 5:1292.

49. Marshall to Douglas, August 13, 1948, ibid., pp. 1309–10.

50. Marshall to Truman, August 16, 1948, ibid., p. 1315.

51. Heller, "Failure of a Mission," p. 523.

52. Marshall to MacDonald, September 1, 1948, *FRUS, 1948* 5: 1366–69.

53. Marshall to Truman, August 31, approved by Truman on September 1, 1948, ibid., p. 1363.

54. Douglas to Marshall, September 1, 1948, ibid., pp. 1365–66.

55. Douglas to Marshall, September 3, 1948, ibid., p. 1373.

56. Marshall to McClintock, September 10, 1948, ibid., p. 1387, n. 2.

57. Troutbeck (Rhodes) to Foreign Office, September 14, 15, 1948, E12017, E12050, FO 371/68586, PRO, and Griffis (U.S. ambassador, Cairo) to Marshall, September 15, 1948, *FRUS, 1948* 5:1398–1400.

58. Persson, *Mediation;* Louis, *British Empire,* p. 550; and Troutbeck to Foreign Office, September 18, 1948, E12162, FO 371/68587, PRO.

59. Douglas to Marshall, September 17, 1948, *FRUS, 1948* 5: 1409–11.

60. Ibid., p. 1410.

61. Ibid.

62. Confidential, unsigned memorandum, July 28, 1948, box 30, Niles Papers.

63. *FRUS, 1948* 5:1415–16.

Chapter 14

1. Lowenthal diary, August 3, 1948, box 27-2, MLP.

2. Epstein to Silver, August 3, 1948 (forwarded to Robert A. Taft), Taft Papers.

3. Divine, *Foreign Policy,* p. 250.

4. Ibid., p. 251.

5. Report in Benjamin Akzin to Rabbi Silver, September 10, 1948, Akzin Papers, 70/9, ISA.

6. Ibid.

7. Ibid., and *FRUS, 1948* 5 : 1380–81. The statements quoted here do not appear in the *FRUS* version.

8. *FRUS, 1948* 5 : 1380–81.

9. Akzin to Silver (see n. 5).

10. Jacob Blaustein to Joseph Proskauer, September 17, 1948, box 81, FAD-1 series, Israel/Palestine, 1945–1948, YIVO Institute, New York. Blaustein, an oil magnate, was chairman of the AJC's executive board for five years and its president in the 1950s.

11. Robert Silverberg, *If I Forget Thee O Jerusalem: American Jews and the State of Israel* (New York: William Morrow, 1970), p. 437.

12. Adler, *Roots,* p. 434, n. 106.

13. Chester Bowles to Clark Clifford, September 23, 1948, folder 1, box 12, Clifford Papers, HSTL.

14. Lovett to Truman, September 24, 1948, *FRUS, 1948* 5 : 1420. The message was transmitted to the presidential train, then touring California and Arizona.

15. E. Orren and G. Rivlin, eds., *Ben-Gurion's War Diary* (in Hebrew) (Tel Aviv: Israel Defence Ministry, 1982), p. 735.

16. Weizmann to Jacobson, September 27, 1948, *Letters and Papers of Chaim Weizmann* 23 : 212.

17. Adler, *Roots,* p. 434, n. 106.

18. See the article on the Jacobson diary in the *Washington Post,* May 6, 1973.

19. Ibid.

20. Ibid.

21. For nn. 21–25, see Lovett, memorandum of telephone conversation, September 29, 1948, and McClintock, memorandum, September 30, 1948, *FRUS, 1948* 5 : 1430–31, 1437–38.

22. Lovett memorandum, p. 1430.

23. Ibid.; emphasis in original.

24. Ibid., and McClintock, memorandum, pp. 1437–38.

25. Text in annex to Lovett memorandum, September 29, 1948, p. 1432.

26. Truman, *Memoirs* 2 : 166–67.

27. Orren and Rivlin, *Ben-Gurion's War Diary,* p. 729.

28. Divine, *Foreign Policy,* p. 253.

29. Sir Oliver Franks (Washington) to Foreign Office, October 1, 1948, E12786, FO 371/68590, PRO.

30. Divine, *Foreign Policy,* p. 253.

31. James B. C. Howe, memorandum, October 5, 1948, folder 1, box 12, Clifford Papers, HSTL.

32. Ibid.

33. Eleanor Roosevelt to Bernard Baruch, October 3, 1948, Baruch Papers.

34. Ben Cohen to Justice Felix Frankfurter, November 6, 1948, microfilm, reel 27, Felix Frankfurter Papers, Manuscripts Division, Library of Congress.

35. Confidential, unsigned memorandum, July 28, 1948, box 30, Niles Papers, HSTL.

36. Epstein to Silver, August 3, 1948, Taft Papers.

37. Dulles (Paris) to Dewey (New York), September 26, 1948, box 36, John Foster Dulles Papers, Princeton University.

38. Dulles to Dewey, September 27, 1948, ibid.

39. Allen Dulles to John Foster Dulles, September 28, 1948, ibid. Allen Dulles was his brother's campaign adviser while John Foster Dulles served on the American delegation to the United Nations in Paris.

40. Rusk to Lovett, October 2, 1948, *FRUS, 1948* 5 : 1448–49, and Rusk to Marshall, October 1, 1948, 867N.01/10–148, NA.

41. Rusk to Lovett and Rusk to Marshall (see n. 40).

42. Ibid.

43. Rusk to Marshall, October 7, 1948, *FRUS, 1948* 5 : 1463.

44. Cf. Lovett to Marshall, October 23, 1948, ibid., p. 1507.

45. Clifford to Truman, 1:05 P.M., October 23, 1948. Clifford's handwritten draft was transmitted to Truman at Pittsburgh; folder 1, box 12, Clifford Papers, HSTL; reprinted in *FRUS, 1948* 5 : 1509.

46. Lovett to Marshall, 1:00 P.M., October 23, 1948, *FRUS, 1948* 5 : 1507.

47. Ibid.

48. Clifford to Truman (see n. 45).

49. Lovett to Marshall (see n. 44).

50. Lovett to Rusk and Marshall, October 24, 1948, *FRUS, 1948* 5 : 1512–13.

51. *New York Times,* October 25, 1948.

52. Ibid., October 27, 1948.

53. Jacobson diary, extracted in *Washington Post,* May 6, 1973.

54. Ibid.

55. Divine, *Foreign Policy,* p. 265.

56. Epstein to Ben-Gurion, October 29, 1948, in Orren and Rivlin, *Ben-Gurion's War Diary,* p. 792.

57. Oscar Ewing, interview, April 29–30 and May 1–2, 1969, Oral History Collection, HSTL.

58. Truman to Marshall, 1:00 A.M., October 29, 1948, *FRUS, 1948*

5:1527, and n. 1. Truman's memoirs give a slightly different statement, dated wrongly as October 17; Truman, *Memoirs* 2:167.

59. Marshall to Lovett, October 29, 1948, 501.BB Pal/10–2948, NA.

60. Lovett to Marshall, October 29, 1948, *FRUS, 1948* 5:1528.

61. Lovett to Marshall, October 31, 1948, ibid., p. 1535.

62. Lovett to Marshall, November 2, 1948, ibid., p. 1540.

63. Lovett to Marshall, October 30, 1948, ibid., p. 1533.

64. Ibid.

Chapter 15

1. Richard S. Kirkendall, ed., *The Truman Period as a Research Field* (Columbia: University of Missouri Press, 1967), p. 94.

2. Weizmann to Truman, November 5, 1948, *Letters and Papers of Chaim Weizmann* 23:221.

3. Truman to Weizmann, November 29, 1948, WA.

4. Cf. Snetsinger, *Truman, the Jewish Vote,* pp. 133–35, and Donald R. McCoy, *The Presidency of Harry S. Truman* (Lawrence: University Press of Kansas, 1984), p. 162.

5. Sir Orme Sargent, minute, October 21, 1948, E14099, FO 371/68593, PRO.

6. McClintock to Lovett, November 5, 1948, *FRUS, 1948* 5:1551–52.

7. Lovett to Marshall (Paris), November 10, 1948, ibid., pp. 1565–66, and Douglas to Marshall, November 12, 1948, ibid., pp. 1570–71.

8. Lovett to Marshall (see n. 7).

9. Lowenthal diary, November 7, 1948, box 27-2, MLP.

10. Ibid.

11. I.e., Truman to Weizmann, November 29, 1948, WA.

12. MacDonald to Lovett, 1:00 P.M., November 5, 1948, *FRUS, 1948* 5:1554. The telegram was delivered to the White House at 4:00 P.M. eastern standard time on November 6, well after the passage of the UN sanctions resolution in Paris.

13. Douglas to Lovett, November 12, 1948, ibid., p. 1574.

14. Douglas flew to Paris to report on the meeting to Marshall; see Marshall to Lovett, November 15, 1948, ibid., pp. 1585–89.

15. Ibid.

16. Ibid.

17. Orren and Rivlin, *Ben Gurion's War Diary,* p. 831.

18. Ibid., p. 833.

19. Ibid., pp. 814–15, 913.

20. Ibid., p. 909.

21. Lovett memorandum, December 30, 1948, *FRUS, 1948* 5: 1701–3.

22. Lovett to MacDonald, 5:00 P.M., December 30, 1948, ibid., p. 1704.

23. Ibid.

24. Ibid.

25. MacDonald, *My Mission in Israel,* pp. 117–18.

26. Orren and Rivlin, *Ben-Gurion's War Diary,* p. 915.

27. MacDonald to Truman, Lovett, 9:00 A.M., January 1, 1949, *FRUS, 1949* 6:594–95.

28. Orren and Rivlin, *Ben-Gurion's War Diary,* pp. 916–18.

29. MacDonald to Truman, Lovett, 11:00 A.M., January 1, 1949, *FRUS, 1949* 6:596.

30. Weizmann to Truman, January 2, 1949, *Letters and Papers of Chaim Weizmann* 23:243–44.

31. MacDonald to Marshall, 8:00 P.M., January 7, 1949, *FRUS, 1949* 6:627.

32. Telephone conversation between Julius Holmes (chargé d'affaires, London), and Joseph Satterthwaite (NEA), January 8, 1949, *FRUS, 1949* 6:627–28; Ilan Pappe, *Britain and the Arab-Israeli Conflict, 1948–1951* (New York: St. Martin's Press, 1988), p. 67; Orren and Rivlin, *Ben-Gurion's War Diary,* p. 935.

33. Pappe, *Britain and the Arab-Israeli Conflict,* pp. 65–67.

34. Louis, *British Empire,* p. 565, and Pappe, *Britain and the Arab-Israeli Conflict,* p. 67.

35. Louis, *British Empire,* p. 565.

36. British Middle East Office (Cairo) to Foreign Office, October 8, 1948, E13124, FO 371/68642, PRO.

37. Sir Ronald Campbell (Cairo) to Foreign Office, January 10, 1949, E454, FO 371/75334, ibid.

38. Franks to Foreign Office, January 13, 1949, E615, ibid.

39. E614, ibid.

40. Orren and Rivlin, *Ben-Gurion's War Diary,* p. 875.

41. Sir Orme Sargent, minute, January 17, 1949, E1273, FO 371/75336, PRO.

42. Ibid.

43. Franks to Foreign Office, January 13, 1949, E1932, FO 371/75337, ibid.

44. Ibid.

45. Sir John Beith, minute, March 22, 1949, E6145, FO 371/75054, ibid.

46. Julius C. Holmes to Marshall, January 18, 1949, *FRUS, 1949* 6:678.

47. Hector McNeil (minister of state at the Foreign Office), minute, January 14, 1949, E18881, FO 371/75337, PRO, quoted in Louis, *Britain Empire and the Middle East,* p. 568.

48. Franks to Foreign Office, January 18, 1949, E883/918, FO 371/75335, PRO, and *FRUS, 1949* 6:691–92. Pappe, *Britain and the Arab-Israeli Conflict,* p. 177, mistakes the State Department draft of January 24 for the actual White House press release.

49. *New York Times,* January 25 and 30, 1949, and *FRUS, 1949* 6:696.

50. *New York Times,* February 1, 1949.

Conclusion

1. Arthur Goren, *Dissenter in Zion* (Cambridge: Harvard University Press, 1982), p. 495.

2. Truman, *Memoirs* 2:169.

Bibliography

Unpublished Primary Sources

The United States

Harry S. Truman Library, Independence, Missouri (HSTL)
  Post-Presidential Files (PPF)
  Post-Presidential Name File
  President's Secretary's Files (PSF)
  Senatorial and Vice-Presidential Files (SVP)
  Miscellaneous Historical Document File
  Official Files (OF): OF 204 Misc., OF 205 Misc.
  Private Papers
    Eben A. Ayers, Clark Clifford, George Elsey, Abraham J. Gran-
      off, Eddie Jacobson, David Niles, Mary Ethel Noland
  Oral History Collection
    Clark Clifford, Mathew J. Connelly, Tom L. Evans, Oscar R. "Jack"
      Ewing, Edgar C. "Bud" Faris, Abraham Feinberg, Abraham J.
      Granoff, Loy Henderson, Mary Paxton Keeley, John A. Ken-
      nedy, Max Lowenthal, Samuel I. Rosenman, A. J. Stephens,
      Harry H. Vaughan, Fraser Wilkins
National Archives, Washington, D.C. (NA)
  Palestine files. 501.BB Pal; 867N.
  Palestine reference files. [Dean] Rusk, [Robert] McClintock. M1175.
    Microfilm.
  Department of State General Records. Record Group 59.
  National Security Agency/Central Security Agency. Record Group
    457.
  Joint Chiefs of Staff. CCS 902.

Library of Congress, Washington, D.C.
  Private Papers, Manuscripts Division
    Emmanuel Celler, Felix Frankfurter, Loy Henderson, Harold
    Ickes, Philip Jessup, Robert A. Taft
Washington National Records Center, Suitland–Silver Hill, Maryland
University and private collections
  Princeton University, Seeley G. Mudd Manuscript Library: Ber-
    nard M. Baruch, John Foster Dulles, Louis Fischer, George
    Kennan
  University of North Carolina, Chapel Hill, Southern Historical Col-
    lection: Jonathan Daniels (#3466)
  University of Minnesota, University Archives: Max Lowenthal
    (MLP)
  University of Vermont: Warren R. Austin
  American Jewish Archives, Cincinnati: Elmer Berger, Morris Laza-
    ron, Lessing Rosenwald
  American Jewish Committee Archives, New York: Joseph Pros-
    kauer, Stephen Wise (AJCA)
  YIVO Institute, New York: Fad-1 series, Israel/Palestine, 1945–
    1948
  Jewish Theological Seminary of America, New York: Paul O'Dwyer
  Abraham J. Granoff, Kansas City (by kind permission of his son,
    Loeb H. Granoff)

Israel

Ben-Gurion Archives, Sde Boker (BGA)
Central Zionist Archives, Jerusalem (CZA)
Hebrew University, Jerusalem, Institute of Contemporary History,
  Oral History Collection
Israel State Archives, Jerusalem (ISA)
  Israel Foreign Office 93.03
  Leo Kohn, Henry Morgenthau
Weizmann Archives, Rehovot (WA)

Great Britain

Public Records Office, London (PRO)
  Prime Minister's Office. Prem 8
  Cabinet Papers. Cab 128, 129
  Foreign Office. FO 371, 800
  Colonial Office. CO 537, 733

Published Primary Sources

Congressional Record. 76th Cong., 1st sess., 1939. Vol. 84, pt. 13.
Foreign Relations of the United States. 1945, vol. 8; *1946,* vol. 7; *1947,* vol. 5; *1948,* vol. 5; *1949,* vol. 6. Washington, D.C.: Government Printing Office, State Department Publications, 1969, 1971, 1976, 1977. *(FRUS)*
Israel Documents. December 1947–May 1948, edited by Gedalia Yogev. Jerusalem: Israel Government Printing Office, 1980. *(ID)*
The Letters and Papers of Chaim Weizmann. 1945–1947, vol. 22, edited by Joseph Heller; *1947–1952,* vol. 23, edited by Aaron Klieman. Jerusalem: Israel Universities Press; New Brunswick, N.J.: Transaction Books, Rutgers University, 1979, 1980.
Public Papers of the Presidents of the United States. Harry S. Truman, 1946, 1948. Washington, D.C.: Government Printing Office, 1962, 1964.

Periodicals

Kansas City Jewish Chronicle
Kansas City Star
New York Times
Washington Post

Unpublished Secondary Sources

Kaufmann, Menahem. "An Ambiguous Partnership: Non-Zionists in America and the Struggle for Jewish Statehood, 1939–1948." Typescript. Institute for Contemporary Jewry, Jerusalem, 1985. Jerusalem: Magnes, forthcoming.
———. "Non-Zionists in American Jewry, 1939–1948." Ph.D. diss., Hebrew University, Jerusalem, 1978.
Kolsky, Thomas A. "Jews Against Zionism: The American Council for Judaism, 1942–1948." Ph.D. diss., George Washington University, Washington, D.C., 1986.
Sachar, D. B. "David Niles and American Policy." Senior honors thesis, Harvard University, 1959.

Published Secondary Sources

Abels, J. *The Truman Scandals.* Chicago: Regnery, 1956.
Acheson, Dean. *Present at the Creation.* New York: Norton, 1969.
Adler, Frank J. Review of *Harry S. Truman,* by Margaret Truman. *American Jewish Historical Quarterly* 62, no. 4 (June 1973): 414–25.

————. *Roots in a Moving Stream.* Kansas City, Mo.: The Temple, Congregation B'nai Jehudah, 1972.

Anderson, Irvine H. *ARAMCO: The United States and Saudi Arabia, a Study of the Dynamics of Foreign Oil Policy, 1933–1950.* Princeton: Princeton University Press, 1981.

Auerbach, Jerold S. "Joseph M. Proskauer: American Court Jew." *American Jewish History* 69, no. 1 (September 1979): 103–16.

————. *Unequal Justice: Lawyers and Social Change in Modern America.* New York: Oxford University Press, 1976.

Baram, Phillip J. *The Department of State in the Middle East, 1919–1945.* Philadelphia: University of Pennsylvania Press, 1978.

Baruch, Bernard M. *The Public Years.* New York: Holt, Rinehart and Winston, 1960.

Bauer, Yehuda. *Flight and Rescue: Brichah.* New York: Random House, 1970.

Ben-Gurion, David. *Israel: A Personal History.* New York: Funk and Wagnalls, 1949.

Bickerton, Ian J. "President Truman's Recognition of Israel." *American Jewish Historical Quarterly* 58, no. 2 (December 1968): 173–240.

Bisgyer, Maurice. *Challenge and Encounter.* New York: Crown, 1967.

Blum, John Morton, ed. *The Price of Vision: The Diary of Henry A. Wallace, 1942–1946.* Boston: Houghton Mifflin, 1973.

Burns, Richard Dean, comp. *Harry S. Truman: A Bibliography of His Times and Presidency.* Wilmington, Del.: Scholarly Resources, 1984.

Burton, William L. "Protestant America and the Rebirth of Israel." *Jewish Social Studies* 26, no. 1 (1964): 203–14.

Clifford, Clark. "The Unique and Inspiring Leadership of President Truman." In *Harry S. Truman: The Man from Independence,* edited by William F. Levantrosser. New York: Greenwood Press, 1986. (Proceedings of Hofstra University International Conference on Harry S. Truman, April 1983.)

Coffin, Tris. *Missouri Compromise.* Boston: Little, Brown, 1947.

Cohen, Michael J. "The Genesis of the Anglo-American Committee on Palestine: A Case Study in the Assertion of American Hegemony." *Historical Journal* 22, no. 1 (March 1979): 185–207.

————. *Palestine and the Great Powers, 1945–1948.* Princeton: Princeton University Press, 1982. (Paperback, 1986).

————. *Palestine: Retreat from the Mandate, 1936–1945.* New York: Holmes and Meier, 1978.

Cohen, W. Naomi. *Not Free to Desist: The American Jewish Committee, 1906–1966.* Philadelphia: Jewish Publication Society of America, 1972.

Cohen, Warren, I. *Dean Rusk.* Totowa, N.J.: Cooper Square, 1980.

Crossman, Richard. *Palestine Mission.* London: Harper and Brothers, 1947.

Crum, Bartley. *Behind the Silken Curtain.* Port Washington, N.Y.: Kennikat, 1969.

Daniels, Jonathan. *The Man of Independence.* Philadelphia: Lippincott, 1950.

Dinnerstein, Leonard. *America and the Survivors of the Holocaust.* New York: Columbia University Press, 1982.

Divine, Robert A. "The Cold War and the Election of 1948." *Journal of American History* 59 (June 1972–March 1973): 90–110.

———. *Foreign Policy and U.S. Presidential Elections.* Vol. 1, *1940–1948.* New York: New Viewpoints, 1974.

Donovan, Robert J. *Conflict and Crisis: The Presidency of Harry S. Truman, 1945–1948.* New York: Norton, 1977.

Dorsett, Lyle W. "Truman and the Pendergast Machine." *Mid-continent Studies Journal* 7, no. 2 (Fall 1966). Special section, pp. 16–17.

Dunar, Andrew J. *The Truman Scandals and the Politics of Morality.* Columbia: University of Missouri Press, 1984.

Eban, Abba. "Dewey David Stone: Prototype of an American Zionist." In *Solidarity and Kinship: Essays on American Zionism, in Memory of Dewey David Stone,* edited by Nathan M. Kaganoff, pp. 27–36. Waltham, Mass.: American Jewish Historical Society, 1980.

———. "Tragedy and Triumph." In *Chaim Weizmann, A Biography by Several Hands,* edited by Meyer Weisgal and Joel Carmichael, pp. 249–313. London: Weidenfeld and Nicolson, 1962.

Eddy, William A. *FDR Meets Ibn Saud.* New York: American Friends of the Middle East, 1954.

Elath, Eliahu. *The Struggle for Statehood: Washington, 1945–1948* (in Hebrew). Vol. 1, *1945–1946.* Vols. 2A–B, *January 1947–May 15, 1948.* Tel Aviv: Am Oved, 1979, 1982.

Feingold, Henry L. "Courage First and Intelligence Second: The American Jewish Secular Elite, Roosevelt, and the Failure to Rescue." *American Jewish History* 72, no. 4 (June 1983): 424–60.

———. *The Politics of Rescue: The Roosevelt Administration and the Holocaust, 1938–1945.* New Brunswick, N.J.: Rutgers University Press, 1970.

Ferrell, Robert H., ed. *Dear Bess: The Letters from Harry to Bess Truman, 1910–1959.* New York: W. W. Norton, 1983.

———. *Off the Record: The Private Papers of Harry S. Truman.* New York: Harper and Row, 1980.

Fink, Reuben. *America and Palestine.* New York: Herald Square Press, 1945.

Flynn, Edward J. *You're the Boss.* New York: Viking, 1947.

Friedmann, Saul S. *No Haven for the Oppressed: United States Policy toward Jewish Refugees, 1938–1945.* Detroit: Wayne State University Press, 1973.

Ganin, Zvi. "Truman, American Jewry, and the Creation of Israel." In *Truman and the American Commitment to Israel,* edited by M. Maoz and A. Weinstein. Jerusalem: Magnes, 1981.

———. *Truman, American Jewry, and Israel, 1945–1948.* New York: Holmes and Meier, 1979.

Garcia-Granados, Jorge. *The Birth of Israel.* New York: Alfred A. Knopf, 1949.

Gardner, Lloyd C. *Architects of Illusion.* Chicago: Quadrangle, 1970.

Gerson, Louis L. *The Hyphenate in Recent American Politics and Diplomacy.* Lawrence: University Press of Kansas, 1964.

Goldmann, Nahum. "On the Road to Statehood: How American Support for Partition Was Achieved" (in Hebrew). *Ha'aretz,* April 4, 1958.

———. *Sixty Years of Jewish Life.* New York: Holt, Rinehart and Winston, 1969.

Goren, Arthur. *Dissenter in Zion.* Cambridge: Harvard University Press, 1982.

Gosnell, Harold F. *Truman's Crises: A Political Biography of Harry S. Truman.* Westport, Conn.: Greenwood Press, 1980.

Grose, Peter. *Israel in the Mind of America.* New York: Alfred A. Knopf, 1983.

Gustafson, Merlin. "Harry Truman as a Man of Faith." *Christian Century* 90 (January 1973).

———. "Religion and Politics in the Truman Administration." *Rocky Mountain Social Science Journal* 3–4 (1966–1967): 125–34.

———. "The Religious Role of the President." *Midwestern Journal of Political Science* 14, no. 4 (November 1980): 708–22.

———. "Truman and Religion: The Religion of a President." *Journal of Church and State* 10, no. 3 (Autumn 1968): 379–87.

Halperin, Samuel. *The Political World of American Zionism.* Detroit: Wayne State University, 1961.

Hamby, Alonzo L. *Beyond the New Deal: Harry S. Truman and American Liberalism.* New York: Columbia University, 1973.

Hartmann, Susan M. *Truman and the Eightieth Congress.* New York: Columbia University Press, 1971.

Heller, Francis H., ed. *The Truman White House: The Administration of the Presidency, 1945–1953.* Lawrence: Regents Press of Kansas, 1980.

Heller, Joseph. "Failure of a Mission: Bernadotte and Palestine, 1948." *Journal of Contemporary History* 14, no. 3 (July 1979): 515–34.

Hillman, William, ed. *Mr. President*. New York: Farrar, Strauss and Young, 1952.

Horowitz, David. *State in the Making*. New York: Knopf, 1953.

Hull, Cordell. *Memoirs*. Vol. 2. London: Hodder and Stoughton, 1948.

Hurewitz, J. C. *Diplomacy in the Near and Middle East*. Vol. 2, *1914–1956*. New York: Van Nostrand, 1956.

Isaacs, Stephen D. *Jews and American Politics*. New York: Doubleday, 1974.

Jessup, Philip. *The Birth of Nations*. New York: Columbia University Press, 1974.

Jones, Martin. *Failure in Palestine*. London: Mansell, 1986.

Kaufmann, Menahem. "From Neutrality to Involvement: Zionists, Non-Zionists, and the Struggle for a Jewish State; Essays in American Zionism, 1917–1948." In *Herzl Year Book*, vol. 8, edited by Melvin I. Urofsky. New York: Herzl Press, 1978.

Kirk, George. *The Middle East in the War: Survey of International Affairs, 1939–1946*. London: Oxford University Press, 1952.

Kirkendall, Richard S. "The Election of 1948." In *The History of American Presidential Elections*, edited by A. M. Schlesinger and Fred Israel, 4:3099–3145. New York: Chelsea House, 1971.

———. "Truman's Path to Power." *Social Science* 43, no. 2 (1968): 67–73.

———, ed. *The Truman Period as a Research Field*. Columbia: University of Missouri Press, 1967.

Klausner, Carla L. "The Zionist Spectrum." In *Mid-America's Promise: A Profile of Kansas City Jewry*, edited by Joseph P. Schultz, Kansas City, Mo.: Jewish Community Foundation of Greater Kansas City, 1982.

Lash, Joseph P. *Eleanor: The Years Alone*. New York: Norton, 1972.

Leahy, Fleet Admiral William D. *I Was There*. New York: Whittesley House, 1950.

Leuchtenberg, William E. *In the Shadow of FDR*. Ithaca and London: Cornell University Press, 1983.

Lorch, Netanel. *Israel's War of Independence, 1947–1949*. Hartford: Hartmore House, 1968.

Louis, William Roger. *The British Empire in the Middle East, 1945–1951*. Oxford: Clarendon Press, 1984.

Lubell, Samuel. *The Future of American Politics*. New York: Harper, 1952.

McCoy, Donald R. *The Presidency of Harry S. Truman*. Lawrence: University Press of Kansas, 1984.

MacDonald, James G. *My Mission in Israel*. New York: Simon and Schuster, 1951.

Marrus, M., and R. Paxton. *Vichy France and the Jews.* New York: Basic Books, 1981.

Mendes-Flohr, Paul R., and Jehuda Reinharz, eds. *The Jew in the Modern World.* New York: Oxford University Press, 1980.

Miller, Aaron David. *Search for Security: Saudi Arabian Oil and American Foreign Policy, 1939–1949.* Chapel Hill: University of North Carolina Press, 1980.

Miller, Merle. *Plain Speaking: An Oral Biography of Harry S. Truman.* New York: Berkley, 1974.

Miller, Richard Lawrence. *Truman: The Rise to Power.* New York: McGraw-Hill, 1985.

Milligan, Maurice M. *Missouri Waltz.* New York: Scribner's, 1948.

Millis, Walter, ed., in collaboration with E. S. Duffield. *The Forrestal Diaries.* New York: Viking, 1951.

Nachmani, Amikam. *Great Power Discord in Palestine: The Anglo-American Committee of Inquiry into the Problems of European Jewry and Palestine, 1945–1946.* London: Frank Cass, 1987.

Nash, Philleo. Untitled article. In *The Truman White House: The Administration of the Presidency, 1945–1953,* edited by Francis H. Heller, pp. 52–56. Lawrence, Kan.: Regents Press, 1980.

Orren, E., and G. Rivlin, eds. *Ben-Gurion's War Diary* (in Hebrew). Tel Aviv: Israel Defence Ministry, 1982.

Pappe, Ilan. *Britain and the Arab-Israeli Conflict, 1948–1951.* New York: St. Martin's Press, 1988.

Penkower, Monty Noam. *The Jews Were Expendable: Free World Diplomacy and the Holocaust.* Urbana and Chicago: University of Illinois Press, 1983.

Persson, Sune. *Mediation and Assassination: Count Bernadotte's Mission to Palestine.* Lowell, Mass.: Ithaca Press, 1979.

Podet, Allen. "Anti-Zionism in a Key U.S. Diplomat: Loy Henderson at the End of World War II." *American Jewish Archives* 30 (1978): 155–87.

———. *The Success and Failure of the Anglo-American Committee of Inquiry, 1945–1946.* Lewiston, N.Y.: Edwin Mellen, 1987.

Poen, Monte M., ed. *Strictly Personal and Confidential.* Boston: Little, Brown, 1982.

Proskauer, Joseph M. *A Segment of My Times.* New York: Farrar Strauss, 1950.

Redding, John M. *Inside the Democratic Party.* Indianapolis: Bobbs-Merrill, 1958.

Robbins, Jhan. *Bess and Harry: An American Love Story.* New York: G. P. Putnam's Sons, 1980.

Rogow, Arnold A. *James Forrestal: A Study of Personality, Politics, and Policy.* New York: Macmillan, 1963.

Rose, Norman A. *Chaim Weizmann: A Biography.* New York: Viking, 1986.

Sachar, Abram. *The Redemption of the Unwanted: The Post-Holocaust Years.* New York: St. Martin's/Marek, 1983.

Schwarz, Jordan A. *The Speculator: Bernard M. Baruch in Washington, 1917–1965.* Chapel Hill: University of North Carolina, 1981.

Shwadran, Benjamin. *The Middle East, Oil, and the Great Powers.* New York: Transaction, 1973.

Silverberg, Robert. *If I Forget Thee O Jerusalem: American Jews and the State of Israel.* New York: William Morrow, 1970.

Snetsinger, John. *Truman, the Jewish Vote, and the Creation of Israel.* Stanford: Hoover Institution Press, 1974.

Spanier, J. *American Foreign Policy since World War II.* New York: Holt, Rinehart, Winston, 1977.

Steinberg, Alfred. *The Man from Missouri: The Life and Times of Harry S. Truman.* New York: Putnam's, 1962.

Stember, Charles, et al. *Jews in the Mind of America.* New York: Basic Books, 1966.

Strum, Philippa. *Louis D. Brandeis: Justice for the People.* Cambridge: Harvard University Press, 1984.

Truman, Harry S. *Memoirs.* Vol. 1, *Year of Decisions.* Vol. 2, *Years of Trial and Hope.* New York: Doubleday, 1955, 1956.

Truman, Margaret. *Harry S. Truman.* New York: William Morrow, 1973.

Tschirgi, Dan. *The Politics of Indecision.* New York: Praeger, 1983.

Wasserstein, B. *Britain and the Jews of Europe, 1939–1945.* Oxford: Oxford University Press, 1979.

Weizmann, Chaim. *Trial and Error.* New York: Schocken, 1966.

Weizmann, Vera (as told to David Tutaev). *The Impossible Takes Longer: The Memoirs of Vera Weizmann.* New York: Harper and Row, 1967.

Westerfield, H. Bradford. *Foreign Policy and Party Politics: From Pearl Harbor to Korea.* New Haven: Yale University Press, 1955.

Wilson, Evan M. *Decision on Palestine.* Stanford: Hoover Institution Press, 1979.

Wyman, David. *The Abandonment of the Jews.* New York: Pantheon, 1984.

———. "The American Jewish Leadership and the Holocaust." In *Jewish Leadership during the Nazi Era: Patterns of Behavior in the Free World,* edited by R. L. Braham, pp. 1–27. New York: City University of New York, 1985.

Index

Abdullah, King, 213, 232, 233, 234, 235
Abu Ageila, 264
Acheson, Dean, 55, 89, 104, 105, 130, 133, 135; and Bevin, 142; and Goldmann, 138, 140, 142; Marshall replaced by, 270; and Morrison-Grady plan, 135, 136; and Proskauer, 141; and Yom Kippur speech, 144
Adler, Frank, 164–65
Africa, Allied battle for North, 288n.19, 289n.46
Al-'Arīsh, 264, 266
Alfange, Dean, 208, 252, 311n.37
Allon, Yigal, 264
Alsop brothers, 180
American Christian Palestine Committee, 86, 208, 252. See also Alfange, Dean
American Council for Judaism (ACJ), 50, 51, 56, 65, 103–5, 106, 109; and Committee for Justice and Peace in the Holy Land, 181; and DPs, 110, 113, 114–20, 276, 279 (see also Citizens Committee on Displaced Persons); and Palestine trusteeship, 192–93; and U.S. immigration policy, 278. See also Rosenwald, Lessing J.
American Jewish Committee (AJC), 37, 52–53, 55, 56, 102–3, 105, 168; and Jewish DPs, 112, 119–20, 276; and partition, 139; strategy of, 62–63; trusteeship plan of, 192; and UNSCOP, 192. See also Proskauer, Joseph
American Jews, 101; anti-Zionist, 65, 102–6, 109; and Bergson boys, 39, 42; and Biltmore resolution, 46; electoral clout of, 89, 178, 279; financial clout of, 69–75, 279, 281; and Holocaust, 101; and Israel (see Zionist[s]); and 1948 election, 258–59; voting habits of, 60–62. See also American Council for Judaism (ACJ); American Jewish Committee (AJC); American Palestine Committee; American Zionist Emergency Council (AZEC); American Zionist Movement; B'nai B'rith; Jewish War Veterans Association; Zionist(s)
American Palestine Committee, 45, 85–86
American Zionist Emergency Council (AZEC), 42, 45, 85–86, 127, 141, 158, 164, 243
American Zionist Movement, 46, 48, 51, 53
Anderson, C. T., 248
Anderson, Irvine H., 95
Anglo-American committee on Palestine, 54, 123–37, 150, 209, 222, 233, 261. See also Crum, Bartley; MacDonald, James; Morrison-Grady plan
Anti-Semitism, 61; Forrestal suspected of, xii, 163; as ongoing American Jewish fear, 101, 102, 114; postwar Polish, 117; Truman and, 8–10, 13; in U.S. Congress, 118–19; on Wall Street, 163
Anti-Zionism. See Zionist(s), enemies of
Appeasement, Chamberlain's govern-

Jackson, Robert, 85
Jacobs, Izzie, 33
Jacobson, Bluma, 13, 16, 74
Jacobson, Eddie, xii, 50, 102, 158, 170, 172, 253–54, 274, 276; aid to Jewish refugees by, 29–31, 32; bankrupt, 15, 16; death of, 285 n.47; and DP problem, 110–11; efforts on behalf of Israel by, 62, 63, 64, 157, 164, 165, 168; and Granoff, 165–67; and Hilldring appointment, 205; as non-Zionist, 110; as Truman army crony, 8, 10, 12–13; as Truman business partner, 8, 11, 13–16; as Truman fund-raiser, 74; and Truman-Weizmann meeting, 183–87; and Weizmann, 186–87, 191, 203, 245–46, 280; and Zionism, 17–18, 110
Jacobson, Gloria, 16
Jaffa, 159, 260, 262
Javits, Jacob, 228–29
Jenkins, Douglas, 30
Jerusalem, 232, 233, 235; internationalization proposed for, 172, 236, 237; UN and, 149
Jessup, Philip, 197, 220, 263
Jewish Agency, 112, 137, 138–40; and partition, 138–40, 144, 182; and recognition of Israel, 218. *See also* Epstein, Eliahu
"Jewish problem," 28–43; final solution of, 34–35 (*see also* Holocaust)
Jewish War Veterans Association, 67, 241, 242
Jews: and Israel (*see* Zionism; Zionist[s]); persecution of European, 28–43; Truman and, 7, 275–76, 281 (*see also* Granoff, Abraham; Jacobson, Eddie; Truman, and Israel; Truman, and Palestine; Truman, and Zionists); U.S. (*see* American Jews); U.S.-based Palestinian, 38. *See also* American Jews; Anti-Semitism; Holocaust; Israel; Judaism; Yishuv
Jobes, Harry, 14
Johnson, Edwin, 41
Johnson, Herschel, 159, 160, 168
Johnson, Louis A., 72, 73, 75
Johnson, Lyndon, 225
Joint Emergency Committee on European Jewish Affairs, 36, 37
Judaism, 55

Kansas City, Mo., Truman in, xii, 5, 10, 11, 13–18
Kaplan, Sidney J., 79

Kaufmann, Edmund I., 72–73
Kaufmann, Menahem, 290 nn.24,25
Kayserling, Leon, 83
Keeley, Mary Paxton, 283 n.1
Kennan, George, 177
Kennedy, John A., 215–16, 312 n.68
Keren Hayesod, 142
King David Hotel, bombing of, 137–38
Klein (Democratic congressman), 301 n.43
Klein, Arthur G., 228, 314 n.18
Klein, Julius, 67, 132, 241–43
Knox, Charles F., Jr., 230
Kohn, Leo, 134–35, 136
Kook, Hillel. *See* Bergson, Peter
Kristallnacht, 28

La Guardia, Fiorello, 115, 124
Laval, Pierre, 33
Lehman, Herbert, 102, 145, 209, 254; and recognition of Israel, 215
Leventhal, Harold, 307 n.35
Levison, George L., 104, 105, 192
Levy, Paul, 32
Liberia, and UN partition vote, 160, 161, 169
Lie, Trygve, 220
Lilienthal, David, 83
Lobby: American Council for Judaism's anti-Zionist, 109; oil, 93–100 (*see also* Aramco); Truman White House (*see* Clifford, Clark; Lowenthal, Max; Niles, David; Rosenman, Sam); Zionist (*see* Zionist lobby)
Loewy, Siegfried, 32
Louis, William Roger, 99
Lovett, Robert, 77, 118, 154, 157, 196, 248, 250; and Bernadotte report, 244; and Clifford, 193, 216–17, 218–19, 225, 246–47, 252, 255, 260–61; and Dewey letter to Alfange, 252; and Epstein, 227; and Franks, 270–71; and Hilldring, 205; and Knox, 230; and MacDonald, 231; and Marshall, 255, 256; and Negev, 159; and 1948 election, 256; and recognition of Israel, 209, 212, 213, 216–17, 219, 221; and Truman, 160, 161, 260, 316 n.14
Lowenthal, Max, xii, 63, 64, 66, 75, 77–82, 102, 168, 189, 195, 227; and Brandeis, 78, 80; and CIO, 80; and Clifford, 63, 78, 81, 146, 189, 206, 208, 212, 225, 279; and Connelly, 214; and Feinberg, 76; importance of, 279; and Niles, 82, 91–92, 206,

Compositor:	G&S Typesetters
Text:	11/13 Baskerville
Display:	Baskerville
Printer:	Maple-Vail Book Mfg. Group
Binder:	Maple-Vail Book Mfg. Group